REVOLUTION in HUNGARY

REVOLUTION
in HUNGARY

by PAUL E. ZINNER

Columbia University Press

NEW YORK AND LONDON 1962

Copyright © 1962 Columbia University Press
Library of Congress Catalog Number: 62-17062
Manufactured in the United States of America

To

JUDY

JOHN

BILLY

and

VICKY

Foreword

PROFESSOR Zinner's essay on the Hungarian revolution and its background is the first major publication sponsored by the Columbia University Research Project on Hungary and based preponderantly on the interviews and other materials assembled by that Project. In welcoming the publication of this perceptive and informed contribution to our understanding of the contemporary Communist world, I should like to take this opportunity to express my appreciation to those who helped make possible this book and the other undertakings of the Project. The Ford Foundation provided a generous grant in support of the undertaking. Alexander Dallin served as Director of the Project during the first year, the active period of planning and interviewing. Robert L. Fischelis was Executive Officer for the overseas operations of the Project. Andre Varchaver was Executive Officer in the United States. The interviewers, in the United States and in Europe, were: Joseph Altman, Stephen Borsody, Joseph Brunner, Stephen Gorove, Desider Holisher, Peter Horvath, Anthony Jasay, John Kosa, Geza Kuun, Leslie Laszlo, Judith Le Bovit, Marian Low, August J. Molnar, Jr., Imre Nemethy, Nicholas Nyary, Anna Oren, Laszlo Pastor, Marta Rezler, Livia Turgeon, and Paul E. Zinner. Professor Zinner also served, with Professor Dallin and me, on the editorial committee that planned the program of publications. Rainer Koehne was Research Associate, and Jonathan Harris, Elinor Murray, William Safran, Henry Stockhold, Luciana Visentine, Alex Weinstock, and David Winter were Research Assistants in the United States. Eliana Covacich, Florence C. Dallin, Elizabeth Fontana, and Judith Saly guided the secretarial and bookkeeping chores. The late John

Kotselas, Christopher Herold, and Erik Wensberg contributed their editorial skills. To all these men and women, warmest thanks!

HENRY L. ROBERTS
Director, Columbia University
Research Project on Hungary

New York
March, 1962

Preface

WHEN, as an aftermath of their defeated revolution, some 200,000 Hungarians, representing a little over 2 percent of the total population, streamed across their country's frontiers seeking asylum, they bore eloquent witness to the brutal fate that befell their motherland. They also carried with them invaluable information about the operations of a totalitarian system and the reasons for its failure. Before the suppression of popular uprising by military forces brought in from the Soviet Union, the government had collapsed under the onslaught of an enraged public. The revolution had been victorious; in its moment of glory, it had swept away its domestic Communist tormentors and it had neutralized the permanent garrisons of its mammoth neighbor whose presence had long been thought to have served first to install and then to insure the survival of the Communist regime.

The revolution exploded a prevailing myth which held that highly developed political consciousness, together with absolute monopolistic control of the means of coercion, persuasion, and production, effectively immunized Communist totalitarian governments against rebellion.

To gain greater insight into what had happened, Columbia University undertook an interview project sponsored by the Ford Foundation. Never before had it been possible to talk freely to so many people with so intimate an involvement and so immediate a memory of life under Communism. Among those who fled there were anti-Communists and Communists who in varying degrees had opposed the existing government and participated in its overthrow. Altogether 250 respondents, comprising a representative sample of the refugee population, were interviewed in the spring and summer of 1957 both in the United States and in Europe.

Information was sought concerning a wide range of topics under three major headings: (a) the pattern of Communist policies including the internal evolution of the Party; (b) popular reactions to Communist rule; and (c) the revolution as a result of the interaction between (a) and (b) as well as a discrete historical phenomenon.

Interviews lasted from two hours to three days and in rare cases even longer. Their content varied from informal discussion of a single phase of events to comprehensive coverage of an individual's life experiences and attitudes on the basis of a long, detailed questionnaire designed to insure comparability.

I participated in the interviewing in the United States and abroad. In addition I had an opportunity to talk informally with many respondents, to round out the data they had already supplied, and with other persons who fled from Hungary after the revolution, to discuss in detail certain social, political, economic, and cultural trends in their country.

This interpretive essay is an outgrowth of the interview Project. But it is both less and more than a summary of the findings. It does not exhaust the full potential of the data for quantitative social analysis of personal and group attitudes, although it sketches such attitudes on the basis of qualitative appraisal of the respondents' testimony.

The study, however, reaches beyond the interview material for factual information. The memory of the respondents obviously was faulty. They did not accurately remember dates, names, and other relevant facts that lay outside their experiences, and frequently they erred about matters of immediate concern to them. It would be impossible and from a scholarly point of view unsound to reconstruct developments in Hungary from 1945 to 1956 on the strength of their statements alone. Although it was not my aim to write a detailed history, the structural frame for the functional relations which I have attempted to project had to be provided.

The perusal of documentary sources helped to accomplish this task and served to check on distortions in the accounts of the respondents that were due either to inexact recollection or to bias. A bibliographical note evaluating these sources is appended.

The interpretation of the events and the explanation of the behavior of the participants are the result of my reflections.

Although the revolution is a natural focal point of interest and is treated in commensurate detail, nearly two-thirds of the study are devoted to an examination of the antecedents. This was not to demonstrate an inexorable or pre-determined pattern of developments, but to shed new light on some old problems and to make Hungary's whole experience with Communism more intelligible.

My primary objective was to portray the evolution of Hungarian society in all its complexity from the collapse of the old order in the Second World War to the breakdown, eleven years later, of the totalitarian system that had taken its place. It seemed important to convey the profound interdependence and the changing character of relations between social forces and among individuals, and to show their effect as well as that of planned policies and their unintended consequences, and of tangible, stable factors and intangible, accidental elements on the shaping of Hungary's destiny in a period of intense social, political, economic, cultural, and psychological transformation.

The study is divided into three parts. Part One depicts the condition of Hungarian society upon emerging from the Second World War, the seizure of power by the Communists, and the imposition of totalitarian dictatorship by them. Part Two covers the period of reassessment and reevaluation that followed the death of Joseph Stalin in which genesis of trends eventually cluminating in a violent outburst against the authorities can be discerned. Part Three gives an analysis of the physiology of the revolution, not only its anatomy.

While this was not meant to be a comparative study, wherever possible I indicated similarities and differences between Hungary and other East European countries under Communist domination to suggest causes that might account for converging and diverging patterns of development and to stimulate further, methodical inquiry along these lines.

The spelling of Hungarian words, including proper names of persons, geographic locations, and titles of documents, was preserved except for the diacritical marks. To insert these appeared to be an exercise in unwarranted pedantry, adding little to the authenticity of the work while making the printer's task more difficult and possibly irritating the reader. Specific references to data obtained from published sources are noted in the text. Information taken from the interview material, however, is not footnoted out of deference to the desire of many respondents to safeguard the anonymity which they frequently stipulated as a condition before agreeing to talk without restraint.

PAUL E. ZINNER

Davis, California
December 6, 1961

Acknowledgments

ALTHOUGH the views expressed in this study are mine, as is the responsibility for them, I owe a debt of gratitude to many persons who assisted me in a variety of ways.

The responsible officers of Columbia University made generous allocation of the funds provided by the Ford Foundation and released me from regular duties in order to devote myself to this enterprise.

I am particularly beholden to my colleagues on the interviewing staff who worked selflessly and untiringly to amass the material on which I have drawn so heavily. While all of them contributed immeasurably to the successful collection of data, the consistent high quality of Marian Low's work commends itself for special mention.

William McCagg, Jr. assisted me ably by compiling information about the Communist Party. Bernard Klein supplied useful statistics which I requested and Zoltan Sebestyen drafted an excellent background paper on the Hungarian economy.

I benefited from the comments of Paul Kecskemeti whose explorations during the past years have closely paralleled mine. The late John Kotselas lent his editorial talents to a portion of the manuscript and J. Christopher Herold went over the whole work with a discerning eye and sharp pen. Myra S. Zinner offered many valuable suggestions for improving the style and helped with the proofreading. Cornelia Marwell, Kathleen McDermott, Kathy Stone and Sharon Towne acquitted themselves nobly of the typing chores.

Henry Wiggins and Gustave Niles of Columbia University Press saw the manuscript through the most difficult stages of production.

Contents

PART ONE

The Communist Seizure of Power
1945-1948

1. Hungary Leaves the War

AT THE conclusion of the Second World War, Hungary was devastated. It had suffered incalculable moral and physical damage. Its traditional political and social values were discredited. Its institutional framework and economic structure were shattered. Its material wealth was sapped. Its cities, especially its capital — the mind, the very heart, as it were, of a small country — lay in shambles. In Budapest not a single bridge across the Danube remained serviceable. The country also sustained fearful losses in manpower, although some of these were to be restored. During the closing phases of the war 320,000 Jews were deported; of these 205,000 perished.[1] An additional 500,000 to 700,000 persons — no accurate figure has ever been made available — most of them adherents and officials of the native fascist clique that ruled Hungary from October, 1944, until March, 1945, either fled westward before the advancing Soviet armies or were forcibly removed from the country by the retreating Nazi forces. Many of these returned in the following year and a half.

The effect of the losses suffered by Hungary was the more incisive as the collapse came swiftly.

Until March, 1944, when German troops moved into Hungary in large numbers, the country had enjoyed relative tranquility. Hungary's direct military contribution to the Axis war effort had been modest. Its economy, though exploited to an extent in behalf of the Axis powers, was not overly strained and supported an adequate domestic market. The population did not especially

[1] The figures cover only Jews from the pre-1938 territory of Hungary. The large Jewish population of territories annexed by Hungary in 1938, 1939, and 1940 is excluded here.

feel the hardship of war. Even the Jews, who were the subjects
of many restrictions, were spared extreme forms of persecution
and survived largely intact as a community.

The government of Miklos Kallay, who was called to the premiership in March, 1942, and deposed by the Germans exactly
two years later, was a throwback to the paternalistic regime of
Count Istvan Bethlen, who held sway from 1921 to 1931. While
Kallay's regime scarcely afforded good or representative government, it stopped a drift toward fascism which had set in under the
premiership of Gyula Gombos (1932-35) and had continued at an
accelerated pace under his successors.[2] Kallay's administration
marked the resurgence, for the last time and in enfeebled condition, of the gentry, the magnates, and the aristocracy, who had
been shorn of much effective power in a silent but far-reaching
"revolution" in the early 1930s, coincident with the short-lived
ascendancy of Gombos. Since those days, the traditional landed
aristocracy had been displaced as a ruling class by representatives
of the petty bourgeoisie, military officers of field rank, civil servants,
and a sprinkling of impoverished nobles.

Until the spring of 1943, the Kallay government even tolerated
formal opposition in Parliament. The Smallholders and Social
Democrats on the left and the fascists on the right leveled verbal
criticism at official policy. That their attacks were ineffectual goes
without saying. The Hungarian legislature served as an oratorical
forum, but little that was said within its walls was translated into
action. Parliament was not completely regimented, it was merely
impotent.

In academic and intellectual circles, opposition of a more serious nature was growing. The future of Hungary in the event of
Germany's defeat was discussed with increasing vigor following
the battle of Stalingrad in February, 1943. The Soviet victory
that had broken the fighting spirit of the Hungarian army in
Russia was instinctively recognized as an irrevocable turning of

2 Kalman Daranyi (1935—38), Bela Imredy (1938—39), and Laszlo Bardossy
(1941—42). The two-year period from 1939 to 1941, during which Count Pal
Teleki was Prime Minister, was also an interruption of the drift to fascism.
Teleki committed suicide in March, 1941, after the German attack on Yugoslavia.

the tide of the war. The ultimate defeat of Germany was accepted as a foregone conclusion by all except the staunchest supporters of the government and a small but fanatic pro-Nazi minority.

The need for domestic reforms also continued to be felt and debated, but there was no agreement among the opponents of the regime on the preferred solutions for Hungary's problems. Confusion and uncertainty marked the deliberations, a spate of ideas without a concrete program. Still, the debates showed that under the cloak of a stagnating "political culture" life was stirring.

In March, 1944, Hungary's participation in the war took a tragic turn. While the Regent, Admiral Horthy, at long last wished to sever his country's ties with Germany and prepared to take steps to effect this purpose, Hitler tightened his grip on Hungary, ordering its occupation by German troops and imposing as premier General Dome Sztojay, the former Hungarian Ambassador at Berlin. Internal pressure increased immediately. The Hungarian economy was sapped to invigorate the faltering German war machine. Political persecution was stepped up. Opposition leaders were arrested, and Jews were deported to concentration camps in Germany and Poland. Those among the opposition who managed to evade the authorities went underground, and all organized resistance ceased. At a time when vassals and satellites of the Third Reich were straining to secede and to cleanse themselves of the stain of Axis collaboration, Hungary was being drawn in the opposite direction. Germany's hold on the country grew tighter. Soon Hungary was Germany's last remaining ally.

Still, the Regent, now the only person capable of staving off disaster, hesitated.[3] Wishing to rescue Hungary from its predicament, he yet did not know how and lacked the capacity for decisive action. His fear of Communism matched his horror at the prospect of the country's destruction and of the responsibility he would bear should the fighting front move across Hungary. Paralyzed by indecision, he continued to elicit Hitler's assurances that Hungary would be protected and adequately defended. Clearly, he expected miracles.

[3] For Horthy's account of his activities during this phase of the war, see his *Memoirs* (New York, R. Speller, 1957).

Late in August, Rumania's successful defection from the Axis camp jarred Horthy. Russian armies were approaching Hungary's southeastern border, and Rumania was now at war with Hungary. There was little time left. A change in Premiers brought General Lakatos to the head of the government. The new cabinet, however, was, if anything, even more recalcitrant than the Regent on the subject of a separate armistice with the Russians. Only when the situation had become hopeless, early in September, did the Regent summon to his palace a conference of past and present Hungarian political leaders to take stock. Out of hiding came the venerable Count Istvan Bethlen to preside—at the Regent's request—at what was his last "cabinet meeting." It was also the last state function in which representatives of the traditional "ruling classes" took part. For, in addition to Bethlen, Counts Moricz Eszterhazy, Gyula Karolyi, and Bela Teleki were invited.

Symbolically, their action terminated the existence of the Hungarian state as they knew it, a state they had resurrected from the wreckage of the First World War but which they were not capable of salvaging a second time. The decision they reached was to abandon the hopeless pursuit of the war and to sue for an armistice. One last effort was made to make contact with the West, and only when that failed did the Regent reconcile himself to approaching the Russians.

At the end of September, a delegation was sent to Moscow to sue for terms. Agreements were signed and the announcement of their conclusion was to be made in Moscow simultaneously with a proclamation by the Regent in Budapest. Horthy's moves were both slow and obvious. The result was a badly bungled job. The Germans had every opportunity to take effective countermeasures to prevent Hungary's defection. To be sure, the Regent's proclamation was broadcast to the nation on October 15; but at that very instant, the German army assumed operational command over all of Hungary, and Ferenc Szalasi—the leader of the Arrow Cross Party, who had been impatiently waiting his turn in the wings— was proclaimed Hungary's Führer. Less than twelve hours after his broadcast, the Regent was taken into protective custody by the Germans. A day and a half later he was sent to Bavaria as a prisoner. His last act—performed under duress—was to sign a document retracting his proclamation of October 15, abdicating the regency, and appointing Szalasi as premier. At this hour in history, Hungary, ludicrously, acquired its first, full-fledged fascist dictator.

What ensued defies the imagination. Szalasi and his cohorts, spurred on and aided by the Germans, acted with total irresponsibility. They looted and plundered. They violated every decency. Waves of arrest decimated the Jewish population and struck at all shades of political opinion save the extreme right. Parliamentary deputies, civil servants, former opposition elements were rounded up without discrimination. The Germans meanwhile fought savagely for every inch of Hungarian territory, including the capital. The siege of Budapest by the Russians began on January 1, 1945, and ended only on February 13, 1945, although the left bank of the Danube had been cleared by mid-January. Shortly after the siege began, Szalasi's government fled westward to Sopron. The beleaguered country now had two governments: one in the East, created in Debrecen with Communist participation on December 21, 1944, under the aegis of the advancing Russian armies and laying the groundwork for a new way of life; the other in the West, making sure that nothing of the old would be salvable. The orgy of the Szalasi gang lasted until April 4, when the last German soldier was driven from Hungarian soil.

The defeat of Germany also meant the passing of Hungary's old social and political order. Curiously, it was Szalasi's brief tenure that gave it the *coup de grâce.* On the one hand, Szalasi had persecuted many of its adherents: he was as opposed to the upper-class rulers of Hungary as he was to the Communists. On the other hand, Szalasi's rise to power can be laid to the ineptitude of the old order which he destroyed: the Regent's incompetence, as manifested in his failure to stave off native fascist rule and the German occupation of his country, tends to magnify all the shortcomings of the era that bore his name.

All told, the well-meant but ineffectual last-minute efforts of the Regent to save what he could merely embittered Hungarian public opinion. Whatever prestige the authorities commanded prior to

1944 vanished under the combined blows of German occupation
and Szalasi's reign of terror. Totally bankrupt, the old order was
beyond redemption. Its legacy for the future was that of violence
and demoralization, social disorganization and economic dislocation.

THE RISE OF A NEW ELITE: HUNGARY'S POPULISTS

Countries seldom experience a major political or social overturn without forewarning. Whether the overturn be the result of
war or of internal upheavals, or of a combination of the two, there
usually are forces present that are critical of the existing order and
ready to change it. Hungary was no exception. Even the ruling
authorities realized that with the end of the war in Europe substantial changes in Hungary's political and social structure and
in its foreign relations would have to be instituted.

The ravages of the final phase of the war, however, minimized
the chances of avoiding change of revolutionary scope. Planning
for the future was effectively disrupted, as was the forging of a
new elite capable of assuming responsibility for the country's
affairs.

Least affected by these adverse developments were the Communists in exile. They weathered the worst of the German onslaught in the sanctuary of the Soviet hinterland and were able
to devote themselves singlemindedly to preparation for their return
home. In the end, they alone had a comprehensive program of
internal political, social, and economic reforms.

For the moment, the Communists were not alone in bidding
for the leadership of their country. Despite the difficulty of articulate opposition to the old regime, opposition had existed. It
was largely unorganized and it lacked political experience. In
short, it bore the marks of the environment in which it developed.

The peculiar character of Hungarian authoritarianism during
the interwar period and during the war precluded any effective institutional expression of political opposition. What opposition
parties existed—the Liberal Party, the Smallholder Party, the
Social Democratic Party—either were thoroughly domesticated (as
were the Social Democrats, who abided by the government's re-

strictions on their activities) or quite agreed with many of the premises of the government (as did the Smallholders under the leadership of Tibor Eckhardt). Such "opposition" could scarcely be looked to for effective alternatives to the administration's own policies.

Opposition was expressed in literature and in coffee house criticism rather than through proper political channels. As in other authoritarian systems, notably in tsarist Russia, social and political criticism was disguised in literary form. But even the literary critics of the regime for the most part succumbed to the essence of the official ideology—chauvinism. It had been difficult for anyone to be indifferent to, or to rise above, the great "historic injustice" of the Trianon peace settlement after the First World War, which reduced Hungary to one-third of its former area and separated about 3 million Hungarians from their motherland. This maiming of the national ego supplied much of the motive power and justification to the interwar governments. These fed the passions of irredentism and thus not only diverted public attention from urgent domestic reforms but even suppressed agitation for reforms as damaging to the attainment of national objectives. The emotional urgency assigned to the solution of Hungary's external ills obviously precluded internal reform.

One of the consequences of this state of affairs was the isolation of the critics of Hungary's internal order from democratic opinion in the neighboring countries and in the West—for the Western democracies were by definition identified with the Versailles system. As defenders of the European status quo, they stood in opposition to Hungary's foremost interests. Hungary drifted toward Fascist Italy and Nazi Germany which shared its appetite for revisionism and appeared ready to support it in the restoration of its just frontiers. *Rapprochement* with Germany in turn started a new series of complications. Hungarian public opinion was divided with regard to the nature and even the advisability of close relations with Hitler's Reich, especially if Hungary was to play a subordinate part in the relationship. There was a healthy tradition of anti-German sentiment in Hungary, just as there was an opposite one. In the circumstances, it was obviously impossible to take a stand on any issue of importance in Hungary without simultaneously clarifying one's view of Germany.

Although preoccupation with foreign relations hindered criticism of internal conditions and isolated Hungary from the mainstream of European democratic ideas, a slow warming of political feeling was discernible. The economic crisis of the early 1930s focused attention on domestic issues, especially since it was instrumental in breaking the hold of the traditional ruling classes who had reestablished themselves in power after the revolutionary debacles of 1918-19. With the rise of a new governing stratum, of a "reform generation," Hungarian politics took a decisive turn to the right but the intensity of political discourse increased. Even the government made dutiful pronouncements about internal reforms. Land reform and electoral reform were publicly debated.

It was in this atmosphere that populism came of age in Hungary in the middle 1930s. Led by sociologically oriented writers of peasant stock, the Village Explorers (*falukutatok*), the movement resembled the surge of Russian Narodniks in the 1860s. Hungarian populists, like the Russian, were aroused by the evils of an anachronistic, semi-feudal social and political system and by the squalor of peasant life. They "went to the people" in order to rediscover the past glory and elemental vitality of the peasantry and in order to bring enlightenment to the countryside, which held the key to the nation's happier future.

It is perhaps symptomatic of the peculiar arrested quality of Hungarian social development that articulate populist agitation should begin so late, a half-century or more after its flowering in Russia and elsewhere in Eastern Europe. At that, the serious literary and intellectual efforts of the populist trailblazers attracted little attention.

The urban population turned a deaf ear to a problem "alien" to it. Only the government authorities showed concern. They censored populist writings more heavily than others and persecuted populist writers suspected of radicalism.

The populists were not a coherent group with a firm ideology. Although they unanimously addressed themselves to the fundamental social problem of Hungary—the intolerable system of land ownership—they disagreed on the precise solutions to this and other, only slightly less pressing troubles. Roughly, the populists could be divided into left, center, and right groups, but each term covered a multitude of inconsistencies.

The right, on the whole, was outspokenly anti-Semitic and pro-German. It soon tended to be diffused in the growing native fascist movement and eventually became an integral part of it, losing its populist identity. The center, more moderate in its racial and foreign-policy outlook, for the most part advocated a "third road" ("Neither Russia nor Germany"): relying on her own resources, Hungary would develop her own indigenous institutions built upon a healthy, vigorous, self-reliant peasantry ("Garden Hungary") and led by an elite composed of the Hungarian middle class, descended largely from peasant stock (the "New Nobility").

The left, generally, held the most advanced democratic ideas of any of the populists. It showed the greatest awareness that both agricultural improvement and industrial growth must be promoted in the broad cause of national economic development. (Nevertheless, the economic ideas of all the populists were fuzzy indeed; they never quite came to grips with the practical economic development of a backward agricultural society.) The left also appeared least chauvinistic, advocating some sort of "fraternal Danubian Confederation" to solve the problems of the small states of the area. In actual fact, not even the left populists had any great affinity for the neighboring states; their notions of confederation were mere pieties.

Finally, the left populists had some acquaintance with Marxist writings (which they understood imperfectly) and, most important perhaps for the future, they mingled with Communist fellow travelers. Some of them may have been members, even at that time, of Communist cells—e.g., Geza Losonczy, Ferenc Donath, Gyula Kallai—names that will figure prominently in the latter parts of our narrative.

In 1937, a group of populist writers founded the March Front. An intellectual club rather than a political party, it was the first formal populist organization. According to one of its founding members—Imre Kovacs, who later became a leader of the National

Peasant Party and in 1947 fled to the West—the March Front came into existence more by accident than by design. Nevertheless, it attracted quite a number of young intellectuals and influenced the thinking of university students. While the Front was chiefly a vehicle of the left populists, its periodical attracted a motley group of contributors, including Communists, Communist sympathizers, and others with pronounced rightist leanings.

The Front had no well-defined political creed. It stood for democratic reforms, and its immediate aim was to organize moral resistance to National Socialism. For all its limitations, the Front, because of its broad appeal, was perhaps the most influential democratic opposition group in Hungary at the time.

The potential significance of a radical, left peasant socialist movement (which the Front was not but into which it could develop) was quickly recognized by the Hungarian Communists in Moscow. Their chief ideologist, Jozsef Revai, engaged the left populists in sharp polemic in a tract on *Marxism and Populism*, smuggled into Hungary and issued (in 1938) under the name of one of the young populist-Communists, Gyula Kallai. In the tract, Revai argues and "proves conclusively" the futility of forming a peasant party on populist premises, since such a party would represent an "outdated" agrarian socialism; the urban proletariat and the intellectuals would scarcely be served by a fundamentally provincial rural leadership.

To be sure, Revai did not unequivocally proscribe populist-Communist collaboration within the framework of the Front. His arguments were heeded by a number of young people, including Losonczy, Kallai, and Donath, the so-called Debrecen group, which took its name from the town where they attended university. They wrote articles for the periodical of the March Front but opposed the formation of the National Peasant Party in 1939.

Neither the March Front nor the National Peasant Party was able to attract a mass following, and both withered away early in the war after the briefest of lives. The political climate of Hungary was especially inhospitable to the organized pursuit of democratic reforms.

The late 1930s and early 1940s brought some satisfaction of Hungary's urge for revenge on its neighbors, Czechoslovakia and Rumania. The so-called Vienna Awards of November 2, 1938, and August 30, 1940, engineered by Hitler restored to Hungary much of the territory it had lost in 1918. While this triumph failed to solve pressing social and political problems, it temporarily soothed discontent. The outbreak of the war and Hungary's involvement in it on the side of the Axis further weakened any effective opposition to the government.

The cultivation of an articulate peasant elite nevertheless proceeded apace. In 1941, the government authorized the creation of a Peasant Alliance, a sort of peasant trade union organization. Headed by Bela Kovacs, a well-known Smallholder and future secretary general of the party, the Peasant Alliance in fact became a thinly disguised Smallholder front organization. Populists, particularly those affiliated with the National Peasant Party, did not take kindly to the Peasant Alliance. Although they nominally supported it, they obstructed rather than aided its activities.

The Alliance was admittedly not a radical antigovernment organization given to subversive or revolutionary agitation. But it did more than promote the partisan aims of the Smallholder Party. It enhanced the political consciousness of the peasantry, and furthered the schooling of peasant youths, even if it did not imbue them with populist teachings. The Alliance appears to have had much more appeal to the peasantry than the populists ever had, and this phenomenon has never been satisfactorily explained. Perhaps it was the pragmatic attitude of the Alliance — which, notwithstanding its educational activities, gave priority to the day-to-day problems of peasants and offered practical assistance in improving farming techniques to raise living standards—which earned it its popularity. The populists, by contrast, addressed themselves to general problems and dealt with them on a level of learned discourse not easily intelligible to the peasants.

Populist influence was greatest in a much narrower but also more select circle—the peasant youths who were enabled, often by government stipend, to attend universities. Most of these went to Budapest to the Gyorffy College, which was headed by Laszlo Kardos.[4] Here, they absorbed not only populist teachings but, under Kardos' guidance, also embraced Marxism; subsequently, they joined the Communist Party almost to a man. The importance of Gyorffy College as a cradle of Hungary's postwar elite becomes apparent when one considers that in Hungary's first "free" government, formed at Debrecen in December, 1944, all ministerial secretaries were said to be Gyorffy College graduates.

Populism during the war period reached the peak of its influence at two conferences held at Szarszo, on Lake Balaton, in 1942 and 1943.

These gatherings took place on the premises of a Catholic society (Soli Deo Gloria) and were authorized by the government. The Minister of the Interior, Ferenc Keresztes-Fischer, even agreed to the printing, at government expense, of an expurgated record of the second conference in a limited number of copies, although he knew that nothing good would be said in it about the existing order.[5] He, at least, was aware of the impending doom of the regime he represented, and he wished to promote discussion— within limits—of the shape of Hungary's new order.

The more important of the two Szarszo conferences was held late in August, 1943, and was attended by about 600 persons, who met for five days. It was a milestone in Hungarian history, although its full significance could not have been appreciated by the participants. No assembly of comparable importance had taken place

[4] The very existence of the Gyorffy College (a college in the European, not the American, sense of the word, i.e., a dormitory for university students rather than a self-contained institution of learning) was an oddity of the Hungarian political scene. It was intended by the government to attract rural youths in order to transform them into pillars of the existing social order by giving them a precious commodity that was otherwise beyond their reach — an education. Given the conditions in Hungary at the time, it was not surprising that these youths reached out beyond the confines set by the government in search of solutions for the problems of their country. How Kardos came to be director of the college is not known to me. His Communist affiliations were in any event a well-kept secret. His enormous natural ability might well have recommended him for the post which he then used to exert an influence inconsistent with the preservation of the status quo in Hungary.

[5] *Az 1943 evi Balatonszarszoi Magyar Elet Tabor Eloadas es Megbeszeles Sorozata* (Budapest, Magyar Elet Kiadasa, 1943), 232 pp.

since before the revolution of 1848. None was to follow until the stormy mass meeting of the Petofi Circle on June 27, 1956—the most significant intellectual protest meeting prior to the revolution of 1956. Many of the names appearing in the records of the 1943 conference appear again in the meeting of the Petofi Circle.

Hungary's later political and intellectual leaders passed here in review. Among those who played significant roles at the conference were Jozsef Bognar, Peter Veres, Janos Kodolanyi, Ferenc Erdei, Laszlo Nemeth, Laszlo Kardos, Geza Feja, and Jozsef Darvas, to name only a few. Even the casually informed reader may recognize Veres, chairman of the National Peasant Party and president of the Writers' Association under the Communists; Erdei, who became notorious as one of the chief representatives of the National Peasant Party and who later held important posts under the Communists; Dobi, a Smallholder with strong pro-Communist leanings who eventually became Chairman of the Presidential Council of the Republic—i.e., titular head of state of the People's Republic of Hungary—and who, in 1959, was admitted to the Communist Party in recognition of his many services to it; Darvas, also a National Peasant leader, who went over to the Communists and became Minister of Culture in the Rakosi regime; Kardos, the director of Gyorffy College, a Communist, who later headed his party's "rural people's college movement" [6] and ultimately became one of the spiritual movers of the rebellion against Rakosi; and Nemeth, perhaps the outstanding populist writer of his generation.

The names of many other participants, at the time wide-eyed youths listening to the speeches and discussions of their elders, today have a familiar ring. They achieved public stature especially during the 1956 revolution. In addition, Ferenc Nagy, the future Smallholder prime minister, and Bela Kovacs, the celebrated and controversial secretary general of the Smallholder Party, were also present, observers on the sidelines.

While it would be an exaggeration to claim that the participants at the Szarszo conference spoke for the entire internal opposition, they did constitute its core. Apart from a handful of independents who intellectually were also rooted in the populist movement but

[6] NEKOSZ-Nepi Kollegiumok Orszagos Szovetsege.

who stayed away from it for personal or tactical reasons, there were only two other centers of opposition to the established social order. One consisted of orthodox Communists, most of whom did not reside in Hungary; the other, of western-oriented liberals, chiefly intellectuals of middle-class origin, including a considerable number of Jews. Though this latter group did not scorn the Hungarian peasantry, it was not of it. The political sympathies of its members during the interwar period had tended to favor the Social Democratic and the Liberal parties.

The activities of the Jewish intellectuals were increasingly stifled during the late 1930s and the war years. But even under less repressive circumstances they would hardly have been able to match the populists. Regardless of the abstract appeal of their ideas, the spokesmen for the western-oriented, urban, middle-class group could not aspire to public leadership in Hungary. At best, they could inspire, advise, and influence, but they could not wield political power in their own right. By contrast, the Szarszo group possessed the attributes required of active political leaders in the event of a dissolution of the existing social order.

The populists belonged to the Hungarian soil. They were mostly of humble, rural social origin. Many were Protestants from the east of the country, a region noted for its strong nationalism. The legacy of the Village Explorers could not be challenged as something alien. Their ideology, though far from original in content, had a home-made flavor; it was developed by Hungarians for Hungary.

This is not to say that populism embodied the noblest traits of the nation; rather, it embodied the most typical. In many respects the populists stood by Hungary's ruling groups, but not in regard to the question of land reform. The land-owning gentry and aristocracy would sooner make political concessions and coddle Jews —as the Germans accused some of doing—than yield one inch on land reform or accept representatives of peasant background on an equal footing with themselves.

The major assets of populism were the social origin, youthfulness, vigor, and intelligence of its adherents. Its greatest weakness was that, except for its central idea—the need for land reform—it had neither a well-defined content nor a concrete program to remedy Hungary's ills. The absence of clearly defined concepts was obvious in the deliberations at Szarszo, which were marked by an inconclusive search for a program.

The printed record of the conference not only shows the inability of the participants to agree on a program but also prefigures (when seen in the wisdom of hindsight) future behavior of several key figures in the debates. For example, Veres emerges as an advocate of adaptability in order to survive. His argument is based on the premise that the "internal logic of mass movements is to destroy those who oppose them." Darvas and Erdei reveal themselves as hard realists quite prepared to face up to the risks attendant upon the forcible transformation of society for its own good. Darvas spoke eloquently if somewhat defensively in favor of industrialization. Erdei, in the opinion of some observers the most brilliant of the lot, gave sharp theoretical formulation in terms of Marxist dialectics to the issue that became the focal point of discussion—Nemeth's "third road" concept.[7] "The third road," Erdei said, "can serve only those who are willing to run the risk of being separated from, indeed of being left behind in, political evolution because of their conviction that on the next rung [of historic development] they will have caught up again."

Although the general mood of the assembly was one of discontent and hostility toward Nemeth's formula (in essence the familiar line that Hungary must solve its problems independently of either the Germans or the Russians), no speaker dealt with it as incisively as did Erdei. Here was, in a nutshell, Hungary's dilemma over the next decade or so. What evolutionary path will the country follow? What part will Russia play in Hungarian affairs? More important, what will be the attitude of Hungarians toward Russia's involve-

[7] Nemeth introduced the "third road" concept in his speech before the assembly almost as an aside. Asked to explain what he meant, he said that if, let us say, two powers struggle for supremacy over New Guinea, the Dutch and the British, why not let New Guinea belong to the Papuans? Dissatisfaction with Nemeth's formula reflected a prevailing tendency among delegates toward friendship and cooperation with the Soviet Union and with the political and social movement associated with it, a trend based far less on ideological conviction than on acceptance of practical inevitability. As a result, however, Nemeth was quite a lonely figure at the conference, a circumstance that hastened his withdrawal from public life and his espousal of an almost hermitlike existence in the country.

ment in their affairs? Which of the historic forces will bring about
the reconstruction of Hungary—the proletariat? the peasantry? the
intellectuals? What will be the price of progress and who will pay
it? Answers to these questions were not soon forthcoming.

The general sense of the conference was that the intellectuals
were duty-bound not to dissociate themselves from the masses, that
Hungary's political and economic system would be reorganized
under some form of socialism, and that both peasants and industrial
workers would play key parts in reshaping the country's future.
By limiting itself to these vague generalities, the Szarszo conference
marked a dead end in populist efforts to formulate a clear and
practical program. But the "education" of the populist youth did
not end here. They came increasingly under the influence of
Marxist-Leninist doctrine and of the Communist Party, to which
the amorphousness of the populist ideology and the conditions
under which they grew up had made them exceptionally susceptible.

The intellectual climate of the universities was sterile. Official
policy prevented the formal presentation of some ideas (e.g., Marxism) and permitted others only in thoroughly sanitized form. This
merely whetted the students' curiosity. And, although proscribed
literature was not readily obtainable, it could be had without running undue risks of detection and punishment.

Government propaganda against Marxism-Leninism, the Communist Party, and the Soviet Union grew in intensity as the war
dragged on, but instead of immunizing its audience it achieved the
opposite effect, among the young intellectuals at least. Acting on
the premise that the government which they hated and distrusted
would not denigrate Marxism-Leninism so vehemently unless that
theory had something relevant to offer, the university students
eagerly sought out whatever Marxist literature they could lay their
hands on. Far from approaching it with misgivings, they had a
favorable disposition toward it. In 1943 and 1944, Marxism was
beyond any doubt the intellectual fad of Hungarian university
students in their surreptitious explorations. For example, one respondent, who eventually became a bright star of the Smallholder
Party, at this time avidly translated Lenin's *State and Revolution*

into Hungarian. His choice of party at the end of the war was by no means a foregone conclusion: many of his friends expected him to side with the Communists, as some of them did. Nor was lack of intelligence responsible for the students' uncritical acceptance of Marxism. They read it *in abstracto* with no practical basis for verifying its claims and postulates.

Reading Marx and his followers in this partial vacuum, the young intellectuals were struck first by the comprehensiveness of Communist theories. Here was a complete system with solutions for all problems, firm guide lines to action, and the assurance of scientific certainty. Doubts and reservations were easily dispelled—to the extent, at least, that the students saw no just reason not to give the doctrine and its exponents a fair trial. Many accepted Marxism-Leninism as they understood it and tried to reconcile it with their populist concepts. They also gravitated toward the Communist Party in the belief that it was the most suitable vehicle for the realization of their own goals.

The harshness of the regime toward individual Communists and the forced inactivity of the Hungarian Communists combined to create an idealized conception of the Party. The persecution of individual Communists gave them stature as martyrs of the opposition; the inactivity of the Party as a whole precluded the disillusionment which commonly attends direct exposure to the intrigues, chicanery, and double dealing characteristics of Communist methods of operation.

Other factors that favored acceptance of Communism and of the Communist Party included lack of first-hand acquaintance with democratic politics and the absence of a party system into which the energies of young people aspiring to political leadership could be channeled. The attitudes of the young populists were those of typical zealous neophytes: enthusiasm mixed with a generous dose of naïveté. Their impulse to destroy the old order was more potent than were their positive ideas concerning the construction of new institutions. Most important, they did not particularly abhor violence. How could they? They had been raised under a system that frequently resorted to violence and in which social strife, not social harmony, was the rule. At best, they had a textbook knowledge of democratic virtues. Even if they had understood the importance of reciprocity and of procedural safeguards for the preservation of human liberties—and there is little evidence that they did—they tended to slight these as democratic niceties, luxuries not applicable to the Hungarian situation. Moral absolutes that are indispensable to the working of a democratic political system were neither well understood nor very appealing under the circumstances.

The ordeals that the young populists still had to endure at the hands of the Germans and the Hungarian fascists during the final phase of the war served further to harden their outlook and to intensify their desire for revenge. The fascist Arrow Cross Party, put in power by the Germans in October, 1944, moved against the populist youth almost as savagely as against the Jewish population. Populist university students were rounded up, incarcerated, and deported. In their prison camps, Communist sympathizers and non-Communists mingled freely. They also came into contact with other political prisoners, who had been held for a longer time, among them a number of old-time Communists. Under prison conditions, differentiation among them along lines of political preference was blurred. Human bonds of comradeship were stronger than were political loyalties.

It was against this background that the Szarszo group entered active politics at the end of the war. The Szarszo forces brightened an otherwise bleak national picture. In them, Hungary possessed leadership material unequaled anywhere in Eastern Europe. Considering the size of the country, they were a numerous elite—more than enough to staff command posts in the government and in public institutions. At the same time, they were sufficiently restricted in numbers to know of one another even if they did not know each other personally. Most of them were on first-name terms. This circumstances, however, did not prevent the Szarszo forces from scattering in different political directions immediately after the war.

The political limitations, not to say the disorientation, of the Szarszo group prevented it from even trying to set the tone of postwar reconstruction. Instead, it became an important pool of manpower, contributing something to every political party except the

Social Democratic. Far from dominating the 1945 coalition, the populists became tools, serving the interests of each one of the parties with which they became affiliated.

The bulk of populist support was divided between the Communist and the National Peasant Party—in what proportions we do not know. A smaller number of them gravitated to the Smallholder Party.

They were a genuine asset to the Communist Party, lending it national character and increasing its appeal in the countryside, where the most stubborn opposition to it might have been anticipated. While they did not determine the policy of the Communist Party, they represented a large and potentially powerful element in it and were not suppressed until after the Communist seizure of power was complete. They initiated the people's college movement for rural youths and thus were responsible for the influx in the Communist Party of large numbers of potential leaders with a peasant background.

In the Smallholder Party, populists initially exerted only negligible influence. They were few in number and there was a natural rivalry between the Smallholders and the populists' own vehicle, the National Peasant Party. Nevertheless, persons with populist sympathies—such as Istvan Dobi, Gyula Ortutay, Lajos Dinnyes, Erno Mihalyfi, and others—gradually rose to positions of responsibility. Their rise coincided with the disintegration of the Smallholder Party and its ultimate delivery to the Communists.

The ease with which the Communists infiltrated and subverted the National Peasant Party was due largely to close personal and ideological affinities among their respective leaders. In the absence of clear lines of demarcation, the National Peasants could not be on guard against crypto-Communists in their midst. This explains how two men like Imre Kovacs and Ferenc Erdei, whose political careers took diametrically opposed turns, could share in the leadership of the Party for the better part of two years without Kovacs knowing (though he might have suspected) that Erdei was a Communist agent. It was not a vain boast when Jozsef Revai reported at the founding meeting of the Cominform that the National Peasant Party's "secretary is a Communist, one of the two ministers representing it in the government is a Communist, fifteen of its thirty-two parliamentary deputies are Communists, eight are sympathizers." [8] In 1950, Rakosi even suggested that the Party had been revived in 1944 on Communist initiative. If this was so, it was a clear case of the creation of a "bogus party" as a member of the national coalition in order to bolster Communist influence and to split the forces of the greatest single group of voters—in this case, the peasantry.

The diffusion of its forces and the contribution these forces made to the establishment of Communist hegemony had tragic consequences for the populist movement. It ceased to exert any political and intellectual influence whatever and disappeared from the scene as an active agent in shaping Hungary's destiny. In the heat of political struggle, individual adherents lost track of one another.

Little by little the demands of political loyalty displaced bonds of friendship and personal preferences. By 1948, when Communist victory was total, many populists uncommitted to Communism were either in jail or pushed to the periphery of political life. A few such as Laszlo Nemeth, who neither supported the regime nor suffered incarceration, lived in complete isolation, cut off from the outside world. Populists who joined the Communist Party lost their earlier sense of identification. Some never wavered in their loyalty to the Communist regime. They were its trusted servants and were suitably rewarded by being kept in positions of prominence uninterruptedly. Others—by far the greater number—fared less well, and many eventually became disillusioned with Communism. Yet they gave no outward signs of disaffection for several years. Populism was all but erased from public consciousness.

It was not until 1953, when the monolithic façade of totalitarianism cracked, that the scattered elements of the populist movement once again achieved contact with one another. Those who had been imprisoned regained their liberty; many of those who had joined the Communist Party regretted their choice. In the somewhat freer atmosphere of the "new course," human relations became easier,

[8] E. Reale, *Avec Jacques Duclos au Banc des Accusés* (Paris, Plon, 1958), p. 119. The first and to date the only account of the founding meeting of the Cominform by a participant. The author left the Italian Communist Party after the Hungarian revolution.

former friendships—transcending party lines—were reaffirmed, and something akin to a common ideological platform, inchoate and at first felt rather than articulated, took shape. After almost a decade of diffusion, the Szarszo group reappeared on the scene, though again in a variety of disguises. It contributed to the intellectual ferment that preceded the revolution. The Petofi Circle served as a common forum for the leaders of the wartime generation of university students, Communists and non-Communists alike.

The revolution itself was to provide them with another opportunity to assert themselves.

Emerging from the wings, the young intellectuals shared the center of the political stage, without a sign of explicit prior collusion, in a rare display of unpracticed harmony. They were in evidence everywhere—at the head of revolutionary organizations as well as in the refurbished political parties. Their presence in such a great variety of places accounted for the remarkable homogeneity of the intellectual content of the revolution. This does not mean that they controlled the revolution. But if anyone could, they were in a position to give it guidance.

The crushing of the revolution marked their defeat. Twice losers in little over a decade, they disappeared altogether from the political scene. Many of the non-Communists, having already known the suffering of internment, fled the country. Most of the Communists remained behind. The government accurately assessed their menace to its stability and turned upon them mercilessly.

The tragic Odyssey of the populist intellectuals, together with a handful of their older mentors, testifies to a certain continuity of Hungarian history during the past quarter-century. Whether or not the failures and fortunes, the ideals and goals of the populists constitute the dominant theme in recent Hungarian development is still subject to debate. The discussion continues, abroad among the escapees, and in Hungary where the official cultural organs have launched an extensive campaign of vilification against the populists and their "ideology." The picture presented here is of necessity not definitive. One thing is certain: recognition of their presence and acknowledgment of their importance is indispensable to an understanding of the momentous events of recent years.

HUNGARY'S POSITION IN THE SOVIET ORBIT

Largely because of the unique path of its history during the closing phases of the war, Hungary in 1945 had a singular position among the East European countries that were subjected to Communist encroachment in the postwar period. If we take material destruction, moral anarchy, discontinuous institutions, and intensity of social tensions as criteria for comparison, we find that while in each category Hungary suffered no more than did some other East European countries, in the aggregate none approached Hungary's plight.

Hungary suffered vastly greater human and material destruction than did Rumania, Bulgaria, or Czechoslovakia. Only Poland sustained similar losses. But Poland differed significantly from Hungary in the manner in which it sustained these losses and in the moral aftermath of wartime experiences.

In the discontinuity of her institutions only Poland and to a smaller degree Czechoslovakia are comparable with Hungary. The institutional structures of Rumania and Bulgaria survived the war intact and were destroyed only later. In Poland, no indigenous political and administrative structure had remained since 1939. Czechoslovakia had been dismembered in 1939, and its component parts were placed under three different forms of administration. In the Hungarian case, the distinctive elements were the completeness and the abruptness of the break, which insured the greatest possible turmoil and allowed no time for preparation.

As for social tension, the social revolutionary mood that prevailed in Hungary in 1944-45 was without contemporary parallel. In Poland and Czechoslovakia, anti-German sentiment ran high, informing a revolutionary atmosphere which, though national in character, had profound social and economic implications as well. The Germans filled the roles of both a foreign occupying authority and an oppressing upper class. The native upper classes had lost their status as a result of the German occupation. There were no collaborators to speak of in Poland and very few in Czechoslovakia. In this manner, national and social revolutionary aspirations overlapped. The former, whose intensity was far greater, motivated the institution of extensive reforms that were essentially of social and economic character.

In contrast to Poland and Czechoslovakia, the mood of the Hungarian workers and peasants fed upon long-standing social and economic grievances. Their anger was aimed directly at the native upper classes. In the countryside, there occurred attacks on estates, particularly during the first half of 1945, and recurrent waves of excitement swept through the villages.

The release of social tensions brought with it massive lust for revenge. A year after the cessation of hostilities, angry mobs stormed the gates of the prison yard in Budapest upon learning that henceforth admission tickets would be required to witness the execution of war criminals. Until then, such executions had been public spectacles. Only in Bulgaria was similar excitement generated over the punishment of war criminals. But in Bulgaria the lust for revenge was political; the economic grievances of the Bulgarian peasantry were slight compared with those of the Hungarians.

Poland, too, displayed striking differences from the Hungarian case. Unlike Hungary, which produced no record of effective internal resistance, Poland boasted a powerful underground movement. It was as anti-Communist as it was anti-Nazi. Despite its losses in the Warsaw uprising of 1944, the surviving vestiges of underground forces could exert strong claims during the reconstruction period. The organizational ability, toughness, and poise of the Polish Peasant Party especially (acquired under the Nazi occupation) were responsible for its stiff resistance to Communists until its partial disarmament in consequence of the return of its leaders from London.[9]

[9] Official Communist figures admit the "loss" of 15,000 Party members in struggles in the countryside between 1944 and 1947. (See K. Dziewanowski, *The Communist Party of Poland*, Harvard University Press, 1959, p. 346 n. 13.) The fight might have been even fiercer and more prolonged had the Peasant Party not disarmed itself to a large extent in consequence of the return of its leadership from London. The terms on which that leadership returned required its participation in the Communist-dominated government. Moreover, intentionally or otherwise, the exile leadership created an unduly optimistic impression of solid Western support for the cause of Poland. "Good behavior," i.e., adherence to parliamentary forms and to the coalition as approved by the Allies in July, 1945, appeared to be necessary prerequisites for assistance. Thus were the hands of Peasant Party advocates of rougher tactics effectively restrained, though not the Communists'.

If the Poles tended to view their liberation from German occupation by the Russians as an even exchange between the frying pan and the fire, the Hungarians had no reason to feel so. Their traditional hostility toward Russia was not exacerbated by a partition of their country, or by a Katyn massacre, or even by the physical liquidation, ordered by Stalin, of the entire Communist leadership, as was the case in Poland. On the contrary, it was Hungary that had declared war on Russia; and the Hungarian army, at one time deep in Russian territory, itself had committed atrocities against the civilian population. As a result, many Hungarians felt sympathy for the Russians and Ukrainians, while others were beset by feelings of guilt and hoped that the Russians would not be impelled to retaliate in kind. Fascist terror, coming as it did late in the war and without forewarning, was so acutely felt by many Hungarians as to create a mood of genuine receptivity to the liberating Soviet army. There were, of course, those who dreaded the approach of the Russians. (Their fears were fully borne out. The invading troops raped and looted savagely during the initial stages of the occupation.) But many others—workers, peasants, Jews, and a portion of the liberal middle class—seem to have regarded the approaching Soviet army as a band of saviors of the most desirable ideological persuasion. Their enthusiasm was staggered, at first, in the face of Russian deeds, but the disappointment did not last long. With an improvement in the behavior of the occupation troops, the stock of the Soviet Union rose again.

To pursue the matter of comparison with other countries that were to fall victim to Communist domination, there was a vast contrast between the situation in Rumania and Hungary. Unlike Hungary, Rumania weathered the war virtually unscathed. Its institutions continued to function, its army held together as a fighting force, its government, especially the King, enjoyed a large measure of well-deserved prestige. The King had maneuvered his people out of very tight straits with great skill and luck. Rumania made the transition from an Axis satellite to an Allied partner smoothly, earning gratitude and tangible benefits in the form of a favorable territorial settlement in the dispute with Hungary over Transylvania. The King remained titular head of state until late

in 1947, representing continuity with the past and playing a powerful symbolic role.

The Communists, seeking to make headway, found in Rumania
few issues that they could utilize. Relative economic and social
stability, absence of pent-up hatreds, satisfaction with the performance of the government complicated their task. Traditionally and
tactically of the view that the worse the situation in any country,
the better, the Communist leaders deplored the prevalence of tranquility, the lack of tension and violence. Clearly, they would have
to create their own issues in order to exploit them to their own
political advantage.

Overt Soviet intervention was needed even to gain the Communists respectable representation in the cabinet. Their ultimate
goals could not be concealed, and while the proverbial corruptness
of Rumanian politics and politicians (e.g., Tatarescu), played into
the Communists' hands, there was a notable polarization in sentiment between a small Communist minority and an overwhelming
non-Communist majority of the nation. Not so in Hungary.

The traditional political climate in Hungary had been anything
but favorable to the Communists. Hungary's experience with the
Soviet Republic of Bela Kun, which stayed in power for three
months in 1919, appeared to bar the Communist Party permanently
as an accepted political agent. For a quarter of a century, the nation
was subjected to unceasing fumigation to eliminate all traces of the
Bolshevist infection. Fear of a repetition of 1919 was a national
trauma.

The penalties for clandestine membership in the Communist
Party were so severe, and the skill shown by the Hungarian security
police in ferreting out Communist organizers sent into the country
from the Soviet Union was so great as to discourage all but the most
determined from seeking Communist ties. After a while, efforts to
maintain an organized party ceased. But in the immediate aftermath of atrocities perpetrated by Nazis and native fascists, even
the stigma of 1919 that attached to the Communists faded. Although
the behavior of Russian troops created a profound revulsion of
feeling that affected the Communists adversely, their Party did not
have to contend with intractable emotional hostility.

The Communists returned to Hungary under much more promising conditions than they could have hoped for. The disarray of the Hungarian political and social structure, the release of social pressures, and the surge of social forces, together with the endemic weakness of democratic parties and politicians, gave the Communists in Hungary more to work with than they had elsewhere except in Czechoslovakia, but for very different reasons.

If the Hungarian Communists avoided the mistakes of 1919, if they refrained from imposing their rule hastily and crudely, delayed with transforming all institutions and property relations, and guarded against offending all social classes simultaneously, they stood a good chance of engaging the creative energies of an aroused people.

This they were well prepared to do. Such a stratagem accorded with the over-all "plan" for the gradual seizure of power to which Communist parties adhered throughout Eastern Europe.

2. The Strategy of Power Seizure

THE RELEVANCE of comparing, as we have done, the conditions that prevailed in individual East European countries at the end of the war may be seriously questioned. Regardless of differences, all succumbed finally to Communist domination. Czechoslovakia with its democratic tradition and professed friendship for the Soviet Union fell just as did Bulgaria with its meager democratic tradition and Poland with its strong hostility toward Russia. Hungary with its shattered institutional structure was conquered just as was Rumania, whose institutions were intact at the end of the war. Moreover, the gross pattern of conquest bore remarkable similarities everywhere. An advance, coordinated planning applicable to any country, and applied by the Communists without distinction of place and circumstance seems apparent.

Nevertheless, broadly uniform methods conceal a great many local variations that warrant a closer analysis of their causes and their importance.

The seizure of power was in no instance effected by a single coup. It was gradual and elaborate and took from three to three and a half years to complete. In the end, the use or threat of force—Soviet military, political, economic, or psychological pressure and partisan, if selective, employment of police terror—was decisive in securing victory for the Communists against their democratic opponents. But force was not their only means. The protracted period over which the seizure of power extended called for the application of variegated techniques, designed to coerce and persuade, intimidate and encourage, isolate opponents and win friends.

UNITY OF SUBSTANCE—DIVERSITY OF FORM

The catalogue of devices used to carry out this basic strategy reads like a primer on the systematic conduct of politics with a view to securing permanent supremacy. It deserves attention for the object lessons it teaches. Although it is beyond the scope of our study to make detailed investigation of the mechanics of power seizure even in Hungary, let alone throughout the satellite empire, a summary listing of the fundamental Communist techniques may be useful.

1. Creation of a four-party coalition, including two separate but closely affiliated Marxist parties, whatever a country's previous political makeup. Socialist-Communist cooperation was secured, though not always fully and painlessly, by virtue of agreements between younger left-wing socialists aspiring to leadership in their parties and Communists who underwrote their claims.

The coalition served as a "frame" for the controlled display of every form of political expression. It represented a "national front," whatever its precise designation in a given country, signifying national unity. The national front format itself had restrictive implications, which were worked to fullest advantage by the Communists. Inclusion in the Front meant acceptance of the operating premises presented by the Communists. This limited the freedom of action of parties, especially those of a moderate orientation. Their membership in the Front tended to pull them toward the "left," their supporters in turn exercised a pull toward the "right." In this manner, indecisiveness and splits within parties were promoted. Exclusion from the Front amounted to ostracism from the body politic. The threat of exclusion, of course, hung over democratic parties at all times.

2. Simultaneous promotion of revolutionary aims from above, through Communists in the central executive departments of the government, and, at the same time, from below, through radical reorganization of the local administration immediately in the wake of the advancing Soviet army, when the benefits deriving from the Soviet presence were greatest.

In the government, the Communists strove to secure key ministries, to transform the departments they held into exclusive domains serving partisan interests, and to neutralize departments held by other parties through the institution of deputy secretaries of state and other means of infiltration.

On the local level, the Communists exploited the maximum advantage in mobility they had as one area after another was liberated. They inflated the powers of local authorities—especially to carry out basic economic reforms and to screen local inhabitants for political loyalty. Local officials were appointed on the spot upon hasty assessment of their qualifications—a decisive criterion being a person's distance from the former regime.

The importance of local bodies declined as order was restored and the discretionary powers of the central government were strengthened. But the first few hectic months of unrestricted local rule left a permanent impress on the countryside, completing the social disintegration and political ruin of the survivors of the old order.

3. Arrogation of the voice of the working classes to the Communist Party through the creation of nationwide, ostensibly apolitical mass organizations serving the interests of a particular social group—workers, youth, partisans.

This technique proved spectacularly successful with the workers, in part because of an affinity by definition and in part because of the ease with which the trade union machinery was captured by the Communists. The unions, despite occasionally successful but always belated efforts of the Social Democrats to regain initiative in the workers' movement, remained dependable Communist tools: they mobilized the "street" as a menace to the political opposition; they inhibited, if they chose, certain activities of the political opposition by means of strikes or by refusing to print, to deliver paper, etc., and they acted as the social conscience of the nation, voicing criticism and raising demands on behalf of a social class whose claims' through past injustices could not easily be turned down.

While the Communists did not succeed with other mass organizations in duplicating the mastery they had over the workers, they managed to neutralize them and prevent their becoming effective agencies of anti-Communist action. This was accomplished in a variety of ways, including the denial of legal status to an organization that the Communists could not subjugate.

4. Selective use of "revolutionary justice" as an instrument of political—and to a more limited degree, of social—struggle; utilization of "political loyalty" as a means of maximizing Communist influence (patronage, intimidation); diminution of the economic power and social status of the former "exploiting" classes; and manipulation of public opinion in a variety of ways—through referendums, propaganda, and appeals to moral indignation.

The last mentioned of these deserves special attention. Moral indignation has always been used by demagogues as an effective weapon. It works in various ways, either by arousing public anger against persons and groups accused of moral wrongdoing or by inducing in them feelings of self-doubt and guilt that may lead to loss of will. Moral indignation also serves as an occasion for blackmail and is perhaps deadliest when used in this form to extort silence, docility, compliance, and even service from political opponents. The Communists in Eastern Europe showed great resourcefulness as self-appointed guardians of public morality. In Hungary particularly, they used blackmail to remarkable advantage, for there were few among the natural (class) opponents of the Communists of such integrity as to be immune to embarrassment.

Underlying all Communist tactics was an unswerving attention to securing the sources of power that assured total domination. The organizational aspects of the bid for power, whether in the government, in the unions, or in other institutions (the army) took precedence over any other Communist-initiated maneuver.

The parliamentary form, which the Communists professed, served to mask the real struggle for institutional control. Appeals to public opinion were of a similar character, in that the Communists courted public support but were more interested in its appearance than its substance. At best, they used such appearance of support as an additional weapon in an already rich arsenal designed to achieve organizational mastery over their opponents, but in no case did they use it to achieve genuine popular consent.

In the final stages of their bid for power, the Communists "discovered" with monotonous regularity plots against the safety of the state by democratic politicans, who were accused of having sold out to the "reaction" and of scheming in collusion with the survivors of the capitalist class to abridge the dearly won economic rights of the toiling masses. It was hardly accidental—to use an old Communist turn of phrase—that ultimately democratic leaders in *all* countries were charged with identical crimes against the state. The charges led to the complete elimination of democratic leaders from public life. They were either tried (Petkov in Bulgaria, Maniu and Mihalache in Rumania) or impelled to flee before the threat of imprisonment (Nagy in Hungary, Mikolajczyk in Poland, Zenkl and others in Czechoslovakia).

Variations in the implementation of the common "blueprint" were of several sorts: the speed and scope of nationalization, the exact timing of the annihilation of opposition forces, the handling of elections. Nationalization was enacted faster and on a more comprehensive scale in Poland and Czechoslovakia, where it was applied largely against foreign—i.e., German-owned—property than elsewhere. Opposition forces were dealt with summarily in Rumania, where they were effectually read out of the body politic in the spring of 1945. In Czechoslovakia, they maintained themselves substantially intact until February, 1948.

Hungary and Czechoslovakia held free elections; Rumania, Bulgaria, and Poland did not. In Czechoslovakia, the reason for holding free elections may have been that the Communists were almost certain of winning a comfortable plurality—which they did. In Hungary, their chances did not seem nearly as good—and indeed they lost. It is still unclear whether a free election was held because the Communists overrated their strength, because they made commitments which they could not retract, or because they wished to "impress" the West. A number of explanations have been advanced; none of them is fully convincing.

These and other differences imparted a distinctive character to developments in each country, underscoring Communist slogans about "separate roads to socialism" and in some cases—notably in Czechoslovakia and Hungary—making it possible to maintain for a prolonged period the plausible fiction of a stable compromise between Communists and non-Communists that would lead to the

creation of a political and social order in which socialist and democratic tenets were reconciled.

If force had been the only question, the Communists could have
achieved total domination anywhere in Eastern Europe immediately upon the cessation of hostilities. The Red Army was in full
control, able to suppress any opposition. Besides, revolutionary
excitement ran high in several countries. That the Communists
refrained from seizing power immediately has often been attributed
to Soviet deference at this time to the exigencies of international
relations. An obvious power grab in Eastern Europe would have
jeopardized Allied cooperation. Still worse, it would have impaired
the chances of extending Communist influence—even control—to
some West European countries which did not then appear beyond
reach. So runs the argument, which may be perfectly valid. But
other considerations governed the decision to move a step at a time.

The Communist parties needed time to entrench themselves,
develop cadres, and gain experience in government. They also
were intent on utilizing for their own benefit social energies which
they were able to mobilize, social forces with which they had common aims (albeit temporarily), and social goals with which they
were able to identify themselves. Their preferred aim was to
gain supremacy against minimum rather than maximum public
opposition.

The gradualness of power seizure placed a high premium on the
employment of the "next link in the chain" theory, which figures
prominently in Communist political thinking. What this "theory"
implies is the discovery of a configuration of forces favorable to
Communist intentions and the shift to a different constellation as
soon as the preceding one has served its purpose. The procedure
is repeated as long as necessary.

There is nothing magical or extraordinary about a theory that
counsels getting somewhere by putting one foot in front of another
instead of leaping headlong at a distant and possibly elusive destination. Yet the stadial technique has caused a great deal of confusion
both in the ranks of the Communist Party and among its opponents.
Obviously, it involves a large measure of deception and dissimulation, not to say cynical manipulation, of situations and social forces.

Often, groups whom the Communists select for temporary cooperation misinterpret Communist intentions and accept in good faith
as permanent an arrangement the Communists regard as purely
transitional. Alternatively, tactical moves by the Communists that
seem at variance with their proclaimed ultimate objectives are denounced as sham. Strictly speaking, these moves are not sham: for
the moment, place, and circumstance they are the goal on which
the Communists concentrate singlemindedly.

But Communists themselves find it difficult to abide by the rules
of the stadial technique. Some are unable to concentrate on immediate targets without losing sight of their ultimate aims, and
others pay insufficient attention to intermediate steps at the cost of
ultimate ends. Here lie some of the sources of "right-wing opportunism" and of the "infantile disorder, left-wing Communism."
The distinction between form and substance, opportunism and
"principled compromise," temporary stalemate and permanent
accommodation is not easy to make. The dividing line is thin at
best. Often it is arbitrary. (Nor is there any guarantee that Communists will infallibly identify the "correct" next link. They often
err and have to retrace their steps.) Small wonder that many Communists in Eastern Europe, especially those who had little or no
ideological background (the overwhelming majority of members
and cadres) tended to lose their way and became victims of the
deception their own Party was practicing on its opponents.

Thus while gradualism and the technique attendant upon it
were meant to aid the Communist cause, they also entailed obvious
risks. Aside from the risks already mentioned, there was a diminution in popular excitement that led to inertia and apathy on the
part of the masses. There was also a dissipation of the sense of
purpose and resolution of the Communist parties. Indeed, some
Communists were fearful of having missed the best chance or perhaps even forfeited altogether the opportunity to seize power. This
danger, though not entirely imaginary, was not too serious.

The Communists operated in privileged circumstances. Although
they could not be entirely sure of winning their point in the end,
they could derive much comfort from the knowledge that the Soviet
Union dominated the lands in question. Barring unforeseen and

unlikely changes in the posture of the Great Powers, all Communist parties in Eastern Europe, could expect to be bailed out by the Soviet Union in the event of trouble. The knowledge that the errors they might commit would probably not prove fatal gave local Communists superior confidence. It improved their performance and allowed them a far better appearance than that presented by their forlorn democratic opponents.

The efficacy of the gradualist approach was conspicuously demonstrated in Czechoslovakia. There, the Communists managed to maintain an uninterrupted, if entirely artificial, working parliamentary system while they maneuvered the country to the edge of power seizure. The ease with which the Communists destroyed their opponents and erstwhile allies in one stroke—a deftly executed coup d'état not wholly lacking in the formal elements of a constitutional transfer of power—underscored the complete mastery they had achieved throughout the years over virtually all institutions. The Czechoslovak case is properly regarded in the Communist world as a classic example of "peaceful" power seizure.

The Hungarian Communists came closer to duplicating this feat than did any others in Eastern Europe, and in one respect they bested the Czechs. In Czechoslovakia, the democratic opposition at least roused itself to a final, determined—if futile—stand against the Communists. In Hungary, the opposition—actually, the Smallholder Party—was systematically whittled down piecemeal until it crumbled entirely. No last, defiant effort at staving off domination marked its end.

COALITION POLITICS: DEMOCRATIC ILLUSION— TOTALITARIAN REALITY

In Hungary, the seizure of power began before the capital was liberated, with the creation at Debrecen, in December, 1944, of an artificial coalition of four parties—Smallholders, National Peasants, Social Democrats, and Communists. It terminated with the establishment of complete Communist hegemony during the months between the fall of 1947 and the summer of 1948, when the Communists liquidated the remnants of the political opposition and promulgated comprehensive decrees of nationalization that wiped out all but the small scale artisan sort of free enterprise.

The milestones on the way were two general elections, in November, 1945, and August, 1947. The first marked the zenith of Smallholder popularity, the second its nadir.

The erosion of the Smallholder Party began in earnest in the winter of 1945 with negotiations about the formation of a new government after the Smallholders' electoral victory, followed by the forced dismissal from the party of its leading candidate for the premiership (Dezso Sulyok) and of twenty-one parliamentary deputies in the spring of 1946, the arrest and abduction of the Smallholders' secretary general, Bela Kovacs, in the early spring of 1947, for alleged participation in a conspiracy against the state, and the implication, later in the spring of 1947, of the prime minister and titular head of the party, Ferenc Nagy, in the conspiracy. Given a choice between certain imprisonment and asylum abroad, Ferenc Nagy opted for political exile and resigned from his post. He left the way open for the Communists to administer the final blow to his party, by engineering the appointment of Communist sympathizers to leading positions in it and by forcing it to run in the election on a joint national front ticket with the Communists, Social Democrats, and National Peasants—a move that caused the voters to turn away in disgust from the Smallholders.

Despite an unrelenting drive by the Communists for total hegemony, there was no general sense of doom or foreboding about the national future. Political forces did not appear to be marshaled irrevocably for a mortal struggle. Liberties seldom, if ever, experienced before (free election by democratic franchise, free press, free speech, an intensive formal parliamentary life) were more persuasive than were the warning signals.

The seizure of power in Hungary is best seen as a series of interrelated but distinct developments, affecting various strata of the population independently from one another, in different ways and at different times.

For example, the political struggle within the government did not impede the progress of economic rehabilitation, nor did the

whittling down of the Smallholders' political power correspond to
a concerted economic campaign against the urban middle class or
the peasantry, on whose electoral support the Smallholder Party
relied. Significantly, the groups originally closest to and most
dependent on the Communist Party became disillusioned first, but
they either could not or would not translate their disillusionment
into political action. The groups most distant from the Communists, and incidentally closest to the Smallholders, became disillusioned last. The revolutionary mood subsided in the countryside
long after it waned in the cities. As a result, the peasants, while
far from infatuated with Communism, could not be mobilized into
action on behalf of the Smallholders. Any active attempt at organizing concerted peasant action of any kind was, in turn, vetoed in
the government.

Proposals made by Smallholder parliamentary deputies in the
fall of 1946 for the revival of the Peasant Alliance were vetoed by
the Communists with Soviet backing. The Alliance would have
served as a rural counterpart of the trade unions, with juridical
status and widespread privileges derived from the favored social
status of the peasantry. The formation of the Alliance was dis-
allowed on the spurious legal ground that it was a corporate body
that had flourished under the fascist era. All such associations were
banned by law from public life.

In practice, the Smallholder Party was effectively isolated both
from its supporters and from the other parties in the government
coalition. Perhaps this is merely a complicated way of saying that
Communist policy was based on the principle of divide and con-
quer. But the Communists refined the principle, relying as much
on the compartmentalization of social processes as on the division
of political opponents.

Striking confirmation of testimony to the Communists' success in
manipulating appearances was provided by a former Smallholder
member of Parliament, a staunch anti-Communist, imprisoned in
1948 at the age of twenty-five and referred to by his friends as the
youngest "retired" parliamentary deputy in Hungary. According
to him, "the parliamentary rules and procedures under which we
operated from 1945 to 1947 were entirely satisfactory, and they

corresponded to the requirements of the times. They were on a European level. The liquidation of the non-Communist parties was not the result of faulty rules. It took place by means of back-door tactics."

Such remarks emphasize the gap between the formal structure and procedures of the government, which to all intents and purposes were "on a European level" and impressed the Hungarians as a distinct improvement over the past, and the actual substance of politics, which was revealed largely behind closed doors and which contradicted the very principles of parliamentary politics. There are, of course, in every political system, distinctions between formal and informal methods of decision making, between open and concealed avenues of political influence. Every government has a double operational standard. The question is, how wide is the gap between the two standards and what means are there to rectify abuses of publicly accepted political conduct? In Hungary, the gap was very wide indeed and remedies were lacking. Still worse, few people—even among leading politicians—were astute enough to see the dialectical unity between the apparent and the real, despite the seeming contradictions between them.

The methods used by the Communists in destroying the Smallholders were as simple as they were efficient, alternating between pressure and relaxation, hope and despair, and combining covert pressure with overt permissiveness. It is precisely the technique used by Communists in criminal prosecution, allowance being made for the difference between the totally controlled conditions possible in tormenting an arraigned prisoner and the less rigidly controllable conditions of political relations. But the object in both cases is to weaken the "victim's" resistance by attrition, to cause him to abandon his principles, to manipulate his moods in order to make him susceptible to suggestion, and finally to induce him to incriminate himself by admitting the substantive validity of the charges against him. To a remarkable degree this is what ultimately happened to the Smallholder Party.

The 1945 election and the circumstances surrounding it provided a telling demonstration of Communist tactics. Most analyses have stressed the fact that the Communists obtained *only* 17 percent of the vote—a decisive rejection at the hands of the electorate. Granted that they suffered defeat and that the Smallholders won a resounding victory. Granted also that the victory was not accurately reflected in the subsequent reorganization of the government (though the Smallholders did achieve 50 percent of the ministries) and in the actual power relation between the Communists and the Smallholders. From the point of view of the Hungarian people, these were not the important considerations. What impressed them was that the election was free; it met the highest standards of democracy; it was secret, universal, and direct, and everyone could vote according to his conscience. Hungary had not had a similar election in living memory.[1] Never before had a party aspiring to total power permitted itself to be defeated in an election. The Hungarians were accustomed to the open ballot, to police interference in the balloting, and to automatically insured majorities for the "government" party.

On the basis of the conduct of the election and the reaction of the Communists to its outcome, no one could describe their behavior as anything but impeccable. They obviously did not tamper with the ballot and took their defeat graciously, showing no truculence and inciting no violence. The prospect of productive cooperation within the national coalition had never been brighter. The Smallholders themselves were dazzled by their victory and a little overconfident as to what it meant. Their confidence was also built up by K. Y. Voroshilov, the Soviet chairman of the Allied Control Commission in Budapest, who told Smallholder leaders that "the Soviet Union wishes to base its friendship with Hungary on its relations with the Smallholder Party."[2]

The foregoing is not meant to suggest that the Communists lost the election purposely in order to manipulate the opposition. Far from it. But the Communists exploited their electoral loss to project a favorable public image of themselves while at the same time minimizing the consequences of the Smallholder Party's

[1] Only the first general election after the collapse of the Bela Kun regime in 1919 came close to duplicating the liberal franchise of the 1945 election.

[2] F. Nagy, *The Struggle Behind the Iron Curtain*, (New York, Macmillan, 1948), p. 154. The author is the former Smallholder Prime Minister of Hungary.

victory. In the end, the Communists earned more from their response to electoral misfortune than they might have from an obviously trumped-up demonstration of popularity.

In the negotiations over the composition of the government, the Communists asserted their claim to the Ministry of the Interior and apparently tricked the Smallholders into a tactical error. As the Communists seemed tractable at first, the Smallholders imprudently leaked to the press the announcement of the impending selection of Bela Kovacs for that post. Six days later, when the official government list appeared, Kovacs's name was missing from the roster. In his stead, the Communist Imre Nagy held the portfolio of the Interior. No explanation was offered. The public was left to draw its own conclusion. While some undoubtedly suspected Soviet pressure behind the scene, others, in the absence of any tangible evidence of coercion, interpreted the reversal as a sign of Smallholder weakness and ineffectiveness. To this day we are as ignorant as to what happened behind closed doors on that occasion as we are of the reasons that induced the Communists to permit a free election.

In the spring of 1946, the Smallholders were exposed to alternating pressure and relaxation. They were also forced to choose between two Communist demands that differed only in the degree of their unattractiveness for the Smallholder Party. The Communists demanded the expulsion from the Smallholder Party of a number of outspoken anti-Communists, among them Dezso Sulyok, the party's original choice for the premiership, a man of conservative background against whom a powerful propaganda barrage was built up. Theoretically at least, the Smallholders could resist the Communist demand. In practice, they had to comply with it: the Russian command in Budapest intimated that in the event of their recalcitrance there would be a strong likelihood of a sudden rise in reparation quotas and of a speed-up in delivery schedules. The majority of the Smallholder leadership decided that it could not in good conscience so endanger the economy. Instead, it sacrificed its conservative colleagues and expelled them from the party.

But almost immediately after this humiliation, the Smallholder leaders had their hopes raised by Stalin himself. On the occasion of a state visit by Hungarian dignitaries to Moscow he encouraged them with references to a possible settlement in Hungary's favor of the Transylvanian dispute with Rumania, professing also a desire for "true friendship . . . without endangering the independence of Hungary." The Smallholders left Moscow under the impression that "the actions of the Soviet authorities in the countries occupied by the Red Army were mostly ungoverned [i.e., unknown to and uncontrolled by the Kremlin] and that on the basis of Stalin's statements a firmer position could be taken against them."[3] (The Smallholders also considered the Hungarian Communists among the "ungoverned" elements and felt that relations with the Soviet Union could be normalized over the heads of the Hungarian Communist leadership.)

Two months later, the Smallholders bowed before yet another assault. They stripped two of their deputies (Ferenc Vidovits and Karoly Vertessy) of parliamentary immunity on the insistence of the Communists that these two men be delivered to the police for alleged anti-state activities. The men in question were not very prominent. It was the principle of the action taken against them rather than their persons that counted. The Smallholder Party once again appeared unable and to some extent unwilling to protect its own members. Morale within the party was not strengthened by this. The prestige of political leaders is bound to suffer by open display of weakness or moral uncertainty, no matter what the cause.

Six months elapsed before the Communists mounted a new, final offensive on the battered Smallholder fortress.

This time their target was Bela Kovacs, the Smallholder secretary general. He was simply arrested and abducted by Soviet security agents, but not before the party leadership had agreed to his questioning by the police and urged him to testify. Whether or not his parliamentary immunity was temporarily suspended for that purpose is a point on which no reliable testimony could be gathered. Kovacs was accused of complicity in a plot to overthrow the Hungarian People's Republic, a plot allegedly prepared

3 *Ibid.*, p. 213.

by the Hungarian Unity, a secret society dating from prewar years whose role has been aptly analyzed by C. A. Macartney.[4] The Hungarian Unity at one time had an enormous though objectively undefinable influence. Its membership comprised "racially pure" Hungarian Unity at one time had an enormous though objectively It continued to exert power behind the scenes among Hungarian political refugees in the West, even those who fled after the 1956 revolution.

The Hungarian Unity had a political committee of seven members who, by virtue of their social background and record of service to the Hungarian state, were barred from holding public office. Kovacs could in no way be called a man of the old regime. He was, however, by temperament a fiery uncompromising opponent of Communism, ideally suited for liaison between the Smallholder Party and the Hungarian Unity. With due regard to his political post, he was a "silent" (eighth) member of the Unity's political committee of seven. If his participation in the political committee was a crime, he was guilty beyond doubt. Whether or not participation alone was a crime is another question. The plans of the Unity to overthrow the people's democratic regime were hardly more than vague hopes to place their own people in office again if and when Soviet influence in Hungary should terminate. There were no independent military or political plans for the overthrow of the existing political system. From the Communist point of view, of course, the activities of the Unity were by definition conspiratorial, inimical to socialism, and thus treasonable. Kovacs's "disclosures" under police duress served to implicate other Smallholder leaders. A direct result was the flight of Ferenc Nagy, the Smallholder premier.

Naturally, the Communist success in manipulating the Smallholder Party was predicated on the impossible ground rules that governed the conduct of politics in Hungary. The Communists used the police for their own purposes and changed the rules of procedure in and out of Parliament at will, while denying the

[4] C. A. Macartney, *A History of Hungary* (2 vols., New York, Praeger, 1957); *the* authoritative work on Hungary between the two world wars by the dean of British historians of Hungary.

same rights to other parties. No coalition can function equitably under such circumstances. The Communists themselves, when confronted with similarly rigged conditions, have proved singularly ineffectual.

Communist use of coercion and the public's knowledge of it must be placed in proper perspective.

In Hungary (as in Czechoslovakia), the Communists managed to conceal the police arm for a long time. At first, they hid its real mission under the cloak of rightful retribution against war criminals. In the excitement generated around the trial of war criminals, it was easy to widen the net so as to include marginal cases that would have been cleared in any court of law adhering to traditional norms. Transgressions of this sort stood every chance of going unnoticed. They served a useful purpose in that they intimidated the more forthright opponents of Communism without creating an atmosphere of general terror. After exhausting these possibilities, the Communists could and did resort to police terror on a highly selective basis, concentrating on key individuals and groups in the capital while leaving the rest of the population unmolested. In this manner, they managed to strike fear in the heart of a limited but politically important segment of the people while the rest went about their business unaware of any danger.

Kovacs's arrest was the most dramatic instance of police intervention. It created more of a stir than any previous infraction of legal safeguards, especially in the countryside, where Kovacs was well-known and liked. The peasants, however, lacked the organizational means to protest effectively.

As for the Smallholder Party, it was too weakened and compromised to rise in protest against this monstrous invasion of its ranks.

Even if due allowance is made for coercion, the eminent success of the Communists could not have been achieved without the "collusion" of the Smallholders themselves. One astute observer called the systematic erosion of the Smallholder Party a process of self-liquidation. To a large measure, it was just that. The Smallholders actively contributed to the perpetuation of the myth of political "normalcy," of a working parliamentary order. Their leadership did not alert its followers and the nation to the evils of Communist practices; it deliberately concealed the existence of Soviet-Communist covert pressure not only from the public but even from the parliamentary deputies of its own party. The impression of "politics as usual" resulted inescapably.

The precise reason why news of behind-the-scene pressures on the Smallholders and reverses suffered by them within the coalition cabinet was kept secret has not been satisfactorily explained. A number of conjectures suggest themselves. The most likely cause was genuine perplexity as to how best to handle a matter that was at once delicate and humiliating. Possibly the Smallholders felt that silence was a price they had to pay for remaining in the coalition, and remaining seemed to them the wiser course, despite indignities. Under the ground rules set for the coalition by the Communists, protest led to political oblivion. Yielding point after point, the Smallholders tried to sustain their morale by clinging to what straws of encouragement the Communists and the Soviet Union were holding out to them, by hoping for the genuine improvement of the situation once a peace treaty was signed, and even believing in the imminence of Western military action against the Soviet Union.

It is also possible, of course, that the Smallholders were forewarned by the example of the Rumanian Maniu and the Bulgarian Petkov. Both men stood on their rights and refused to compromise and were excluded for their pains from any constructive participation in their country's politics. Thus the moral issues involved were demonstrated, but the question facing all East European non-Communists was: was this enough? The Smallholders, if they ever explicitly asked themselves the question, arrived at a negative answer.

The concealment of Communist abuses and of the hardships that beset the Smallholder leadership meant that the public was never mobilized to concerted action. The population could not rally to the aid of the party; rather, it viewed the disintegration of the party with lingering bewilderment and a final loss of faith.

Equally serious repercussions resulted from the behavior of all the coalition parties in the distribution of spoils among themselves. None had ever been allowed near the fleshpots of patronage before. They naturally succumbed to the common instinct of all politicians and fought avariciously for the spoils of office. This was well and good. But it obscured the broader struggle against Communism. Self-gratification by politicians scarcely promoted a single-minded and arduous defense of the commonweal.

In the final analysis, the catastrophe that overtook the Small-holders stemmed from Communist pressure, from the peculiarities of the postwar political situation, and from the internal weaknesses of their party.

One of its leaders has said that the party had an unfortunate organization and ideology. It would be more accurate to say that it had no identifiable ideology whatever and that not its organization but its leadership was unfortunate, as were the composition of its supporters and the lack of intensity of their allegiance.

The popularity of the Smallholders was largely artificial. It was due largely to the fact that the political spectrum had been narrowed to the government coalition—the Communist-designed "frame"—which formally represented shadings from extreme left to moderate right-of-center only. The domination of public life by four parties made adherence to one or another of them a basic prerequisite for almost any person wishing to preserve or improve his place in society.

Of the four coalition parties, only the Smallholders and the Communists attracted supporters from a cross section of the population—the Communists in smaller quantity (but perhaps better in the qualities of zeal and talent), the Smallholders in greater quantity (and somewhat more diluted quality). The Social Democratic and National Peasant parties catered to a much more restricted clientele.

The heterogeneous composition of the Communist Party eventually bred serious internal difficulties and led to extensive purges of its membership. For the time being, however, the Communists clung together, concealing the lines along which the Party was divided. Not the Smallholders. They lacked the initial cohesiveness of the Communists and fell apart along the seams of social and ideological difference.

The heterogeneity of the Smallholder Party was well known to the Communists, who struck at its weak points with the intention of dividing it. On one extreme in the Smallholder Party were fellow travelers such as Istvan Dobi, Gyula Ortutay, and others who actively undermined the party's will to resist Communist encroachments. They kept the Communist high command accurately informed of what went on in the Smallholder ranks and helped to influence party policy in favor of the Communists.

At the other extreme were those who constituted a link with the Horthy regime, although they themselves could not be identified with it. This does not mean that the Smallholder Party was a front organization (or fig leaf, as Rakosi once called it) of the "reaction." On the contrary, there is good reason to believe that the "reaction" disdained and distrusted the Smallholders as much too leftist and unreliable. But the more liberal survivors of the Horthy regime who were barred from formal participation in politics on their own account found a natural haven in the Smallholder Party.

Between these extremes were other groupings along lines of class, religious preference, and age. The Smallholder Party did not fully satisfy the demands of any of these elements, as indeed no such broadly based political organization could. In a mature democracy, this sort of ambiguity is no drawback; the harmonizing of otherwise clashing interests is one of the basic tasks of a democratic political party. In Hungary, where the clash of interests continued to have priority over social harmony, disparate groups could not yet willingly reconcile their particular interests with the general good. They gave their support to the Smallholders grudgingly, for want of a more satisfactory vehicle. Thus the Smallholders captured the majority of the Catholic and of the peasant vote. But the party itself did not have a good working relationship with the Catholic hierarchy, whose primate disapproved of Smallholder leaders and policies, and the peasantry itself was lukewarm to it. The peasantry during this time was still too concerned with the land reform to care for anything else. As for the youth attracted to the Smallholders, it was on the whole rather under populist intellectual influence. It was often at odds with the Smallholder leadership over the latter's temporizing measures. The idol of the young was Bela Kovacs, whose voice in party councils, despite his strong personal following and central organizational role, seldom prevailed.

Despite its impressive electoral record, the Smallholder Party inspired little confidence even among its members. It neither matched the political skill of the Communists nor displayed the galaxy of intellectuals associated with the Communist and National Peasant parties. In a true sense, the Smallholders were beneficiaries as well as victims of postwar politics; under normal conditions, they would have attracted a much less imposing array of votes. As things were, their electoral support was of an inchoate character. It was not a clear mandate for a particular course of action and was not negotiable for effective power.

The collapse of the Smallholder Party to all intents and purposes signaled the end of coalition government as well.

In the second general election, in August, 1947, the Smallholder Party, running as an obedient member of the government bloc, polled 769,763 votes (15.4 percent), a drop of 1,900,000 votes since November, 1945. One would have to accuse the Hungarian electorate of incredible fickleness, were it not for the fact that three hastily organized opposition parties, who were permitted to participate in the election, polled almost exactly the number of votes lost by the Smallholders: the Democratic People's Party 820,453 (16.4 percent), the Hungarian Independence Party 670,547 (13.7 percent), and the Independent Hungarian Democratic Party 260,-394 (5.2 percent). The vote cast for these three parties was a more accurate indicator of a crystallization of political opinion than had been the 1945 election. Some of the leaders of these parties were men who had been expelled from the Smallholder Party; others represented more specific political trends, notably a Catholic and conservative orientation, than did the Smallholders. Their showing was the more impressive since they had little time to prepare for the electoral contest and were hampered in their campaign. The election itself, though freer than all elections held between 1919 and 1945, was not exemplary. A considerable degree of ballot stuffing is said to have taken place. Nevertheless, the majority claimed for the government bloc (60 percent) fell far short of the mechanical majorities reported from all the other satellites save Czechoslovakia.

The question again arises why the Communists, by this time in command of the government and bent on eradicating all opposition, failed to insure a more decisive victory for themselves and their satellites at the polls. Possibly, they underestimated the strength of the opposition. If so, they could have corrected matters in the official announcement of the results (as the Rumanian Communist Party did in 1946). That no extensive correction took place betrays an intention more cynical than the mere falsification of electoral returns. The Communists appear to have been anxious to reveal the full face of the enemy in order to mow him down ruthlessly. The fate of the three opposition parties substantiates this conjecture. They were cut down swiftly after the 1947 election, when Hungary entered the final phase of totalitarian domination.

3. Postwar Reconstruction and Foreign Policy

COMMUNIST economic policy in Eastern Europe closely dovetailed with the political. This is normal procedure. The interdependence between politics and economics is a basic tenet of Communist dogma, and it was manifest in a variety of ways.

The latitude permitted the middle class and the peasantry to pursue their own economic interests corresponded closely to the degree of political liberties allowed them. The apparent concern of the Communists with national welfare and the zeal with which they led the reconstruction of war-damaged installations, including churches, paralleled their adherence to the outward forms of parliamentary government. The tight, though veiled, control they exercised over the country's economic life duplicated the stranglehold they had on the political instruments of power. Economic control was founded on the Supreme Economic Council, the secretary general of which was the Communist Zoltan Vas and which superseded all the economic ministries, thereby nullifying formal occupancy of several of these by Smallholders. The overt economic activities and avowed aims of the Communists masked both their covert works (such as the trade agreement with Russia in August, 1945, intended to facilitate the exploitation of Hungary in behalf of the Soviet Union) and their real intent, which was to rebuild the economy speedily in order to set the stage for rapid, planned industrial expansion. Just so their overt political behavior was obscuring their real objective of total domination.

In the economic as in the political sphere, the difference between Communist policies in Hungary and elsewhere in the Soviet orbit was of degree rather than kind. The general patterns were identical everywhere. No government proceeded to collectivize land immediately. No government nationalized all industrial property until after the completion of power seizure. No government discouraged private economic initiative. The grand design called for scrupulous adherence to the classical Leninist formula of gradually narrowing class alliances as the revolution moved from its democratic toward its socialist phase. The Hungarians simply exaggerated the dialectic inherent in the prescribed course. In economics as in politics, they deliberately enlarged the gap between form and substance. They encouraged illusions to dissimulate reality.

Not only was Hungary's economy ruined at the end of the war, but wartime destruction was aggravated by Russian plunder, by the systematic removal of industrial installations as war booty, and by the extraction of reparations. To this must be added such selective measures as the land reform, which compounded economic calamity for one particular social group, the landowners.[1]

Nevertheless, there is general agreement among Hungarians who subsequently left the country that the rate of economic recovery was impressive. Their contention corroborates and in turn is corroborated by statistical evidence. Among those questioned, a majority gave credit for the recovery to the Communists, who handled economic reconstruction with enthusiasm and even a touch of genius. The Communists ingratiated themselves both with specific achievements and with their moderate economic program.

Specifically, the Communist mayor of Budapest (the same Zoltan Vas who later became secretary general of the Supreme Economic Council) won respect for the dramatic and efficient supply of the capital with food in the fall of 1945, when famine threatened. The Communist Minister of Transportation, Erno Gero, won plaudits as the chief architect of the rapid rebuilding of the Danube bridges

---

[1] Land reform was decreed on March 15, 1945. It affected roughly 3.2 million hectares of land (1 hectare = 2.47 acres)—one third of the total agricultural area of Hungary, including forests. The number of farm holdings affected was 120,000. Of these, around 40,000 were large estates that were confiscated outright. Land was distributed among 640,000 claimants. These included 370,000 landless peasant families, 215,000 "dwarf holders," and about 55,000 other beneficiaries.

in Budapest and elsewhere. (A popular slogan in Hungary at the time was "Eljen Gero—Hidvero": Long Live Gero the Bridge Builder.) In order to appreciate the psychological effect of Gero's accomplishment, one must remember the pride the inhabitants of the capital take in their bridges, which they regard as national monuments, like the House of Parliament or the Crown of Saint Stephen. Their symbolic importance even in 1945 overshadowed their strict economic utility. Finally, the Communists received credit for stabilizing the Hungarian currency in the summer of 1946 after a runaway inflation of seven months during which the worth of the pengo dwindled to virtually zero.[2] The inflation itself constitutes a separate chapter in the postwar development of Hungary and will be treated at greater length later.

In a more general sense, the Communists made a favorable impression by both their agricultural and their industrial policies. The land reform was decreed in March, 1945, before the country was fully liberated and while a Communist held the Ministry of Agriculture. Whatever its long-term economic implications, the reform alleviated the land hunger of a large portion of the peasantry. Most important, it sent the peasants into frenzied economic activity. For the first time in memory, they felt that no political inhibition prevented them from striving to improve their position. Free to match their skills against nature, they worked the soil as never before. The land reform, of course, transcended purely economic considerations. It was a social revolutionary measure of supreme importance that ruined the powerful landowners and released a pent-up energy which enlivened the countryside some time after.

The radical policy of land distribution and its social revolutionary consequences had no counterpart in industry and commerce. Instead of nationalizing property on a broad scale, an act that would not have met with serious opposition in 1945, the Communists were instrumental in restoring all but the largest factories and mines to private owners. Those who feared wholesale expropriation were agreeably surprised. A comparison between

[2] At the end of July, 1946, the black market price of one U.S. dollar was 4,600,000 quadrillion pengos.

the scope and pace of nationalization in Hungary and in the other East European countries clearly establishes the backwardness of Hungarian economic planning until 1948, when it caught up with the rest at one bound.

The rationale underlying Communist policy seemed to be that under the existing conditions the speedy rehabilitation of the economy took precedence over the social utility of expropriating the capitalist exploiters, who were insignificant in numbers and who could be cut down at any time and with greater ease than the landowners. Excepting a very few tycoons who controlled industrial empires, the business community was invited to contribute its talents to the economic recovery of the country. Its cooperation was secured by the proffer of the usual capitalist incentive—profit —as was the cooperation of the middle and lower middle classes, professional people, shopkeepers, and artisans, who were either self-employed or worked with a small number of hired helpers. If these entrepreneurial citizens could be induced to apply themselves in behalf of their own welfare, they would incidentally enrich national wealth and without cost to the state. Their acquisitiveness was encouraged, they responded with alacrity, and the results were gratifying.

The great inflation is remembered by Hungarians with a mixture of horror and pride. It was a traumatic experience, but it did set a world record in the worthlessness of a currency.

While the inflation was in progress, it was as much as a substantial portion of the population could do to follow the tedious routine of exchanging currency daily as the changes in rate were released by the government and to plan purchases in such a manner as not to be caught in the squeeze of currency changes.

Naturally, black markets and rackets flourished. The Communists were said to run the largest organized black market through front men in order to replenish the Party's coffers. But they had no monopoly on the market. Illicit transactions were a necessity for many, especially for middle-class people.

Families with no salaried bread winner were forced to engage in complex barter and financial deals to secure basic staples for survival. Far from enriching themselves, they had to dip into whatever reserve wealth they had to make ends meet. Their savings were wiped out in the bargain. This did not prevent the Communists from fanning the flames of class hatred. The ranks of the "reaction" were enlarged to encompass profiteers and black market operators who were accused of enriching themselves at the poor man's expense.

The working people were in fact better off. At the height of the inflation they were being paid in kind, and their minimum subsistence was assured. Payment in kind incidentally turned out to be a highly effective device of labor discipline. No worker could afford to loaf, and absenteeism was virtually unknown. The power of the trade unions to allocate and distribute stocks also induced many workers to join the unions and thus to contribute to the power of the Communists—who had the union apparatus firmly under control.

The peasants, self-sufficient for food and less dependent on the money economy than were the urban classes, were least affected by the inflation. The price structure of agricultural and industrial goods also tended to be to their advantage.

No one has seriously suggested that the inflation was a planned Communist maneuver. But once inflation was in progress, the Communists refrained from halting it in order to find a cheap way of financing the country's economic recovery. The alternative was enormous capital investment. Certainly, Hungary's currency could have been stabilized long before August 1, 1946, when the government overnight introduced a new currency, the forint, that replaced the old worthless pengo at the rate of 1:400,000 quadrillion units.[3]

The inflation over, economic reconstruction proceeded apace. It was at this time that the Communists most blatantly encouraged the middle class to gratify its wants. By the summer of 1947, when the final blow was being administered to Hungary's tottering political coalition, economic conditions were sufficiently improved to provide satisfaction and contentment to a substantial part of the people. Some Hungarians went so far as to assert that at this time Budapest was better supplied with consumer and luxury goods

[3] Stephen D. Kertesz, *Diplomacy in a Whirlpool* (Notre Dame, University of Notre Dame Press, 1953), p. 155.

than was Prague, although a year earlier Prague had appeared to be infinitely more prosperous. Actual well-being thus substantiated the illusion of economic freedom and contributed to the political apathy of the population.

It is not impugning the Hungarians to say that between 1945 and 1947, whether of necessity or choice, much of their attention was absorbed by economic pursuits in their own behalf. All major social groups benefited from the economic upsurge. The workers scored impressive social gains. The middle class was able to recover losses dating back to the closing phases of the war. But the most striking social and economic advances were made by the peasantry.

Communist economic policies contributed significantly to maintaining "alliances" with the peasantry and the middle class. Communist political objectives were enhanced commensurately.

THE SHAPING OF PUBLIC OPINION

In February, 1952, Matyas Rakosi, in a retrospective analysis of the power seizure, paid tribute to the Communist Party for having won the great majority of the "toiling masses" to its side.[4] One need not subscribe to Rakosi's views to grant him some truth. In so far as no strong anti-Communist consensus took shape anywhere in the population, Rakosi was correct.

Hungarian public opinion remained diversified yet deferent to the new conditions until 1948. Group attitudes seemed to be determined with reference to specific needs and interests rather than to the Communist Party. At the same time, the various groups dutifully acknowledged the existence of new sources and channels of authority and adjusted themselves to these without trying to defy or hamper them.

The Communists, for their part, seemed content, even anxious, to maintain an atmosphere of spontaneous diversity. They did not seek to impose a pattern of rigid conformity, to solicit active, organized support for the Party. Instead, they were at great pains to give an appearance of permissiveness and to identify themselves with the objectives of various groups.

4 Matyas Rakosi, *The Way of Our People's Democracy* (English translation by the National Committee for Free Europe, Research and Publication Service, New York, 1952).

In their effort to project a favorable and bland public image of themselves, the Communists seemed quite successful. Witness the startling testimony of a prisoner of the Communist regime of upper-class background. Referring to late 1946 and early 1947, when he was already in prison, he asserted that he and like-minded inmates secretly hoped that the Communists would not be ousted from political power too soon, lest the democratic reforms they sponsored fall victim to the resurgent forces of the reaction. The return to Hungary of about 90 percent of the more than 500,000 people who fled the country ahead of the Soviet army further testified to the prevailing optimistic view that tolerable accommodation with the Communists was possible.

It would be incorrect to infer from the foregoing that any group wholly identified itself with the Communist Party, not even the workers and the Jews, although many individuals had close affinity to it. What developed was essentially a hierarchy of "alliances" between the Communist Party and certain groups, definable by intensity and motivation. In assessing these "alliances" it is well to remember that the exact nature of the relationship need not be consciously recognized by both partners. There certainly need be no explicit agreement for the pursuit of common objectives or formal instruments for cooperation. In the Communist vocabulary, the term "ally" connotes anyone who at a particular time and under particular conditions "objectively" promotes Communist interests, whether this be done actively, passively, consciously, unwittingly, or any other way. Conversely, the term "enemy" connotes not only those who are actively combating Communism but all others who in any sense impede the attainment of Communist goals. The dividing line between ally and enemy is imperceptible. It depends on minute changes in a given situation and on the reading of one's attitude by the Communists. It is quite possible to go to bed, as it were, in the camp of allies and to wake up in that of the enemy, without moving a step oneself. (E.g., Israel: an ally in the struggle against Western imperialism while in quest of its independence, a foe and a lackey of the imperialists immediately upon becoming an independent state.)

As things were, Hungary was full of potential Communist allies. There was a natural "alliance" between the Communist Party and the peasantry, founded on their (temporarily) common goals—the destruction of the landowning class and the distribution of land. The "alliance" was maintained so long as the Communists found it expedient not to interfere with the peasants' enjoyment of the fruits of their own labor. Another and more direct "alliance" existed between the Communist Party and former fascist groups who offered their services in return for forgiveness of past sins.

The predominant attitudes of major groups during the period of power seizure may be summarized as follows:

1. Workers: At first, they were enthusiastically in favor of the Communist Party, although there is some question if they voted for it in overwhelming numbers. The blurring of significant differences between the ideology and the program of the Social Democratic and Communist parties made it possible to support the Social Democrats, the traditional party of the workers, for sentimental reasons, without in any way endangering the winning of long-sought social and economic goals. The Communist Party was, nevertheless, viewed with confidence as a genuine workers' party which, by virtue of its power position, guaranteed the fulfillment of the ambitions of the working class. Working-class unity as represented by the close cooperation between the two Marxist parties was also welcome.

The workers' enthusiasm began to wane as the Communists took a greater and greater hand in the trade union movement. The workers objected less to the domination of Communists there than to the introduction of antidemocratic practices within the union movement, especially in the form of arbitrary discrimination against "rightist" socialists and old-time trade union organizers. A division along traditional lines separating old social democrats from Communists and fellow-traveling "left" socialists began to take shape. But neither the unity nor the strength of the workers' movement were seriously affected by it. The organization of the unions, if anything, grew more solid. Disgruntlement with internal trade union matters did not translate itself into political disaffection for the workers did not as yet question the honesty of the Communists' political intentions and the soundness of their economic policies. Besides, they had no other forum of opinion to turn to. Affiliation with political parties other than the Marxists was unthinkable, as was the creation of an independent union organization free from Communist influence.

2. Peasants: Numerically they were the largest social stratum in Hungary; also, during the period under discussion, they were the most revolutionary. The peasantry was an agent and a beneficiary of sweeping changes in class structure and economic enterpreneurship. Peasant attitudes chiefly reflected satisfaction with the abolition of the oppressive system of landownership, pride in newly won self-respect, and consuming interest in making their own mark as independent tillers of the soil, free of any unnecessary interference. In politics, the peasants showed cautious reticence toward all the parties courting their favor. The more prosperous among them generally voted for the Smallholder Party, the most familiar and most innocuous of coalition parties. But in specific instances in which the Smallholders were locally represented by former members of the landowning class, no matter how liberal in disposition, the peasants were mulishly stubborn in opposing them. "Dwarf holders" and new owners generally were more likely to associate with the National Peasant and the Communist parties.

Despite the bonds of common interest, the peasantry (even without the large landholders, who formed a class of their own) was not and had never been a homogeneous stratum. It was composed of several, perhaps as many as ten, subgroups—each identifiable by the jobs held by its members, by their mode of living, and even by their habits of speech—in a strict hierarchical order, with sharp lines of demarcation, somewhat comparable to the color shadings of American Negroes.

If the size of their holdings is taken as the main criterion, the various subgroups, such as they were after 1945, can be classified in three categories: middle peasants (over 15 yokes [5]), smallholders (8-15 yokes), and dwarf holders (less than 8 yokes). The new owners—those who received all their land after 1945—joined the smallholders and dwarf holders.

There were great differences between the economic potential of the middle peasants and of some smallholders on the one hand (in their implements, experience, diligence, etc.) and the dwarf holders

[5] 1 cadastral yoke equals 1.42 acres.

and new owners on the other hand. The middle peasants and the better-to-do smallholders did very well economically. They produced for the market and benefited from the favorable price relations between agriculture and industry. They became the new peasant aristocracy.

The less prosperous smallholders, the dwarf holders, and the new owners, in general, scarcely managed to produce for the market; the size of their holdings was uneconomical; and they received no government assistance to improve themselves. They continued barely to subsist, sometimes living even below the miserable standard of their former servant status. Here, a new "class conflict" in the countryside was taking shape. The land reform, far from solving the economic and social problems of the peasantry, simply transferred them upward. The countryside did not achieve social harmony overnight. The differentiation that took place recalls the emancipation of serfs in Russia in the 1860s and the further revision of class in the 1920s during the NEP period. But in the brief interval between land reform and the seizure of power, few of the new tensions produced genuine stress, and the farming population worked on in the sun of liberation.

3. The middle and upper classes: The concept of the middle class as a predominantly entrepreneurial power group was not applicable to Hungary. The Hungarian middle class was small. Its composition and its politics are better discussed according to more specific occupational and political determinants. The groups about which information is available comprise Jews, white-collar employees in industry and commerce, and former fascists.[6] The

6 Such obvious groups as Catholics and Protestants were omitted from the discussion for reasons other than oversight or deprecation of their significance. These two religious groups comprise over 90 percent of the population (roughly in a ratio of 2:1 between Catholics and Protestants). They cut across many lines of demarcation between various groups. It was felt that subsuming Catholics and Protestants under other categories in which the dominant reference was to occupation or social status would not unduly demean religion as an element determining behavior and attitude. By contrast, differentiation based primarily on religious grounds would detract from and obscure social, economic, or political influences. On the whole, Catholic peasants acted more markedly with reference to the religious factor than any other identifiable group in Hungary. Church influence was most pronounced among them, and they seemed to be commensurately resilient to Communism.

upper class, also subject to division into several subgroups by social
origin and occupation, though more familiar with power, will be
treated even more summarily than the others because of the paucity
of information about it.

a. Jews: The consideration of Jews as a separate group is justified
by the part they played, or are believed to have played, in the
Communist regime. Hungarian Jews, as those of many European
countries, did not think of themselves as a separate group; they
were thoroughly assimilated. They were nationalistic to the point
of sharing the Horthy regime's irredentist foreign policy orientation. Their political ideas were not particularly liberal with regard
to domestic politics. Rather, they had a profound disdain for the
masses—workers and peasants alike. A benevolent paternalistic
government that did not discriminate against Jews would have
suited their tastes.

Despite their own predispositions, their "distinctness" from the
rest of society (and, by the same token, their group identity) was
forcefully brought home to them by racial, discriminatory legislation, especially from the late 1930s on, and by a rising tide of
physical terrorism which got completely out of hand in the closing
months of the war.

At the end of the war, the Jewish community had every reason
to look to the Communists as its protectors. But it would be false
to say the Jews were pro-Communist. By virtue of their traditional
economic status and their fervent wish to regain it, many Jews
had an ambivalent attitude toward the Communist Party. They
sought its favor and feared it at the same time, lest it enact radical
economic reforms that would stifle individual initiative. When it
became clear that Communist policies did not seek to make inroads
on private property, these apprehensions were quieted.

In the end, the Jewish community in Hungary held two general
attitudes.

Independent businessmen and members of the free professions
(doctors, lawyers) looked upon the Communists with mixed feelings
of relief and distrust. They regarded them as natural guarantors
against any abridgment of civil rights on religious grounds. But
they disliked the Communists for their suspected rowdyism and

their economic doctrines. Politically, this segment of the Jewish population tended to affiliate itself with the Social Democratic Party as a sort of reasonable compromise between the Communist Party (direct association with which seemed below their dignity) and the other two parties, neither one of which looked particularly attractive. The National Peasants had the odor of latent anti-semitism. The Smallholders, especially in Budapest, where the vast majority of Jews were concentrated, looked too much like slightly disguised successors of the old regime.

In contrast to the business and professional people, Jewish intel-lectuals and artists, youngsters in their teens (regardless of their parents' occupation and political preferences), and those who had been in concentration camps were eager to join the Communist Party.[7] Seeking outlets for their talents, recognition for their rights, and revenge for past dishonor, these groups gave their services un-stintingly to the Party. To them the Social Democrats looked namby-pamby. Only the Communists appeared sufficiently forceful and radical. Moreover, only the Communists satisfied their psycho-logical needs for security and belonging.

b. White-collar employees: This segment of the middle class was made up of people of diverse religions and social backgrounds, from different regions of the country. They had one thing in common, a profound sense of deference to authority. Scarcely self-reliant, dependent on the good graces of their superiors, profes-sionally unprepared to change employment, they clung to their positions and in order to safeguard their status eagerly adjusted themselves to the prevailing hierarchy of power and values. For-merly haughty, rightist, and imitative of the mannerisms of the upper class, they now curried the favor of the new "powers" in industry and commerce—the Social Democrats and Communists. The Social Democratic Party became the chief repository of their

---

7 The attitude of the teen-agers deserves special mention. Under the impact of the war they matured very early. Having been exposed to the Hungarian secondary school system at its worst (antisemitic and chauvinistic), they de-veloped a genuine, burning hatred for the old regime. The normal radicalism of youth was thus increased, and these young people quite naturally sought out the Communist Party—the antithesis of the old regime and the only political group unsullied by compromise with it. The "purity" of the Communists in this sense added to their attractiveness.

favors—as it did of some other middle-class groups—because of the quaint combination of respectability and influence it offered. It was leftist and Marxist and thus unexceptionable in the prevailing political climate. At the same time, it had an aura of gentility about it by virtue of its long history as an accepted, "housebroken" opposition to the Horthy regime.

As the influence of Social Democracy in economic enterprises faded and the Communists took command ever more openly, many white-collar employees transferred their membership to the Communist Party, hoping to enjoy the protective benefit of the party label.

This group, from which technically trained people (engineers, technicians, even bookkeepers) have to be separated, but which shared common traits with the government bureaucracy, on the whole displayed a gift for opportunism. Lacking in principle, it ingratiated itself with its new masters and conformed in speech, in behavior, and even in dress to the style of the new political order.

c. Fascists: This group included former officials of the Horthy regime identified specifically with the law enforcement agencies, i.e., gendarmes, military officers, and certain types of civil servants, as well as with the scum—mostly of lower middle-class origin—that rose to the surface during the Szalasi terror. If not incarcerated, these elements were deprived of their customary means of livelihood. Having no reserves to fall back on, they made do as best they could. Necessity and, on occasion, lust for violence led some of them into the services of the Communist Party. On the whole, however, this group lived on the fringes of society, in disgrace.

d. The upper class: This group included nobility by birth and attainment, the upper gentry, the former political and military leaders of the country, the financial and industrial magnates associated with the Horthy regime. From its ranks came many of the major war criminals, tried by revolutionary tribunals and dealt with, on the whole, very harshly. The remaining members of this group retired from public life. Some viewed their retirement as temporary and entertained ideas of a political comeback. Their illicit political activities (in which they engaged more from habit than conviction) had a comic opera character. Shorn of their traditional bases of power, faced with a restive population on the move toward the realization of long-sought reforms, these relics of the past had scant hope of reasserting their authority. Their plans, if they can be called such, were pitiful, based entirely on the voluntary and permanent withdrawal of Soviet power from Hungary. Others of this group believed that the "state of siege" under which they lived would be of longer duration. They simply dug in to make the best of a very bad situation and to survive as long as possible.

THE MAKING OF HUNGARIAN FOREIGN POLICY: EMBELLISHING THE DEMOCRATIC FAÇADE[8]

The end of the war once again found Hungary in an unenviable position in the international concert. It had no friends among its neighbors, whom it had alienated by repossessing territory from them during the war and by other misdeeds such as the 1942 massacres in Bacska (a territory "regained" from Yugoslavia in 1941). It had no well-wishers among the victorious Great Powers, with whom it failed to ingratiate itself by any noticeable act of statesmanship aiding the Allied cause. The truth of the matter was that Hungary remained Germany's loyal ally to the bitter end. This would prove difficult to live down.

The prospect of retaining any of the territorial gains made in 1939 and 1940 appeared slim. It seemed certain that Hungary would shrink back to its truncated, "Trianon" size, an injury to the national ego which supplied much of the motive power and emotional appeal to the inter-war governments.

In 1945, the mood of irredentism was somewhat muted by the rational realization that Hungary had forfeited its claims to the permanent restitution of the territories it first lost in 1918 and by the emotional precedence given to internal problems. Saving all that could be saved nevertheless became the keystone of Hungarian foreign policy, which was built around two major issues: prepara-

[8] The material of this section is largely based on a memorandum supplied by Gyorgy Heltai, the Communist Political Director of the Ministry of Foreign Affairs from 1945 to 1949, when he was arrested as a "Rajkist." Mr. Heltai is currently director of the Imre Nagy Institute of Political Science in Brussels.

tion of the peace treaties and normalization of relations with the West. By a curious twist of historic circumstances, Hungary's relations with the countries undergoing political and social transformation similar to its own were strained. This affected the attitudes of the respective Communist Parties as well.

The Hungarian Communist leadership did not officially condone any semblance of irredentism. Rakosi himself is said to have been mortally afraid of incurring the Soviet Union's disfavor over the question of national chauvinism. He recoiled from every suggestion that he make demands on neighboring Communist-dominated countries. But obviously, on questions of national interest, there were divergent opinions among individual Communist leaders. Party policy, in keeping with its avowed purposes, could not afford to appear less concerned for the national welfare than did other political parties. Finally, even the more internationalist Communist leaders, including Rakosi, did not cherish the thought of being bested by their foreign comrades-in-arms, especially if being bested implied one's relative standing in Moscow's good graces. The conspicuous absence of unselfish fraternal feelings among the East European Communist leaders became plain in these early squabbles over the settlement of issues that had plagued their bourgeois and reactionary forerunners. As for Hungary's professed desire to establish close relations with the West—that too was in part motivated by hopes for merciful treatment at the peace table. In part, it was a natural corollary of the general policy of maintaining democratic appearances. Foreign policy afforded a unique opportunity to earn respectability abroad at virtually no cost and to strengthen the credibility of claims made in behalf of the domestic order the Communists pretended to be building.

The evolution of Hungarian foreign policy and of the foreign policy apparatus duplicated the main features of the general trend in the political system. The Communists did not control the Ministry of Foreign Affairs, but they exercised decisive influence in it and had effective veto power over the foreign policy commitments of the government.

The very organization and staffing of the Ministry offers valuable insights into the management of affairs in Hungary at this time.

The Minister, Janos Gyongyossi, was nominally a Smallholder. He had been picked for the post by Soviet Marshal Rodion Malinovsky, in 1944 and held it until the summer of 1947.[9]

During his tenure, Gyongyossi did not set the tone of foreign policy. Not especially popular and influential in his own party, he had real fear of the Communists and catered to their wishes as well as to those of the Social Democrats. He was essentially a mouthpiece of the political appointees serving under him. Among these, the Communists were most influential, although they did not constitute more than 10 to 15 percent of the staff of the Ministry prior to 1947.

The staff of the Ministry was made up of diverse elements. Its core at first consisted of former employees of the Ministry and of old-line career diplomats. The reason for keeping these was not entirely expediency. In one of the many anomalous developments that characterized Hungary, the foreign service happened to be relatively free of Nazi and fascist sympathizers. It was, in fact, a hotbed of anti-Nazi activity during the war. Many of its higher-ranking officials of upper-class background were politically enlight-ened Anglo- or Francophiles. A number of them had been jailed by the Germans and the Szalasi regime. Due to their unimpeach-able wartime record, their reinstatement in government service—if they wanted it—was a foregone conclusion. Most of them were eager to serve again in order to apply their diplomatic talents to the promotion of Hungary's cause at the peace conference. Reli-able and competent as they were, they were unrepresentative of the prevailing alignment of political forces. The major parties thus assigned their own trusted representatives to the Ministry. This practice unnecessarily hampered the work of the experts and at times, it seems, led to the duplication, triplication, and even quad-

---

[9] When Russian troops occupied the Eastern portion of Hungary, Gyongyossi was the publisher of a Smallholder-oriented newspaper at Bekescsaba. The pro-Soviet tone of the paper attracted the attention of the Soviet command. Gyongyossi was pressed into service at the Soviet field command at Szolnok. Two months later, when the new postwar government was formed, he became Foreign Minister. The key to his selection probably lies in his distant political past. A professor by training, he was somehow (no one seems to know precisely how) involved in the 1919 Red regime. Compromised, he was unable to continue in his profession and became bookseller and journalist in turn.

ruplication of assignments. Chaos eventually was brought under control. By this time, however, Communist infiltration of the Ministry was proceeding swiftly, and a new, far less desirable type of political appointee was making his appearance on the scene.

Hungary's foreign policy toward the West found tangible expression in the choice of heads of mission dispatched to the various Western capitals after the war. Not one of them—and all were appointed with the consent of the Communist leadership—was a Communist or even a Communist sympathizer. The Minister in Washington, Aladar Szegedi-Maszak, was a career diplomat. He had been jailed by the Nazis. The Minister in Paris, Pal Auer, was a well known Smallholder lawyer. The Minister in London, Istvan Bede, was a former deputy press chief of the government and a personal choice of the Social Democratic leader Arpad Szakasits. If not immediately, then in the course of the next two years, the Communists placed their own reliable appointees in more or less innocuous posts in all legations in order to check up on the activities of the chief of mission.

The device of sending personally and politically acceptable ministers to Western capitals was clever. It produced the commercial treaties and foreign loan arrangements Hungary desired to conclude during this period. It perpetuated a falsely pleasant picture of Hungary. More important, in an indirect way, it got people to do the bidding of the Communist Party who normally would never consider such an affiliation. The risk of defection on the part of these people was, of course, to be reckoned with. But it was planned for. Their defection indeed coincided with the completion of the power seizure, at which time the Communists dropped their earlier pretenses all along the line. The first series of resignations in the Hungarian diplomatic corps were occasioned by the so-called Hungarian Unity trial which touched off the final assault on the Smallholder Party.[10] As a consequence, the ministers in Washington and Paris resigned. But it was characteristic of the political climate of the country that even at this late date the Communists were able to dredge up respectable replacements. The Paris post

10 See pp. 42-43 above.

went to Count Mihaly Karolyi, the first president of the ill-fated Hungarian Republic of 1918-19, who had been swept out of office by the Kun regime. Blacklisted by Horthyite reactionaries, he was tried and convicted *in absentia*, losing his property and civic rights. He lived in exile throughout the Horthy era, a personal symbol of persecuted liberals. He returned to Hungary in 1946. The Washington post went to Rustem Vambery, a "gentleman of the old school," a political liberal, by profession a lawyer; he had defended Rakosi before the Hungarian tribunals in 1936. The façade, though crumbling, was not wholly demolished. It was not until well after the completion of the power seizure that wholesale Communization of the foreign missions took place. The occasion was another trial, that of Laszlo Rajk.

Hungary's foreign policy toward the East was less conspicuously successful. Despite frantic efforts to enlist Soviet support in behalf of some of Hungary's claims, the peace conference ended in what was for Hungary a total fiasco. None of its territorial aspirations were honored. The hated Trianon frontiers were reaffirmed. The bitterest pill of all, particularly for the Communists, was the attitude of the Soviet delegation. It was thoroughly hostile to Hungary's claims after what appeared to be—at least in the estimation of Hungarian politicians, including Rakosi—an implicit suggestion by Stalin himself that a favorable adjustment of the border with Rumania would be sympathetically considered by the Russians. This was the only instance that we know of (although there must have been others) in which Rakosi permitted himself to be duped to the point of letting down his guard and authorizing premature, public disclosure of what he took to be a promise. On returning from Moscow, Jozsef Revai, who headed the Communist Party's foreign policy commission, triumphantly announced the good news at a mass rally in tones strident with old-fashioned irredentism. One can imagine Rakosi's shock and anger when he was informed of the outcome of the peace negotiations.

Although Hungary was slighted in its quest for territorial restitution, it obtained some satisfaction from its neighbors concerning the rights of the ethnic Hungarian minorities in their respective countries. The situation was especially delicate vis-à-vis Czechoslovakia, which wanted to expel its Hungarian minority as it did the German. Neither at Potsdam, where the expulsion of the Germans was explicitly authorized, nor at the Paris Peace Conference did the Great Powers condone such a move. Yet the Czechoslovak authorities proceeded unilaterally and attempted to force a decision on the Hungarians which the latter vigorously resisted. Ultimately, in 1947, an agreement was reached that was about as equitable as could be expected. These national issues, aside from being negotiated on the government level, were subject to inter-party discussions. In the course of these, both sides were acerb, the Hungarians remonstrating with the Slovaks that they were flouting the Marxist principle of national self-determination, formulated by none other than Stalin, and the Slovaks retorting that while the Hungarians were appealing to staid dogma, they (the Slovaks) went straight to the oracle, Stalin himself, who gave them the nod. Relations between Rumanian and Hungarian Communists would have been equally strained but for the fact that the Rumanian Communist Party urgently needed the cooperation of Communists of Hungarian ethnic descent living under Rumanian jurisdiction. Agreement was reached that the Hungarian minority in Rumania would enjoy broad cultural rights. In return, the Hungarian Communist Party would refrain from exerting influence on Rumanian Communists of Hungarian origin and would advise them that they were to be faithful and loyal servants of the Rumanian Party.

Relations with Yugoslavia developed in a most curious fashion. Territorially and ethnically the Hungarians could make no demands on Yugoslavia.[11] Despite the traditional hostility between the two countries, the Yugoslavs espoused Hungary's cause at the Paris Peace Conference and offered to mediate in the dispute with Czechoslovakia. The importance of the Belgrade post—in contrast to the other East European capitals—appeared to be underscored by the size and composition of the Hungarian mission there. While neither Prague nor Bucarest had Communist mission chiefs, Bel-

11 Because of the atrocities perpetrated during the war by Hungarian authorities against the Serbian population in the Bacska region, Hungary could not advance territorial and ethnic claims against Yugoslavia nor could it engage the Yugoslav government in tenacious negotiations similar to those conducted with the Slovaks.

grade was the recipient of Zoltan Szanto, a redoubtable veteran of high standing who at one time served as secretary general of the Hungarian Communist Party. His staff included a number of other Communists as well.

The reasons for the friendship the Yugoslavs appeared to be forcing on the Hungarians have never been fully revealed. Possibly Rakosi himself resented what to him might have seemed a patronizing attitude on the part of Tito, who at this time was considered the Kremlin's favorite in Eastern Europe. It is known that the Yugoslavs broached the subject of a South East European federation most confidentially, so that only an inner circle of Communist leaders knew about it. The response of the Hungarian leaders has not come to our attention; but in the distant aftermath of the hectic events that followed, it has been asserted that Rajk and other "nationalist" Communists were not hostile to the idea, while Rakosi opposed it, more for personal reasons (he was afraid of being overshadowed by Tito) than for national considerations. Just why Rajk, a nationalist, rather than the internationalist Rakosi should have welcomed federation with a group of Slavic nations has not been satisfactorily explained, except in terms of personal preference, temperament, and the like. The story of the Hungarians' reaction, for all we know, may be apocryphal. That the question was discussed can be taken for granted. When Tito was excommunicated from the Communist family, Rakosi turned viciously against him.

Cursory examination of Hungary's foreign policy and of the role played in it by the Communists leads to the following conclusions:

1. The Soviet Union allowed Hungary some latitude in pursuing national objectives. Foreign policy was not subject to minute daily supervision. Similarly, Hungarian Communist leaders were not privy to Soviet foreign-policy decisions.

2. The Communist leadership, especially Rakosi, though exceedingly cautious in advancing foreign-policy claims that might alienate the Russians, did not block the pursuit of aims manifestly in the interest of the nation. Good relations with the West, though feigned rather than sincere, were consonant with the maintenance of democratic appearances.

3. The foreign-policy personnel of Hungary was a mixture of old

career diplomats and new political appointees. Even the latter were not exclusively "party hacks." The Ministry of Foreign Affairs maintained something of an *esprit de corps*. It also enjoyed a measure of functional autonomy. Proposals were often initiated in the Ministry, and while they did not always carry the day, they were frequently given a hearing even by the Communist high command. The Communists did not exercise tight, microscopic control over the Ministry. They were, for a time, satisfied with the political loyalty of their Party members as sufficient guarantee against "irregularities." Only as the time table of power seizure moved forward did greater numbers of Communist functionaries infiltrate the Ministry. Eventually, the original echelons of Communists, themselves suspect of national deviation and bourgeois sentimentality, not to say of acute espionage on behalf of the Western Powers and of Tito, were almost to a man replaced by "aparatchiki."

4. Hungarian foreign policy toward the West was eminently successful in normalizing contacts with all Western countries. Hungarian foreign policy toward the East was less successful. It revealed a lack of harmony among the leaders of the respective Communist-dominated states.

4. The Communist Party

It is neither frivolous nor paradoxical to say that the Hungarian Communists had power thrust on them in 1945 even before they had an organized Party.

For a quarter of a century, from 1919 to 1944, the Hungarian Communist Party led a threadbare existence in the shadow of the disaster that overtook it as a result of the collapse of Bela Kun's Soviet Republic. At times it disappeared altogether, and Communist activities were confined to more or less isolated, self-trained groups that sprang up here and there. These lacked neither zeal nor talent. They attracted a measure of sympathy among people whose moral sensibilities were outraged by the inequalities of Hungarian society and by the miscarriages of Hungarian justice, but who did not dare declare themselves openly for the Party.

Meanwhile, many Communists who had fled from Hungary immediately after the 1919 debacle, found asylum in Soviet Russia. Their revolutionary venture, though it ended in failure, had made them heroes in the Communist International. For years, they enjoyed the confidence of the Comintern and received responsible assignments in it.

Eventually, the prestige of the Hungarian Communists abroad also declined. Their leader, Bela Kun, fell from grace in 1937, a victim of Stalin's blood purges. He dropped out of sight and it is presumed that he was summarily executed. Some of his colleagues were exiled to Siberia. Others escaped with milder reproof and merely exercised self-criticism, recanting their ideological errors. A few went unscathed. For example, Erno Gero served as a Comintern hatchet man in the Spanish civil war.

Although the Hungarian Communists in the Soviet Union temporarily lost any semblance of cohesiveness as a group, many of them survived the purges. They became assimilated in their new, seemingly permanent environment. No Hungarian, not even a Communist, ever fully loses his national identity. But these people melted into the Soviet scene. They acquired Soviet citizenship and worked in Soviet institutions. Some married Russian girls. Their children went to Soviet schools.

These veterans formed the core of the Party when it was reactivated in 1941 under the leadership of Matyas Rakosi.[1]

Their ranks, scarcely replenished by new arrivals for about twenty years, were augmented by a small number of defectors and prisoners of war captured in 1942 and 1943. Among the defectors were Party members and Social Democratic trade union organizers who had been sent to the Russian front by the Hungarian army in punitive labor battalions consisting of Jews and politically unreliable individuals. Defectors and prisoners of war who had been won over to Communism after their capture received hasty indoctrination, and being more expendable than the Party's old stalwarts, several (e.g., Antal Apro and Istvan Kossa) were sent on dangerous missions in enemy-occupied Hungary to begin indispensable organizing work, especially in trade unions. The veterans of the movement stayed behind in Russia to plan grand strategy for seizing political power. They returned to Hungary in the wake of the liberating Soviet armies.

Attempts during the war to improve coordination between the Communist movement in Hungary and in the Soviet Union were

---

1 Rakosi had spent some time in Russia in the early 1920s as a member of the Secretariat of the Communist International. But he had had the misfortune of being sent back to Hungary as an organizer. Apprehended by the police, he spent sixteen years in prison. He and Zoltan Vas, a fellow Communist prisoner, were released by the Hungarian government in 1940 and "exchanged" for a group of tattered military pennants of sentimental value only. These flags had been in Russian possession since 1849 when Tsarist troops put down the Hungarian national rising against Habsburg rule. The "exchange" was one of several initiated by the Soviet government which took advantage of the benign climate of its "honeymoon" with Nazi Germany to arrange for the release and emigration to Russia of prominent Communists held captive in a number of East European countries closely allied with Germany. For example, the Rumanian Ana Pauker was released under circumstances similar to Rakosi's.

ineffectual. The alertness of the Hungarian police helped to prevent the establishment of dependable channels of communication, thus increasing the ideological confusion of the local Communists.[2]

In reality, there were two separate Hungarian Communist movements—one at home and another abroad in the Soviet Union. They did not unite until the liberation of Hungary was well under way. High-powered organizers from Russia (Gero, Nagy, Revai, Farkas) appeared in Hungary for the first time in the fall of 1944 to revitalize the Party and to impose the stamp of Moscow's leadership on it. But owing to the piecemeal liberation of the country and to the disruption of its communications and transportation systems, two Communist centers sprang up—one in Debrecen, where the provisional government was temporarily seated, and another in Budapest. Each had its own directing Central Committee. They formally merged on February 25, 1945.[3] The forging of a Party was their most pressing task.

BUILDING THE PARTY

Communist membership policy followed the dictates of the strategy and tactics of power seizure. These called for rapid expansion into a mass Party with widespread appeal to the population. The customary high degree of selectivity, geared to the requirements of a conspiratorial elite, was abandoned in favor of open recruitment. Inadequate social background and lack of ideological conviction were no bars to admission. The Party tried to make itself

[2] The difficulties of the Hungarian Communists were endemic throughout Eastern Europe save Czechoslovakia. Persecution, inadequate contact with the headquarters of international Communism in Moscow, personal and ideological rivalry arising from the strains of underground existence, and geographic separation were a common fate of Communists in Bulgaria, Rumania, and Poland, affecting the development and character of their parties and causing dissension among their leaders long after their illegal existence ended. The Hungarians were merely harder hit than were others by these adversities.

[3] Source material on the very confused antecedents of the rebirth of the Communist Party in Hungary can be found in Dezso Nemes, *Magyarorszag Felszabadulasa* (The Liberation of Hungary; Budapest, 1955 and 1960). This is a standard text by a durable ideological expert. Additional information may be found in A Magyar Szocialista Munkaspart Kozponti Bizottsaganak Parttorteneti Intezete, *A Magyarorszagi Munkasmozgalom 1939-1945-ig* (Budapest, Kossuth, 1959-60). This is a publication on the Hungarian Workers' Movement from 1939 to 1945, prepared by the Institute of Party History of the Central Committee of the Hungarian Socialist Workers' Party.

attractive to as many people and for as many reasons as possible. It accommodated the idealist and the opportunist. It offered solace to the disoriented and power to the ambitious. It soothed the injuries inflicted upon Jews by the old regime and at the same time employed the talents of former fascists.

Marxist doctrine, presented in a bland way that emphasized its universality and humanism, was far from repugnant to Hungarians. Anyone could accept it without offending moral precepts and disturbing deeply imbedded historical self-images. The young in particular found Marxism appealing. They helped make it the most stylish doctrine in vogue. The effectiveness of Marxism as a social myth once again received telling confirmation.

Doctrine aside, the Party's manifest sense of purpose, its demonstrated organizational ability, and the quality of its leadership were important in attracting followers. Resoluteness and efficiency, though they may be decried as harsh and impersonal qualities, invariably command respect in politics. As for the Communist leaders, they stood head and shoulders above the parochial types which were the best the other parties were able to produce. Of course, the tremendous positional advantage of the Communists tended to make them look "good" as compared with the futile non-Communists, who acted from positions of weakness.

Rakosi, who was later violently denounced for his "inhuman" character, at this time cast a magic spell with his forthright manner and his great intelligence. Some people regarded him as a genius or near genius, almost too big to have only the cares of a small country like Hungary entrusted to him. Erno Gero impressed with his devotion to work, escetic personality, and mode of life. He was untiring and ubiquitous in personally supervising the economic reconstruction of Hungary. He took journalists, including non-Communists, with him on his unending journeys and seemed to take them into his confidence. Revai was deemed an intellectual giant, eccentric perhaps, but a giant all the same, with qualities unequalled by any other official party ideologist.

The most glamorous of all was Gyorgy Lukacs, the world-renowned Marxist theoretician and philosopher. The return of the virtuoso of dialectical materialism was all the more welcome because the ranks of Hungary's notable intellectuals had been severely depleted by successive waves of emigration and extermination. With Lukacs—and in the context of the situation this may strike the reader as somewhat ironical—a fresh breeze of European culture blew into Hungary's fetid intellectual atmosphere. Under his guidance, new generations of Marxist intellectuals, unexcelled by those of any other nation, could grow up.

Of course, Lukacs was on display. He wielded no effective power in the Party. There is no evidence that he was aware of being a tool of the political leadership, but, judging by his subsequent conduct, it is doubtful that he would have behaved differently had he known that he was being used as "bait."

The Party's membership swelled rapidly from an estimated 2,000 in the fall of 1944 to 30,000 in February, 1945, and to 150,000 in May of the same year. In mid-1947, there were 700,000 registered Communists, and two years later, after the merger of the Communists and the Social Democratic Party, more than twice that number. Imposing as these figures were (and their accuracy was, as a matter of principle, open to doubt), even at face value they did not fully justify Rakosi's assertion that the Party had become the leading force of the nation. But this is relatively unimportant. What mattered was the attractiveness of the Communist Party and the strength and quality of that attractiveness.

In its recruitment policy, the Party was anxious to absorb the advocates of violent revolution or simply of violence. In the countryside, it cultivated the lowest ranks of the agricultural proletariat, whose animosities were useful in demolishing the landowning class.

The Party was equally intent on capturing the allegiance of the patriotic element, i.e., the political prisoners and all others who could even remotely be classified as underground or partisan fighters against the Germans. Granted that their numbers were small and their qualifications as partisans meager. The Hungarian resistance had been pitifully anemic. All the more reason why anyone giving signs of militancy should be aligned with the Communists, to bolster the Party's own corps of militants and to deny to the other parties these remnants of spirit and energy. "Patriots," it is known, were offered retroactive membership in the Party that would entitle them to more substantial privileges and would swell the Party's own prestige. To heighten that same prestige and to tie their hands, leaders of the academic world and of the professions were also approached to join.

Other groups which the Communists showed particular interest in capturing were the youth and the women of the country, who had no prior political experience and involvement. Several respondents related that fifteen-year-old youths, too young to be admitted as Party members, volunteered their services and aided the Party in a variety of menial ways, so as to establish the preconditions for their joining later. The concentrated effort of the Party to acquire an ideological monopoly over the youth brought forth an ostensibly apolitical, nationwide youth association, the MADISZ.[4] While the attempt to capture the allegiance of all the youth failed, the Communists met with greater success in addressing themselves to the rural youth through the network of people's colleges (*nepi kollegiumok*) which offered a genuine possibility for social advancement.

The people's college movement was well received in the countryside and brought the Party closer to the country people than any other program it sponsored. But it was, by its very nature, a double-edged weapon. Its active organizers, themselves barely out of school, were not deeply steeped in Marxism-Leninism. They had come to the Communist Party via the route of populism, and the populist influences they had absorbed still showed. Under their direction, the NEKOSZ movement assumed a populist, not to say national-Communist, tinge. Their spontaneous enthusiasm and their program of instruction were highly unorthodox from the Communist Party's point of view. To be sure, the Party was acquiring valuable recruits. But what was the character of these recruits?

The Party's efforts to enlist the support of women were handsomely repaid. The women's mass organization, MNDSZ,[5] proved an excellent starting point. The female recruits of the Party showed extraordinary zeal for self-effacing, devoted, and efficient service. Feminine functionaries were a new phenomenon on the

4 Magyar Akademiai es Demokratikus Ifjusag Szovetsege.
5 Magyar Nok Demokratikus Szovetsege.

Hungarian scene. The explanation for their extraordinary efficacy is, probably, partly self-evident. The participation of women in politics had powerful connotations of social emancipation.

Party members were not at first indoctrinated with Marxist-Leninist theory. Before 1948, there was no systematic indoctrination program even for functionaries, let alone for rank and file members. Such a program would have been inconsistent with the public image of the Party, in which the ideological element was minimized. Indoctrination would have drawn attention to the discrepancies between the Party's real beliefs and its avowed program for Hungary. Full-scale indoctrination would also have overtaxed the Party's capacity. It simply did not have trained propagandists by whom a program could have been developed.

The number of "convinced" Communists could at no time be ascertained. At least, there is no way of extrapolating this information from the available testimony. A great many Communists were reported convinced so soon after 1945 as to cast doubt on the probability that they were ideological converts or, for that matter, on the sincerity of their conviction.

The reasons for joining the Party were many. Foremost among them seemed to be considerations of practical benefits to be had from Communist membership. Some people saw the Party card as a protective shield against possible persecution. Others viewed it as job security. Still others considered it as the best guarantee for social advancement.

The Party itself did not much care why people signed up for membership. It worked on the simple precept that any degree of involvement with Communism was better than none. The filling of positions of power by Communists, be their membership ever so nominal, was preferable to having non-Communists fill these posts. Thus, irrespective of underlying motives, the bonds tying member to Party and Party to member were for the moment strong enough to promote the fulfillment of the immediate goals of both.

The Party got what it wanted. Through the multitude of its members—by 1947, 2 out of 7 families had a Communist in their midst—it melted imperceptibly into the masses. It was not sequestered from the rest of the nation. For a totalitarian party, proximity to and distance from the social environment which it seeks to control and mold in its own image is at all times of crucial importance.

The ordinary Communist member, on his part, had no reason for complaint. The Party made only minimal demands on him. It did not make acceptance of its values a condition of membership. It merely set general and loose norms of accepted and forbidden behavior, attitudes, etc., without prescribing adherence to them in detail. Nor did the Party engage in *ad hominem* criticism. Criticism and self-criticism in the customary Communist meaning was not yet on the public docket. Even in deriding petty-bourgeois attitudes, the Party acted gently and impersonally.

The average member was at this time under no strain as a result of his Communist affiliation. His privileges exceeded his duties. He was seldom asked to do anything that did not accord with his conscience. It was possible for him to be both a good Communist and good Hungarian, or even a good Communist and good Christian. His intellectual and moral sensibilities were not unduly ruffled by the Party's own deeds. He could rationalize the occasional political excesses of the Party as being in the public good. The noble claims of the Party had not yet been shown to be spurious. Often truth was on the side of the Communists.

The satisfactory symbiotic relation between the Party and its members held dangers for both. It is a special feature of the dialectic method to magnify one obstacle while lowering another.

Members, on the whole, joined the Party on suppositions that were later shown to be mistaken. The latitude the Party allowed them was only temporary. After the seizure of power, their relation to the Party was placed in proper perspective. They were under heavy pressure to conform in behavior and attitude to Communist norms and to mouth Communist values. They were trapped in situations of conflict which they could best resolve by rationalizing their own position or by accepting uncritically even the most absurd rationalizations of the Party. This was nothing short of total enslavement. The alternatives to it were ejection from the Party for not following its dictates (which entailed hardships ranging from the loss of livelihood to imprisonment) or exacerbation of inner conflicts (which often led to personal breakdown).

The preconditions for rationalization were firmly established as early as the immediate postwar phase, when members were not subjected to a rigorous regimen of indoctrination but conditioned themselves psychologically to become good Communists. Their conversion took the form of ever-deeper involvement with the Party. It began with self-censorship to meet standards of behavior, if not thought, which the Party expected or was believed to expect. In the early stages of their involvement, members tended to be stringent self-censors, their stringency being increased by the Party's own moderation. They were successively led to resolve their doubts in favor of the Party and against themselves and finally to accept uncritically the Party's rationalizations.

This process of ingestion of Party members applied primarily to intellectuals of middle-class background. They were especially sensitive to the necessity of rejecting their former social environment and modes of thought. They were apt to go to exaggerated lengths in cleansing themselves of petty-bourgeois attitudes. Even without the Party's prodding, they had a natural tendency to struggle against petty-bourgeois traits which held a particular odium for them and with which they knew, or sensed, that they were thoroughly infested.

Intellectuals are not necessarily accurate models of the rest of society. In terms of predisposition and sensitivity, but even more in the articulation of experiences and the propensity they have for *post hoc* rationalization of behavior, the intellectuals represent a special case. There is no assurance that the ordinary member of peasant and working-class background, about whom we possess much less information, followed the paths of rationalization of the intellectual. Some peasants and workers, being of much simpler mind than intellectuals, were supine before the Party's indoctrination and conditioning. Other peasants and workers for the very same reasons never got the Party's message. Like the Marquis de Sade's Justine, they came through a succession of corrupting experiences innocent.

The Party, of course, fully expected to readjust its relationship with its members as soon as the seizure of power was completed. The sacrifice of quality for quantity was, however, not without risks. It was bound to complicate the future transformation of the

Party into a disciplined, ideologically sound, and tightly organized instrument of rule. The self-deception of the members also had potentially explosive implications. It robbed the Party of any ground for genuine and spontaneous loyalty on the part of its members as soon as its true face was revealed. But the Party, conscious of its great power, was probably confident that it could handle any problem that might arise from its loose and dishonest membership policy. This calculation was not altogether mistaken. For a long time, while the Party moved forward with the restructuring of Hungarian society on a large scale, terrorizing the population but displaying at the same time seemingly irresistible strength and a swift, revolutionary dynamic that had its own iron logic, the Party easily held its members in check. Yet, in the end, the Party endured terrific humiliation at the hands of its members.

By its self-examination, initiated under Imre Nagy's "new course" (begun in 1953), the Party revealed its true face and caused profound feelings of revulsion among its members. Feeling variously guilty, ashamed, frustrated, or cheated, the members turned against the Party as the perpetrator of a monstrous hoax, although rightly they should have blamed only their own stupidity for their troubles. The Party, caught in internal turmoil, its will undermined, its power at an ebb, lacked the means to recapture and hold the loyalty of its members. This helps to explain the Party's loss of prestige among its own members after 1953 and its collapse during the revolution, when its membership simply evaporated.

THE MAKING OF COMMUNIST INTELLECTUALS

Hungary's intellectuals played an important part in aiding the Party's bid for power. They included writers, journalists, broadcasters. The core of those sampled in the study is made up of writers who eventually became leading dignitaries in the Writers' Association (i.e., Party hacks) and of journalists who clustered around the Party's official daily organ, *Szabad Nep*.

From the evidence available, one must infer that a disproportionately large number of these intellectuals were of Jewish background. They were also very young. They had almost no prior professional experience and, more important, no opportunity for mellowing.

They were impetuous and reckless. Their judgment was tempered neither by compassion nor wisdom. Almost all suffered from acute psychological difficulties. They were profoundly alienated from the society in which they lived. They also passionately rejected their immediate family environment. Conflicts with their parents (or one of the parents) and with the old society led them straight to the Communist Party. There they found shelter ideally suited to their needs. The Party provided them with a sense of belonging, purpose, and direction, yet it relieved them from direct responsibility for their actions. Their services were performed at the request of the Party and were used by it at its pleasure. The greater the distance between the values of the Party and those of their former environment, the better. Individualists at heart, they nevertheless enjoyed the spontaneous spirit of camaraderie many of them now knew for the first time. There was also real adventure and excitement in what they were doing. They were building a Communist propaganda apparatus where none had existed. They were creating, without apparent interference from any outside authority.

This propagandistic intellectual realm—in contrast with Lukacs' world of scholarship—was Jozsef Revai's exclusive domain. This was especially so at *Szabad Nep*, the Party's daily newspaper, whose editor-in-chief he was. The budding generations of writers and journalists were entrusted to his care. He mesmerized them with his talent, enthusiasm, and energy.

The Communist press had advantages in plant facilities, newsprint, and the like, but it had no monopoly. If it was to be successful, it had to sell itself by the quality and persuasiveness of its product. Colorful, imaginative writing was called for. The drab, stereotyped format of *Pravda*, which was later imposed on all Party journals, did not have to be conformed to at this time. The question simply did not arise. Nor was the intellectual *sanctum* invaded and regulated by Party bureaucrats. It was functionally autonomous, enjoying unusual privileges because of the significance attached to its mission and the conditions under which it had to work.

Wherever possible, the abilities of individuals were "rationally" utilized. Someone with particularly strong anticlerical leanings would be assigned to write stories smearing the clergy. Someone else with particularly anti-aristocratic bias would be selected to do background research for stories aimed against a former cabinet minister. As a result, the stories, tendentious and distorted as they often were, were lively and readable. They had genuine passion behind them that showed in their composition.

Party intellectuals also received outlandishly high emoluments. No other group lived so well. Employees of the Party's administrative machinery who had responsibilities roughly equivalent to those held by writers and journalists worked much longer hours, studied much harder, and lived much more frugally. Only the top leaders of the Party and secret police officers lived on a standard comparable to that of these upstart intellectuals.

Youths barely out of their teens were catapulted to positions of prominence. They were pampered on a diet of bohemian excesses. They did not grasp the implications of the doctrine they were mouthing. They failed to consider the consequences of their actions and to appreciate the absurdity of their hedonistic mode of life. The real issues affecting the future of the society which they helped to mold escaped their attention. The content of their intellectual discourse was incredibly shallow. They were a frightening example —the gilded youth of the period, high-flying, irresponsible, arrogant, destructive. Small wonder that the more sensitive among them eventually experienced a remorse of conscience and repented for actions that had contributed to the perpetration of monstrous crimes against their fellow men.

ORGANIZATION

The structure of the Party and the initial functioning of its lower units reflected the already familiar pattern of feigned democracy. Although it was hierarchically organized in the form of a simple pyramid of territorial units (of which the region, coinciding with the major administrative subdivisions of the country, each dominated by one of the larger towns, was the most significant), the Party did not impart the impression of operating according to the strict tenets of "democratic centralism."

The hastily founded and still incomplete network of Party units was adapted to rapid expansion and initiative from below. The units were loosely organized. They had elective committees whose composition was not determined in advance by the senior official of the next highest administrative unit, but corresponded to the consensus of the membership. Committee members participated actively in deliberations affecting Party policy on their particular levels. Each committee had one or two functionaries assigned to it who acted in an administrative capacity. For the time being, they did not make the weight of their influence felt unduly. In most cases they also were recent recruits with scant experience. They had to be trained on the job, so to speak.

Within twelve to eighteen months, a shift toward concentration of power in the hands of appointed functionaries was noticeable on the intermediate, district level, but local units still retained an open character. Centralization on the regional and national levels progressed much more rapidly. But it would be a mistake to visualize the Party leadership as perfectly coordinated and of like mind.

THE HIGH COMMAND

The Party leadership was made up of diverse and distinct elements. It is not idle Kremlinology to divide the leadership into three major groups or factions, respectively labeled "Muscovite," "home-grown" or simply "home," and "Western," and to seek in them the keys to an understanding of the course of events under consideration in this study. Although factional strife did not rack the Party in the initial postwar phase, the existence of separate groups and the relations among them affected the composition of the leadership and outlined the shape of future conflicts.

The major factions themselves were neither homogeneous in composition nor unitary in outlook. The "Muscovites" were reportedly rent with dissension of a personal nature (Rakosi vs. Gero, Revai vs. Nagy). The "home" Communists showed greater cohesiveness, but they were also subdivided into more specific groups—old bolshevik 1919ers who had not emigrated to the Soviet Union or to the West and who had fallen into obscurity between the two world wars; "home" Communists proper, mostly younger people who were active in Budapest and Debrecen in the 1930s (Rajk, Kadar, Kallai,

Donath, Losonczy, Zold); and wartime recruits among whom were "populists" (Kardos *et al.*), disgruntled, cashiered junior military officers of the Hungarian Army (Palffy *et al.*), and others. The "Westerners" represented an even odder mixture. Many of them had been expelled from the Party in the 1930s for ideological deviation, especially Trotskyism. They found sanctuary abroad, in France, Switzerland, England, and even the United States, and were now returning home impelled by patriotic fervor. Their readmission and assignment to positions of trust was perfectly consistent with current policy and most useful in swelling the thin ranks of old wheelhorses.[6]

In addition to "geographic" factions, the Party also was divided into factions along the familiar triad—left, center, and right—which sometimes cut across the other factional divisions; thus the "Muscovite" Gero and the "home" Communist Rajk, both leftists, were once aligned against the "Muscovite" centrist Rakosi.

The picture grew still more complex with the absorption of the Social Democrats (in 1948), who themselves harbored two or three distinct factions (right, left, and crypto-Communist), and with the promotion of new cadres recruited after the war.

In sum, the Party leadership was a mosaic, not a monolith. Nor did its composition remain static. The general trend observable in it pointed to a steady if unspectacular consolidation of the hold of "Muscovites" on key positions in the central apparatus, which they seized first as the country was liberated and while many "home" Communists still languished in prisons and detention camps.

Between the "Muscovite" and "home" factions, there was a dichotomy rooted in the history of the Hungarian Communist movement. The "Muscovites" were, for the most part, Party veterans dating from 1919. Although they were few in numbers and were strangers in their country, they formed a redoubtable general staff of the Party. They were tough, hard, "professional revolutionaries." They had an abundance of schooling in ideological and organizational matters and knew the Soviet Union. With few exceptions,

[6] The reappearance of "Trotskyite renegades" occurred in all East European Communist parties, notably the Czech.

they had absorbed the practical lessons taught by the great transformation of the Soviet Communist Party at Stalin's hand. They had respect for the Stalinist system. As a group they had the confidence of the Kremlin.

The "home" Communists included many younger elements. They were short on ideological training and organizational experience. They had no direct pipeline to the Kremlin and were probably distrusted there as unknown. They had little appreciation of the substance of Communism as practiced in Russia. But they had earned credit by keeping the Party alive as best they could under extreme hardships. They had courted considerable danger (many had been arrested). Familiar with conditions in Hungary, they were in every sense native.[7]

There was considerable ground for friction between these two groups. Nevertheless, their qualities complemented each other. Both were indispensable to the success of the movement. Mutual accommodation and a division of labor between them was as necessary as it was desirable for the good of the Party. From 1945 to 1948, intraparty squabbles were subordinated to the winning of the struggle against the bourgeoisie. Various factions in the Party acted in harmony, recognizing their interdependence and losing themselves in the passion of work that was to lead to the realization of long-cherished dreams. This was not the time to indulge in family quarrels, to air ideological disagreements, or to settle personal feuds.

Before 1948, only one instance of public dissent within the Party is on record. The question at issue was serious. It concerned the method and timing of power seizure. Significantly, Rakosi lifted the veil from intraparty disagreements. In an address (reprinted in the Party journal) before the first "mass" meeting of 147 functionaries in May, 1945, he excoriated "the comrades of 1919 ... and those who worked in illegality" for being unable to understand that they must "persuade and convince" instead of "forcing their will

---

[7] The two factions also differed in religious background. The "Muscovites" included an inordinate number of Jews, while the "home" Communists (Party functionaries, not intellectuals) were preponderantly Protestant. But there is little evidence that religion any more than any other issues that existed or arose between the "home" Communists and the "Muscovites" interfered with their harmonious collaboration for the seizure of power.

on others by pressure or threat." He went further to offer an explanation, though not an excuse, for "the sectarian behavior" of those
who had worked illegally, by saying that as a result of their past
they had developed "habits of work, secretiveness, and suspiciousness" of which they could not rid themselves. "The bitter struggles
in which they engaged with the Socialists and other democratic
parties" did not permit them to switch easily to the proper execution
of "the Party's new and correct policy." [8] Returning to the same
theme seven years later, when he stood at the zenith of power, having long since successfully eliminated the 1919ers and the "home"
Communists from the contest, he added that they had turned to
him with dismay and disbelief over the Party's soft tactics, over its
failure to seize power immediately. But no explanations had been
tendered at the time, for fear of prematurely tipping the Party's
hand to its foes. (Note the admission of conscious concealment
within the Party itself.)

That a divergence of opinion existed over the seizure of power
is beyond dispute. The depth and seriousness of the disagreement
is subject to debate. There is no evidence that the 1919ers and the
"home" Communists were inclined to remonstrate with their "Muscovite" superiors over high policy. Even if they did not fully comprehend the rationale behind the policy (no reliable information
exists as to whether they did or did not understand it), they fell in
line with its execution without showing disgruntlement. Rakosi's
motives for revealing, and very likely magnifying, the "rift" therefore gain added interest.

It would seem that his "revelation" was intended to serve several
purposes. It reinforced in a credible manner the general propaganda line of the Party which specifically sought to disavow the
terror and speedy installation of a dictatorship of the proletariat in
1919, implying that the reenactment of such horrors was the far-
thest thing from the Party's mind. It put Rakosi in a favorable
light as the protagonist of moderation, absolving him of any culpa-
bility in the excesses which Communists perpetrated during the first
few months after liberation. It also served notice on the Social
Democrats to let bygones be bygones and to reciprocate the new

8 *Szabad Nep*, May 23, 1945.

spirit of friendship and solidarity fostered by the Communist leadership. Finally, it set the stage for the elimination of the 1919ers and other "home" Communists from positions of leadership.

The last-mentioned motive might well have been the most important. Conscious of the threat the "home" Communists represented to his leadership, Rakosi tried to undermine their popularity by associating them with the harsher manifestations of Party policy and by arrogating to himself its beneficial aspects. Without accusing them of disloyalty, which would have been absurd at this time, he gave good cause for barring their elevation to top rank. He attributed their failings to the hardships they had had to endure as underground revolutionaries and suggested that in fact they had outlived their usefulness and should be retired from active politics to enjoy their just rewards. This position carried the clear intimation that there would be disciplinary ground for their elimination unless they conformed to Party policy.

The top Party organs and their members between 1945 and 1948 were:

1. A Secretariat, consisting at first of five members. It was headed by the secretary general and was entrusted with general administrative responsibilities for and in the Party. The Secretariat was officially formed in May, 1945, at a meeting of Party functionaries. In November, 1945, two posts of deputy secretary general were created within the Secretariat. In October, 1946, the administrative functions of the Secretariat were vested in an Orgbureau. The secretary general and his two deputies retained their titles and positions.

2. A Politbureau, confirmed at the first conference of Party functionaries in May, 1945, and reelected with modified membership at the Congress in 1946. It was the Party's supreme deliberative body.

3. An Orgbureau, formally elected at the Congress in 1946. It was the highest administrative body of the Party, responsible for the implementation of Politbureau policy within the Party apparatus.

4. A Central Committee, elected at the May, 1945, conference and enlarged at the Congress in 1946. It was a larger deliberative

body, formally the repository of the confidence of the Party masses —their elected assembly—and the organ of power during the intervals between Congresses. Actually, it was from the start a consultative and advisory rather than a decision-making body.

Matyas Rakosi held the post of secretary general uninterruptedly. One of the deputy secretary generalships was held, also without interruption, by Mihaly Farkas, a "Muscovite." The other deputy secretary generalship was held by "home" Communists—Rajk from November, 1945, probably until May, 1946, and Kadar from October, 1946, until the seizure of power.[9]

The names of the Politbureau members and their alternates selected in 1945 were not published. The Politbureau elected at the 1946 Congress had nine full members (Rakosi, Farkas, Gero, Revai, Nagy, Apro, Kossa, Rajk, and Kadar) and three alternates (Kovacs, Horvath, and Szobek). Of the nine full members, five were "Muscovites" (Rakosi, Farkas, Gero, Revai, Nagy); two belonged to the prisoner-of-war group (Kossa and Apro); and two were "home" Communists (Rajk and Kadar). The alternates were all "home" Communists.

The Orgbureau, elected in 1946, had five full and three alternate members. They were Rakosi, Farkas, Kovacs, Apro, Olt (full members), and Kobol, Dogei, and Urban (alternate members). Each headed one of the important departments of the central apparatus of the Party. Of the five full members, there were two "Muscovites" (Rakosi and Farkas) one "POW" (Apro), and two "home" Communists (Olt and Kovacs). The three alternate members were all "home" Communists. Conspicuously missing from this body was Kadar, although he was a member of the Secretariat.

The Central Committee elected in May, 1945, had twenty-four members and five alternates. Among them were seven "Muscovites" (Rakosi, Farkas, Gero, Revai, Nagy, Nogradi, Vas), fourteen "home" Communists and three "POWs" as full members, and five "home" Communists as alternates. The Central Committee

---

9 It is not clear whether Rajk retained his position until October, 1946, or relinquished it sooner. In any event, no replacement for him was announced until Kadar's appointment was made public.

of 1946, considerably enlarged, had thirty-one full members and ten alternates. It included nine "Muscovites" (eight full members and one alternate, Erzsebet Andics), twenty-nine "home" Communists (twenty full members and nine alternates), and three "POWs."

The Party's representatives in the government included three members of the Politbureau—Rakosi (Deputy Premier), Gero (Minister of Transportation), and Rajk (Minister of the Interior)—and two members of the Central Committee—Vas (Secretary General of the Supreme Economic Council) and Molnar (Minister of Public Welfare). Another member of the Politbureau, Imre Nagy, held the Ministry of Agriculture (until November, 1945) and then the Ministry of the Interior (until March, 1946).[10]

The Parliamentary delegation of the Party, numbering seventy, had an overwhelming number of "home" Communists in it. Thus the inner councils of the Party were dominated by "Muscovites," while the outer councils had a heavy representation of "home" Communists.

Of the individual Party leaders, Rakosi and Farkas, as secretary and deputy secretary general of the Party respectively, occupied posts of preeminence. They alone sat both in the deliberative Politbureau and in the administrative Orgbureau. (One alternate member of the Politbureau, Apro, also held full membership in the Orgbureau.) Rakosi's stature was further emphasized by his deputy premiership. He was the ranking Communist in the Party and the government, an exceptional concentration of formal power in one person in Eastern Europe at this time. As a rule, responsibility for Party and government work was divided between two people, possibly as a prudent safeguard against the accumulation of too much influence in the hands of a single leader.

No explanation for the unusual situation in Hungary has been advanced. Perhaps there was an exaggerated concern over sharing real power with the "home" Communists. Indeed, had the two

10 For a brief period, from December, 1944, to May, 1945, Jozsef Gabor, a "Muscovite" but otherwise an innocuous Communist, held the Ministry of Transportation. He retired because of ill health and died soon after.

top posts been divided, one of them would have had to be assigned to a "home" Communist.[11]

Rakosi's selection as Hungary's leading Communist also seems strange because he is reported to have been in Stalin's bad graces. Gero, his "Muscovite" rival, would have been the logical choice for the post. The answer suggests itself that Rakosi was chosen precisely because he was not fully trusted by Stalin, on the sound psychological assumption that a person who did not enjoy the old dictator's confidence would serve him more faithfully than another more trusted individual. History is full of examples of betrayals by confidants. Stalin preferred to surround himself with subordinates who owed their status entirely to him and were totally dependent on him, rather than by friends who had any independent claim to prominence.

Rakosi strove hard to earn the honor of being Stalin's best pupil. To this end, he borrowed a leaf from the Russian tyrant's book. In fact, an invaluable key to Hungary's postwar history is to be found in Rakosi's apish imitation of Stalin's "style" from 1945 to 1956. During this time, and despite a temporary eclipse (from 1953 to 1955), Rakosi was the kingpin of the Communist movement. Initially, Rakosi, like Stalin, was in a minority position in his Party, surrounded by individuals and factions hostile to him. Ultimately, Rakosi, like Stalin, parlayed the post of secretary general into an unassailable citadel. In the process, Rakosi, like Stalin, showed a capacity for ruthless intrigue. He manipulated contending factions, acting as a sort of balance of power between them, effectively preventing any single faction from achieving a majority without his support, and guarding all the while against their combining in opposition to him, until he had whittled them down to insignificance. He kept the Party leadership in a state of flux, diluting or concentrating its membership as it suited his purposes, purging and then balancing the effects of his own purges. It was a tribute to his skills that he retained control of the Hungarian Party long after the death of his mentor

11 Only in Czechoslovakia did two "Muscovites," Gottwald and Slansky, hold top honors in the government and the Party. But the Czechoslovak situation, particularly as it related to the internal development of the Communist Party, was based on historic precedents for which there was no parallel anywhere else.

and that he was the last of the Stalinists to be purged from office in Eastern Europe. In the end, although he was totally discredited, it still required forceful outside intervention to remove him. His Party was powerless against him. In the earlier stages, however, Rakosi refrained from tipping his hand. He maneuvered with all deliberate speed, cautiously, circumspectly with due regard to the limiting influence of the political setting.

Farkas, almost completely unknown in Hungary in 1944, ranked a close second to Rakosi. He served briefly as Deputy Minister of the Interior in 1945 and then was assigned to Party work as head of a special department of the Secretariat, responsible for Communist personnel in police and security forces. But he was entirely a creature of the Party apparatus. He was as deferent to his superior as he was disdainful toward his subordinates and ruthless toward his victims. A stranger in Hungary (his domicile was in Slovakia where he lived until the Second World War), he stood conspicuously apart from the "home" Communists, among whom he had no friends. Isolated, he was ideally suited for the performance of tasks that demanded distance from and lack of feeling for the social environment.

None of the other top "Muscovites" (Gero, Revai, Nagy) consistently held administrative posts in the Party. They lacked the formal attributes of power held by Rakosi and Farkas. Of the three, Nagy played the most curious, and, in some respects, the most innocuous part. Initially, he seemed to be one of the ruling inner circle. His assignment to the Ministry of Agriculture during the period of land reform and land distribution had primary significance. His elevation to Minister of the Interior in November, 1945, might have been intended as a sop to the non-Communists. The presence of a "mild" Communist in formal command of that dread ministry might have made Communist control of this coveted department more palatable to their opponents. Nagy's removal from the ministry in March, 1946, is said to have marked the beginning of his eclipse. If so, it was temporary and partial, for, in May, 1946, Nagy was appointed chief administrative officer of the Party's Secretariat, a position of responsibility, although limited in power. In October, he was one of two keynote speakers at the Party Congress. (The other was Rakosi.) After the Congress, he retained his position in the Politbureau and served as leader of the Communist Party's parliamentary fraction. Despite the high posts he held, Nagy seemed to have no well-defined sphere of authority and no tangible bases of power in the Party. He was prominent, but not influential.

Gero and Revai, by virtue of their public posts and of the functional autonomy of the departments for which they were responsible, compensated for some of the disadvantages of having no entrenched positions in the Party apparatus. Although Gero's authority in the economic sphere was to some extent encroached upon by Zoltan Vas, the secretary of the Supreme Economic Council, a staunch supporter of Rakosi, both Gero and Revai had an opportunity to build up personal followings. They also acted prominently in policy making as senior members of the Politbureau, which at that time functioned very much as a deliberative body. Revai, for example, was chairman of the Party's foreign policy commission.

By contrast, Rajk and Kadar, the top-ranking "home" Communists, held formal positions of much more modest influence.

Rajk, on returning home, was made secretary of the Budapest Party organization, an important post because of the size and influence of the Party membership in the capital. Six months later he was made deputy secretary general of the Party. He appears to have lost that position shortly after his appointment to the Ministry of the Interior in March, 1946, although there is no record of a public announcement of his dismissal from the deputy secretary generalship. Of course, on being made Minister of the Interior, Rajk had to relinquish his position of secretary of the Budapest Party organization, which demanded full-time attention. He retained only his membership in the Politbureau.

As Minister of the Interior, he was occupied with governmental problems and could not devote much time to Party affairs. Moreover, the Minister's powers did not correspond to the importance of the Ministry itself. The security police, which was nominally under the Ministry (it became an independent department in

1949), was headed even then by Gabor Peter.[12] It was also tightly supervised by Farkas's special department in the Party's Secretariat. There is good reason to believe that its orders came directly from the secretary general of the Party and his deputy (Farkas) rather than from the Minister of the Interior. In his post, Rajk had little opportunity to accumulate any real power, and if anything, his public standing diminished. The Minister of the Interior personified police suppression and thus was unpopular.

Kadar, the second ranking "home" Communist, followed in Rajk's footsteps. At first deputy police chief of Budapest (under Ferenc Munnich), he then took over from Rajk as Budapest Party secretary and still later became deputy secretary general of the Party. In 1948, Kadar became Minister of the Interior when Rajk, already on the decline, was removed from that post and assigned to the Ministry of Foreign Affairs. The implications of Kadar's step-by-step replacement of Rajk in Party and government posts will be examined presently. It was part of a design by Rakosi to rid himself of Rajk, his chief rival for authority in the Party.

The conflict between Rakosi and Rajk has become distorted in the perspective of history, which has made Rakosi the villain and Rajk the martyr. This judgment was probably inevitable in the light of disclosures that definitely established Rakosi as Rajk's murderer through a purge trial based entirely on fabricated evidence. But the image of Rakosi as a sinner and Rajk as a saint does not correspond to the facts at the time the conflict took shape. Both were hard Communists dedicated to the destruction of their ideological opponents. No injustice is done to Rajk's memory if he is remembered as less than a paragon.

The easiest and best way to view the contest between the two men is as a clash between "spontaneity" and "consciousness." Rakosi represented consciousness *par excellence;* Rajk, spon-

[12] Gabor Peter, though a "home" Communist properly speaking, had had some training in Moscow in the 1930s and possibly again in 1943–1944. He had carried out security functions in the Party as far back as the 1930s. The personal antipathy he had harbored toward a number of Hungarian Communists from that time on translated itself into purge action against them after 1948.

taneity. In terms of personality (shrewd, cold, patient, calculating, and thoroughly two-faced) as well as training and status in the Party, Rakosi epitomized the Communist secretary general as that office and the person of its holder fused in the Stalinist model.

Rajk was outgoing, fiery, volatile, excitable, direct, guileless. Controlled schizophrenia, an essential attribute of all successful Communists, was not in his make-up. His training was far inferior to Rakosi's. It is easy to comprehend his impatience with a policy of slow, methodical power seizure, and his displeasure over coddling "enemy classes." He not only wished to make short work of them; he also deplored the hypocrisy involved in slow seizure. Ferenc Nagy, the Smallholder prime minister, described Rajk as a "fanatical, half-educated Communist . . . with a passion for civil strife . . . a continual trouble maker." Not so the suave Rakosi.

Rajk, then, prior to the power seizure, stood far to the "left" of the "moderate" Rakosi. By the same token, after the power seizure, Rajk's artless ideas about proletarian dictatorship collided with the elaborately contrived and ruthlessly implemented policy of class war that was foisted on the country. As far as Rajk was concerned, class war should precede power seizure, not follow it, and it should be mercilessly applied against the class enemy, not against the masses. After the power seizure, Rajk stood to the "right" of Rakosi, who, by deft maneuvering, remained in the *center* of the stage. The makings of at least an ideological conflict between Rakosi and Rajk were clearly present.

Rajk also had an abundance of personal acquaintances, friendships, and contacts—which Rakosi lacked. Even without formal authority in the Party, Rajk claimed the loyalty of many functionaries whose services were needed for the development of a solid core of efficient Party bureaucrats. This was particularly true in the Budapest city organization of the Party, a redoubt of the "home" Communists.

Rajk was, therefore, in a better position than anyone else to challenge or to undermine the secretary general. Whether or not he wanted to do this is another matter. There is no solid evidence that he did. But Rakosi, if the assessment of his personality presented here and elsewhere is correct, must have seen in Rajk an obstacle to the smooth functioning of the Party and a threat to himself. When the opportunity to destroy Rajk presented itself after the power seizure, Rakosi found in Janos Kadar a perfect instrument for his plans.

Kadar had a following among the working class. His replacing Rajk aroused no serious suspicion that "home" Communists as such were being discriminated against. All one could say was that Rajk's personal position was being undermined. Yet moves that appeared to have merely personal significance had much broader consequences. The "home" Communists were gradually deprived of their most forceful representative. Relations between Kadar and Rajk became strained. The unity of the "home" Communists was impaired. They began to separate along lines of personal preference. Most important, Kadar became increasingly dependent on Rakosi, until he was completely in the latter's tow and served as his tool.

The testimony of persons who knew Kadar bears out the supposition that he was well suited to act as Rakosi's unwitting hatchet man. They describe him as a weakling, less aggressive, less intelligent, less self-reliant, and also less "romantic" than Rajk; in the words of one knowledgeable respondent, he was a "mediocrity" who needed guidance and was quite suggestible.

Kadar's role turned out in the long run to be nothing short of tragic: an essentially good-natured, simple man, he twice served his masters in the perpetration of vicious crimes—first, by acting as Rakosi's tool in the framing and execution of Rajk, second, by betraying the revolution in setting up a Soviet-supported government counter to Nagy. During the period of power seizure, neither he nor Rajk appeared to be unduly concerned over what was happening to them. In fact, "home" Communists generally were not disturbed about the unequal distribution of power in the Party. They accepted Rakosi's leadership and stood in awe of him.

In the meantime, the allocation of responsibility on operational levels also presaged discord and conflict. This was especially true in two areas—propaganda and security, particularly in the military establishment

The problem of the Party propagandists has already been

touched on. Writers and journalists—recent converts to Communism—disdained the Party bureaucracy and made themselves obnoxious to it. The bureaucrats felt frustrated at not being able to extend their power over these irresponsible, nonproletarian Communists whom they envied and to whom they felt inferior in social origin, education, status, and income.

The situation in the security organs was different, and even more complex. The security police represented a curious patchwork: "Muscovites," Jewish ex-prisoners of concentration camps, anti-Semitic career police officers with past fascist affiliations. But this crazy quilt was actually a cleverly conceived device: its internal divisions would reduce the danger of the police developing into an independent power, and, at the same time, it made it possible to utilize the talents of people of diverse backgrounds. Rajk served as a good front man, while "Muscovites" controlled the actual security work. Jews made excellent interrogators by virtue of their own experiences and their trained and precise minds. (According to an eyewitness—whose opinion may not be completely accurate but is typical—at secret police headquarters at Budapest, "all interrogators were Jews.") Former police officers were well suited for the more distasteful physical aspects of criminal prosecution.

The pattern of organization and staffing in the armed forces was different. The public posts of control with which the Communists neutralized the army as a potential striking arm against them and rendered it convertible at the proper time, went without fail to a group of young cashiered officers of the Horthy era. All had graduated from the *Ludovika,* the Hungarian West Point, in the late 1930s. Most of them had been directly or indirectly affected by the anti-Jewish legislation of the late 1930s.

Outstanding among them was Captain (at the time of his dismissal in 1940) Gyorgy Palffy-Oesterreicher, who was separated from the service reportedly because of the religious and family ties of his Jewish fiancee, the niece of Tibor Szamueli, a long-dead Communist of the 1919 period. During the war, Palffy was in the employ of one of the largest industrial combines of the country, the United Incandescent Works. In 1944, he joined the

Peace (Communist) Party. In 1945, at the initiative of the Russians, he was made chief of the Military-Political Division of the Ministry of Defense. He was then thirty-six years old.

Within a year, during which the number of "orientation officers" and counterintelligence agents grew enormously, Palffy was in command of the entire counterintelligence system of the armed forces. It rivaled in importance the security police under the Ministry of the Interior. In 1946, Palffy was elevated to the command of the Frontier Guards, a force of fifteen battalions representing the bulk of the combat-ready troops available to Hungary. In 1947, he became Inspector of the Army, with the rank of Lieutenant General—a position that carried with it virtual command of the entire army; a spectacular career for a man under forty years of age and of less than four years standing in the Communist Party. Subsequently, his star waned as rapidly as it had risen. He was hanged as one of Rajk's co-conspirators in September, 1949.

Along with Palffy and at his initiative, men with backgrounds strikingly similar to his soon were placed in the armed forces. Captain Gusztav Illy became Chief of Personnel. Captain Imre Radvanyi became liaison officer between the government and representatives of foreign powers. Lieutenant Istvan Beleznay became Chief of the Training and Education Department of the Ministry of Defense. This meant effective command of the political officer corps disguised under the title of "orientation officers" at that time. (Beleznay was relieved of his command in May, 1947. His place was taken by Ferenc Janosi, Imre Nagy's son-in-law.)[13] Captain Laszlo Solyom, at first entrusted with work in the police force, eventually became Chief of the General Staff.

Within three years, these men and several others of similar background rose to general's rank. Although their power was checked by trusted "Muscovites" in the Party apparatus (Nogradi, Revesz, Farkas), they represented an important enclave in the army and had means to assert their influence. This was especially

[13] Janosi had scant qualifications for the job. Allegedly a one-time student of theology, he defected to the Russians while serving in the Hungarian army on the Southern Ukrainian front. His rise to prominence seemed to be a direct consequence of family ties.

true of Palffy's counterintelligence corps, which played a major part in the detection and actual arrest of the members of the Hungarian Unity conspiracy. Normally, in a Communist system, counterintelligence functions are entrusted to a chain of command in the Ministry of the Interior (or Security), as was the case in Hungary after 1949.

By their social origin and professional training, these army officers were as different from the traditional breed of Communist as one can find. They were linked to the Party by the grudges they bore against the old regime. Their loyalty to Communism was a function of opportunism and driving ambition. But once in positions of prominence, would they subordinate themselves to the demands of Party discipline? Or would their ambition drive them further? A closely knit "in-group," they were potential factionalists. Their temperamental affinity for the leading "home" Communists made them even more unreliable. (Palffy and Rajk allegedly were good friends.)

For the moment, however, they could be depended on to be pitiless toward their former tormentors. Familiar with the old army structure and acquainted with many of the top army leaders, they were invaluable in sifting undesirable elements from the officer corps. The available evidence indicates that they fulfilled their destructive mission with zeal and efficiency. The question was whether they would be equally suitable in the creation of a politically indoctrinated worker-peasant army. Could they ever overcome their social biases? Could they adopt a proletarian *Weltanschauung?* Or would their stiff-backed, Magyar *honved* tradition continually reassert itself under the new Communist insignia?

Ultimately adjudged a source of weakness, the very diversity and organizational looseness of the early Party—even of its leading cadres—was a source of strength. Far from being soft or from seeming amorphous, the Party exuded strength and vigor. It had not yet become ossified under the weight of enforced conformity. Its impulses had not yet been reduced to a monotonous cascade of commands, accepted unquestioningly by a sycophantic horde of officials and a thoroughly browbeaten mass of members. And in most respects—the notable exception being the nerve center of the Party, its central Secretariat—the Communist Party closely corresponded to the public image it sought to create. It made up in spontaneity what it lacked in consciousness, and that was precisely what was called for under the circumstances.

Few guessed and even fewer grasped the meaning of this tolerated spontaneity. The "home" Communists, though undoubtedly on temporary probation until their trustworthiness was determined by the Russians, threw themselves into Party work enthusiastically. They contributed heavily to the early successes of Communist strategy. The "Muscovites" held the reins of power. They also provided an aura of superior wisdom and guidance. Many, surprisingly many Hungarians succumbed to the spell.

PART TWO

From Stalinism to Revolution

1948-1956

5. The Party Against the People, 1948-1953

MATYAS RAKOSI aptly labeled 1948 a year of transition.[1] Between the fall of 1947 and the spring of 1948, all Communist parties in Eastern Europe concluded their power seizure. The more laggard, like the Czechs and Hungarians, caught up with the others. The Czechs broke the back of organized political opposition in one swiftly executed coup. The Hungarians stepped up the tempo of liquidation of scattered remnants of political opposition.

Forced mergers of Social Democratic and Communist parties, in the spring of 1948, brought about the "unity of the Marxist left" and terminated the process of political power seizure.[2] Sweeping decrees of nationalization all but eliminated private enterprise and secured for the Communists the economic heights of power. The road was clear for "socialist construction."

The transition from power seizure to socialist construction was not precipitated by urgent needs in any East European country. But gradual as the seizure of power was, it had to come to an end sooner or later. By 1948, after the lapse of about three years, power seizure had run its course. The parties were marking time.

Meanwhile, East-West diplomatic relations steadily deteriorated. In 1947, for the first time since the end of the war, the Red tide that threatened to spill over into Western Europe was halted with any degree of decisiveness. The Communists suffered major political setbacks in France and Italy. The United States launched a monumental program of economic rehabilitation of the Continent.

[1] The Hungarian expression "fordulat," used by Rakosi in a political context, connotes violent, decisive overturn or turnabout.

[2] Actually the Social Democrats were absorbed by the Communist parties, although the "new" parties adopted the name of Workers' or United Workers' parties everywhere except in Czechoslovakia.

Soviet attitudes hardened correspondingly. Intensified "cold war" was the result. The position of the borderlands of Soviet power suddenly grew precarious and required fortification.

A smoldering ideological conflict between Stalin and Tito also came to a head. It led to the expulsion of Yugoslavia from the Communist family. The dispute bore directly on the ordering of relations between the Soviet Union and its East European satellites. The issues at stake ran the gamut from social organization to national sovereignty.

The shape of things to come was actually foreshadowed by the creation of the Cominform in September, 1947.[3] From it could be inferred greater stress on organizational controls over East European Communist parties, stronger emphasis on uniformity of policies, and speedier implementation of Communist goals. Unfortunately, the protocols of the founding meeting of the Cominform did not penetrate public consciousness for a long time. Local Communist leaders themselves did not immediately comprehend all that was expected of them.

The implications of socialist construction were far from clear. Only an insignificant minority of the population in any country, including Communists, anticipated the breadth and depth of changes that were to affect institutions, cultural values, social relations, and the daily lives of citizens. The scope of changes turned out to be truly revolutionary. They were put into effect rapidly, under duress, and caused hardship to all. The Communist parties labored under severe restrictions imposed by the Soviet Union. The societies dominated by the Communists, in turn, were remolded in the image of the prevailing socialist (Soviet) model.

Separate references to the Communist parties and to the societies they dominated are meant to underscore their parallel and inter-dependent development. Frequently the evolution of Eastern Europe after 1948 has been seen as an undifferentiated process of totalitarian oppression of more or less uniformly recalcitrant peoples by monolithic parties. This is a dangerously simple view. For one thing, the totalitarian subjugation of Eastern Europe was

3 See Reale, *Avec Jacques Duclos, passim.*

not as undifferentiated as its Soviet protagonists wanted and as many Western observers perceived it to be. For another thing, the Communist parties never quite succeeded in shutting out environmental influences and in achieving complete coordination of their own ranks.

Each Party carried with it into the period of socialist construction a spate of unresolved internal problems, personal rivalries, ideological disagreements. Some of these were of distant origin; their settlement was held in abeyance during the power seizure period. Others stemmed precisely from the conditions attendant upon the seizure of power. Now, as the Communist parties were confronted with the awesome task of governing, they also had to resolve their internal difficulties and to adapt themselves to dictation by the Soviet Union, which imposed high and rigid standards on their conduct. The freedom they had enjoyed in preceding years was sharply curtailed. The power they wielded was derivative in character. They had limited authority to make decisions and to exercise independent judgment.[4]

The transformation of Communist parties into suitable "instruments of rule" under Soviet prodding took precedence over the transformation of societies. The two processes were about equally stormy. Forcible resolution of conflicts within the parties through purges did not quell the sources of discontent and antagonism. It merely repressed them, just as the terror applied by the parties suppressed public discontent without eliminating it. The crisis of society in each country was duplicated by a crisis of the ruling Party.

In the end, the conditions prevailing within the several Communist parties—their stability or instability, the harmony or discord among their individual leaders, the cohesiveness and technical competence of their leading cadres—had a decisive influence on the turn of events in their respective countries. This was dramatically demonstrated in the upheavals that rocked Hungary and Poland in October, 1956. Without profound internal decay in the Hungarian Party, no revolution would have taken place regard-

4 In sociological terminology, the Communist parties would be identified as power agents rather than power subjects. They administered power in behalf of an outside agency.

less of the amount of popular hatred against the regime. The Polish Party, on the other hand, could not have averted revolution had it not at the last minute found a way to restore its badly tattered internal unity.

The years of socialist construction, from 1948 until the middle of 1953, a few months after Stalin's death, are embedded in the memory of those who lived through them as a dark age. Instead of avoiding the rigors and privations that had become associated with the construction of socialism in the Soviet Union, the East European countries seem to have been exposed deliberately to the same hardships.

A stringent universalism replaced the relatively tolerant particularism of the preceding years. Any allusion to national exclusiveness was condemned as heretical, and recognition was demanded for the universal applicability of the Soviet model. The preservation of national individuality was denounced as retrograde and equated with the restoration of capitalism. Progress was identified with steadfast, unquestioning emulation of the Soviet example.

The Communist parties which previously had identified themselves with spontaneous aspirations of varied groups now imposed their own set of goals on all social classes and groups. These goals (and the means used to achieve them) denied the gratification of wants and frequently of basic needs as well.

Selective terror, brought to bear against political opponents of "progress and democracy," gave way to pervasive threats to the personal safety of all, regardless of class and party affiliation. Coercion became the chief instrument in the hands of the government for exacting conformity and compliance with official policies.

Economic targets were determined without regard to national interests and national capacities. Exaggerated industrialization caused large-scale social dislocation, a permanent state of mobilization of human resources, and a decline in consumption standards. Collectivization was accompanied by intense human suffering and inefficient production.

Class conflict was artificially aggravated in the cities and in the countryside, where political expediency rather than economic considerations led to the "invention" of kulaks where none existed. Last but not least, systematic suppression of the national ego imparted to socialist construction an air of national exploitation on behalf of a foreign power.

Sovietization became a synonym for totalitarian transformation in word and an analogue in fact. It accentuated the alien character of the Communist parties, a stigma which they earlier tried to eschew. Sovietization often went to ridiculous extremes, which, at best, could contribute little toward the success of basic objectives and which, in practice, had the opposite effect. Affront to national self-esteem and assault on individual dignity combined to form powerful psychological irritants.

Foisting "socialist realism" on artists and writers was obnoxious; but it could be explained as an inevitable part of established Communist ideology. The same could not be said in favor of denigrating national traditions and long-dead national heroes, trampling upon national myths and symbols such as emblems and flags, erecting vulgar memorials to Soviet domination, introducing Soviet symbols (army uniforms, newspaper formats), extolling the universal superiority of Soviet achievements and of the virtues of "Soviet man." These were gratuitous insults to peoples whom national self-identification had in the past served as a well-spring of survival and who, rightly or wrongly, considered themselves to be a notch or two more "civilized" than the Russians.

Perhaps it was the very strength of national feeling in some East European countries that induced the Soviet Union to adopt wholesale, ruthless methods to lower national self-esteem and to demolish traditional patterns of national self-identification. But the practitioners of these policies could not have been unaware of the probable repercussions of their deeds. Nationalism became the last rallying point, the final refuge of solidarity of masses of people who were otherwise badly torn asunder by social, economic, and political differences.

Despite great pressure, the Procrustean mold forced on Eastern Europe produced neither monolithic societies nor a monolithic international order. It would have been astonishing, indeed, if in the short span of five years the Communists had been able to reduce a heterogeneous region such as Eastern Europe to a common denominator. Surface similarities that caught the eye hid national differences. The rhythm of change varied quite distinctly from country to country. Collectivization of land was accomplished faster and more ruthlessly in some places than in others. Religious denominations were persecuted more vigorously in some areas than in others. Leading Catholic prelates in Poland, Czechoslovakia, and Hungary were brought to heel in entirely different manners. Intraparty disputes were settled with more or less bloodletting. Cultural "Sovietization" was pressed with greater or lesser intensity. Even political institutions were adapted to the Soviet model at different times and in varying degrees.

The reasons underlying these variations cannot be easily determined. Nor can the significance of diversity be assessed accurately. Conscious and unconscious resistance by the Communists themselves probably accounted for some of the variations, as did imperfections in the system of transmission of orders from Moscow to satellite capitals. The redoubtable Stalinist system did not work with push-button efficiency. Neither communications nor controls were perfect enough to assure flawless performance.

As to the causes of "local variations," one can hazard only guesses. Thus Czechoslovakia avoided the worst pitfalls of super-industrialization and escaped economic ruination probably because it had at its disposal a large reservoir of technically skilled personnel and an advanced, diversified industrial economy which absorbed shocks that crippled less developed economies. Similarly, the Czechoslovak Communist Party preserved a large measure of organizational stability despite widespread purging. It had a large, trained pool of reserve manpower consisting of unemotional, competent administrators with long years of service in the Party who took the purges in their stride and stepped into posts vacated by their predecessors without disturbing the conduct of daily business. The Czechoslovak Party owed its special character to the historic conditions in which it grew up.

The Poles, by contrast, carefully avoided a blood bath in their ranks. No Polish Communist leader lost his life in the course of purge trials. Very likely, the Polish Communists remembered the brutal liquidation of virtually the entire Party leadership on Stalin's orders just before the Second World War. They must have abhorred the thought of additional fratricide. In addition, Polish Communists treated their political opponents with restraint (once the struggle for power was over). No one was "stood up against the wall." Polish economic policies, though far from realistic, acknowledged the enormity of the peasant problem and refrained from pushing a program of collectivization at a fast clip. Polish Church policy, in deference to the staggering burden of subjugating the "mother Church" of upwards of 95 percent of the population, also showed signs of moderation not apparent elsewhere.

The Hungarian Communists acted less prudently than the Poles in every respect, although they faced problems of similar magnitude and although, unlike the Czechs, they had no adequate reserves on which to fall back. The Party purges were bloodier in Hungary than elsewhere. Economic policies were more adventurous than those of other Communist regimes, although the Hungarian economy was highly vulnerable to super-industrialization. These comparisons, though they are crude and must be used with caution, nevertheless suggest a situation of very high tension in Hungary, marked by great brutality in the treatment of the population and by an extraordinary failure of the economy.

Indeed, testimony given by respondents underscores the enormous contrast between conditions during the process of power seizure and those prevailing under socialist construction. All hopes for harmonious social evolution, reconciliation of the interests of various social groups, and stabilization of democratic political institutions were shattered. The sense of political liberation felt at the demise of the old regime gave way to new despair. The feeling of social emancipation of workers and peasants withered as they were cast into bondage again. The creative energies of the population sagged commensurately.

The gap between promise and fulfillment, expectation and reality, usually gives a reliable measure of popular disappointment, disillusionment, and disaffection. In Hungary, the gap was very large, and Communist propaganda kept alive consciousness of it by extolling Marxist social ideals as if the daily practices of the Party did not bely them.

Communist parties always have problems in handling avowed Marxist social ideals. A Hungarian ex-Communist historian cogently noted that "Soviet [Communist] power cannot definitively renounce the basic social ideal, the task to substantiate the Marxist historical necessity, because this task is the justification and origin of its being. To renounce this task would be [tantamount] to losing its legitimacy." [5]

The Hungarian Communist Party had a stronger ideological orientation than most others. It also had greater cause to be concerned about its "legitimacy."

In the course of socialist construction, the Party tightened its grip gradually, as was its wont. Not until 1950 did the whole population feel the impact of political and economic deprivation.

In the first half of 1948, the Hungarian Communists still acted circumspectly. They concentrated on absorbing the Social Democrats (a maneuver surrounded by much intrigue, because Rakosi chose to use it in order to dilute the top leadership of the Party as a preliminary step to consolidating power in his hands), but this process met with tenacious opposition from other quarters. The merger accomplished, Rakosi turned his attention elsewhere.

During the second half of 1948, terror became intensified. Sweeping changes took place in government offices, economic institutions, and social organizations. A large proportion of the country's natural elite (the technical and administrative intelligentsia consisting of younger people with university training and a strong populist bias) was eliminated from public life at this time, partly by demotion to menial positions, partly by incarceration. A trial of leading members of this group appeared to be in the making— the first show trial in Hungary. However, plans were abandoned as attention turned to Jozsef Cardinal Mindszenty instead.

Arrested in December, 1948, the Cardinal was brought to court in February, 1949, in a vulgar display of self-indictment. The

[5] Balazs Nagy, "Reflections on Soviet Power and Historical Materialism," *The Review*, (No. 3, Brussels, January 1960), p. 39.

Cardinal's ordeal caused widespread revulsion of feeling in Hungary and abroad, but the Communists had risked these predictably adverse reactions because they determined to use the Cardinal to teach a basic object lesson to all their would-be domestic opponents.

By the end of 1948, Cardinal Mindszenty was a lone symbol of personal defiance around whom anti-Communist sentiment could crystallize. At odds with most politicians (democrats and Communists alike) and with some of his subordinate bishops, who counseled greater flexibility in dealing with the government, he was yet an imposing, magnetic figure who commanded fierce loyalty. His removal from public life was an indispensable political necessity for the Communists, as was his isolation from his flock. But to achieve these ends the Cardinal could have been sequestered in a monastery without being subjected to public humiliation.

The method chosen by the Communists indicated that they wanted more than merely to isolate the Cardinal, who was reputed to be exceptionally strong and unbending. Clearly, they wanted to destroy belief in his personal integrity and to demonstrate their own determination to brook no opposition. They wanted to demonstrate convincingly that no agency—domestic or foreign—could intervene in behalf of so prominent a person as the Prince of the Roman Catholic Church, and that no individual, regardless of the moral fortitude and spiritual resources at his disposal, could withstand police pressure. If a man of the Cardinal's stature could be broken, resistance to the regime was obviously futile.

The effectiveness of the intended object lesson cannot be satisfactorily determined. The trial did, however, shed significant light on the turn of mind of the Hungarian Communist leaders.

The shock of the trial had hardly worn off when the country confronted another spectacle, in its own right more terrifying than the defamation of the Cardinal. In June, 1949, a scant four months after the conclusion of the Mindszenty affair, Laszlo Rajk, the leading "home" Communist, was arrested. Three months later he and several alleged accomplices (all prominent Communists) were tried, sentenced to death, and executed. While his liquidation had the earmarks of a personal vendetta, it unleashed a mass purge of "Rajkists," Communists of all types of persuasion, conveniently accused of being Rajk's friends or of sharing his ideas, in order to facilitate their removal from office, and imprisonment.[6] Terror struck deep in the Party and, by the middle of 1949, gripped the entire country.

At this time, economic privation was not yet universal. A three-year economic plan, begun in 1947, was allowed to run its course. It was designed to rehabilitate Hungary's damaged economy, not to restructure it. The first five-year plan, aimed specifically at rapid industrial expansion, went into effect in 1950. As if to make up for lost time, it set highly ambitious targets. To meet them, maximum national efforts had to be exerted. In 1951, industrial goals were revised upward as a result of the drain of the Korean war, which necessitated greater sacrifices on the part of all East European countries. To make matters worse, collectivization was also stepped up.

In 1950-51, Party purges cut down former Social Democrats (Marosan, Szakasits) and additional "home" Communists including Janos Kadar, Geza Losonczy, Ferenc Donath, and Gyula Kallai.

In the same period, scores of thousands of Budapest residents of middle-class background were peremptorily "deported" to remote villages. Although punitive in character, the relocation of middle-class residents was not politically motivated. It was the government's answer to an acute housing shortage that arose from the influx of workers from the countryside. There is no evidence that enough living space was liberated to ease crowding.

In January, 1951, selective rationing of consumer goods was introduced to forestall economic chaos. Several forced-labor camps were installed to accommodate a rapidly expanding prison population.

In 1952, for the first time in four or five years, no new hardships were inflicted on the population, although terror did not taper off and economic conditions remained unalterably grim. Purges in the Party came to a temporary halt, and for reasons that are still unexplained, a number of leaders who had been eclipsed but not imprisoned in preceding years were brought back to formal prominence. Among them was Imre Nagy.

[6] For a fuller treatment of the Rajk purge in the Communist Party, see below pp. 131-34.

Faint signs of awareness in the Communist high command of the ruinous effect brought about by its economic policies became discernible. With just a slight stretch of the imagination, one could detect the distant rumblings of impending change in the Communist camp.

TERROR IN CONTROL

Relations between the Party and the people developed under the aegis of comprehensive political and economic controls that combined to brutalize human sensitivities.[7]

The shift from power seizure to socialist construction multiplied

[7] Functionally, relations between the Communist Party and the population developed in close conformity with what is probably the "classical" Soviet pattern, noted particularly in the Harvard studies of the Soviet social system (Kluckhohn, Inkeles, and Bauer, *How the Soviet System Works*; Bauer and Inkeles, *The Soviet Citizen*). These studies, like the present work, base the core of their findings on data gathered in the course of interviews with former residents of the country in question. It is not surprising that testimony by Hungarian escapees about the 1948-53 period corroborates reports of former Soviet residents. Although they spoke from very different time perspectives (the Hungarians, soon after they left their motherland; the former Soviet citizens, after an interval of ten years or more), they drew on memories of corresponding phases of development and described identical totalitarian syndromes (Stalinoid, early industrial) in somewhat different settings.

Similarities in the type and intensity of actual and perceived pressures, sources of deprivation and dissatisfaction (as well as satisfaction), patterns of individual adjustment (adaptation) to life situations created by Communist totalitarianism in Russia and in Hungary, raise anew the question of universality and particularity in the totalitarian process. The problem is to define the relative importance of social and psychological constants as opposed to cultural, ethnic, religious, and political variants.

Data collected from Hungarian refugees suggest a high degree of cultural, ethnic, and political neutrality in the totalitarian process, notwithstanding the intensity of nationalist sentiment as a motivating force.

It may well be that Communist totalitarianism, which has a functional bias in its approach to human problems, is not entirely wrong in regarding social and psychological constants as a "base," and cultural, ethnic and other variants as a "superstructure." But it is a mistake to assume that societies can be altered successfully by manipulating the base alone without reference to the superstructure. Similarly, social analysis falls short of its mark if it limits itself to information derived from measurable social and psychological constants and fails to assign due value to the influence of ethnic, cultural, and other variants, despite the formidable methodological difficulties that are involved.

Exhaustive social analysis of the Hungarian experience and detailed comparison with the results of the Harvard studies require special attention in a separate monograph. In the context of this study it is possible only to summarize functional relations between the Party and the population in order to gain insight into the forces that shaped the destiny of the country.

contacts between the authorities and the people and made them more intimate. The Party's interest now extended over the whole range of human activities. It restricted personal privacy, autonomy, and spontaneity. This resulted in friction, tension, and alienation.

Large-scale social engineering is inconceivable without regimentation and coercion. The initial efforts put into restructuring a society invariably exceed the rewards in which people can share. Gratification tends to lag a considerable distance behind, even if the available fruits of labor are equitably distributed. But enthusiasm, hope, and identification with long-range objectives help to mitigate early hardships.

When socialist construction began in Hungary, these mitigating circumstances were present. Communist behavior made them disappear rapidly. The extent of brutalization of human sensitivities cannot be explained by the manifest or latent hostility of the Hungarian people to Communism. Middle-class groups proved more supine than the Communists could hope for. The good will of the workers was not quickly dissipated. Peasants were no more recalcitrant than in other countries. No social class or group possessed political power to resist Communism. None had institutional means to promote its interests.

The universally reported brutalization of human sensitivities therefore must be attributed to a deliberate preference of the Party. The rational motives underlying it are not clear. Possibly Rakosi thought that Stalin would be pleased with nothing less. Possibly he gave free reign to his own penchant for violence and inhumaneness, which he had long kept in check. He is said to have expounded his philosophy of government in terms of a "law of large numbers." This, he explained, meant "killing some and corrupting the rest." The account of Rakosi's explanation may be apocryphal. His policies, however, appeared to have been based indeed on the premise of "killing some and corrupting the rest."

Police terror ranked first among the instruments that brutalized human sensitivities. It was both pervasive and indiscriminate.

By crude calculation, one family in five crossed paths with the police through the arrest of one of its members or of a close friend.[8] Actual imprisonment, however, was not the prevalent means of terrorizing people, nor was terror used primarily to punish overt acts of defiance. Its real mission was to prevent such acts from occurring.

In the countryside, police surveillance was perforce intermittant, despite the fact that the regime waged severe battle against class-alien "kulaks." But the occasional nature of police raids did not guarantee the security of villagers. Police interfered in their lives just as arbitrarily as in the lives of urban dwellers. Flying squads of secret policemen (the dread blue-uniformed AVO) swooped down on villages, usually to "aid" with the organization of a collective farm or to "improve" compulsory deliveries of crops. The techniques they employed were simple and effective. Beating or placing a person on a hot stove usually sufficed to soften up resistance to joining a collective or to surrendering hoarded grain.

The physical aspects of terror against workers are less explicitly documented. However, large numbers of workers (mostly former trade unionists and "natural leaders" with a sense of independence) were held in prisons. Rakosi, as if to underline the persecution of this allegedly "privileged" social stratum, once boasted that "there are more workers in prisons than intellectuals."

As applied against the middle class, terror took the shape of persecution, harassment, and often blackmail in order to enlist a person's services as informer. The alternative to informing was imprisonment. The secret police, in seeking the assistance of "class aliens," counted on the low resistance of people who had no reasonable expectation of a bright future. But recruitment of informers was by no means limited to middle-class elements.

No statistics are available on the number of informers and on the use the police made of their services. All respondents alluded to the presence of informers in their place of work or domicile. They often referred to "built-in" people *(beepitett emberek)* in casual conversation. The expression became one of the more

[8] The total number of political prisoners in Hungary, including Communists and non-Communists, has been estimated as high as 200,000. The number of executions has been placed at about 2,000.

common figures of speech in Hungary. It pointed up the institutionalization of the practice of informing.[9]

While many Hungarian refugees confirmed the wide spread of the practice, they disparaged its efficacy. They claimed that informers were easily spotted and ostracized by their fellow workers. Actually, the system was far from ineffectual. For the known or suspected presence of informers helped to create an atmosphere of suspicion, to sow distrust, even among close friends and toward customarily respected persons, and to inhibit free association and exchange of information by word of mouth. The net effect was to dissipate group solidarity and to perpetuate a feeling of isolation. Informers were instrumental in "atomizing" society and in encapsulating discontent in individuals—both major objectives of the regime.

Next in order to terror, invasion of privacy in a variety of ingenious and highly irritating ways was used to brutalize human sensitivities. Work schedules, compulsory participation in supervised social activities, including seminars and lectures in factories and offices just before the beginning or after the termination of the normal work day, and an increase in the ratio of gainfully employed persons per family unit reduced the amount of leisure time of individuals and the opportunity of families to be together away from probing scrutiny of their behavior.

A poet characterized conditions in Hungary at this time as being devoid of love. Others said essentially the same thing more prosaically. Life situations were so rigged as to cause maximum discomfort for the population and allow a minimum of time for private, unsupervised pursuits. Fatigue, a function of overexertion and anxiety, became a universal feature of life.

Obsessive preoccupation of the authorities with the social and occupational background of all employees added a new twist to the invasion of personal privacy. It was as if the whole working population were under continuous security investigation. Personnel

---

[9] Dossiers located at secret police headquarters during the revolution (but for lack of time not counted) also bore sad testimony to the existence of a formidable network of informers.

files were kept meticulously to determine the class origin and occupational history of job applicants and to record entries about their political loyalty and personal demeanor. Called cadre cards (*kader lapok*), they were repugnant instruments of intimidation in the hands of their usually zealous custodians. They were in fact police files whose very existence put people on guard and impeded social and occupational mobility.

The cadre card was first of all a weapon in the unrelenting struggle against the middle class. It barred middle-class applicants from finding desirable employment, unless they were willing to falsify information about their social status and risk being unmasked. But other than middle-class persons were also victimized by the cadre card. Preoccupation with cadre status became so prevalent that expressions like "good cadre" and "bad cadre" passed into common usage.

The economic process occupied a central place in socialist construction. The five-year plan was intended as an instrument to transform society. Economic policies profoundly affected popular welfare in the total context of the term, not in its narrow, materialistic meaning.

Although it is true that day-to-day hardships growing out of the economic process were keenly felt, material deprivation had greater psychological than economic effects. In one way or another, families and individuals managed to get by. In 1951 and 1952, the cost of food and clothing rose sharply, but, at the same time, the earning power of families also grew. On the average, more members per family unit worked than ever before. What hurt, therefore, was not so much an absolute drop in purchasing ability as a relative impoverishment in terms of the equivalent effort needed to procure certain goods (and a deterioration in the variety and quality of goods available).

The same is true of the hated system of norms. In general, even the most advanced norms set for workers were not incommensurate with Western industrial standards. The production rate of workers certainly lagged behind the West. But Hungarian workers started off with incredibly "soft" norms, and such "hardening" as took place was not rewarded with extra pay. In the end, in their own terms of reference, Hungarian workers produced more for the same pay. In a period of three to four years, norms increased as much as 50–60 percent, while real income declined.

Extreme rigidity in the operation of the economy, a corollary of stringent political controls, also created psychological irritants. The handling of wage funds is an example. Elsewhere in Eastern Europe and in Russia, at corresponding stages of economic growth, wage funds constituted a flexible element in the total production picture. The manipulation of wage funds (overspending) helped managers to secure (and even to hoard) workers needed for production. Wage funds expanded faster than authorized by plan and created inflationary pressures. But they also helped to perpetuate the "money illusion" of workers and had a beneficial effect on their morale. Not so in Hungary, where wage funds were so tightly controlled that managers could not hire the work force they needed to meet production targets. The absence of a "money illusion" had an adverse effect on all wage earners. Inflationary pressures, in turn, arose from other disproportions in production. To counteract them, price increases were ordered. But instead of draining off buying power by raising (hidden) turnover taxes, the government relied heavily on mandatory deductions from pay for so-called "peace loans." The "peace loan" quotas, deducted from pay at the source in ten monthly installments in each calendar year, increased year by year and created tremendous resentment.

Concomitantly with wage funds, labor turnover was also held to a minimum. While a high labor turnover is not desirable from the regime's point of view (fluctuation in the labor force has been the bane of socialist construction everywhere except in Hungary), it does reflect a certain measure of freedom and initiative and leads to a higher degree of job satisfaction that enhances worker morale. In Hungary, strict enforcement of work-book regulations virtually chained workers to their jobs.

To complicate matters, relative and absolute standards of living of different social strata varied considerably, and not necessarily in accordance with official expectations. "Class enemies" of the regime often lived better than socially "favored" elements. The urban middle class and the rural kulak, though faced with eventual economic extinction, temporarily managed to maintain themselves by living off accumulated capital. They drew heavily on fiscal and other real assets and on family assistance. Middle-class persons, though their current earnings were often inadequate to meet more than the barest essentials of subsistence, had surplus clothing and durable goods (appliances, home furnishings) to last a number of years. Although part of their living quarters had been confiscated, they still enjoyed comfortable if modest lodging. Workers were not nearly as well off.

The situation contained a strong element of social tension. Those whose standards had been reduced held the regime responsible, and those whose low standards had not risen as expected also blamed the government and envied the relatively higher standard still enjoyed by "class enemies."

But more important than the day-to-day hardships endured by the population was the patent failure of the planned economy. Every facet of the economic process revealed irrationality, ineptness, ill will, or rank stupidity on the part of the authorities.

Few people gained an overall view of the economy. None could judge it in total perspective. Statistics concealed the truth. Verification was impossible. But every person caught a glimpse of a particular phase of the economy that was sufficient to impart to him an awareness of wrongdoing. An outstanding example of this was the building of the Budapest subway system, into which the government poured one billion forint without getting any returns. No interpersonal communication was necessary to prove it a blunder, since it was common knowledge that the subsoil of Budapest was honeycombed with artesian wells and streams that made the construction of a subway system impractical.[10]

The causes of the over-all failure of economic planning and some of the consequences that grew from it can be summarized as follows:

1. The rates of projected growth were excessive, the apportionment of investments between heavy and light industry, between industry and agriculture, was unbalanced. Hungarian industrial

[10] Another example was the construction of Sztalinvaros, a huge industrial center for the production of iron and steel, that was never completed.

·production is said to have expanded by 210 percent in five years (1949–53). Comparable figures for Poland are 158 percent; for Czechoslovakia, 98 percent; for East Germany, 92.3 percent; for Rumania, 144 percent; for Bulgaria, 120 percent.[11] While these percentages require a great deal of interpretation to be meaningful, they do give a rough estimate of the exaggerated pace of development of Hungary. Investment ratios between heavy and light industry increased steadily from a very high figure of 9.1:.9 in 1950, to 9.3:.7 in 1951, and 9.4:.6 in 1952.[12]

2. Industrial branches designed for growth were improperly identified and inadequate attention was given to balancing raw-material requirements with the marketability of finished products. Certain industrial branches (e.g., foundries, iron processing) were developed without heed to the unavailability of domestic sources of raw materials.

3. Hungary showed a great predilection for the construction of huge new production units to the detriment of smaller, more economical ones and the expansion, renovation, and even maintenance of existing plant facilities. The entire conception of planned industrial growth seemed faulty. Investment schedules called for strongly unbalanced outlays for new plant facility. The short-run consequences in terms of industrial returns and in wasted manpower were disastrous.

According to statistics, the seventy-five new enterprises constructed during the five-year plan contributed less than 5 percent of the total industrial production (2 percent in 1950, 2.9 percent in 1951, 3.8 percent in 1952). This clearly implies that existing plants bore the brunt of increased production.[13]

While the short-run results may have been gratifying in a sense, since they showed tremendous increases in production with existing plant facilities, they were achieved at the cost of virtual ruination of equipment, which was not properly maintained or replaced, so

[11] Imre Nagy, *On Communism: In Defense of the New Course* (New York, Praeger, 1957), p. 185.

[12] *Statisztikai Evkonyv,* 1956 (Statistical Yearbook, 1956, Central Statistical Bureau), p. 53.

[13] *Adatok es Adalekok a Nepgazdasag Fejlodesenek Tanulmanyozasahoz 1949-1955,* Budapest, 1957 ("Data for Studying the Development of the People's Economy between 1949 and 1955"), p. 79.

that early breakdown threatened and industrial safety deteriorated to a point of grave danger to the working force.

Emphasis on construction also meant that disproportionately large numbers of new workers were absorbed in the building trades, where the type and the conditions of work (especially in the absence of advanced mechanization) cause low labor discipline and a high percentage of waste. (Between 1949 and 1951, the number of workers in construction grew by 125,000 whereas the rest of the industrial labor force increased by only 58,000. In 1952, an additional 49,000 workers were engaged in construction, bringing the total to 244,000, while only 88,000 new workers were added to the industrial labor force.)

4. Technical manpower talent was squandered owing to the primacy of political considerations in allocating manpower. The country's trained technicians and managers were relegated to unimportant posts. Rapid promotion of untrained but politically loyal personnel lowered efficiency of management and led to a pyramiding of costly economic errors.

5. Economic controls were too rigid. They did not allow the substitution of informal arrangements for prescribed procedure in order to meet production targets. But controls, by necessity, were not comprehensive enough to prevent widespread juggling of economic indicators to cover up shortages and failures to meet planned objectives with regard to all relevant specifications (volume, quality, composition). The practices that developed did not violate the letter of the economic plan but vitiated its intent. Although these practices were not actually illegal, they were disruptive of the economy.

The total economic picture was one in which the detrimental features of capitalist economics were compounded. The presumed social anarchy that characterizes the capitalist economic process at its worst (lack of central direction, irrational utilization of resources, inequitable distribution of wealth, uncertainty of economic expectations) was not replaced by a rationally operated system of planning on a social scale. But the efficient operation of individual economic units that marks the capitalist economy yielded to near anarchy under socialism.

Responsibility for this dismal state of affairs rested entirely with the Communist leadership. The presuppositions on which the economic plan rested appeared incredibly primitive. They aimed at making little Hungary, deficient in essential industrial raw materials, a country of iron and steel, *self-sufficient* in the *production* of these basic industrial ingredients.[14] Current experience indicates that countries with planned economies in the early stages of industrial expansion tend to succumb to a sort of gigantism and project unrealistic rates of growth. Hungary, however, was not that primitive to begin with and it had at its disposal, if not a large staff of economists, some of the world's best. The blunders of Hungarian economic planning are all the more puzzling. The blame for them must be laid to the political leadership whose megalomania was bound to have disastrous repercussions. They did not match means to ends. They struck out to accomplish too much too fast, forgetting that not even a totalitarian country can afford to bankrupt itself for the sake of future achievements.

Economic failure was an objective cause of difficulties that demanded rectification. It also produced corollary social and psychological evils. Some of these were possibly of transitory nature. But they helped to introduce what, for the moment, were new categories of social tension.

In factories, conflict between workers and management gained a sharpness previously unknown. The resentment felt by workers toward their new managers exceeded their dislike for their former "bourgeois exploiters." Workers considered them incompetent, unfit for the jobs they were holding, and accused them of betraying the working class. An additional source of friction in factories was the influx of large numbers of new laborers from the countryside. They formed their own gangs, behaved raucously, and disrupted industrial discipline and solidarity.

Tensions of a similar nature developed on the collective farms. The managerial personnel consisted of industrial workers or, still worse, locally disdained "scum" (*Lumpenproletariat*) who were

[14] The problems of Hungarian economic planning are discussed in a number of works; outstanding among them are Bela A. Balassa, *The Hungarian Experience in Economic Planning* (Yale University Press, 1959), and Janos Kornai, *Overcentralization in Economic Administration* (John Knapp, transl.; Oxford University Press, 1959). (The original Hungarian version of this book was published in Hungary in 1957.)

unsympathetic to the plight of the peasant and ignorant of the ways of farming. Strife arose among collective farm members as well. As a social unit, the collective farm brought together industrious, self-reliant peasants, and lazy riffraff. The latter tended to benefit from the rules that governed life in the collective, particularly the method of remuneration in labor-day units. Finally, the presence of a collective farm in a community contributed to strife between collective farm members and members of individual farm households. The former, regardless of their actual feeling about membership in a collective, were under a cloud of suspicion. The latter, especially if they did well, could not help eliciting the envy of the collective.

In offices and schools as well, friction was common between declassed technicians and administrators on the one hand and the political beneficiaries of the system on the other hand. Frequently, the feeling of inferiority of the latter rather than the rancor of the former was responsible for friction. Indeed, the incompetence of Communist officials, due to a lack of formal education and of job experience, was one of the major irritants in the entire social system. For example, university students who eventually protested against various aspects of ideological and military indoctrination actually objected less to the principle and content of indoctrination than to the "uneducated rabble" whose lectures they had to endure. The government tried through education to raise the standards of its personnel, but supply never caught up with demand. It could not train adequate numbers of functionaries fast enough. Education was the regime's long range answer to the overwhelming problem of competent staffing.

THE EDUCATIONAL SYSTEM:
A SOURCE OF GRATIFICATION

The educational program of the government was one of the few bright spots of the Communist system. Although parents and children alike (especially on the grammar school level) frequently bemoaned the lack of religious training and the massive distortion of truth that went on at all levels of instruction, the benefits of the educational facilities that were now open to those who had in

the past been unable to better themselves outdistanced the disadvantages. On the level of secondary schools (including trade
schools and high schools preparing for advanced study) and in
institutes of higher learning, the students belonged to a privileged
caste. The prospect of full employment under an expanding
economy and the growing demands for engineers, technicians, managers, etc., mitigated for them some of the negative features of the
political system under which they lived.

This is not to suggest that these young generations raised under
Communism were more materialistically minded than their elders.
Nor is it to imply that they accepted Communist values wholeheartedly and became ideologically convinced servants of the totalitarian state. What they did accept was the premise that their
worth to the Party and, coincidentally, their own personal welfare
were a direct function of their social utility to the government and
not of political considerations. (This was the easier to do since most
career opportunities were in fields of low political content. The
situation in specialized branches of learning in the humanities,
literature, art, and social sciences was somewhat different.) On this
basis they arrived at a mutually satisfactory (if tacit) understanding
with the authorities. They found it quite possible to put up with
the required quota of ideological indoctrination as a necessary but
marginal evil. They did not seem to be unduly taken in by it, but
neither did they chafe at being deprived of traditional educational
fare, including exposure to Western scholarship, art, culture, and
science.

The evidence is admittedly scanty and the subsequent record of
demonstrated hostility toward the regime on the part of students
of all ages would seem to contradict the foregoing assertions. But
student unrest set in only later, after the end of the Stalinist period,
and then often for very peculiar reasons. For the time being, students did seem the best hope of the Communist regime to anchor
itself in the matrix of society. The absence of protest and observable
restiveness on the part of students in this period, of course, should
not be mistaken as a sure sign of acquiescence and approval.
Silence, everyone soon learned, was a precondition of survival. On
the other hand, it would be erroneous to equate the silence of

students with a thunderous desire to speak out in protest. This was simply not the case.

It was for good reason that youths who were barred from attaining higher education because of their middle-class family background did everything within their means to gain entrance to a university. A surprisingly large number of them succeeded despite the strict application of quotas against them. Those who failed, naturally opposed the regime.

THE CONTROL SYSTEM EVALUATED

Notwithstanding the exaggerated aspects of terror, informing, cadre supervision and the pecularities of the economic process, the Hungarian Communists were not known to utilize other than standard instruments and techniques of totalitarian control. The immense hostility and profound anxiety that spread through the land were due to the character of the control system as a whole rather than to its special features.

The system of controls was highly efficient and remarkably rigid. It allowed little room for maneuver either in behalf of government interests or against them. Hungary's economic failure is partly explicable by the lack of an informal mechanism that circumvents ponderous formal command channels, cuts through the maze of bureaucratic prescriptions, and gets things done.

The population, however, suffered more acutely from the absence of informal means to promote personal interests and obtain redress from injustices suffered at the hands of the authorities. Going through "legal" channels was hopeless, and other means, such as bribery, "fix," "contacts," or "protection," which form an essential (existential) part of the paraphernalia of every social order, also failed. People were naked before the government, without recourse against it. They felt helpless, isolated, at the mercy of a ruthless, high handed, abusive, arbitrary Leviathan.[15]

The feeling of helplessness exaggerated an already existing sense

---

[15] Arbitrariness is a spurious form of normlessness. Unlike genuine normlessness, it reinforces rather than relieves the coercive element of institutional behavior. It introduces a large element of uncertainty into general life situations that enhances "voluntary" conformity to prescribed norms and always favors the prevailing system, never the individual citizen.

of frustration that arose from conflicts between individual goals and societal objectives. If harmony between basic human motives and overt behavior is a measure of liberty, Hungary was indeed a society bereft of any shred of freedom.

Theoretically, there were no restrictions on individual responses to the institutional structure. In practice, overt defiance amounted to self-destruction. Evasion entailed extreme hazards that few people cared to brave. Outward conformity was a minimum condition of survival. The Hungarian population conformed assiduously. The distinction between genuine and feigned conformity was difficult to make. Those who only feigned conformity, without really subscribing to the goals and means approved by the regime, had to devise means to preserve their personal integrity. Overt compliance, covert resistance became an unspoken rule of thumb by which they attempted to guide themselves. Psychologically, it was not a very satisfactory solution. It failed to preserve that which it was intended to safeguard.

The strain of maintaining a double standard was very considerable. Continual dissimulation necessitated unrelenting vigilance. It damaged self-respect, not because it failed to gain approbation by others but because it led to self-doubt and induced feelings of guilt and shame. Internal tensions built up and found no release. Aggression either had to be sublimated (with unpredictable psychological results) or suppressed as long as possible. When it could no longer be contained, it had to be released in disguised form that did not invite retribution. Aggression could not be directed against the real sources of tension and hostility, only at "safe" targets. Instead of ventilating their anger on the government, people grew hostile to one another, rioted during soccer games, engaged in barroom brawls, street fights, etc. This kind of release provided only temporary and unsatisfactory relief.

This general condition affected people in all walks of life, regardless of the actual harassment to which they were exposed. There were individuals in all strata who came through the entire period of socialist construction unscathed. But no major class or group enjoyed privileged status. The astonishing situation arose whereby a system of government founded on principles of collectivism completely disdained group interests and promoted a truly rampant if somewhat bizarre form of individualism.[16]

In this sense, the system had a self-reinforcing quality. All told, the strong "individuation" of society was a signal victory for the Communists. They managed to break down the social fabric of Hungary and to ensure themselves against any challenge to their authority. Resistance was nonexistent. The very success of disintegration of the social fabric, however, vitiated other, equally important positive objectives. There was no sign of reintegration of society through new, approved associations and organizations commanding loyalty and solidarity.

The network of negative sanctions was not adequately reinforced by positive sanctions. The obvious bad faith of the government, demonstrated at every step of the way, undercut if it did not nullify the persuasiveness of Communist indoctrination. Glaring discrepancies between propaganda images and reality, between words and deeds, provided an unhappy standard by which to evaluate Communist propaganda. The torrent of lies that flowed from official sources, the necessity of overtly acknowledging lies as truth, and of lying in turn to dissimulate true personal attitudes, led to a profound revulsion of feeling.

For the moment, the absence of positive sanctions was not catastrophic for the regime. Their lack would be keenly felt only in the event of a significant change in the system of coercion. But the unshakable stability of the system was more apparent than real. Surface calm concealed tremendous stores of latent hostility and aggression.

The question of how long a totalitarian system can go on increasing the pressure of negative sanctions before it reaches an objective breaking point in rebellion or functional breakdown has yet to be answered. There has been considerable speculation about a point at which coercion begins to yield diminishing results or even becomes self-defeating by retarding social processes it is meant to advance. Communist totalitarianism has never really been put

[16] By a curious inversion of practices, interpersonal contacts were freer in forced labor camps than anywhere else. Only in such camps was anything like unsupervised group consensus known to exist. The explanation probably is that the inmates of the camps were never expected to reenter society.

to the test, for as pressures mounted toward a point of danger, something usually intervened to divert attention from the main issues or to alleviate tension just enough to rekindle hope in the future and revitalize flagging energies.

Stalin in his earlier years skillfully manipulated tensions to achieve optimum results of compliance and performance. He lost his touch toward the end of his life and became less flexible. The loss of elasticity was reflected in the process of totalitarian construction in Eastern Europe and brought both the Soviet Union and the men controlled by it to the brink of despair. But this time it was Stalin's death that brought about relaxation, reassessment of policies, and readjustment in relations among Communist parties, within the Communist parties, and between the parties and the societies they controlled. It remained to be seen how well the Hungarian Communists would adapt themselves to new conditions—conditions which amounted to a carefully regulated process of decompression with all that implied: criticizing the past, balancing coercion, incentive and persuasion as instruments of manipulation, relieving pent-up hatreds, redressing some injustices, and redirecting energies into creative channels.

6. The Party Against Itself

ON THE EVE of the actual seizure of power, evidence began to accumulate of restiveness in the Communist leadership as well as among the rank and file at the slow pace of progress. But the resolutions of the Cominform meeting at Szklarska Poreba in Poland, in September, 1947, presaged a new era. The pulse of Communists quickened. Revai, Gero, Rajk, and others came forward with plans and schemes aimed at "opening the gates of progress." Gero clamored for intensified socialist production and stiffer labor discipline. Revai strained for a showdown with the Catholic Church. Rajk dreamt of a purified Party at the center of a reorganized national front leading the way to socialist glory. All wanted to move speedily toward the next phase, socialist construction, though it is doubtful if any one of them had a clear conception of what this would entail.

Of the top leaders, Rakosi seemed least in a hurry. Sensing that a coalition against him was in the making among the Party leadership, he conveniently became "ill," went off to Moscow, returned "cured" a few weeks later, went off again in March, 1948, accompanied by the Social Democrat Arpad Szakasits, and came back after a few days, confident of having assayed the situation and primed to make his bid for absolute leadership in the Party.

The time was right. Internationally, Stalin's struggle with Tito was nearing the showdown stage, and Rakosi guessed its outcome correctly. Internally, the merger of the Communist and Social Democratic parties provided an ideal occasion for "fishing in troubled waters."

The terms of the merger (what they actually were is unimportant), gave the secretary general an opportunity to embroil the

Party in political intrigue and to befuddle his opponents. He bought off Gero by agreeing to speed up nationalization. He trundled Rajk off to Moscow, expecting that Rajk would irritate the Soviet "comrades" and corroborate Rakosi's appraisal of his personal faults. (This is what happened. Rajk pleaded with the Russians to remove Rakosi. He gave a very bad account of himself as a headstrong and independent individual. His fate was probably sealed on the spot.) Finally, Rakosi ingratiated himself with the Social Democratic leaders whose side he took against the Communists in their dispute over methods of merging the two parties.

Rakosi emerged victorious from the skirmish: the top leadership of the united "Workers' Party" was scrambled and diluted beyond recognition by Social Democrats.[1] Rakosi now moved swiftly to consolidate his gains.

The party merger, which completed the power seizure, took place in June, 1948. Hungary still lagged behind other East European countries in economic and social change, but Rakosi had already struck hard and fast to mold the Party in his own image. In internal political transformation, the Hungarian Workers' Party was well ahead of its counterparts in other satellite countries. Rakosi intended to synchronize the Hungarian Communist command structure with Stalin's own as rapidly and faithfully as possible. To this, he devoted unflagging energy. He succeeded beyond his fondest dreams.

From this time on until the end of the Stalinist era in 1953, the Communist Party underwent more or less permanent purging until its cadre structure was thoroughly rebuilt from raw, politically immature recruits who were loyal to the institution that elevated them and totally dependent on its good will, regardless of the amount of incidental power that it vested in them.

In less than five years, Rakosi reduced the Party from a vibrant

[1] The Social Democrat Szakasits was chairman of the Party, Rakosi is secretary general. One of the three deputy secretaries general was a Social Democrat (Gyorgy Marosan); the other two were Kadar and Farkas. Two of the 8 members of the Secretariat (Szakasits, Marosan), 4 of 13 in the Politbureau (Szakasits, Marosan, Ronai, Harustyak), and 21 of 65 in the Central Committee were Social Democrats.

if heterogeneous and undisciplined organism to a soulless, stream-lined instrument. The purges eliminated the flower of "home" Communists, the "Westerners," and the genuine national element, rooted in populism, that had affiliated itself with Communism during and after the war. In a sense, the Party consciously estranged itself from the population. It assumed an alien character; for those whom it selected for high office, though mostly of a humble social origin, were regarded by the population as sons who had forsaken their native land to serve a usurping power.

The transformation of the Party along the lines chosen by Rakosi was as necessary as it was brutal. Eventually all Communist parties followed suit, replacing their prerevolutionary cadres with post-revolutionary ones. New conditions called for new talents, and a change of guard in the Communist high command followed. Younger people, products of the society they were serving and governing and not creators of that society, were preferable to old war horses. But Rakosi's methods, as usual, were brusque and dehumanizing. To infuse the Party with new blood he did not have to kill off the old leaders. And, although rational considera-tions may have underlined the purges, they were indefensible as measures ridding the Party of disloyal, treacherous elements.

The Communists who were killed, imprisoned, or shunted to the side lines held a variety of convictions but none inimical to the Party. Few, if any, entertained "revisionist" ideas or nurtured excessive humanitarian sentiments. That was not the issue. They happened to be in the way of the secretary general and so were removed.

Rakosi personally presided over the purges and seemed to take great delight in them. The Rajk case was the greatest coup he engineered. His behavior bordered on the pathological. Unfortu-nately, it went undetected for what it was until much later.

THE PURGES

Rakosi went to extraordinary lengths to corrupt those connected with the Rajk case, probably to protect himself against recrimina-tion. He dispatched Kadar, supposedly one of Rajk's best friends, to induce Rajk to confess "for the good of the Party" and promise him that he would not be executed, but would be sent off to Russia where he could contribute to the movement under an assumed name. As if this were not enough, Rakosi had the entire conversation between Kadar and Rajk monitored and kept a (doctored) tape recording of it on hand to implicate Kadar. (Kadar's opening words: "I have come at the request of Comrade Rakosi" were erased from the tape.)

But aside from this, Rakosi feigned such indignation at the "monstrous discoveries" of Rajk's crimes as to convince his listeners of sincerity in a case which was wholly fabricated from beginning to end on his orders. He kept a thick file purported to contain the record of the police interrogation of Rajk on his desk and at opportune moments flung it open to read from it passages of confessed acts of treachery by Rajk. In the face of such "evidence," who could doubt Rajk's guilt and Rakosi's genuineness?

Despite the publicity that accompanied it, the details of the Rajk case have never been satisfactorily explained. Rajk's influence had been declining since 1948. His removal from the Ministry of the Interior to the Ministry of Foreign Affairs in August, 1948, was an unmistakable sign of demotion. It was a thankless assignment for anyone at a time when mass defections from the foreign service could be expected and when the Ministry could easily be implicated in alleged plots with foreign powers against the People's Republic. The importance of the Ministry meanwhile declined, for, after 1948, the East European states lost what little independence they still had in foreign policy matters. It could be argued that Rajk was appointed to the Ministry to preside over the liquidation of the old staff and to tighten security, but this was patently not so. A "Muscovite" watchdog, Andor Berei, was placed under Rajk as Deputy Minister. The Ministry was also invaded by secret police types who had no connection with Rajk and did not take their orders from him. He was a lonely figure surrounded by strange people in a hostile environment.

In November, 1948, Rajk was dropped from the Secretariat of the Party, and although his appointment, in the spring of 1949, as secretary general of the Independent People's Front might have been considered a victory for Rajk, it was not that. Most likely

Rakosi engineered it to give himself a plank in his frontal attack on Rajk. Indeed, one of the more telling charges later brought against Rajk was his alleged "Titoist" view of the role of the Party in relation to the National Front. Tito was just then under heavy fire for perverting the leading role of the Party, allowing it to be absorbed in the National Front, an inchoate, shapeless, mass organization that deprived the Party of its separate identity and thwarted it in the performance of its historic mission. Whether or not there was any connection between Rajk's and Tito's views is not known. Rajk may have been impressed with some of Tito's ideas, or he may have arrived independently at similar conclusions. We know that Rajk had some artless thoughts about the shape of the Hungarian political structure that did not correspond to the "proven" Stalinist pattern. In the circumstances, this was enough to establish him as a criminal.[2]

The time and setting were ripe for a Titoist trial in Hungary. Xoxe, in Albania, had already been tried, and Kostov, in Bulgaria, was readied as a sacrificial victim. Stalin, infuriated by Tito's defiance and anxious to substantiate his view of the perniciousness of Titoist deviation, was searching for "proof" of the international tentacles of the Titoist conspiracy. Rakosi was eager to oblige. He produced a first-rate victim with a watertight case against him.

Soviet and Hungarian security authorities cooperated closely in preparing the trial. They even went to Austria to kidnap "Rajkists" and bring them back to Budapest. In general they followed a well-established pattern of interrogation, but a few novelties were

[2] Rajk's family ties and his past activities also militated against him. They gave his opponents a ready opportunity to question Rajk's motives and his loyalty to the Party. It was said that Rajk was spared long imprisonment for his Communist activities in the early 1930s because of the intervention of his brother-in-law, a police official. But, in return, Rajk betrayed some of his Communist friends to the police. Similarly, in 1944, Rajk's elder brother, an adherent of the fascist Arrow Cross movement, supposedly intervened on his behalf. After the war, Rajk interceded for his relatives and saved them from being tried for their political misdeeds. In the late 1930s, Rajk fought as a volunteer in the Spanish civil war. He thus belonged to the select group of "Spaniards" who were highly regarded in the immediate postwar period and whose talents were put to best use in the police and security forces that were being raised by the Communists. But, in connection with the break between Stalin and Tito, the "Spaniards" as a group came under a cloud. Stalin accused them of having come under the spell of imperialist countries and ordered a wholesale purge of their ranks.

added—notably the staging of repeated rehearsals of the trial, as of a theatrical production in which all the actors, including the prosecutor, the witnesses, and even some of the spectators learned their part by rote. If the testimony of several of the respondents can be believed, the defendants themselves did not know which one of the "performances" was the actual trial. General Bielkin, chief of Soviet security forces in South East Europe, took personal command of the operation.

More incredible than the fabrication of the whole Rajk affair was the fact that it was believed and condoned by Party members.[3] Not a single former Communist among the respondents reported having had more than fleeting and superficial doubt about Rajk's guilt. None questioned the Party's right to do as it pleased. The lesser victims of the Rajk purges admitted that they failed even to register inner protest against their fate. For a long time, most of them attributed their own detention to a mistake but thought that others who were imprisoned were in fact guilty. They had effectively divested themselves of independent judgment and entrusted their moral conscience to the Party for safekeeping. They did not believe in inviolable personal rights, in justice for the individual. The greater good of the social movement took precedence over that of the individual. They took it for granted that the dynamic surge of a large-scale social movement was destructive of the personal welfare of its affiliates as well as its opponents. There was no time to stop to investigate individual grievances at the risk of slowing the forward march of historic forces. Concern for the individual is a luxury of mature and settled social systems that have put their stormy, revolutionary phase behind them.

Only after long imprisonment did "Rajkists" make the discovery that they thought identically about themselves and others and that in fact none had committed the crimes for which they were allegedly being punished. This led them to examine the basic premises underlying the Party's methods and goals.

Nevertheless, it must be noted that terror had approximately

---

[3] Rajk himself apparently cooperated with the prosecution. Two witnesses, independently from one another, reported that in the course of their interrogation the police confronted them with Rajk. In both cases Rajk is said to have confirmed charges made by the prosecution against himself and the witnesses in question, although the witnesses denied these.

the same effect inside as it had outside the Party. What group solidarity there was broke down. Interpersonal communications, other than of official nature, stopped. Every individual stood alone before the impersonal monster that was the Party. Factionalism was out of the question. Few people had the inclination to help others in trouble; even fewer could. The police arm of the Party struck without forewarning. There was no appeal against it. The story is told of Jozsef Revai's being informed by telephone of the arrest of Laszlo Gacs, his brother-in-law.[4] Revai, obviously surprised and shocked by the news, paled visibly and managed to stutter no more than, "That was close, that was close, you are striking dangerously near," to the voice on the other end of the wire.

The Rajk trial and the purgest that accompanied it unquestionably opened fissures in the Party, but these remained carefully concealed for a long time. The Party had hardly buried Rajk when it faced the gigantic task of implementing the five-year plan. The succession of events came so rapidly that it allowed little time for introspection.

The purges continued until the middle of 1951 without abatement, although their cadence varied. In due course, the Party grew accustomed and indifferent to them. The arrest of personalities such as Losonczy and Kadar caused no stir whatever. The Party no longer was intent on teaching object lessons. These had long since been learned.

No reliable count of the number of persons purged has ever been made, but they must have been in the thousands, including at least five hundred upper-echelon bureaucrats.[5] (Gero, reporting on the progress of "rehabilitation" in 1956, mentioned 474 cases that had been reviewed. These included only persons of some importance in the Party.[6])

---

[4] Gacs is said to have been expelled from the Party over some irregularities in the 1930s. He was not immediately readmitted after the war and because of the animosity between him and Peter, he was always in a precarious position. His arrest was one of numerous instances of a political "settlement" of personal rivalries and dislikes that riddled the Communist Party.

[5] "Purged" as used in this context denotes people who were imprisoned. The number of those expelled from the Party was, of course, many times larger.

[6] P. Zinner, ed., *National Communism and Popular Revolt in Eastern Europe* (New York, Columbia University Press, 1956), p. 351.

Group purges (as distinguished from individual actions, which were continuous) took place in the following order:

1949: The Rajk purge that began before the arrest of Rajk himself in June and continued well into the fall after he was sentenced. It reached into government offices (Bela Szasz, Gyorgy Heltai), the Party apparatus (Tibor Szonyi, Andras Szalay), the army (General Gyorgy Palffy, Colonel Bela Korondi), and other institutions. It affected Rajk's family and friends (e.g., his widow, Mrs. Julia Rajk, was separated from her infant son and imprisoned from 1949 until 1954). It truncated, among other things, the burgeoning NEKOSZ movement which by this time had acquired a nationwide network of 150 colleges with a total enrollment of some 10,000 students. Terming them nationalist and populist in character, the Party disbanded the colleges and scattered its leaders (Laszlo Kardos, Antal Gyenes, Balazs Nagy). Some were imprisoned; others were assigned to menial jobs; a few sold out to the Party leadership. The cohesiveness, ideological affinity, and comradeliness that marked the movement were smashed. Thus, during this year, the most promising, if unorthodox, native experiment of the Hungarian Communist Party came to an abrupt, unhappy end.

1950: Purge of Social Democrats and further purge of army officers. In the first half of the year, all but a few "left" Social Democrats such as Ronai and Harustyak were dismissed from public office and arrested. Included in this "action" were Arpad Szakasits, Gyorgy Marosan (erstwhile deputy secretary general of the Hungarian Workers' Party), Istvan Ries (former Minister of Justice), Imre Vajda, Pal Schiffer, and many others. Later in the year, a new wave of purges hit the high command of the army, virtually wiping out the remnants of the officer group that rose to prominence in the immediate postwar period. Most of these, it will be remembered, were old-line officers trained in Horthyite Hungary. The chief victims were Generals Laszlo Solyom, Gusztav Illy, Laszlo Kuthy, Kalman Revai.

1951: A final convulsion of mass arrests that cut down "home" Communists whose affiliations with the Party dated back to the 1930s. Prominent among the victims were members of the Debrecen group,[7] many of whom had risen to great heights in the Party and government apparatus. Although they were of intellectual background, they made their mark as Communist functionaries. Included among them were Geza Losonczy, who first served as deputy chief editor the Party journal *Szabad Nep*, then had a brief stint as secretary in the Prime Minister's office (1948-49), and finally moved to the Ministry of People's Culture as Secretary of State under Jozsef Revai, where he stayed until shortly before his arrest; Ferenc Donath, a member of the illegal Central Committee of the Party in 1943-44, Secretary of State in the Ministry of Agriculture after 1945, and chief of Rakosi's personal secretariat in 1949; and Szilard Ujhelyi, a high official in the Ministry of Social Welfare. Sandor Haraszti, Losonczy's father-in-law and a highly respected old-time Communist journalist, was also arrested. Sandor Zold, who served in the Party Secretariat and who, in June, 1950, took over as Minister of the Interior from Janos Kadar, committed suicide as he was about to be arrested.

The imprisonment of Janos Kadar and Gyula Kallai in May, 1951, terminated the mass purges in the Party. Kallai had replaced Rajk as Minister of Foreign Affairs in June, 1949, and held that post until his arrest. Kadar had held the Ministry of the Interior from August, 1948, to June 24, 1950. Assigned to "important Party work" at that time, he possibly headed the "special department" of the Party Secretariat which, however, gradually declined in importance. He retained his seat in the Party Secretariat, the Politbureau, and the Orgbureau, and he was the most illustrious "home" Communist in these bodies. He was reelected to these posts in February, 1951, shortly before he dropped out of sight. Whether he wielded any power was another matter.

The Rajk affair put Kadar in an awkward position, both for the part he had taken in persuading Rajk to confess and for his original intention to abstain from voting in favor of Rajk's execution. He had a serious run-in with Rakosi in January, 1950, over fundamental questions of cadre policy. In January, 1951, Kadar made a self-critical speech at the Party Congress. It was his swan song. At Rakosi's mercy for some time past, he had outlived his

[7] See above, p. 12.

usefulness. It had long since become superfluous to adhere to the
fiction of respectable "home" Communist representation in leading
Party organs. Kadar is said to have been charged with attempted
escape to the West, confronted with two "witnesses" to the deed
(who had known nothing of it until they heard the accusation),
and imprisoned. His dismissal signaled the final ignominy of the
"home" Communists.

MEMBERSHIP POLICY AND IDEOLOGICAL CONTROLS

Besides purges, the Party took other measures to impose conformity and to improve its cadres and members. The membership
policy and indoctrination program of the Party cannot be evaluated here in detail. During the Rajk purge (actually from September, 1948 to November, 1949) the Party was closed. No new
members were admitted, and a thorough check of membership rolls
helped to pare these down from a reported high of 1,500,000 to
less than 1,000,000. After the Party was opened to new members
on a differential basis (discriminating in favor of workers and
working peasants), the effect of changed attitudes to Communism
became apparent. There was a dearth of new applicants from the
"proper" social strata. In January, 1950, Rakosi argued for a more
liberal admission policy, opening the Party to former bourgeois
elements on an individual basis, provided that they met stiff quali-
fication tests. It was on this point that he clashed with Kadar.
Despite these inducements, Party rolls increased very moderately
until 1952, when the transfer of 130,000 members under twenty-
four years of age to the Communist youth organization DISZ
reduced the membership to 800,000. The transfer may well have
been decided upon to give the youth organization a much needed
transfusion, since its appeal to the young was strictly limited.

With all this, the Party zealously guarded the ideological content
of Communist literary and artistic output. Non-Communist
artists and writers, of course, could produce only at the tolerance
of the Party. Most of them, especially the writers, were silenced
altogether. The cultural policies of the Party were as stringent
as its economic and social policies. Ties with the West were sev-

ered. Hungarian plays and musical compositions with a national-istic flavor, reminiscent of past glory, were banned.

For the enforcement of ideological purity, the Party maintained a large Agitation and Propaganda Department and a formidable Ministry of People's Culture. The latter was headed by Jozsef Revai, the former by Revai's erstwhile deputy at the Party journal *Szabad Nep*, Marton Horvath. (The staffs of both the Agitprop Department and the Ministry were said to have trebled between 1949 and 1950.) Together, these two policy-making and supervisory organs ruled over the intellectual output of Communists with dra-conic severity.

Szabad Nep now became a Hungarian replica of *Pravda*. It also became the domain of Matyas Rakosi rather than of Jozsef Revai. Revai, chief editor of the paper, was relieved of this function in June, 1949, when he moved to the Ministry of People's Culture. His deputy and successor in the editorship, Marton Horvath, also severed his relations with the paper when he became chief of Agitprop. His place was taken by Oszkar Betlen, an unknown journalistic neophyte on the Hungarian scene.[8]

Under Betlen, the editorial staff increased in size from forty to about a hundred people. Among his closest collaborators were several secret police agents. The top editorial board assisting Betlen retained the services of one member of the immediate postwar crew only (Miklos Gimes). Other members of the board were Mihaly Kulcsar, a former typesetter, Laszlo Juhasz, a secret police agent (he committed suicide in 1953, when his friend and patron Gabor Peter was arrested), and Laszlo Sarkany, Betlen's deputy, a non-descript type (he became lecturer in journalism at the university in 1953 and in 1956, after the revolution, took a post as colonel in the Kadar regime's security forces). Under Betlen's management, several stalwarts of the young journalistic guard who joined *Szabad*

[8] Betlen acquired notoriety for his vindictive and vulgar nature. He is said to have boasted about the part he had in unmasking Ferenc Donath and other intellectuals such as Gyorgy Adam and Pal Lendvai. He was a Hungarian from Slovakia, where he befriended Mihaly Farkas. He is alleged to have served a seven-year sentence in the Oswiecim concentration camp. Following his liberation, he spent a brief time in Moscow and "returned" to Hungary rather than Slovakia where strong anti-Hungarian sentiment prevailed even against former Communists.

Nep immediately after the war were separated from the journal, e.g., Miklos Vasarhelyi, Gyorgy Nemes, Tibor Tardos, and Miklos Molnar. Molnar, who married into the "Muscovite" nobility, soon found a better position with the newly founded *Irodalmi Ujsag*.

The creation of *Irodalmi Ujsag* [Literary Journal] on November 2, 1950, represented still another step in the direction of blind emulation of the Soviet Union. (By an odd coincidence it was exactly six years later that the last memorable revolutionary number of the journal was printed.) The Journal modeled itself on the Soviet periodical by the same name (*Literaturnaia Gazeta*), which served as an outlet for the Soviet Writers' Association. The Journal's editor-in-chief was Bela Illes, a "Muscovite" literary hack who was particularly disliked by Hungarian writers.

TWO CAUSES CELEBRES: GYORGY LUKACS AND TIBOR DERY

Day-to-day control of Communist intellectual life was punctuated by two *causes célèbres*—the so called Lukacs debate in 1949 and the Dery debate in 1952. Each was intended to lay down firm ideological guide lines for intellectuals generally and writers particularly.

The famous Lukacs debate, for all the heat it generated, was mostly an exercise in rhetoric.[9] Its purpose was to cut Lukacs down to size and to forestall his becoming, despite his own intentions, a focal point of interest among Communists, lest he impair the ideological monopoly of the Party's political leadership. In an age of conformity that demanded blind obedience to the Party's crude theoretical postulates, the very features that had made Lukacs a strong Communist drawing card in the past became dangerous.

The philosophical fare he handed out was not injurious to the cause of Communism, even in its Stalinist incarnation. As far as he was concerned, the virtues of the whole, taken as a unit in a very broad sense and projected onto a time scale of historic proportions, outweighed the transitory faults of its parts. In this sense,

---

[9] The implications of the debate have been dealt with at length in other works, e.g., I. Meszaros, *La rivolta degli intellettuali in Ungheria* (Turin, Einaudi, 1957).

he taught his disciples a more profound type of allegiance to Communism than the Party ever expected; for he instructed them to accept Communism critically and to reconcile themselves to it personally as to a way of life superior to others.

The strength of such a rational acceptance of Communism, including the necessary brutality that accompanied its early growth, was not appreciated by the Party. It feared that the faculty of thought which Lukacs sought to impart to his students would make their loyalty always questionable. Who was to tell to what uses they would put the critical habits of rationality they learned from Lukacs? His own unswerving allegiance to Communism was no guarantee of that of his followers.

It was therefore decided to chastise him, to diminish his prestige, and to discourage close affiliation with him.

The attack on him was a thinly disguised accusation of cosmopolitism. His European orientation and the rigor of his philosophical postulates came under fire. He was particularly called to task for underestimating the importance of Soviet literature. In the course of the debate, Lukacs dutifully exercised "self-criticism." The Party was satisfied. His students seemed bewildered. In answer to their queries, he is said to have denied that he prostrated himself before the Party—for, as he put it, he did not recant anything about the rock foundation of his philosophical system, Hegelianism. The point might well have been too fine for most people to comprehend. In any event, Lukacs was not eliminated from public life. His nimbus was tarnished but not demolished.

The Dery debate in some ways resembled the campaign against Lukacs. For Dery, a writer on a much more urbane level than Lukacs, also accepted Communism with all its faults. An old, prewar member of the Party, he had remained faithful to it through thick and thin. But he did not see why a spade should not be called a spade even under socialism. His positive heroes, according to Party criticism, were not virtuous enough. His negative heroes were not sufficiently villainous. They were lifelike characters with relative merits and demerits in a complex world. Dery was by nature a nonconformist and a lone wolf. This too irritated the

Party. (Revai, it is said, once urged him to "cease being a fellow traveler in the Communist Party" and join the crowd).[10] Upon the publication of the second of a projected four-volume work, in which Dery hoped to trace the career of a working-class youth from the 1930s to 1948, the Party struck. It organized a great debate, presided over by Revai, in which it pilloried the offending Tibor Dery, who, although severely censured, was not imprisoned.

It is difficult to assess the impact of the Dery debate on his fellow writers. Some claim that it really marked a turning point in their spiritual orientation. In its attack on Dery, they say, the Party overplayed its hand and for the first time revealed itself to them as the monster it was. According to them, the entire writers' community was saddened by what transpired in the great debate and even those whose disillusionment was not yet complete tended to withdraw farther into themselves and to communicate less with the outside world.[11] A period of "internal emigration" is said to have set in.

If these claims are even partially true, they bespeak a significant change of heart on the part of Hungarian writers from the preceding year. In 1951, no writer was able to dredge up any sympathy for the purged Losonczy and Haraszti. And the first Congress of Writers later in the year was held under the aegis of exemplary orthodoxy. Perhaps the lessons of the Dery debate boomeranged in an unexpected way. To the outside observer, the exercise through which the Party put the writers was superfluous. Dery, to be sure, was a man of integrity and therefore dangerous. He was generally liked in a community that was marked by fierce factional and individual strife. But he did not have any influence over his fellow writers. They were quite content to go their own way and that was, almost to a man, the path staked out by the Party. They needed no reprimand to stay in line; their enthusiasm exceeded the limits of necessary overt conformity. Their attitudes toward one another and toward their fellow men generally were beneath contempt.

The Communist writers grouped in the Writers' Association did

---

10 T. Aczel and T. Meray, *The Revolt of the Mind* (Praeger, 1959), p. 104.
11 For a discursive account of the debate, see *ibid.*, pp. 94-118.

not form a coherent unit with a common philosophy of life and an *esprit de corps*. They were divided into quarreling factions that held each other in mutual disdain and outbid each other for the favors of the Party. As they themselves later admitted, this was a time of "clique" struggles that the Party fully utilized to its ends. In the words of one of them, now abroad: "During that period . . . we were full of personal hatred for one another, each clique hating the other; X had been a friend of mine all my life, but in that period I hated him."

There was a "Muscovite" clique headed by Bela Illes, Sandor Gergely (an official of the Writers' Association), and Gyula Hay. (Hay, who spent many years in Berlin before settling in the Soviet Union, was sometimes identified as the head of a "Berlin clique." In any event, he was less important than the other members of the "Muscovite" group and somewhat removed from them.) In addition, there was the clique known as the "young gentlemen" (because of their bourgeois background); it included Gabor Devecseri, Tamas Aczel, and Ferenc Karinthy. An "opposition" clique (so named because of its opposition to the "young gentlemen") included Laszlo Benjamin, Zoltan Zelk, and Lajos Tamasi. Still other, less well defined cliques formed around Istvan Orkeny, Istvan Kiraly, and others.

It is difficult to say what separated these groups from one another except obvious differences in background, personal dislike, and rivalry.

Of them all, the "Muscovites" behaved least objectionably. They represented the "mother church" and enjoyed senior status. They acted as *ex officio* guardians of Hungary's literary life and did what they had to to administer the Party's domain. They had all been through a hard school, knew how the system worked, and harbored few illusions. Yet, personally (with the possible exception of Gergely), they seemed to be more subdued and "decent" than their younger native comrades.

Sycophantic odes praising Stalin, panegyrics hailing the virtues of socialism flowed from the pens of younger, domestic literati in disgusting profusion. In so doing, they betrayed a cherished tradition of Hungarian writers and totally divorced themselves from the nation. Accepting the Party as the voice of national social consciousness and as the dispenser of fame and fortune, they willingly buried their own social consciousness and abandoned their individual consciences.

This was the greatest crime of the Hungarian writers, and at the same time the source of future redemption for some.

THE PARTY COMMAND

Extensive purging changed the composition of the Party command. It accentuated the preponderance of "Muscovites" in positions of control, effectively eliminated "home" Communists from prominence, and rapidly raised new cadres close to the apex of the Party's pyramidal structure. But the composition of the Party's leadership did not remain stable for long. Minor adjustments (which, however, did not entirely lack in significance) were taking place almost continually even after the purging subsided.

The structure and functioning of the power system in Hungary cannot be satisfactorily derived either from organizational charts or from depositions given by respondents. Organizational charts give some idea of the outline of the power structure but contain no clues to the distribution of power among office holders. The listing of a person's name indicates no more than that he was at a certain time not in total disgrace, although he could already have been earmarked for liquidation. Even his continuing presence in "high Party circles" was no clear indication of his standing in the power structure. Imre Nagy, for example, was never far removed from the center of power; yet, for over a year he was on the brink of disgrace.[12]

The Communist high command kept itself purposely isolated, inaccessible, and enigmatic. Compartmentalization of information and knowledge is a familiar trait of all security-conscious organiza-

---

[12] Similar conditions existed in the Soviet Union. If Khrushchev's account of Stalin's arbitrary rule is believable, K. Y. Voroshilov, though in name a full member of the Politbureau, was for years barred from attending its meetings and from reading Politbureau material. *The Anti-Stalin Campaign and International Communism* (Columbia University Press, 1956), p. 84.

tions, and none excels the Communist in this respect. Whether circumstances warranted it or not, a conspiratorial atmosphere pervaded all Communist parties during this period, to a greater degree perhaps than at any other time in their history. This was much to Rakosi's liking. He exaggerated secrecy beyond all reasonable measure to mask his manipulations more effectively. Conditions discouraged overt inquisitiveness and inhibited the covert exercise of natural curiosity lest it lead to inadvertent self-betrayal. The system worked remarkably well. Even highly placed officials were amazingly ignorant about Party affairs that were not of immediate concern to them.

Because of scant information, only tentative conclusions can be drawn about the distribution and exercise of power in Hungary and about power relations between the Hungarian Communist hierarchy on the one hand and the Moscow center, including its local emissaries (technical and military advisers), on the other hand. The impression one gains is that there was a notable absence of firmly delegated and properly defined power throughout the Hungarian Party and state administration. The system was probably kept vague on purpose to facilitate autocratic rule by a single individual, Rakosi, and through him, by the Soviet Union.

The derivative or dependent nature of power in Hungary held the key to the awesome strength and the abysmal weakness the system demonstrated under widely different circumstances.

Ultimately, it can be said that power was vested in the person who could order the arrest of another and have it carried out. This only Rakosi seemed able to do. But even he did not have free rein. There were persons whose arrest he could not order. And, to this extent at least, his authority was not total.

The secret police, the executive arm of "law enforcement," though a formidable instrument, was not a significant locus of power in its own right. A state within a state, detached from all institutional affiliations since the fall of 1949, directly responsible to the Council of Ministers (but in fact to the general secretary of the Party), it could intervene with immunity in any public institution or any household, protected by the knowledge that there was no recourse against its actions. Yet it was completely at the mercy of those who directed its activities from above. It had no defenses whatever against intervention in its own ranks. Its personnel suffered as high a rate of attrition as that of any other institution.

Russian technical advisers constituted a significant enclave in the power structure. They stood apart from Hungarian officialdom. But no one has been able to clarify the precise operational responsibilities of the Russian advisers vis-à-vis the departments and institutions to which they were assigned and the top Communist leadership of Hungary. There seems to have been no overall pattern of "interference" by Russian advisers. The influence they exerted and the manner in which they exerted it varied from one department to another and depended on the personalities involved as well as the problems to be solved. The managers of joint Soviet-Hungarian companies, of course, exerted the most direct influence in their own spheres of competence.

The capacity of "Muscovite" Communists to survive the purges requires closer attention. While they did not share power equally among themselves, they came through the harrowing years of Sovietization intact as a group. One or two (notably Nagy and Revai) had to indulge in self-criticism, but this did not seriously affect their immediate careers.

The reasons for the "Muscovites'" powers of survival must not be sought in any strong bonds of solidarity among them, although these were not wholly absent.[13] The fact that they managed to preserve themselves against the sniping of their detractors was due primarily to the "contacts" they had in Moscow. What these "contacts" were and how they came into play at opportune moments are questions we cannot answer. Possibly Stalin himself had a hand in maintaining "natural rivals" in competing offices so as to set one off against another. This was his technique in the Soviet Union. It could have extended as far as Hungary. It is not unlikely that he encouraged Communists to spy on one another and to inform

13 For example, Rudas, rector of the Economic University of Budapest, offered Nagy a professorial chair in the fall of 1949, when the latter was deprived of his political functions. Such instances, however, were rare.

Moscow. In any event, some credence must be placed in the oft-repeated, though never substantiated, contention that several "Muscovites" were saved at one time or another by their patrons in the Kremlin. Some obviously had independent channels of communication with friends in Moscow to whom they appealed when in need.

It was long before his spectacular appointment to the premiership in June, 1953, that Imre Nagy began to make his comeback. Expelled from the Politbureau in August, 1949, he was a university professor until his recall, in December, 1950, to government service as Minister of Crop Collections. At the Second Party Congress, in February, 1951, he was reelected to the Politbureau and made a member of the Secretariat of the Party as well. In November, 1952, he relinquished his Ministry and was advanced to a deputy premiership (one of five created at the same time). The stages in his "rehabilitation," many Kremlinologists have noted, coincided with Malenkov's ascendancy in the Soviet Union.

The domination of "Muscovite" Communists left a deep mark on the Party and, in the public eye, stigmatized Communist rule as alien. In no other country were "home" Communists so blatantly eliminated from public positions of prestige and power. Rakosi, of course, was the king pin of the whole movement. Gero was titular head of the economic administration. Other prominent officials in the economy who in fact helped to balance Gero's influence were the "Muscovite" Istvan Friss (head of the economic department of Rakosi's secretariat) and Zoltan Vas (chairman of the State Planning Office). Jozsef Revai presided over ideological and cultural matters; others active in this area were Illes, Gergely, Betlen, Zoltan Biro (Rakosi's brother), who was in charge of the education department in the Party's Secretariat, Laszlo Rudas, and Erzsebet Andics (Andor Berei's wife). In the military establishment, Mihaly Farkas held sway. Working with him were "Muscovites" such as Sandor Nogradi who headed the Main Political Administration of the Army, and Generals Geza Revesz and Istvan Bata.

At the top of the hierarchy of Party officials, far ahead of the rest, was the "quartet": Rakosi, Gero, Farkas, and Revai. These four were viewed by the public as chief exponents of the Communist regime, and when the time for reckoning came, they were so identified by Stalin's successors as well. It was not in any sense through affiliation in an institution from which all others were excluded that they acquired their special status. They were, of course, members of the Politbureau and Secretariat of the Party, but so were others (e.g., Rajk, Kadar, Marosan, and Szakasits before their respective arrests, as well as Nagy, Hegedus, and Kristof later on).

The "quartet" was not known to act as an informal committee that arrived at decisions by collegial process of consultation and deliberation.[14] Nor did its members carry equal weight in the Party and state administration. But the formal spheres of jurisdiction which they divided among themselves covered all important areas of the public realm—political, military, economic, and cultural.

Of the four, Revai was the least influential. Repeatedly he was in political and ideological difficulties. Attempts were allegedly made to implicate him in the Rajk trial.[15] In point of fact, Revai abstained from voting in the Politbureau in favor of Rajk's execution. As penance, he was made to write the indictment. He was also caught off guard on the question of theoretical interpretation of the character of People's Democracy in 1948 and had to recant.

In 1949, Revai was separated from *Szabad Nep*, where he might have exercised direct control over the editorial contents of the paper. True, as Minister of People's Culture he had enormous scope, and the occupancy of the chairmanship of the Agitation and Propaganda Department by another person than himself did not necessarily limit his authority, especially since the chief of Agitprop, Marton Horvath, a man of little independent prestige, was his former underling. Still, the question remains whether Revai was merely a more glorified mouthpiece of the Party than were others or a participant in major decisions. Viewing his career in retrospect, one would be inclined to say that he had strongly limited discretionary authority and was, from Rakosi's point of view, expendable at any time.

[14] For a time before 1951 the members of the "quartet" and Kadar constituted an inner secretariat of four deputy secretaries general and one general secretary. The title of deputy secretary general was dropped in 1951 coincidentally with Kadar's arrest.

[15] Two victims of the Rajk purge reported independently of one another that the police interrogated them closely about possible ties between Rajk and Revai.

Revai's ministry was a strange haven for "home" Communists with a populist background. Some of his close assistants, e.g., Losonczy, for whom he obviously had more than a professional tolerance, were "shot out from under him." This could not possibly fail to have unpleasant repercussions for him. Personally, though he was the epitome of orthodoxy (as it was then demanded by the Party), he retained a discerning aesthetic sense which he did not hide from others in private. He had a taste for good Western literature, a trait unbecoming the Grand Satrap of Soviet literary supremacy. He also seemed more sensitive to the issue of Hungarian populist literary tradition than were his peers. In some inchoate way he tried to fuse populism with the prevailing current of "socialist realism." It is doubtful if he knew how this could be done, but he was neither unaware of nor totally indifferent to the dangers courted by callous flouting of "native" literature and folk art.

Farkas was thought to be all-powerful in the military establishment. Appointed Minister of National Defense in August, 1948, he performed invaluable service presiding over the Sovietization of the armed forces. He acquired a reputation as a talented and ruthless organizer. His personal brutality and that of his son, Vladimir, a high ranking official of the secret police, became legendary.

Nevertheless, his powers were limited. For one thing, Soviet advisers in the armed forces made their presence known more obtrusively than elsewhere. For another thing, he had a rival in the person of Sandor Nogradi, who had good connections in Moscow and exerted influence in his own right as chief of the Main Political Administration of the armed forces and head of the military department of the Party Secretariat.

Some significance may be attached to the fact that in 1951 Farkas was dropped from the Orgbureau, in which he had served continuously since 1946, although he remained in the Secretariat and the Politbureau.

Gero, the second ranking member of the "quartet," found himself in an anomalous, thankless situation. It was almost designed to demolish him in the long run and thus to rid Rakosi of his foremost rival. As economic czar of the country—he headed the People's

Economic Council—Gero was the workhorse of the team and a natural target of abuse for failures. At the time, he was kept away from the strictly political realm and thus was in no position to develop a "power pyramid" of loyal adherents in the Party organization. To prevent him from entrenching himself in the economic hierarchy, Rakosi took care to surround him with stalwart aides (Friss and Vas). In the agricultural sector, a spontaneous conflict between him and Imre Nagy lent itself to exploitation. In 1949, Nagy had advocated moderation in the collectivization program, for which he was censured. His severest critic was Gero, who thus laid himself open to future attacks.

Gero was in trouble as early as 1951, when a high-powered Soviet delegation headed by Jeno Varga appeared on the scene to reexamine Hungarian economic targets and plans. In fact, it is possible that Nagy's return to the government as Minister of Crop Collections in December, 1950, signaled the first step in a campaign to cut Gero down to size. For Gero had moved into the agricultural sector with particular vigor, cleaned it out of Nagy's supporters, and established a real stronghold there, with Andras Hegedus, probably his most faithful protégé, in direct charge.

In 1952, as the economic crisis deepened, Gero's position grew more precarious. True, Rakosi jettisonned Vas as head of the Planning Office.[16] But, with the abolition of the Economic Council, Gero lost his main forum. In the government reorganization in November, 1952, Gero had to be content with being named one of five deputy premiers, sharing status with Imre Nagy, Karoly Kiss, Arpad Hazi, and Istvan Hidas, none of whom were his associates.[17] At about the same time he was forced to acknowledge publicly shortcomings in the economy. At a production conference in February, 1953, Gero and Nagy clashed vehemently over agricultural policies. In the Party bureaucracy, only Andras Hegedus counted

[16] Vas was sent off to manage a coal syndicate. He made a comeback under Imre Nagy's premiership. From then on, his fortunes were tied to those of the premier, although his support of Nagy was equivocal. The rise and fall of Vas's fortunes have never been satisfactorily explained. Originally a close associate of Rakosi, as a result of a friendship formed in prison, Vas, like so many other people, seemed to have lost the confidence of the secretary general and suffered the consequences.

[17] Two of the five, Arpad Hazi and Istvan Hidas, were Rakosi's creations.

as a faithful supporter of Gero. Toward the end of the Stalinist period, Gero's fortunes were at a low ebb.

By contrast, Rakosi towered head and shoulders above the other members of the "quartet." Unencumbered by departmental responsibilities, he devoted himself to directing over-all policy. He alone guided the affairs of the Party. In the Party proper, he maneuvered almost at will to bring to the fore new cadres, chosen by him. He deployed them to check his opponents and each other, so that none would accumulate real power and gain a sense of permanent security in office. In 1950 and 1951, as the last important victims of purges fell, Rakosi's men began to appear in the highest Party circles, just a notch below the "Muscovites." Men like Istvan Kristof, Arpad Hazi, Istvan Hidas, Lajos Acs, Bela Szalai, Jozsef Mekis, Laszlo Piros, achieved meteoric success due to their affiliation with Rakosi. Several had joined the Party only at the end of the war. None had any prior claim to such rapid rise to prominence.

Rakosi himself never seemed in danger of being seriously challenged. He weathered a minor threat to his leadership in 1947 and successfully parried what was rumored to be Soviet criticism of his conduct late in 1951; by August, 1952, when he assumed at long last the title as well as the power of a premier, he united in his person the direction of Party and government.

The question in Rakosi's case was not whether he ranked first among Hungarian Communists but how much indigenous power he concentrated in his hands—how independent of the Russians he was. Opinion on this subject varies. In the view of some persons, Rakosi outmaneuvered and outwitted even the Russians with his superior intellect and propensity for ruthless intrigue. For example, it is said that he precipitated the trial of Rudolf Slansky in Czechoslovakia against the wishes of the Czechoslovak Communist leadership (whom he threatened to blackmail) and with only lukewarm Soviet support. This contention may well be far-fetched, at any rate, in time his standing with the Russians grew stronger. He proved a master politician, possessing both acumen and instinct, that gave him advantages over his rivals and permitted him to anticipate impending shifts in Moscow's policy and mood speedily and accurately. He read Stalin's mind better than did any other Hungarian—well enough to stay in power and develop an apparatus of his own, more formidable than that of other East European Communist leaders. Within the personal autocracy of the Stalinist empire, using the same techniques, he built a personal autocracy in Hungary in which he had some operational autonomy.

Although the power of the individual members of the "quartet" was not always what it seemed to be, no other Communist even approximated their status. Imre Nagy arrests attention not because he played an outstanding part but because every facet of his long career is of interest in view of what history had yet in store for him.

Unquestionably Nagy was a senior citizen among the "Muscovites." A person of lesser stature might well have been completely silenced for the heretical views he held about the rate and method of collectivization in Hungary. Nagy was but temporarily retired to academic life. The decision to allow him to teach was not altogether in the Party's best interests, for Nagy became immersed in an agricultural environment and taught subjects related to agriculture. Of course, no one could foresee the future and act with prescience, but it is clear in retrospect that during his academic tenure Nagy developed a better understanding of the thinking of Hungarian populist youth and established close personal links with a number of former populists who, like himself, had been shunted to the sidelines. He also became acquainted at first hand with the problems of Hungarian agriculture, an education other Communist leaders spurned.

For the moment and for a long time to come, Nagy was first and foremost a loyal Party member. He entertained no idea of creating a personal coterie or of engaging the Party in a polemic about its agricultural policies. Devotion to the Party and a high sense of discipline made his political rehabilitation easy. No one needed to fear that Nagy would sabotage the Party in his ministerial post or that he would suddenly grow ambitious for power. Indeed, he justified the confidence placed in him. He was loyal. His speeches and published writings at that time contained nothing to which the Party could have taken exception. If he had any mental reservations, he kept them to himself and did not permit them to interfere with the performance of his duties to which he attended with meticulous care and unimpeachable orthodoxy.

Aside from Nagy, only Antal Apro, Karoly Kiss, and Marton Horvath were durable members of the top command. None wielded any particular power. Apro was a perennial Politbureau member, although he suffered a decline in 1952, when he was relieved of the secretary generalship of the trade unions and appointed Minister of the Building Industry instead. Kiss was chairman of the Party Control Commission from 1948 to May, 1951, when he became Minister of Foreign Affairs and a member of the Politbureau. As chairman of the Control Committee, he was head guardian of Party purity. In actual fact, he had no say about purges and was singularly ill informed as to what went on in the Party.

THE RISE OF THE NEW CADRES

Less spectacular but in the aggregate more important than the shuffling and reshuffling of the top dozen or two leaders was the shaping of a new bureaucratic elite, second and third echelon executives, military commanders, and managers, on whose shoulders the administration of the Party's affairs ultimately rested.

At the Second Congress of the Hungarian Workers' Party, held in February–March, 1951, Rakosi proudly reported that 100,000 cadre members of working-class and peasant background had been raised to positions of leadership in the state administration, the economy, and the people's army since the Communist seizure of power.[18]

Although every word in Rakosi's statement requires close definition, it gives some indication of the scope and rate of social change in Hungary. It matters little whether the figure was 80,000 or 120,000. Nor is it of particular significance to know the exact social origin of the new leading cadres (workers from the bench, children of working-class parents, foremen, artisans, petty bourgeois, landless peasants, middle peasants, etc.) and the precise statistical range of positions to which they were assigned. The main point is that in a very short time a very large number of persons, generally of low social origin, with only rudimentary educational

18 *Szabad Nep*, February 26, 1951.

background and no managerial experience [19] were raised to high status (both relatively and absolutely) solely through the good offices of the Party and largely on the basis of criteria of selection that stressed political reliability and personal favoritism rather than universal standards of technical competence.

For a country the size of Hungary, the creation of a new elite of about 100,000 in less than two years was truly a revolutionary undertaking. It was as if the United States in a comparable period filled roughly 1,700,000 positions of prestige and influence in all walks of life from the ranks of socially and educationally underprivileged persons.

The 100,000 leading cadre workers represented the Party's investment in the future and its bulwark against upheaval. They were a new service nobility, creatures of the regime and its main source of strength.[20]

Too little is known about the composition of the new leading cadres to draw any far reaching conclusions from it. Detractors of the Communist regime have spoken disparagingly of the new elite as being made up preponderantly of worthless, brutal dregs of society, gangsters, thieves, idlers, murderers, dedicated to plunder and exploitation. This is a patently biased picture, though not wholly incorrect, in that the Party had in it a high proportion of unsavory types who rose to the top and maintained themselves there because of the prevailing political conditions. Yet, it was not the Party's ultimate aim (and it would not have been consistent with its best interests) to seek out the *Lumpenproletariat* as the mainstay of the new order. The Party strove to attain excellence. It wanted to select able, hard-working persons and to provide them with adequate

19 The term "managerial" is used here in a very broad connotation to denote any type of supervising responsibility.

20 It is interesting to note here that the overall figure of 100,000 remained static in references from 1951 through 1955 (according to Rakosi at the Third Party Congress in 1954 and *Szabad Nep*, March 27, 1955). This means either that the 1951 figure was grossly exaggerated or that the number of leading cadres reached a plateau in 1951 from which it changed only insignificantly throughout the next few years. Since the ensuing period was largely one of readjustment and rationalization of production and employment of human resources, the latter supposition is more likely to be correct. This does not mean that the same people held on to their jobs. On the contrary, fluctuation was considerable and its consequences far-reaching. But the basic figure remained about the same.

training to make of them competent executives and commanders. But such people could not be found or trained in a hurry, and the Party was eager to get on with social transformation. In this, as in other areas, it showed excessive impatience and exaggerated political bias that vitiated any rational program of cadre training. It promoted too many people too fast, maximizing the disruptive effects of the social and political transformation it was staging.

The problem of balancing considerations of technical competence (in whatever area of endeavor) and political loyalty was not unique in Hungary. Every Communist regime has had to deal with it as indeed must every revolutionary regime that represents or purports to represent underprivileged strata of the population who have had no access to education and status prior to their rise to political power. The ultimate solution, of course, is to raise a new "intelligentsia" that combines technical skills and political loyalty, but in the meantime the issue is to reconcile competing and even contradictory interests.

The choice made by the Hungarians was more radical than that by other Communist parties. They opted recklessly for political reliability as a standard in the selection of new cadres and disdained the services of bourgeois technicians because of their social taint and presumed disloyalty. But the standard of selection was loosely defined and eluded systematic policing. It encouraged rank partisanship. Within a framework of subjective preferences, many abuses in the nature of personal favoritism and nepotism arose.

The error of excessive haste and partisanship was compounded by chains of repercussions set off by the appointment of "wrong" cadres to responsible posts. Aside from being incompetent and thus detrimental to the proper implementation of the Communist program of industrial expansion or police surveillance, new cadres often exacerbated a sense of social friction and caused both irritation and disillusionment. The least fit Party officials tended to behave most brutally and autocratically, partly to cover up their incompetence, partly to extract compliance by force where they failed to command respect.

The result was an estrangement between the Party and the population. Communist officials became ever more isolated from their environment. They resorted to paper administration and shunned personal contacts. To a large degree, alienation between official-dom and the population was promoted by the Party itself, which keenly appreciated the need for distance from the surrounding environment in order not to succumb to its pressures. But the isolation of the Party was excessive.

This is not to imply that Communist cadre policy revealed itself immediately and unmistakably faulty or that the leading cadres experienced a sense of futility. Far from it. As is the case in every ideologically and organizationally closed system, those within it have a distorted sense of reality and a tremendous capacity for progressive self-deception based on an accumulating feedback of tendentious information. The Hungarian Communists were no exception. They lived in a world of their own that was logically consistent and thus intellectually reassuring. They were caught up in a dynamic situation with no time for idle thought. Waste motion or purposeful action impart identically satisfying feelings as long as the lack of purpose is not discerned. Whatever can be said about the Stalinist system in the Soviet Union and Eastern Europe, it did not lack in dynamism and had a perverted logic of its own. Party functionaries easily became mesmerized by it and accepted it as a way of life which was not subject to facile alteration and from which they could extricate themselves only with great difficulty.

The Party held its cadres in bondage by a combination of corrupting influences, among them a shared sense of power, material well-being, and moral irresponsibility.

Party officials were encouraged to act recklessly. They had no fear of retribution from the population. They were imbued with a deep sense of the irreversibility of the situation in which they found themselves. The old order would never rise again. Their memory of it was sufficiently vivid to lend them conviction in extirpating its last remnants. The necessity for ruthlessness was easily explained to them in terms of the injustices committed by the defunct social order and of the inevitability of injustices in the initial stages of the new. Material well-being proved a powerful incentive to most, and they accepted their economic privileges in the midst of nation-wide austerity as an emolument due them for their former privations and their current services.

Conspicuous consumption became typical of the new leading cadres. In the capital, at the top of the hierarchy, second and third echelon officials lived very well indeed. In four to five years or less, they had risen from obscurity to deputy-ministerial posts and the like. Their achievement was in no small way due to hard work, including study at forced pace in Hungarian and Soviet institutions. Their original investment of effort and austerity, however, paid incredibly high dividends in a very short time. Villas in fashionable suburbs, servants, lavish furnishings, and a social life to match, all were placed at their disposal and became a natural part of their existence. They were not a leisure class (this distinction belonged to writers and artists alone) for they continued to work long, arduous hours. But they were definitely a class of conspicuous consumers who took their mode of living in stride, without giving signs of being aware of its incongruity. They emulated the social habits of the despised bourgeoisie which they had just deposed. While they learned their lesson well—that they must not inherit the bourgeois state apparatus and the bourgeois political and economic institutions but smash them and erect their own—they disdained the same rules when it came to imitating capitalist social habits.

On the whole, the Party succeeded in inculcating in its new leading cadres a spirit of buoyancy, optimism, and instrumental loyalty to the regime. The image of the new Communist cadre had not yet become clearly focused and was certainly full of flaws, but a service generation sharing many of the characteristics of former nobilities of autocratic courts was rapidly maturing. It was centripetally oriented, cushioned against the shocks of discovery of the real misery of the downtrodden masses, impervious to pleas for consideration, assistance, and mercy, haughty, arbitrary, cruel, and, above all perhaps, oblivious to its recent past, its social origin, and its surviving blood ties with the outside world. In 1952, a year in which danger signals were already discernible, a deputy minister and his wife, both of impeccable proletarian background, ceased to have any contact whatever with their respective families, who still lived in squalor, while they occupied a spacious villa. At the same time, a writer of bourgeois background, all wrapped up in the mysteries of "socialist realism," disdained *his* parents and, on addressing them in writing, priggishly affixed his signature to the bottom of his letter as Dr. X. Such was the human measure of estrangement between the cadres of the Party and their social environment—a terrible and, in the long run, debilitating isolation of the rulers from the ruled.

For the moment, there was nothing to shake the confidence of the new leading cadres, despite the ever-present threat of quick demotion and possible extinction at the hands of those who bestowed favors as well. They seemed to accept the built-in insecurity of their status as an inevitable occupational hazard that did not affect their loyalty to the Party. They owed everything to the Party. As long as all went according to expectation, they would give the Party staunch support. But like the equilibrium of a spinning top, the internal stability of the Party was predicated on maintaining a great if not unbroken momentum. In 1953, with the death of Stalin, adjustments in the Soviet power structure and the policies of the new Soviet leadership followed. The rhythm of socialist construction was interrupted, if only partially and temporarily. The frequency and modulation of impulses emanating from Moscow changed. A new, unanticipated situation arose that deeply affected all East European Communist parties. Familiar conditions of internal stability were suddenly altered. Adaptability to novel circumstances was at a premium. The Hungarian Communists found themselves in precarious straits.

7. Prelude to Revolution, 1953-1956

THE DEATH of Joseph Stalin on March 5, 1953, ended an epoch of terroristic dictatorship. For a few months, Hungary and some other East European countries (notably Czechoslovakia) continued their frenzied drive for socialist construction as if nothing had happened. In East Germany, a highly sensitive area, signs of decompression and of popular unrest appeared quickly. A full-fledged uprising broke out on June 17, 1953. It had to be put down by the Soviet military.

In Czechoslovakia, the workers of Plzen, a major industrial center, rioted on June 1 in protest against a drastic currency evaluation that cut down their earning power. Although order was restored in one day and the rioting did not spread to the rest of the country, the government desisted from further planned wage reforms that would have had an even harsher effect on the earning capacity of industrial workers. Disturbances and unauthorized strikes were reported from other countries as well.

Clearly, a period of readjustment and reassessment was at hand. The first concern of Stalin's heirs was to prevent violence and to head off possible inroads by outside enemies. To this end, they offered concessions at home and abroad while they settled problems attendant upon the transfer of power from a system of personal government whose principal features they could not assimilate easily.

The East European countries followed the lead of the Soviet Union. The Communist parties adopted the principle of collective leadership, dividing the responsibilities of the first party secretary and the prime minister between two people. They decreed limited amnesties for political prisoners and refurbished their legal procedures to soften harsh arbitrary standards of justice. They also moved to revitalize moribund national fronts, and they organized elections to national legislatures and local representative bodies. They revised industrial targets (spurring the production of consumer goods within modest bounds), slowed down—and in some cases suspended—further collectivization of agriculture, reduced consumer prices, forgave back taxes and food deliveries owed by peasants to the state, and encouraged private initiative in small-scale artisan enterprises.

Initially, the scope of policy changes varied from one country to another. For example, in Hungary, an abrupt and sharp break with past practices was announced on July 4, 1953, by Imre Nagy, the newly appointed Prime Minister. In Poland, signs of adjustment were barely discernible. Further developments in the East European states also bespoke a certain degree of diversity in respect to the timing and the magnitude of reforms initiated by the government and to the expression of discontent by different groups of the population.

All East European countries were in need of a relaxation of tensions, but not all Communist leaders were convinced that the psychological moment for a change from the set pattern of controls was opportune for them. They were afraid of the consequences that would follow from a replacement of the techniques of coercion with subtler and more complex methods of manipulation. To ease the tempo of totalitarian restructuring of societies without incurring a loss of direction, and to relax the vise in which the people were held without losing grip on them, were indeed efforts that challenged the abilities of the Communist parties.

In addition, relations between the various Communist parties and the new Soviet leadership also came under review. Stalin's successors apparently encouraged local Communist leaders to take more initiative and to grow more self-reliant, without, however, violating the tenets of proletarian internationalism that demand the subordination of particular, national interests to those of the whole socialist camp. Moscow continued to intervene in the affairs of East European Communist parties often and forcefully, but with less consistency than in Stalin's time. This lack of consistency was due to the uncertain and even pragmatic evolution of Soviet policies and to the struggle for power in the Kremlin.

In the absence of clear and unmistakable signals from Moscow the East European Communist parties tended to become confused. Their leaders curried favor with one or another faction in the Soviet Union while personal and group rivalries in their own midst once again rose to the surface. The Polish and Hungarian parties, which had the gravest internal conflicts, suffered most acutely.[1] The Soviet Union, for its part, did not always assess local situations accurately, preoccupied as it was with its own internal problems. This was especially true in 1956, in the wake of the strong condemnation of Stalin's cult of personality—a euphemism for the terroristic aberrations of Stalin's personal dictatorship—which N. S. Khrushchev made in a secret speech before the delegates of the Twentieth Congress of the Communist Party of the Soviet Union (CPSU).[2]

Khrushchev's attack on Stalin personally and on his methods of government was an absolute necessity in terms of the Soviet domestic situation. But it reverberated throughout the Communist world and touched off a chain reaction of unexpected proportions in Poland and Hungary, which the Soviet Union did not manage to contain in time. The disarray of the Communist parties in Poland and Hungary communicated itself to the people, reinforced popular discontent, and set the stage for upheavals in the

---

[1] According to one former Hungarian Communist, the disintegration of the Party was entirely due to the unusual situation which arose in the wake of Stalin's death.

In his view, navigating the political waters under Stalin had been simplicity itself. All one had to do was to zero in one's political compass on Stalin's whims, kowtow to him in sycophantic adulation, and all was well. Under the new conditions, anticipating Moscow's pleasure became a complex art. For one thing, in view of a struggle for power among the Soviet leaders, it was necessary to choose sides. For another thing, policies had to be evaluated without the firm guidance once provided by Stalin's insistence on rigid conformity. Success or failure thus came to be dependent on "extrasensory" perception in attuning oneself to the prevailing powers in Moscow. In this game Rakosi lost. While this explanation is both too cynical and too simple, it contains an element of truth that cannot be overlooked in analyzing the antecedents of the revolution.

[2] *The Anti-Stalin Campaign*, pp. 1-89.

fall of 1956—transfer of power from Stalinist to nationalist Communists in Poland (which helped to stave off the threat of an uprising) and popular revolution in Hungary.

In Hungary, the course of events from the death of Stalin to the outbreak of revolution was distinct from that in any other East European country. Hungary was the first to renounce Stalinist policies, and it did so in the sharpest terms and with the greatest fanfare. It was the last to implement comprehensive and permanent reforms and to achieve an orderly adjustment of the relations between the governing power and the population. It was Hungary which witnessed the most protracted struggle for control of the Communist Party between sectarian, Stalinist forces and a reform-minded, right-wing opposition.[3] Hungarian Communists had to cope with the most acute problems of decompression and proved least capable of handling them.

In retrospect, these three and a half years emerge as a coherent whole, a period of incubation (this apt label, as far as the author knows, is Paul Kecskemeti's), in the course of which the classical symptoms that are associated with the progressive decay of political and social orders, and thought to be necessary preconditions for all major revolutions, gradually came into evidence—alienation of the intellectuals from the existing order of things, serious disorganization within the ruling circles, and massive social unrest. In the end, Hungary was a caricature of the Marxist image of capitalist society in its final stage of dissolution.

This is not to presume a conscious, deliberate, or preordained movement toward revolution. On the contrary, social and political developments proceeded haltingly. Nevertheless, the decisions and commitments made by the participants in these developments, independently and in response to one another, intermeshed in a manner that strongly enhanced the likelihood of a tragic, violent climax.

The entire gestation stage of the revolution can be subdivided

3 The terms "sectarian" or "left sectarian" and "right wing," "right-wing opposition," or simply "opposition," will be used here in the context in which they were applied by rival Communist factions to one another. The labels are not necessarily accurately descriptive in the traditional sense in which Communist "sectarians" have been identified.

into three distinct phases that correspond to the premiership of Imre Nagy (July, 1953–April, 1955), the resurgence of Rakosi (April, 1955–February, 1956), and the anti-Stalin campaign following the Twentieth Congress of the Communist Party of the Soviet Union in February, 1956.

THE PREMIERSHIP OF IMRE NAGY

In the second half of June, 1953, (the exact date has never been revealed) the Soviet leadership summoned four leading Hungarian Communists (Rakosi, Farkas, Gero, and Nagy) and one non-Communist (Dobi) to Moscow, sharply berated the "quartet" for its adventurous policies and sectarianism (raising among other things serious objections to the disproportionately large number of Jews in the Party command), and ordered changes, including the appointment of Nagy to the premiership, but retained Rakosi as first secretary of the Party. Nagy saw in the attitude of the Soviet leadership a vindication of his own views, especially in economic matters; for, as he records it, the "key members of the Soviet Communist Party" recognized that the country was on the "verge of catastrophe" and that the Communists stood a good chance of being "summarily booted out" (the expression is attributed to Khrushchev) unless "prompt and effective measures were taken to bring about a change." [4]

The decisions reached in Moscow were acted on by the Central Committee of the Hungarian Communist Party in Budapest a few days later, and on July 4 Nagy presented himself to Parliament. In a speech of unprecedented content and delivery,[5] he sounded a ringing condemnation of past policies and promised major innovations that accorded with the desires of the population. Nagy articulated grievances felt by millions of people against superindustrialization, hasty and brutal collectivization, and police terror. He admitted that the "objectives of the accelerated Five Year Plan" had been "beyond [Hungary's] strength." The implementation of the plan "vastly overtaxed [Hungary's] resources . . .

[4] Imre Nagy, *On Communism*, p. 66.

[5] Many Hungarians heard the broadcast of the Prime Minister's address. They were struck by his use of "rich native idiom" instead of the customary Communist jargon.

hampered the growth of the material foundations of the country's welfare and . . . resulted in a deteriorating standard of living."

In Nagy's view, it was "imperative" for the new government to "reduce the exaggerated rates of industrialization, especially the overly rapid pace of development of heavy industry, and . . . to increase the production of consumer goods." Similarly, Nagy attacked the method and manner of growth of producers' cooperatives (i.e., collective farms), which "endangered the physical and material security of the peasantry." He deemed it "necessary to slow down [this] development," and pledged his government's assistance to members of collective farms who "wish to withdraw from producers' cooperatives," provided they first met their current obligations to the farms. Finally, he declared that the government would authorize the dissolution of collective farms "in which a majority of the members express such a desire."

Turning to police terror, Nagy excoriated the preceding government for its "grave mistakes," proclaimed the "consolidation of the rule of law [to be] one of the most urgent tasks of the new government," and expressed an interest in abolishing "the system of internment camps" and in "regularizing the position of the deportees." [6]

The speech electrified the population and jarred the mass of Party functionaries who had had no inkling of its message. The impact of his address was the greater because it came without prior warning. Important government declarations were usually well advertised in advance. Their texts were printed in the Party journal as Central Committee resolutions, denoting the primacy of the Party over the government. Not so this time. The Party information media were controlled by Rakosi's adherents. They deliberately suppressed news of the Central Committee meeting which had confirmed Nagy's appointment and had set down guidelines for his policy program.[7] They evidently hoped to minimize the importance of both the person and the program of the new Premier by ignoring them.

[6] *Szabad Nep*, July 5, 1953.

[7] The resolution which the Central Committee adopted and which served as a basis for Nagy's programmatic announcement was never published by the Communists, although in subsequent years they often referred to it.

The silence of the Party press produced the opposite of the intended effect. It made it seem as if the Party had not given its prior approval to the program, an impression that was reinforced by Nagy's infrequent references to the Party. The unusual circumstances of its delivery turned the speech into an extraordinary (and unintended) tribute to Parliament. No program of significance had ever been introduced there under the Communists. It appeared as if Nagy had deliberately chosen this forum to go directly to the nation over the heads of the Party and to underscore his aim of governing through constitutional organs. Actually, he had no such thought in mind. He had to make the best of an awkward situation because the Party refused him the normal amenities due a Prime Minister. He even had difficulty in obtaining statistical information from the Party Secretariat. His slight of the Party was not intentional. It was an example of his guilelessness, which sometimes made him appear less loyal to the Communist cause than he was.

Whatever might have been his intentions, the speech made history. It introduced a "new course" in Hungary's political life. Although Nagy did not prevail in the end and his program was never fulfilled, he broke the momentum of large-scale social engineering, which, once interrupted, never regained its earlier dynamism and consistency. He tore off the Party's false mask of monolithism and profaned previously unassailable idols. The fissures he revealed in the "granite-like unity" of the Party were never repaired. They grew deeper until they split the Party completely. From this time on there were two versions of interpretation of the past, laudatory and defamatory. There were also two champions of good and evil (Nagy and Rakosi) around whom supporting casts gathered.

Nagy's address was popularly regarded as a fresh breeze in a fetid atmosphere. But it understandably alarmed Rakosi. Wasting no time, he called a meeting of activists of the Greater Budapest Party organization to rally the Party cadres around him and to reassure them, in turn, that they need not fear any serious intrusion in their authority. The activists' meeting was well publicized in advance. When it convened on July 11, Rakosi rectified some of the misconceptions to which Nagy's speech might have given rise. He explained that it had been a mistake to "depart from the custom of informing the public first of all in the name of the Party." [8] But he told his listeners that Nagy's program had been "worked out on the basis of the decisions of the Party's Central Committee"; i.e., Nagy was under Party discipline and obligated to abide by the Party's orders.

Rakosi then proceeded to dull the cutting edge of some of Nagy's remarks and to give his interpretation of the meaning of the new program. While agreeing that peasants could leave collective farms if they wished "at the end of the economic year," he reaffirmed the Party's determination "not to change its policy of assistance to producers' cooperatives . . . and to do all in its power to consolidate and develop these," for this was the only "correct road to the socialist transformation of the countryside." He emphasized the need for continuing "vigilance . . . to counter any tendencies toward capitulation," and quieted the apprehensions of functionaries concerning a "clean sweep" of the Party cadres by telling them that those "comrades who lost their positions in the Politbureau and the Council of Ministers will without exception continue to work in suitable positions in the Party and the government." To Rakosi, then, the new program represented no change in direction, as many had thought. It conformed to the "unchanging aim of the Party to build socialism" and merely outlined better ways of doing it.[9]

Nagy dutifully seconded Rakosi in putting at ease the troubled minds of the assembled officials. He "agreed fully" with the "review of comrade Rakosi," paid tribute to the Party, pledged unity between the government and the Party, and, in the end, lashed out against "hostile inciters" who would wreck the entire collective farm system by urging peasants to abandon their stations immediately.[10] This was the first of several such reversals in which Nagy played the part of Rakosi's straight man.

8 *Szabad Nep*, July 12, 1953.

9 Although this explanation was specious and logically untenable, it gave Party functionaries a formula for sabotaging the real intent of the new program while paying lip service to it.

10 *Szabad Nep*, July 12, 1953.

The activists' meeting helped to bolster morale in the Party and restored a more accurate perspective on the state of affairs in Hungary. It marked the beginning of a seesawing battle in which Nagy fought Rakosi on uneven terms for twenty months. At no time during this period did Nagy achieve mastery in the Party or in the government.

In the reorganized Politbureau, the membership of which was trimmed from fourteen members and four alternates to nine members and two alternates, Nagy's one staunch supporter was Rudolf Foldvari, a new appointee and temporary secretary of the Budapest Party organization. By contrast, Rakosi managed to pack this body with his minions (Lajos Acs, a new member, Istvan Kristof, and Istvan Hidas, all three of whom were promoted from alternate to full membership, and Bela Szalai, a newly appointed alternate member.[11] Two members of the "quartet" (Farkas and Revai) lost their Politbureau seats and their ministerial posts, as did Apro, another stalwart of the leadership. The disgrace of Farkas and Apro was, however, temporary.

Farkas was restored to the Politbureau in August, when he was also made secretary of the Central Committee and put in charge of the Agitation and Propaganda Department. He maintained himself in these positions until the end of Nagy's tenure of office. Less influential and certainly less effective than he had been as Minister of National Defense, Farkas nevertheless remained in the inner circle of the Party command.

Apro, a lesser figure, was restored to the Politbureau in October, 1953.[12] Only Revai was cast into more permanent oblivion. (He was not resuscitated until July, 1956, when Rakosi was dismissed from office.) Revai's retirement from public life is inexplicable

[11] This is not to say that Rakosi's leadership was accepted unquestioningly. Several Politbureau members (including General Farkas) are said to have wavered from time to time in their loyalty to him, but their attitudes seem to have been determined by their assessment of Moscow's preferences and as quickly as they could they swung back in line behind Rakosi.

[12] The Politbureau elected at the Third Congress of the Party in May, 1954, also consisted of nine members and two alternates. The distribution of power in it was even more unfavorable to Nagy. Foldvari was no longer a member. The full members were Rakosi, Farkas, Gero, Nagy, Apro, Hegedus, Hidas, Acs, and Szalai; the alternate members were Bata and Mekis.

except in terms of the great hostility that existed between him and Nagy. He was the least offending member of the "quartet" and might have found means of communication with the intellectual forces in Hungary whose cooperation the regime either sought or could have used.

His retirement had a devastating effect on Revai. He is alleged to have undergone a profound personal crisis, punctuated by fits of raving bordering on dementia. He apparently blamed Rakosi rather than Nagy for his personal misfortunes and agitated from the sidelines (e.g., in advice he gave to journalists at the *Szabad Nep*) to expose Rakosi and bring about his downfall. He is also said to have castigated the Party leadership in private for its ruinous mistakes, which threatened to demolish the people's democratic system. For all this, however, he could not bring himself to join forces with Nagy and remained his fanatical enemy. Revai's obstinacy served both men ill. The course of events in Hungary might have taken a different turn had they been able to unite.

In the government, Nagy was surrounded by foes. His deputies were Gero[13] and Hegedus, who also held the Ministry of the Interior and the Ministry of Agriculture respectively. The Minister of Heavy Industry was Istvan Hidas, and the Chairman of the State Planning Office Bela Szalai.[14]

Nagy succeeded in placing some of his friends into positions of influence only after much delay. It took him several months to arrange for the return of Zoltan Szanto, an old "Muscovite" with views somewhat similar to his own, from Paris, where Szanto had served as ambassador. He became chief of a newly established Office of Information in the Premier's chancellery. The deputy chief was Miklos Vasarhelyi, a journalist who was one of Nagy's

[13] Gero, whose fortunes sagged at the end of the Stalinist era, was saved by the reorganization of the Party and government apparatus. As in the past so now, in the face of a common danger, he and Rakosi set aside their differences to their mutual if temporary benefit. Gero relinquished the portfolio of the Interior in the summer of 1954. His replacement, Laszlo Piros, was also a Stalinist.

[14] Nagy succeeded in dismissing Szalai in October, 1954, but he then accepted the suggestion of the Soviet ambassador to appoint the "friendly Muscovite" Andor Berei to that post. It will be remembered that Berei served as watchdog of the Ministry of Foreign Affairs for many years.

early and steadfast supporters. Zoltan Vas was brought back from banishment to the provinces and made secretary of the Cabinet Council. Perhaps out of gratitude, he became a strong supporter of the new Premier. Ferenc Janosi became secretary general of the Patriotic People's Front, one of Nagy's favorite projects, which he finally managed to launch in October, 1954. Miklos Gimes, another journalist who sympathized with Nagy's views, was re-called from Paris in December to become editor of *Magyar Nemzet,* the official publication of the Front.[15]

Lacking strength in the Party and the government, Nagy turned to the Patriotic People's Front (a new name for the Independent People's Front) to gain for himself a much-needed forum and to create an organization that could help to draw the masses out of their lethargy and into active participation in politics. It is un-likely that Nagy envisioned the Front as a rival to the Party, still less as a substitute for it. But he staffed it with his supporters, and it attracted people who sympathized with his program. The possibility existed that the Front would, in time, acquire sub-stance and become the institutional base of forces inimical to the Party.

Inevitably, his venture aroused strong opposition from the Party apparatus and for this reason did not progress beyond the organ-izing stage. Dabbling with national fronts has always been fraught with danger in Communist countries. Most parties have shied away from it, because of organizational complications and ideological repercussions that were sure to follow. While the revival of national fronts was one of the accepted means of reducing political tensions throughout Eastern Europe in the post-Stalin era, it was not a serious effort anywhere. Nagy's genuine interest in the Front was suspect and he was eventually chastised for it.

The lack of success he had with his political plans was fully matched by the failure of his economic program.

15 Oszkar Betlen remained chief editor of *Szabad Nep* until June, 1954, when Marton Horvath was reappointed to that post. Horvath, a vast improvement over Betlen, was nevertheless only a fair-weather friend of the Premier. Betlen was sent to Bucarest as Hungary's representative on the staff of the Cominform journal.

To carry out his economic program, Nagy had to have the cooperation and good will of all concerned as well as much luck. The Party cadres undermined his efforts, and different groups of the population that actually benefited from his endeavors did not contribute to the success of his policies. The attitude of the masses was understandable. Nagy promised them a better life, and they did whatever was possible to insure it for themselves. With the taming of terror, they grew bolder, and instead of showing gratitude for the concessions made to them, they demanded more. Many peasants abandoned collective farms ahead of the scheduled time.[16] They tended their own plots, hoarded, and bartered. Their actions further crippled agricultural production. In the cities, there was a marked decline in labor discipline. Absenteeism and labor turnover increased, while labor productivity dropped. Workers slacked on their jobs, collected their pay, stole what they could, and engaged in private blackmarket enterprise. The damage inflicted was probably marginal, but, under the prevailing conditions, even minor infringements caused an unduly grave strain on the economy.

The objective economic causes of trouble were even more serious. Fundamental among these was the narrow base of the economy, which provided inadequate support for rapid and extensive alteration of the commodity structure of production. A cutback in producer items and expansion in consumer goods had an adverse effect on foreign trade. The import of goods, mostly from Western countries, could not be paid for by exports. This created an acute shortage of hard currency which required quick remedial action. The scarcity of domestic financial resources called for austerity (unless foreign loans could be obtained—which was not the case), and not for increased expenditures for social welfare, to which Nagy had committed himself. By 1954 the economy was in dire straits. The harvest was bad and industrial production was faltering. Although many causes of the economic difficulties could be traced to the disastrous policies of the Stalinist period, it was easy to lay the blame on Nagy. Current problems were his to

16 During the first six months of Nagy's administration, an estimated 200,000 peasants, representing two-fifths of the total membership, withdrew from collective farms.

handle, and his mistakes invited criticism from his detractors.

Amid the many issues that caused discord in the Party, none was more explosive than the question of the rehabilitation of Communist political prisoners. It was Rakosi's Achilles heel, which he fought savagely and, for the time being, successfully to defend.

The consequences of carrying the policies of the "new course" to their logical conclusion must have been clear to Rakosi. He opposed on ideological grounds any changes whatever and was unable on personal grounds to bring himself to recommend anyone that suited him for the premiership. Yet, he knew that changes of almost any kind could be thwarted and their intent distorted, and he also knew that personalities could be engaged in struggle with a fair chance of defeating them. What Rakosi could not bear was an investigation of the purges he had carried out in the Communist Party. For if the truth were revealed about Kadar, Kallai, Losonczy, and Szakasits, let alone about Rajk, his own fate would be sealed. He was, therefore, above anything else, opposed to political rehabilitation. He delayed and obstructed moves in this direction for the better part of a year while he prepared the way for step-by-step retreat if it should become necessary. He was ready to offer sacrificial victims at opportune moments so as to draw attention away from himself. Gabor Peter was one (his trial opened in March, 1954, just before the beginning of rehabilitations);[17] Mihaly Farkas was another.

Rakosi was playing for time. He expected that liberalization was a temporary expedient that would give way to Stalinist orthodoxy once the Soviet leaders settled questions of personal rivalry among themselves. Rakosi knew he would be immune to all danger as soon as this was done. In the expectation of this event, he continually probed for weaknesses in Nagy's armor and repeatedly sought to blacken him in the eyes of the Soviet leadership.

[17] Rakosi had ordered Peter's arrest in the uncertain period between the Nineteenth Congress of the CPSU in October, 1952, and Stalin's death, when symptoms became discernible that hinted at an impending purge of secret police cadres as the first step in another major bloodletting planned by Stalin. To protect himself, Rakosi wasted no time in ridding himself of Peter and of many other high-ranking officers of the secret police.

Throughout the better part of 1954, Rakosi's efforts bore no fruit. In the spring, when Hungarian Communists paid one of their frequent visits to Moscow, Rakosi was again reprimanded for his obstructionism, but no sanctions were invoked against him. The Third Congress of the Hungarian Workers' Party, held after some delay in May, 1954, was a standoff between him and Nagy. Meanwhile, review procedures preparatory to the rehabilitation of unjustly imprisoned Communists had begun despite Rakosi's opposition, and, in a few months, the first group of prisoners was released.

In the autumn of 1954, Nagy actually seemed to be in the ascendancy. At a meeting of the Central Committee in October, his policies received unusual endorsement.[18] According to observers, he was at the zenith of his popularity and at the psychological peak of his determination to push his program and himself as Hungary's leader. Inasmuch as the Party press again gave inadequate coverage to the event—it had failed to publish the Premier's address to the Central Committee—Nagy took to the pages of *Szabad Nep* in a signed article in which he restated in essence the views he had propounded behind closed doors.[19]

This was the signal for Rakosi to counterattack. He set off for Moscow to feel out the prevailing climate. With as keen a sense of timing as he had ever displayed, he denounced Nagy's economic heresies. A campaign built around identical issues was in the final stages of preparation there, intended to serve both as a platform and as a shield for Party Secretary Khrushchev in his assault on Prime Minister Malenkov. Rakosi's views were accepted by the Soviet leadership. He returned to Budapest at the end of November, jubilant in the knowledge that he had dealt a mortal blow to Nagy.

Although the charges Rakosi brought against Nagy were not without substance, a judicious examination of all the issues would have shown his economic policies to be far less extravagant than they were made out to be. It would have revealed the complexity

[18] This is said to have been the only instance on record of a majority of the Central Committee backing Nagy against recommendations made by the Politbureau.

[19] *Szabad Nep,* October 20, 1954.

of the country's economic problems, and suggested possible compromises for the reconciliation of needs, wants, and capabilities in heavy and consumer industries and in agriculture. But the mood in Moscow just then was inhospitable to judicious argumentation. Soviet domestic interests demanded a forceful reassertion of dogmatic economic views. Rakosi benefited from them; Nagy became their victim.

Immediately after Rakosi's return, a broad campaign of vilification against Nagy's economic policies was unleashed. Nagy's isolation in the Communist leadership was plainly evident at the celebration of the tenth annivarsary of Hungary's liberation, held at Debrecen on December 21. Although he was one of the speakers, he kept entirely to himself, and, at the informal festivities that took place in the evening, he sat at a table with writers and journalists, not with the Party high command.

In January, 1955, Nagy was ordered to Moscow, and there the accusations Rakosi had leveled against him in Budapest were read out to him almost verbatim. Although he remained Prime Minister in name for another three months, his status was irrevocably undermined. In February (only a few days after the dismissal of G. M. Malenkov as Premier of the Soviet Union), a medical bulletin issued by Rakosi informed the Hungarian population of Nagy's inability to perform his duties because of an acute heart condition. (In point of fact, Nagy did at that time suffer from a heart condition.) In March, the Central Committee convened and heard Nagy being indicted in the presence of M. A. Suslov, an emissary of the Soviet Communist Party.

The resolution adopted by the Central Committee sharply attacked the recent "tendency to right-wing opportunist deviation . . . concerning socialist industrialization" and flatly asserted that, "should this right wing, opportunist policy . . . become victorious, our country would ultimately be pushed into the ranks of the backward nations."[20]

About six weeks later, Nagy's dismissal was officially announced. The Central Committee adopted still another resolution, which catalogued all of Nagy's alleged deviations and condemned him

[20] Imre Nagy, *On Communism*, p. 103.

unequivocally. While the March resolution dealt with the Party
program (officially it pretended to continue unbroken the program
mapped out in June 1953), the April resolution addressed itself
primarily to the person of Imre Nagy and likeminded right-wing
oppositionists; it asserted among other things:

> Comrade Imre Nagy, as a member of the Politbureau and as the chair-
> man of the Council of Ministers, represented political opinions which were
> sharply opposed to the over-all policies of our Party and inimical to the
> interests of the working class, the working peasants, and the people's de-
> mocracy. Comrade Nagy tried to throttle the motor of socialist building,
> socialist industrialization, and especially the development of heavy indus-
> try, and in the provinces the movement of agricultural cooperatives, which
> is the decisive method of socialist rebuilding of the villages. He tried to
> obscure and force into the background the Party leadership, and he at-
> tempted to pit government agencies against one another, and the Patriotic
> People's Front against the Party. Comrade Nagy by all this prevented the
> building of a solid basis for increasing the welfare of the people.
> These anti-Marxist, anti-Leninist, anti-Party views of Comrade Nagy
> form a comprehensive system, an attitude which spread to the various
> fields of political, economic, and cultural life....
> In the interest of realizing his rightist, opportunist policies, Comrade
> Nagy resorted to un-Party like, anti-Party factional methods that are
> completely incompatible with the unity and discipline of the Marxist-
> Leninist Party.[21]

The censure of Nagy was unwarranted. If anyone was guilty
of factionalism, it was Rakosi. Nagy did not think of himself as
the leader of the opposition, and he found it distasteful to be cast
in that role by other persons who sympathized with him. He
placed loyalty to the Party above all other considerations and was
willing to cooperate in good faith with Rakosi, but the latter made
the terms of cooperation unilateral surrender.[22]

The opposition label, conveniently descriptive as it is, must be
applied with great caution. The opposition evolved tortuously,
from a frame of mind shared by an undetermined number of
Communists in isolation from one another, into a conscious community of interest with a program of action. Originating deep in

21 *Ibid.*, p. xliii.

22 It is said on good authority that Nagy informed Rakosi of his willingness
to retire from public life and to take up his professorial duties if that would
help to restore the unity of the Party. But even these terms were unacceptable
to Rakosi, who wanted to destroy Nagy.

individual consciences, it emerged in more or less coherent groups only a few months before the revolution. Never did it achieve the status of a structured organizational entity. At the beginning of 1955, it was far too early to speak of it in such terms.

Despite the attractiveness of Nagy and of his policies, there was no noticeable rush either among the masses or among select groups to fall in line behind him. The people remained on the sidelines of what shaped up as a contest in the Party. Select groups, especially writers and journalists, were slow to awake from their torpor.

During the first year of the "new course," they were busy discovering themselves and the world around them. They acted like people emerging from total darkness into brilliant sunlight. Dazzled, they could not quite believe what they saw. Through clever manipulation, the Party machine embroiled them in quarrels among themselves. This drew some fire away from the Party and retarded the coalescence of writers into a purposeful opposition to Rakosi's leadership. The Party pretended solicitude for the problems of the Hungarian countryside and encouraged an examination of the plight of the villages. In a manner quite unorthodox for Communists, the ills of socialist agriculture were dramatized before and above anything else. This helped to renew hostility between populist or populist-oriented writers (including some major figures who were fast fellow travellers but not members of the Party, such as Peter Veres and Pal Szabo) and Communists of urban descent.

Unfortunately the religious issue also intruded here. Populist types and Communists of peasant stock tended to take out their venom on writers of middle-class background whose failure to report properly on conditions in the countryside they blamed on their urban, Semitic, cosmopolitan outlook.

The clique struggle raged for the better part of a year, during which sides were taken either in favor of the peasants or of the urban middle class (i.e., the mass of *déclassé* elements).[23] Sur-

[23] Miklos Molnar, who was then editor of *Irodalmi Ujsag*, places the cessation of internecine struggles in the Writers' Association at the beginning of the summer of 1954. See M. Molnar and L. Nagy, *Imre Nagy Réformateur ou Révolutionnaire* (Geneve, Droz, 1959), pp. 90-91.

prisingly, the situation of the workers went largely unnoticed. No one championed their cause. It was only in the summer and fall of 1954, when the writers and journalists were confronted with victims of Communist terror, whom they had helped to convict or whose guilt they had believed to be true, that they comprehended the monstrousness of their past behavior. Their attitudes then began to change. According to one writer, "the Writers' Association arrived at a turning point in October, 1954, when it was discovered that the Rajk trial had been completely fabricated and that the holy war preached against Yugoslavs was founded on a tissue of lies. . . . It became evident to the great majority of the writers that they had helped to crush revolutionaries, that they had glorified calumnies, that as a result they had been put in an impossible situation before the reading public." [24]

This turning point coincided with Nagy's brief breakthrough in the Party. Dery, one of the soberest writers and one who had a clean bill of health (as far as crimes against his fellow men were concerned), responded to Nagy's article in *Szabad Nep* with an unmistakable expression of confidence in the pages of *Irodalmi Ujsag*.[25] The journalists at *Szabad Nep* also endorsed the Premier's views. Their belated help was, however, without effect.

To the end of his tenure of office, Nagy was in an anomalous position. The Soviet leaders did not follow their recommendation for "prompt and effective measures" with any action. They permitted the Party cadres to sabotage his program, and, in the end, they agreed to his dismissal. Their attitude toward him was mistaken at best (since they did not give him the support he needed to save the Communist Party from catastrophe) and disingenuous at worst (since they used him as a front man without ever seriously anticipating a role of effective leadership for him). This duplicity exacerbated conflicts in Hungary.

THE RESURGENCE OF RAKOSI

The first round of skirmishing ended in triumph for Rakosi and

[24] Otto Major, "Reflections after the General Assembly of the Writers," *Irodalmi Ujsag*, September 29, 1956.

[25] Tibor Dery, "Open Letter to Imre Nagy," *ibid.*, October 22, 1954.

for the forces aligned with him. He moved to reintroduce stringent economic policies and to resume collectivization. But he did not abolish small scale private artisan enterprises. More important, he continued the rehabilitation of the victims of political terror, albeit at an agonizingly slow rate.

The reorganization of the government resulted in the promotion of Andras Hegedus to the premiership while the reshuffling of the Politbureau brought about the demotion of Mihaly Farkas, which had long been overdue. Rakosi branded Farkas as "an accomplice" of Nagy and punished him for his cowardly behavior which had led him to support Nagy when he thought that Moscow was backing the Premier. Nor was Revai reinstated. Rakosi could not forgive the slanders he had heaped on the Party leadership.

The ex-Premier and his followers were silenced.[26] Nagy was released from all official posts and sent into retirement. He lived in seclusion at home, recuperating from his heart ailment and drafting memoranda for the attention of the Central Committee in which he attempted to vindicate himself. All but the most intimate and the most courageous of his friends avoided him. His house was kept under surveillance by the police. The manner of his discharge from the Party and from the government temporarily damaged his reputation. The rapid decline he suffered after his apparent ascendancy just a few months earlier was incomprehensible to anyone lacking intimate knowledge of Rakosi's machinations. His inactivity after his October victory was all too reminiscent of his earlier failure to assert energetic leadership. Not having the facts at their disposal and not being inclined to take intra-Party conflicts at face value, people questioned Nagy's motives. It was not until a later time, when the impact of Rakosi's policies made itself amply felt, that they revised their opinions about Nagy and looked upon him with favor. Rakosi meanwhile pressed forward to liquidate the "new course" and to bury his opponents so that he could make up for time lost in the socialist construction of Hungary. At this point, however, his usual political sense abandoned him. He mistook the character of his victory

---

26 Szanto was sent abroad as ambassador to Poland. Janosi became a museum director, and Vasarhelyi was demoted to a minor editorial position.

over Nagy and misinterpreted the meaning of Khrushchev's defeat of Malenkov.

Apparently he imagined that with the removal of Malenkov, the apostle of moderation, and with the resurgence of economic orthodoxy in official Soviet literature, Stalinism was about to be restored. He acted accordingly and overplayed his hand. He did not count on the possibility that Khrushchev would borrow a leaf from Stalin's book and adopt the policies of his opponent once he had rendered him harmless. Rakosi either thought that Khrushchev was a Stalinist or that the dogged Stalinist veterans in the Soviet Presidium were using Khrushchev to their own ends and were about to reassert themselves.

In the absence of any solid evidence, it is possible only to speculate about Rakosi's trend of thought. Yet, it is easy to imagine that he—as almost anyone else of strong dogmatic convictions—was the victim of his own predilections and simply could not break out of the limiting sphere of his own prejudices. He lacked the plasticity which henceforth characterized Khrushchev's operational methods. The policies he pursued diverged steadily from those followed by Khrushchev. This was particularly true in regard to Rakosi's conception and use of the police apparatus. He depended on coercion as the main supporting pillar of his system and could not reconcile himself to the curtailment of the police arm as an instrument of rule. Socialist legality, a major plank in Nagy's reform platform, was anathema to him.[27] He did not perceive, or did not believe in, the permanence of the steady contraction of the overt role of the coercive apparatus in the Soviet Union, following Beria's arrest in July, 1953. He was at a loss when it came to substituting more complex but less dehumanizing social controls in the place of the simple, efficient, and brutal methods of the secret police. He tried to restore a police regime in Hungary, but he succeeded only partially.

It was now his turn to be thwarted by the Soviet leadership,

[27] Socialist legality does not imply anything like the adoption of Western democratic standards of justice. But it does mean the abandonment of gross arbitrariness in the operations of the judicial organs of government and it delineates the area of political criminality which they must eschew in order to stay on the "right side of the law." It imparts a considerable sense of certainty to the citizenry that it will not be punished either unjustly or for crimes it did not commit.

which by some action outside Hungary, if not by explicit orders to him, stayed his hand. Although it had opted in his favor, the Soviet leadership was committed to a policy of liberalization that neither accorded with his views nor suited the objective conditions in Hungary in all respects.

On May 15, the Great Powers signed the Austrian State Treaty. According to existing international agreement, this removed the juridical basis of stationing Soviet troops in Hungary. However, the formation on May 14 of the Warsaw alliance of eight socialist powers anticipated the change of status and provided an alternative legal cover (though in fact none was necessary) for garrisoning Soviet troops in Hungary indefinitely. But the Vienna treaty included provisions for the permanent neutralization of Austria. Perceptive, though somewhat unrealistic Hungarians, immediately seized upon this as a possible solution for the problems of their country. Imre Nagy's tracts, which he drafted in 1955, strongly reflect this trend of thought.

At the end of May, Khrushchev made his pilgrimage to Belgrade to achieve a reconciliation with Tito. The Yugoslav leader's vindication was a direct slap at Rakosi. Any hint of sanctioning Titoism as an accepted variant of Communism was poison to him, and, while this did not quite come about, the circulation of Titoist ideas and the use of Titoist slogans to promote a national trend among Communists could not be suppressed with impunity just then. Hungarian intellectuals rejoiced on the sidelines. Some believed that Tito might demand Rakosi's head as a price of reconciliation, and they looked forward to the first secretary's downfall. Others merely felt relief at the prospect of restraints on the restoration of full-fledged Stalinism. Slowly, they began to use previously forbidden Titoist ideas for their own ends.[28]

The Summit Meeting in July rekindled hope in Hungary of an

28 The actual influence that Tito's brand of Communism had on Hungary has never been satisfactorily clarified. Respondents gave conflicting estimates. On the whole, they contended that Tito's example appealed to them only in part. They applauded his independence from Moscow and paid lip service to some forms of social organization developed in Yugoslavia. But their ingrained hostility toward Yugoslavia as a country prevented them from giving Tito's methods and programs closer attention. A small number of perceptive intellectuals went so far as to recognize that Tito's internal reforms had fallen short of Nagy's program.

international *détente* that would make life easier for the captive nations of Eastern Europe. Soviet initiatives for the meeting were popularly interpreted as a sign of weakness in the face of the palpable military preparedness of the NATO powers, of which Communist propaganda ceaselessly warned Hungarians. Whatever impelled the Soviet leaders to seek a summit meeting with President Eisenhower, they appeared anxious to promote international good feeling from which they hoped to reap world-wide propaganda benefits. These intentions did not accord with the resumption of terroristic practices. Although Rakosi's policies were anything but soft, he was forced to mark time. He also had to fall in line with a Soviet-sponsored campaign to induce former nationals of East European states to return to their homelands. The Hungarian government adopted a decree amnestying certain categories of political exiles who had been tried *in absentia*. Although this was feigned amiability, it was incompatible with the unleashing of terror.[29] Rakosi had to bide his time.

In the autumn Khrushchev's attention was drawn to the preparation of the forthcoming Party Congress, at which he was to make his historic denunciation of Stalin. The international climate showed signs of congealing rapidly after the Summit Meeting. The Conference of Foreign Ministers held at Geneva from October 27 to November 16 saw an unyielding Molotov set forth principles and proposals on Germany and on the problem of European security that were plainly unacceptable to the Western powers as a basis for negotiation. Circumstances seemed opportune to Rakosi for a showdown with his oponents.

First he lashed out against Imre Nagy, ordering Nagy to be expelled from the Party. The former Premier was now in total disgrace. This done, Rakosi turned against the writers, whom he had been stalking for some time.

The dismissal of Nagy from the premiership plunged the writers and journalists into deep gloom; they had to reconsider their stance. Rakosi's policies clarified the issues for them, and they would have liked to assist the deposed Premier. But they did not know how. It

---

[29] In July, 1955, Cardinal Mindszenty's release from prison was announced, although he was not set free but was placed under house arrest instead.

was not customary in the Communist Party to go to the aid of a fallen comrade. They lived too close to the Stalinist era to have forgotten its lessons. So for a time, they lay low. Their passivity did not deter Rakosi from wreaking his vengeance on those who had supported Nagy. He cracked down on the editorial board of *Irodalmi Ujsag,* dismissing the responsible editor, Miklos Molnar. He then shifted his attention to the staff of *Szabad Nep* and discharged a number of talented young journalists from that newspaper; at the same time he arranged for the return of the notorious Oszkar Betlen to the chief editorship. But these piecemeal measures failed to satisfy his hunger for revenge. His fanaticism drove him to seek more reprisals.

To cover up the heinous crimes he had committed, he needed to commit additional crimes in an endless sequence. So far, only the intellectuals knew the truth about Rakosi's blood purges. But unless draconic measures were taken soon, word might spread to the population and to the Party cadres, and they might start to ask questions. This contingency had to be avoided at all costs. It was not enough to sweep under the carpet the filth that had been uncovered in the process of rehabilitating the victims of the purges. If possible, all traces of it had to be removed. But how? People were still being released from prisons. The danger of public disclosures of past atrocities was growing. Rakosi tried to put the blame on Peter and even on Farkas, but to no avail. He had to look for other remedies. If he could muzzle the writers and, preferably, if he could make an example out of them before the nation by imprisoning a number of them and even by executing some, the rest of the population would hardly dare to ask more questions.

In part because of Rakosi's relentless stalking and in part because of encouraging symptoms in Soviet policy that presaged continuing liberalization, the writers gained self-confidence and ever so cautiously began once more to probe the Party's armor. In an article published in *Irodalmi Ujsag,* Gyula Hay pleaded with the Party to desist from imposing arbitrary bureaucratic restraints on artistic creativity.[30] The article aroused the ire of the

[30] Gyula Hay, "Freedom and Responsibility," *Irodalmi Ujsag,* September 10, 1955.

Party leaders, and they ordered the confiscation of the next issue of *Irodalmi Ujsag*, ostensibly because it contained two stories that were deemed defamatory to Communist personalities.[31] The responsible editor, Gyorgy Hamos, who had been in the job for a few months only, demurred and was promptly dismissed. Several writers rose to the defense of their colleague, and a rebellion in the Writers' Association was under way.

This rebellion consisted of the drafting and forwarding of a memorandum of protest to the Party leadership, in which the writers took exception to "recent manifestations of gross encroachments of artistic freedom." Taking refuge in the resolution adopted by the Central Committee in March, which "integrally affirmed the decisions of June 1953," the writers noted with "deep anxiety . . . the recourse to sinister authoritarian methods that had been repeatedly condemned by the Central Committee itself and by the Party Congress." They catalogued these encroachments and, significantly, listed in addition to the purge of *Szabad Nep* personnel and the confiscation of *Irodalmi Ujsag*, the Party's proscription of notable classics and of works by non-Communists, such as Madach's *Tragedy of Man*, Nemeth's *Galileo*, and Bartok's musical piece, *The Miraculous Mandarin*.

The memorandum expressed the "conviction that so long as the Central Committee does not put an end to such unsavory practices, our cultural life will not be able to make any progress, and, still worse, the youthful hopes that were called forth by the liberation of Hungary in 1944 will be smothered." For these reasons, the signatories "respectfully" asked the Central Committee "to terminate these antidemocratic methods of certain Party organs and functionaries that disfigure the Party's cultural policy, paralyze intellectual life, and sap the prestige and influence of the Party."[32]

Forceful as the language of the memorandum was (certainly for the given conditions), it did not violate Party rules. It was carefully phrased, it referred continuously (though at times with tongue in cheek) to resolutions and decisions of the Central Com-

---

[31] Purged of the offending stories, the issue of *Irodalmi Ujsag* was released for circulation.

[32] The full text of the memorandum can be found in *La Verité sur l'affaire Nagy* (Paris, Plon, 1958), pp. 150-51, and also in Aczel and Meray, *The Revolt of the Mind*, pp. 345-48.

mittee, and it sought to promote Party interests. It did not transgress the legitimate interests of the writers. It made no reference to Imre Nagy and kept silent about broader economic and political issues. Its contents, however, were divulged before a plenary session of Communist Party members of the Writers' Association on November 10, and signatures were solicited for the memorandum in the Writers' Association and outside it, among leading Communist intellectuals. Altogether fifty-nine persons are said to have signed the memorandum, but some cultural leaders, such as Gyorgy Lukacs, refused.[33] These steps constituted a clear infraction of Party rules, which prohibit the voicing of criticism "outside channels." Reading the memorandum before a plenary meeting of Party members and divulging its contents to persons outside the organization directly concerned called for disciplinary action against the writers on procedural grounds if not for substantive reasons.

The initiative for the memorandum had come from the dean of Communist journalists, Sandor Haraszti, an old member of the Party, a respected and even a beloved person, jailed by Rakosi and forsaken by his friends in his hour of trial. It was he who coaxed, bullied, and shamed writers in good standing in the Association into cooperating with him in a venture of which most of them were afraid. He chose a psychologically opportune moment, for a few weeks earlier Laszlo Benjamin, one of the repentant Stalinist poets, in a fit of moral remorse penned a truly touching poem to Haraszti, begging him for forgiveness. Written in September, 1955, the poem was finally published in June, 1956, but its contents had become known much sooner to the writers among whom it had circulated by hand. It opens with this stanza:

> Sandor, this is how we are! Lies
> Cast you into hell. This cry,
> I hurl at you from the hell into which I plunge!
> I am guilty, I who believed you a criminal!

Its closing lines are:

> And although impossible, I want to fight unto death
> To repair that which cannot be undone!

Not all writers shared these sentiments. Benjamin was one of the

33 For the names, see *ibid.*, pp. 348-50.

more sensitive, if not the most brooding, among them; but, in the climate of opinion created by Benjamin's soul-searching, it was difficult to deny Haraszti's pleas. His was the voice of conscience.

Actually, according to one of the chief participants in the collection of signatures, the writers were "scared stiff." They lived "from Party resolution to Party resolution which determined [their] entire frame of mind, mode of living, tactics, everything."

They had good reason to be worried. Rakosi had a ready pretext, if he needed one, to lower the boom on them. He called a monster meeting of Party activists from the greater Budapest area for December 6, to which he invited some twenty of the more vociferous writers. The meeting assembled in the huge hall of the Iron and Steel Workers' Union, the very place where the Rajk trial had been held. The atmosphere was indeed that of a trial, and the memorable session was commonly referred to by the writers as a "lynch trial." For in the time-honored fashion of rigged meetings, Rakosi had the entire program arranged, and a resolution condemning the writers (supposedly proposed at the meeting) had been drafted and printed in advance.

Rakosi cleverly exploited the antagonism between functionaries and intellectuals and brought the full weight of officialdom to bear against a handful of frightened writers. He correctly anticipated that the mob of functionaries would quickly warm to the fare offered them and would support with genuine, passionate derision, hatred, and scorn the accusations made from the dais against the writers. None of the writers save Gyula Hay (the only "Muscovite" to join in the writers' revolt) rose to speak in self-defense. Hay was laughed off the rostrum. He was made the object of pitiful ridicule by Rakosi's well-coordinated claque.

The resolution adopted at the meeting condemned the writers for their anti-Party attitude and mentioned some by name—Gyula Hay, Tibor Dery, Zoltan Zelk, Tibor Meray, and Tamas Aczel.[34] The writers left the meeting thoroughly beaten, intimidated, and expecting to be arrested. Arrests did not materialize, but the Central Control Commission of the Party in individual hearings with the offenders managed to persuade all but eight of the fifty-nine

[34] The resolution was printed in *Irodalmi Ujsag*, December 10, 1956.

who had signed the memorandum to withdraw their names. The eight were Haraszti, Dery, Losonczy, Vasarhelyi, Benjamin, Zelk, Aczel and the composer Szervanszky. The Party expelled some of these and deprived others of their regular means of livelihood.[35] But even those who withstood the Party's pressure had to plead guilty to an infraction of the rules of conduct. Others, though they were brave before the Control Commission, proved so fearful of the consequences of their actions that they quickly burned portions of Nagy's manuscript, which he had circulated among intimate friends for comments. The writers were in full flight.

Their clash with Rakosi occupies a unique place among the events that preceded the revolution. Yet, it was not a titanic struggle for power, but a tame intramural affair, the importance of which was exaggerated entirely out of proportion by Rakosi himself, since he wanted to use it as a springboard for a final assault on the writers. In a totalitarian system, any sign of opposition is a serious matter, mostly because the rulers choose to make it so.

The writers had no support whatever among Party cadres and they had no thought of challenging the Party leadership. The public knew nothing of their endeavor (it was informed about it only after the fact by Rakosi's resolution), did not much care, and could not have done anything to help had it known or cared. Rakosi's victory was not final for only one reason—he could not obtain Moscow's approbation to proceed as he wished. Preparations for the Twentieth Congress were nearly completed. The kind of punitive practice to which Rakosi wanted to resort was about to be scathingly condemned. The writers thus won a reprieve.

The manner in which Rakosi had engaged them revealed his dangerous dogmatism. He fought them too well but not wisely enough. His use of the bludgeon instead of the rapier was mistaken. He could have "bought off" the writers even at this advanced hour by offering them a modest amount of artistic freedom and by promising moderate reforms. They desperately wanted to believe in the people's democratic system and hoped to continue

35 Haraszti and Vasarhelyi were expelled from the Party. They were reinstated the following spring. Aczel, a former darling of the Party, had to support himself for several months by using his private automobile as a limousine for hire.

living within its framework. Greater sophistication and especially greater tolerance on his part would have yielded much better results. It was his very intransigence that ruled out any possible compromise and served as convincing proof that changes needed to be made and that these changes involved, in the first place, his removal from control over the Party. He helped to polarize issues between himself and those who stood in his way, and, as a result of his incomplete victory, the struggle against him became more muted but also more embittered.

His incessant attacks on Nagy helped to make the ex-Premier appear to be a more formidable foe than he really was in the eyes of some people, and a veritable martyr (which he was not by any standard of measurement) in the eyes of others. With less attention from Rakosi, Nagy would have attracted less attention from others as well, and he might have slowly sunk into oblivion. His expulsion from the Party was entirely gratuitous.

Rakosi's behavior and his policies contributed enormously to the proliferation of hostility throughout the Party and the nation. His choice of means to strengthen the Party's authority weakened it instead. He did not succeed either in restoring any appreciable cohesiveness in its ranks or in instilling any degree of confidence in its cadres. These followed him obediently out of fear and because they had no alternative, rather than out of conviction. Under his administration, the mild ferment that had set in earlier turned into decay and rot that menaced the Party's capacity to function properly, although for a certain period this could be hidden. With terror, Rakosi could have maintained himself in power, and he might even have succeeded in patching the weakest parts of his control system. In the absence of pervasive terror, it was bound to become increasingly evident that the society over which he presided was held together by nothing.

8. The Intellectuals, the Cadre Elite, and Public Opinion

HUNGARIAN intellectuals have been identified as the progenitors of the revolution. The part they played in precipitating revolutionary developments has been compared to that of the French *philosophes* in laying the foundations for the great French Revolution. The comparison is flattering to the Hungarians, though not entirely groundless. Massive disaffection of intellectuals is a standard pre-revolutionary symptom everywhere, and probably the least contestable of the necessary preconditions for revolutionary risings. But a point-by-point correspondence between the motives and the behavior of intellectuals in eighteenth-century France under royal absolutism and those of their twentieth-century counterparts in Hungary under Communist totalitarianism should probably not be sought.

The biggest single difference between Hungary and France (and between Poland and France) was the intimate involvement of the Hungarian and Polish intellectuals with the social system against which they rose. The French *philosophes* had been born under royal absolutism and were able to survey it with a measure of rational detachment which the Hungarian Communist intellectuals could not duplicate. The latter helped to create the totalitarian system and were part of it. They not only helped to shape it but also were its favored beneficiaries. To attack it meant to attack themselves.

The primacy of psychological factors and the central place that feelings of guilt held in them were distinctive features of the protest of Hungarian intellectuals. (Polish intellectuals, for good reason, were not so severely affected by feelings of guilt as were the Hungarians.) The slowness of the awakening of Hungarian intellectuals from the totalitarian torpor into which they had lapsed is partially explained by psychological resistance to painful self-discoveries.

The sense of guilt played a particularly important part in the "conversion" of writers and journalists. They had assisted the regime in commiting criminal acts much more directly and on a greater scale than had the technical-administrative intelligentsia. Haunted by living ghosts who sought their revenge and who did not let their tormentors rest on easy consciences, writers and journalists who were capable of experiencing moral remorse succumbed to deep internal crises—witness the high incidence of lyric and allegoric poetry written in Hungary in these years that is plainly of penitent and self-defamatory character.

Psychologically motivated, intellectuals reacted in a variety of ways. At one extreme were those who turned against the regime outright to save their integrity. At the other extreme were those who suffered overwhelming remorse and repudiated themselves. In between there was room for a gamut of motivations, some highly opportunistic. A great many intellectuals sought to buy themselves back into the favor of the nation. At the same time, they did not want to give up their Communist affiliations. They hoped to accomplish both objectives by disavowing an odious faction of the Party and by denouncing policies which they had learned were unpopular. Others just hedged, uncertain of the outcome of the power struggle in the Communist Party and fearful of being on the wrong side. After all, it took extraordinary foresight or deep conviction to adhere to a program of reforms for which there was no precedent in the annals of the Communist movement.

In the long run, spurious and genuine motives produced identical postures of opposition. From observation alone, it was difficult to differentiate between them. It is safe to say that a crassly opportunistic journalist and a grievously conscience-stricken poet made much the same practical contribution to the cause of opposition.

The stages of growth of the intellectual protest correspond closely to the phases of revolutionary incubation. Each stage represented a qualitative advance over the preceding one. But growth was very slow, and the protest movement did not attain heroic dimensions before the spring of 1956. Until then, far from dictating the tempo of change, the intellectuals took their cues from political events which they had no part in influencing and followed cautiously along trails blazed by Soviet and Polish writers. They were consistently about a year behind the Poles.

The laggardness of Hungarian intellectuals was due to several reasons, including psychological difficulties and the restrictions imposed by a still powerful Party machine. Important among them was the dominant part played by Rakosi in all Hungarian events. As long as Rakosi remained the key figure in Hungary, any progress depended on his consent or on his removal from office. Thus, the energies of those who desired reforms concentrated less on substantive issues than on the frustrating problem of dislodging Rakosi. To attack him openly was dangerous and difficult. To undermine him required a political skill of which reform-minded intellectuals were not overly possessed. The circumstances in which Hungarian intellectuals lived interposed great obstacles to sustained introspection and to the kind of unhampered, general ideological debate that would have led to a "thinking through" of problems.

No systematic exploration of the content of the ideas of Hungarian intellectuals during this period is as yet possible. Contemporary records are few and *post factum* testimony tends to include a great deal of spurious "wisdom." By inference from serious discussions with some participants (and taking into account what they said and left unsaid) it is possible to suggest that the discourse among Hungarian intellectuals was shallow and unoriginal. It did not match that of the Polish writers, poets, philosophers, and historians, some of whom probed deeply into the social determinants, philosophical premises, and ethical absolutes that form the basis of a "good society."

For example, nothing comparable to Adam Wazyk's "Poem for Adults," published on August 19, 1955, in *Nowa Kultura,* the official organ of the Polish Writers' Association, was printed in Hungary. It is doubtful if a poem of similar scope was conceived by any Hungarian poet. This is not to question the ability of Hungarian intellectuals to plumb depths reached by their Polish counterparts, but simply to record what appears to be a fact.

The distance from the descriptive exposition of the evils of the system to the prescription of remedies was a long one. Hungarian intellectuals took much time to traverse it; most of them never reached their destination. Only a very small minority, the core of which consisted of Communists who had been imprisoned, broke its affiliation with Marxist thought completely. Curiously enough, some members of this group continued to think of themselves as Communists; others did not. In any event, they made the long journey to the discovery (or rediscovery, as the case might be) of moral imperatives governing human relations, and they drew the conclusion that formal institutional and procedural safeguards, cumbersome as these might be, were indispensable preconditions of a system of government guaranteeing both freedom and justice.

The great majority of those who were at odds with the system made no break with its fundamental Leninist premises. They developed neither an independent political platform nor a distinct ideology. They were content to associate themselves with the June Program of Imre Nagy. They shared a growing revulsion of feeling against the Communist system as they knew it. In its place, they envisioned a more or less ideal model of Communism, adapted to human needs generally and to Hungarian national requirements specifically. They did not want to abolish one-party government, but to reform it.

They wished to eliminate the entrenched Communist leadership, which had become personally obnoxious to them, introduce greater freedom and democratic practices in the Party, tone down the harshness of Communist rule, assure greater legal protection against arbitrary persecution of Communists and non-Communists, and devise more equitable economic policies which, though they did not follow the dictates of the "market," took account of the normal appetites of people for gratification. Finally, they wished to create a political instrument (such as the Patriotic People's Front) that would draw the population into at least symbolic participation in the management of its own affairs. They did not want genuine government of and by the people. But, at least, they wanted government for the people not against it.

This predominant trend of thought rested on questionable logic and reflected emotional and wishful thinking. It made for partial solutions of problems and tended to glorify a hybrid system of government whose capacity for survival yet remains to be tested. Neither was it compatible with the canons of Leninism, no matter how charitably these are interpreted, nor did it meet the acid test of real freedom. The inconsistencies of thought and emotion of a majority of the intellectuals that opposed Rakosi caused further differentiation among them, especially in the heat of revolution, which revealed that many of the views they held were incompatible with one another. Some, who were already susceptible to democratic ideas, capitulated to them completely. Others were driven back to the acceptance of a line of reasoning more consistent with orthodox Leninism. The former joined the revolution. The latter stayed neutral in it and later found it possible to serve Kadar.

In the promotion of protest among intellectuals, rehabilitated victims of Communist terror played a preeminent part. They were ahead of the rest of the intellectual community in their thinking about the deficiencies of the Communist system. They had been through their purgatory and had no reason to harbor guilt feelings. All were restored to good standing in the Party. This was an honor some did not particularly cherish, but it could not be refused. Many found occupations commensurate with their talents at universities, institutes of learning and research, libraries, publishing houses, journals, and periodicals. Although a few were invited to take on political jobs, all declined except Janos Kadar, who became Party secretary in a working-class district of Budapest and gradually worked his way up the ladder of the hierarchy. Because they had been political prisoners, they could not be elected to executive posts in any social or mass organization. But they had opportunities to circulate rather more freely than most people and to exert influence informally, often using the added prestige of their incarceration to best advantage. They made a fetish of referring to themselves as "enemies of the people."

Some of them displayed human qualities that only one or two of those who had not been in prison possessed—an obsessive determination to fight the sectarian leadership to the end and a courage verging on recklessness. Geza Losonczy and his father-in-law Sandor Haraszti were cases in point. Haraszti went about like a man possessed (though he was far from demented), buttonholing people and informing them of the absolute necessity to remove Rakosi from office. He was the *spiritus movens* of the writers' memorandum of 1955. He conceived the idea, wrote the draft, and coaxed writers in good standing (e.g., Tamas Aczel) into collecting signatures for it. Losonczy, in turn, flatly rejected Rakosi's advances to enlist his services in the cause of the Party. And it was at his home that the dispirited writers found overnight refuge after their harrowing "lynch trial" in December, 1955. He was not afraid to offer asylum to those whom the Party had just ostracized. Of those who had not been in disgrace during the Stalinist era, only Miklos Vasarhelyi showed similar mettle.

Several rehabilitated intellectuals (Ferenc Donath, Geza Losonczy, Gyorgy Heltai, Szilard Ujhelyi, Jozsef Szilagyi) sooner or later clustered around Imre Nagy and became his faithful and intimate friends. Not all of these had been in prison, and they did not form an organized group. A few had close affiliations with writers and journalists. Others stood closer to the Petofi Circle, the nascent organizational vehicle of the technical-administrative intelligentsia. Their activities were far from spectacular. Nevertheless, they formed a Communist political reserve to staff high Party and government posts should the opposition prevail.

Apart from them, two major groups in the protest movement of intellectuals had to be distinguished—the writers and journalists on the one hand and the technical-administrative intelligentsia on the other.[1]

There was no lack of spontaneous rapport between the two groups, but overt collaboration was ruled out by Communist organizational controls. Even covert contacts remained sporadic up to the spring of 1956. Until then the technical-administrative intelligentsia was condemned to silence; it had no ready outlets for its ideas and the scientific or professional topics of concern to it could not be debated in public.

[1] Academic personalities, in the author's estimation, fit into the second group in accordance with their disciplinary identification—historians, economists, etc.

Only journalists and writers had access to communications media and could articulate protest in a variety of guises, some of which had a chance of eluding censure. The government encouraged straight journalistic and literary exposition of conditions in the country. Furthermore, the writers and journalists could inferentially universalize demands for human liberties by subsuming these under their own legitimate quest for artistic self-expression and for freedom from authoritarian bureaucratic interference.

But until the spring of 1956, the literary product of active members of the Writers' Association was meager and uninteresting. For self-protection they often had recourse to Aesopian language which obscured the meaning of their message. Because of their Stalinist past, they met with suspicion and skepticism. Although several writers reacted strongly to conditions they found among the masses and wrote about them with feeling, even they did not succeed in ingratiating themselves with the public, which preferred the revival of Hungarian classics and the restoration to good standing of "reactionary" writers such as Nemeth, Kodolanyi, Sinka, and Kolozsvari-Grandpierre.

The writers remained isolated in the nation and in the Party. They had only tenuous contacts with Nagy. They had few trustworthy friends among Party functionaries. Those they could count on were not highly placed. The most that could be expected of them was to keep the writers informed about happenings inside the Party.

The writers were thus discoursing mostly among themselves—in reality, a small group of two or three dozen *engagés* whose activities went almost unnoticed except by the Party command and by like-minded intellectuals in the capital. The situation of the journalists was still more difficult. Although they had the best opportunity to reach the public through the daily and the periodical press, they were under constant surveillance by the Party, which could and did take effective reprisals against them either through outright dismissal or through transfer to a post in an environment that inhibited criticism altogether. Several journalists were sent to the provinces. Others were sent abroad, where they were, of course, out of touch with events in Hungary. Their dispatches were easily "sanitized" before they reached the public. Scattered, the journalists were deprived of the first requisite for coalescing into an opposition group—an organizational base. The writers were more fortunate in this respect.

The Writers' Association made its main contribution to the development of protest against Rakosi as the first and for many months the only sanctuary in which oppositional ideas could be nurtured. This service was invaluable. For it, the Association earned the gratitude and gained the respect of all opposition-minded intellectuals. These eventually sought advice and guidance from the writers to advance their own struggle against the first secretary.

THE ROLE OF THE TECHNICAL-ADMINISTRATIVE INTELLIGENTSIA

The participation of the technical-administrative intelligentsia in the opposition to Rakosi is even more difficult to determine than that of the writers and journalists. It was a larger and more diffuse group, scattered throughout all institutions of the Party and the state, and unable to articulate views in any easily communicable manner. The evolution of its ideas can be charted from the growth of the Petofi Circle, which became its forum.

The Petofi Circle was officially "founded" only in March, 1956. It was then that it revealed itself to the public and acquired status as a recognized institution. But it had been in existence since the winter of 1954, and it had played an important part even in its incipient stages of development. It was established at the very end of the premiership of Imre Nagy as an informal "circle" of friends within the Kossuth Club, a debating society for intellectuals which was a part of the Society for the Dissemination of Scientific and Political Knowledge—a center for mass enlightenment patterned after a Soviet organization of the same name.

Unlike the Writers' Association, whose membership was professionally determined and limited, the Petofi Circle attracted intellectuals from all walks of life—from the universities, the professions, the arts and sciences, government offices, and economic institutions. It reached important layers of the Communist Party membership and even functionaries in various institutions. Further-more, it could (and did) act as a clearing house for contacts between Communists and non-Communists. It was in and around the Petofi Circle that the wartime Gyorffy College and the postwar NEKOSZ groups of Communists and populists were able to con-gregate once more to renew acquaintances and to exchange opinions. The core of the Petofi Circle consisted of this amalgam of Com-munists and populists.[2] Here, in informal quiet discussion, old friends who had been separated for years rediscovered a community of thought about social, political, and economic issues. They also learned quite unexpectedly that their views were largely shared by still younger generations of Communist officials with whom they had no prior acquaintance.

Although the Circle accommodated Communists in good stand-ing, it was to a far greater extent frequented by those who had been cast out. It had been from its inception a focus of opposition in which the national element was coequal with, if not predomi-nant over, the Communist element. The same could not be said of the Writers' Association, whose members had become seriously alienated from the nation. For these reasons the Petofi Circle always had a greater potential than had the Writers' Association for becoming a political center of opposition. Within it, Hungary's forgotten children of destiny, the country's natural political elite, found haven. The thin, worn thread of continuity in Hungary's modern awakening and search for fulfillment, which for years had been lost from sight, reappeared here.

It was not by accident that in the spring of 1956, when the struggle between the opposition and the sectarian Communist leadership reached its crucial phase, the Petofi Circle at one stroke developed into "the second leading center" in the country, chal-lenging the authority of the duly constituted Party center.[3]

Initially, the Circle survived because its modest activities barely

[2] As soon as it became an official organization, formal membership in it was, of course, restricted to Communists.

[3] It was Erno Gero who labeled the Petofi Circle "the second leading center" (in Communist parlance a term with a very definite meaning) in July, 1956. He could have paid no more glowing tribute to the Circle had he deliberately set out to do so. See P. Zinner, ed., *National Communism*, p. 345.

aroused attention. As the Party leadership began to sense the attraction the Circle had for opposition-minded Hungarian youths, it tried not to smother it but to make it an instrument of policy that would help to draw young people to Communism. A many-sided struggle followed between Party satraps, who wished to extend their influence over the Circle, and the original core membership of the Circle, which fought with skill and determination to retain the autonomy of their organization.

Without the close personal friendship and the trustworthiness of its small nucleus of leaders, the Petofi Circle could not have withstood that intricate struggle. By the time the Party, in exasperation, decided to annihilate the Circle—in July, 1956—it was too late.

THE ROLE OF THE PARTY CADRES

The part played by the leading cadres of the Party during the period of revolutionary incubation is perhaps less well understood (and has received far less systematic attention) than that of any other group in Hungary. They had no spokesmen of their own, and few among their members fled Hungary after the revolution to tell their story. Yet they played an important and ambiguous role, important in part because of its ambiguity.

They were dubbed the "praetorian guard" of the Party and as such were regarded as its main source of strength. That they defended the Party is true beyond doubt, but all Communists did that, each in his own way. The question was whose Party was being defended—Rakosi's, Nagy's, or some one else's?

At first, the Party cadres lined up solidly with Rakosi. They had nowhere else to turn. Being Party cadres, under the strictest discipline, most exposed to the whims of the leadership, and least capable of broadening their vistas of the political situation in the country, they had no independent opinions. They lacked the power to turn against the Party leadership even if they had been inclined to do so. A "revolt of the clerks" is the least likely occurrence in a highly structured, hierarchial organization. The impulse for a shift in allegiances followed by action usually comes from the top, from among highly placed persons who have become disaffected.

But it was precisely this eventuality against which Rakosi guarded by the ruthless elimination of all prominent "home" Communists during the preceding years. Native cadres were tied to the "Muscovite" leadership and dependent upon it.

Imre Nagy's well-meant but maladroitly staged entrance upon the scene in July, 1953, drove the Party's cadres still further into Rakosi's arms. They were thoroughly alarmed at Nagy's intentions and at the implications of his program. Rakosi, it will be remembered, hastened to their aid—not out of altruism, but because he depended on their support more than they depended on his.

From this point on, through the backing and filling of the ensuing years, Party cadres were under incessant multiple pressures that weighed heavily on them—from the sectarian Party command, from the reformist opposition, and from the mass of the population. While the pressure from the sectarian leadership was greater than that exerted by the reformist opposition and the people together, it would be incorrect to assume that Party cadres did not respond to the revealed plight of the population. Their alienation from the social environment was in most cases substantial but not yet complete. They had not forsaken their origins irrevocably or severed their ties with the people and with the groups from which they came.

This is not to say that they were moved by humanitarian considerations. But once the premises upon which they acted during the Stalinist period were withdrawn, as they were during the incubation stage of the revolution, inner conflicts which until then they had suppressed (or of which they had not been aware) rose to the surface.

They now had to face up to conflicting values and motives within themselves. They found that they were accountable for their deeds after all, to the people and not only to their Party bosses, and that the situation which they had been led to believe was irreversible, if not reversible was certainly subject to change and to reevaluation in an unaccustomed light.

As the overall position of the Party cadres vis-à-vis their environment deteriorated, their insecurity over their status within the Party increased, while outside the Party they had to deal with a more hostile population. In effect, the Party cadres were made to bear the brunt of the blame for mistakes and were manipulated in such a way as to take the heat off the top command. Usually the cadres least responsible for policy (that is the lowest-placed functionaries) were under greatest pressure. They were under crossfire from the people, with whom they had daily personal contacts, and from the Party, which demanded increasingly distasteful services while offering less effective protection.

This unhealthy state of affairs had adverse repercussions on the loyalty of cadres. In time, they began to discover that they were being used by the leadership. They were chagrined to learn that the leadership had no loyalty toward them. In most cases, these discoveries came late, at the end of 1955 or more likely in the spring of 1956. They led Party cadres to a further realization: that they could dissociate themselves from the leadership and that, if the Party offered them no protection against the people, they could seek it themselves.

Lower-level officials began ingratiating themselves with the people. Higher-level officials became more tractable. They broke out of their social isolation, saw old "reactionary" friends again, and occasionally admitted being disoriented and concerned about their personal future. Even secret police officials were known to curry the favor of their former victims so as to have a ready defense just in case. In jails, the treatment of prisoners grew more humane. Small services (for bribes, of course) that are normal fare in most prison systems but that had been inconceivable in Hungary under Stalinist terror were now gladly provided.

It took a long time and many bitter experiences before Party cadres even began to abandon the "Muscovite" leadership. They lagged behind the intellectuals by about eighteen months in thawing out from the posture into which they had been frozen in the Stalinist period, and they never progressed far enough to join forces with the right-wing opposition. Their morale deteriorated rapidly during the months preceding the revolution, and although their state of mind did not reach a disaster point before the actual outbreak of violence, it contributed appreciably to the disorganization of the Party. Certainly without these psychological antecedents, the behavior of Party cadres in the revolution would be incomprehensible. For when the "praetorian guard" was most needed, it was not to be found.

THE ROLE OF THE POPULATION

Until they rose in wrath against the government, the contribution of the masses to their emancipation from Communist tyranny was negligible. Over the entire period of prerevolutionary thaw, neither peasants nor workers showed a marked propensity for social action. This is not said by way of disparagement, for the opportunities for organized social action were lacking, and no group of people may be judged for failing to act recklessly.

Paradoxical as it may appear, their apathy was due to their alienation from the system. Only a few people among the many who felt exhilarated by Nagy's words in 1953 translated their enthusiasm into positive action. Most people took their cues from the Party, and, since it did not energetically espouse the promised reforms, they felt constrained to satisfy themselves with minor acts of self-seeking. Political indifference was in no sense incompatible with active probing for the satisfaction of individual material wants. Disenchantment with and estrangement from the regime grew in proportion to the successive frustration of every new hope and the repeated failure of the Party to redeem its promises. At best, the people thought that the struggle within the Party (in so far as they were aware of it or interpreted intra-Party developments as a struggle) was of no concern to them. At worst, they looked at it as a sham that was designed to hoodwink the population.

This astonishing distance increased with time, despite some amelioration in the conditions of daily life. It was the salient feature of the Hungarian political scene up to the day of the revolution. Every new policy of the government had a deleterious effect on popular attitudes and moods.

The intended cure for grave economic ills that beset the country as a result of the adventurous policies of the Stalinist era proved in some respects worse than the disease. The removal of certain intolerable pressures that had derived from the unreasonable pace of industrialization created new pressures of a different kind. As a result of the contraction of the rate of economic expansion, the threat of technological unemployment arose. University students, high school graduates, and students of trade schools suddenly faced a spectre they had thought was not known to socialism. This had a devastating influence on their loyalty toward the regime. A high school teacher reported a disastrous drop of discipline and rise of delinquency among his students in 1954 and 1955, as their fears of finding no employment mounted. Similar worries, though perhaps expressed in different behavior, gripped university students. They had simply taken it for granted that the government owed them good jobs when they finished their education.

But not only students were affected. Workers whose expectations of upward mobility were thwarted also felt cheated, as did managers and administrators who lost the positions they had already attained. Improper staffing with inadequately trained personnel was a bane of the Hungarian economy recognized by everyone. To correct it, a sweeping program of "rationalization" was decreed in 1954. It was, in the opinion of an ex-Communist refugee, a "cruel" step. It created havoc among privileged members of the society the Communists were building. Forgetting that their rise in status was undeserved to begin with, they now bore a deep-seated grudge against the regime that first had raised and then dropped them to a level more befitting their talents. A number of peasant and worker youths were adversely affected by these decisions and turned into bitter enemies of Communism. The beneficiaries of "rationalization" were for the most part "declassed" middle-class experts, managers, and technicians. Although they were grateful for the favors bestowed on them and were surprisingly well received in their new environment, they did not become ardent supporters of the regime but remained politically neutral.

Above and beyond economic policies, the subsidence of terror under Nagy's administration and the imposition of new restrictions under Rakosi had a profound influence on the attitude and the behavior of the masses.

With the attenuation of terror, fear changed to contempt and dissimulation gave way to evasion. Informal channels could again be tested to obtain satisfaction outside and against official prescriptions, and it was possible to seek redress for wrongs done by the authorities. The imposition of new restrictions forced people to abandon practices to which they had been growing accustomed and to become submissive once more toward officialdom. This made them angry and exacerbated their aggressive feelings toward the Party.

An important development of the prerevolutionary period was the reappearance of at least the rudiments of an autonomous public opinion. Its growth was stimulated by a gradual dissipation of distrust and suspiciousness and by a better understanding of the forces that controlled the people's daily lives. Nagy had given them an invaluable standard by which to judge the performance of the system. The ideas he had propounded could not be eradicated from consciousness even after they were condemned. Once people had begun to talk to one another, they tended to reinforce and confirm their convictions. The psychological importance of the knowledge that one shares views with others needs no explanation. The people's terrible sense of isolation was somewhat relieved. This was an essential prerequisite for any meaningful social integration and for expressive behavior directed through institutions. Hungary never quite reached that point before revolution broke out.

Group solidarity developed slowly. The social fabric of the nation had been too severely damaged under Stalinism to be repaired in short order and under the difficulties interposed by the semi-Stalinist government of Rakosi. Egocentrism remained the hallmark of the prerevolutionary period, but interpersonal conflicts now diminished in relation to hostility directed against the system, and the people concentrated their energies on improving their welfare, instead of being reduced to struggling merely to preserve their psychic integrity. Exasperation, too, had a quality of impatient anger rather than of resignation or despair.

The mood that seized the population is not unfamiliar, although its intensity probably exceeded anything normally experienced. A partial release of controls in the presence of pent-up desire for gratification tends to create greater disturbance than continued denial of gratification. The problem of decontrol is always to avoid a stampede. No satisfactory solution has yet been devised to minimize this danger. Voluntary restraint is not a quality possessed by the masses except under unusual circumstances of perceived necessity. There was no reason why Hungarians should be patient with the government and have a superior sense of responsibility toward it, especially since it gave repeated evidence of its bad faith, denied them any meaningful participation in the management of their own affairs, and treated them as if they were totally irresponsible.

The regime arrogated to itself all power of decision and acted in behalf of everyone. It was natural to blame it for everything, in turn, including evils which were not of its making. People tended to rationalize their own failures and disappointments by attributing them to some real or imaginary act of the authorities. Their feelings of dissatisfaction were often incommensurate with the actual deprivation from which they were currently suffering. They reflected an accumulation of past grievances and unfulfilled hopes. Their expectations exceeded anything that they could provide for themselves or that the government could reasonably give them even under ideal circumstances.

All told, a deep discontent saturated the whole society. Of and by itself, it was insufficient to cause an upheaval. It could not be expressed in an orderly, organized manner. But precisely because of its diffuseness, it was like a highly inflammable substance that needed only a spark to ignite and flare up into uncontrolled conflagration.

9. The Anti-Stalin Campaign

KHRUSHCHEV's secret address before the Twentieth Congress of the the CPSU, in which he dwelt at length on the evils of the cult of personality, was meant to do more than merely denigrate Stalin and blame him for past horrors. It was designed to liquidate Stalinism as a form of government and to rout its exponents throughout Soviet officialdom. It was a promise of permanent change in the style of government and a pledge against the recurrence of the arbitrariness that threatened the personal security of all. It was a summing up of accomplishments since Stalin's death and a projection of a course of action for the future.

The speech was made in closed session. No text of it was published in the Soviet Union or any other Communist-dominated country. Yet it was a turning point in the history of the entire international Communist movement. It precipitated a general moral crisis in the Communist world. Nowhere were its effects more explosive than in Hungary, perhaps because nowhere else was Stalinism still as firmly entrenched as there.

The content of Khrushchev's speech rapidly became known to Communist functionaries, among whom it spread consternation. They now sensed that a major shake-up in the command structure of the Party was inevitable. From the functionaries, the intellectuals and other opposition elements also learned about the speech. They welcomed it as a mandate for bold action against Rakosi. For the first time, they felt courageous enough to carry the fight to him and to force issues instead of waiting for openings made by others.

Between March and October, 1956, events in Poland and Hungary developed along parallel lines, but, on closer examination

contrasts come to light that yield valuable clues for an understanding why that tumultuous period ended so differently in the
two countries.

One important distinction was due to chance. In Poland, the
post of first secretary of the Communist Party was vacated on
March 12, 1956, as a result of the death of Boleslaw Bierut, the
country's chief Stalinist. The new secretary, Edward Ochab, was
not precisely reform-minded, but he was not as deeply committed
to Stalinist practices as his predecessor had been. In Hungary,
Rakosi remained at the head of the Party and blocked every
attempt at a liquidation of Stalinism. It took four and a half
months to remove him from office.

Thus in Poland the anti-Stalin campaign gained immediate
momentum and pointed toward broad political, economic, and
cultural reforms and toward changes in leadership, while Hungary
still inched ahead toward the removal of the remnants of Stalinism.

A meeting of the Polish Council of Culture and Arts on March
24-25 and a membership meeting of the Hungarian Writers'
Association on March 30 recorded the temper of intellectuals in
both countries. While the Poles scathingly attacked past cultural
policies,[1] the Hungarians showed their defiance of the regime by
soundly defeating the Party's candidate for the secretaryship of
the Writers' Association. They elected instead by almost unanimous vote (103-2) Geza Kepes, a poet and former member of
the National Peasant Party.

In April, expectations of vast improvement mounted to fever
pitch in Poland. The session of the Sejm (Parliament) which
opened on April 23 witnessed unprecedented expressions of hope
that the legislative body would develop into a meaningful organ
of government. In his opening speech, the Prime Minister, Josef
Czyrankiewicz, a defender rather than a critic of the administration,

---

[1] E.g., Jan Kott: "Whenever facts stood in the way, they were changed. If
genuine heroes were obstacles, they evaporated. . . . The false theory of the
mechanical rotting of art in bourgeois society in the imperialist epoch was
accompanied by a theory of the automatic flourishing of art in socialist society."
Or, Antoni Slonimski: "The history of philosophy knows few periods in which
intolerance had so greatly increased as that of the last few years." P. Zinner, ed.,
National Communism, pp. 48-49.

declared: "It would be naïve to deny that the Sejm . . . has not properly discharged its constitutional functions. . . . The Sejm began to fulfil that role only during these days. . . . Today we have conditions enabling [the process of democratization] to proceed with increasing speed. . . . We are beginning to work out proper forms and proper practices. We want the Sejm really to become . . . the supreme legislative body, supervising the activity of all lower state organs." [2]

Although public mood ran well ahead of the Party at this time, and although the exaggerated hopes attached to the role of the Sejm stemmed largely from spontaneous expressions of strongly revisionist, not to say liberal, deputies, the authorities themselves seemed to encourage debate and were not unalterably opposed to Parliament's becoming a sounding board for criticism. This contrasted sharply with the attitude of the Hungarian Party.

The dismissal of Stalinist ministers from the Polish government, followed by the resignation (on May 6) of Jakub Berman, the *eminence grise* of Polish Communism, from the Politbureau and from the government, in which he held a deputy premiership, gave the public assurance that the diehards were being weeded out.

In Hungary, no comparable events took place. The duel between the intellectuals and Rakosi, however, increased in intensity, with both the Writers' Association and the Petofi Circle taking the offensive.

After two months of thaw, both Ochab and Rakosi tried to stem the rising flood of criticism and to restore the authority of the Party. They took to the pages of *Pravda*. Ochab's article of April 29, however, was much milder and defensive in tone than was Rakosi's evaluation of May 2.

At the end of June, the Petofi Circle in Hungary (June 27) and the workers of Poznan in Poland (June 28) staged minor rebellions against the government. The Petofi Circle organized a so-called journalists' debate—the last of a series of public discussions exposing the nature of the Rakosi regime—which attracted an audience of several thousand and turned into a demonstration against the government. The Poznan workers rioted against the authorities and

2 *Ibid.*, pp. 95-96.

smashed government property, including the local police station. Theirs was an act born of exasperation over repeated failures to win a hearing for their economic grievances. Though triggered by material discontent, it had far-reaching political and social implications.

Both parties reacted instinctively with strongly worded condemnations of the disturbances. The Poles assailed the Poznan riot as a provocation by foreign agents. The Hungarians, in turn, compared the Petofi Circle meeting with the Poznan riot as an act of defiance. They hastily issued a Central Committee resolution condemning the Petofi Circle and all those connected with it. The resolution set the stage for reprisals against offending intellectuals.

The Poles quickly gained second thoughts about the nature of the workers' dissatisfaction, toned down their condemnation, admitted that the rioters had justified economic grievances, laid the blame for these to fossilized bureaucrats, and promised improvements.

Apparently the Polish Communist leadership took the Poznan riot very much to heart as a warning of deep-seated unrest and decided to do something about it. The plenary session of the Polish Communist Central Committee that opened on July 18 reflected this chastened mood. The resolution adopted by the Central Committee was a forward-looking document that reflected the spirit of popular demands.

In a move of still greater importance, the Central Committee reinstated Wladyslaw Gomulka, Poland's leading "national Communist," the Party's erstwhile secretary general, who had been in disgrace since 1949. A special communiqué announced his reinstatement on August 4. At the same time, two of his associates, Marian Spychalski and Zenon Kliszko, were also exonerated of charges of national deviation. Kliszko was made undersecretary of state in the Ministry of Justice, and another rehabilitated national Communist, General Waclaw Komar, was made chief of the police forces under the Ministry of the Interior.

Time did not stand still in Hungary either. On July 18, the Communist Central Committee also convened. To everybody's

surprise, Rakosi was cashiered. His plans to deal with the opposition came to naught, but, even without Rakosi, the Communist
leadership could not quite come to terms with justified demands
for reforms. No concessions were made to Imre Nagy and his
supporters. Nagy was not readmitted to the Party, and none of
his associates were elected to the Party leadership, although some
rehabilitated Communist functionaries were (e.g., Kadar, Kallai,
Marosan). Gero took up the cudgels against the intellectuals where
Rakosi had dropped them. The resolution adopted by the Central
Committee contained a disappointing conglomeration of familiar
themes phrased in stock Communist terminology. The hoped-for
breakthrough did not materialize.

With the head start it had gained during the spring and early
summer, Poland had a better chance than had Hungary of avoiding
popular upheaval as a means of resolving internal problems. In
Poland, there was some release of tensions over a period of time,
and also some tangible evidence of improvements. In Hungary,
tensions mounted, and the government continued to temporize.
The Polish Communists seemed to have a finger on the pulse of
public opinion, while the Hungarians did not. In the end, the
Polish Communists managed, though not without difficulty, to
adjust power relations among themselves and to stay on top of a
rapidly evolving situation. The Hungarians failed abysmally on
both counts.

ANTI-STALINISM IN LOW GEAR: MARCH-JUNE, 1956

Availing themselves of the opportunities created by the Twentieth
Congress of the CPSU, Hungarian intellectuals mounted a two-
pronged offensive against Rakosi—through the Writers' Association
and through the Petofi Circle. The writers used *Irodalmi Ujasg*
to good advantage in articulating their grievances. In a short
time, their mood communicated itself to the people, who also
understood that a fundamental change in the presuppositions
underlying the operations of the Communist system had occurred.
The people now cast away their reserve toward the writers and
began recognizing in them genuine representatives of their own
aspirations for greater freedom. At last, the discourse among

Communist intellectuals transcended the confines of the Party. Some of the writers (e.g., Tibor Dery) gained nationwide prestige. *Irodalmi Ujsag,* in turn, enjoyed previously unknown and unimaginable popularity. Every issue was snapped up at newsstands as soon as it appeared. People were anxious to see each new installment of the writers' struggle with the Communist leadership. Issues of the journal were at a premium in the countryside as well.

The Petofi Circle, in its own right, helped to popularize antiregime views and to mold public opinion in a series of debates and reunions it sponsored. The leaders of the Circle decided that at this stage their usefulness would be enhanced if they emerged from obscurity and revealed themselves to the public.[3]

To introduce itself, the Circle organized a Hungarian-Yugoslav friendship evening; the political connotations of that event required no explanation. About two hundred persons attended. The Petofi Circle was launched on its public career.

There followed a series of scientific and scholarly lectures on Marxist political economy, historiography, and philosophy. These topics were purposely chosen to eschew strictly practical political issues, which in the judgment of the Petofi Circle's leaders were even at this time too risky. The debates were meticulously prepared. Discussion leaders were selected in accordance with their political reliability from the point of view of the opposition. The manner of presentation and even the discussion that was to follow were prearranged in considerable detail through prior consultation with the designated participants. Of course, each debate had to be authorized by the Party leadership. Great care had to be taken to present it as innocuously as possible.

The first debate, on political economy, was a huge success. About four hundred persons attended. It broke up at midnight and had to be continued a week later when an audience of six hundred turned up and filled all the rooms of the Kossuth Club. Ferenc Donath, Tamas Nagy, and Kalman Szabo were the dis-

3 At the turn of the year, the informal "circle" became a formal organization, an adjunct of the Communist Youth Association (DISZ). In this capacity, it organized evening discussions of limited scope. They were attended by two or three dozen persons. This phase of the Circle's activity terminated in the middle of March.

cussion leaders. The discussion ended in a complete rout of the official representatives of the Party, including Istvan Friss, who at the time headed a section in the Planning Office. Friss, called upon to answer the critical comments of the participants, declined.

By way of rebuttal, the Party, three days later, organized a debate about the proposed five-year plan at which the same Friss was the main speaker. He viciously attacked the Petofi Circle, but hecklers in the audience demanded to know why he had not spoken up at its debate. The Party's attempt to smear the Circle failed. If anything, it gave the Circle welcome publicity.

The second debate, on problems of historiography, was attended by six hundred people and it too had to be resumed on the following day, for, at midnight of the first evening, twenty-five discussants had not yet had their say. The Party's official representative, Erzsebet Andics, who was then in charge of the cultural section of the Party's Secretariat, suffered a defeat as humiliating as that of Friss.

The third debate, on Marxist philosophy, held early in June, was presided over by Gyorgy Lukacs. It attracted a mob of over a thousand. (Since they could not be accommodated in the Kossuth Club, the meeting was shifted to a nearby university.) In his address, Lukacs noted the "bankruptcy of Marxism in Hungary." With the philosophers' debate, the first phase of the Petofi Circle's overt activities ended.

Immediately after the conclusion of this cycle of scholarly lectures, there followed a number of public reunions of much greater political relevance. These lasted through June. A reunion of Gyorffy College alumni brought together some of the younger members of the Party and government leadership with former close associates who were now in the opposition. The latter reportedly seized the occasion to remonstrate with the Party officials for betraying the common cause to which they all had once been dedicated.

Another meeting of old Party workers and young intellectuals was attended by about a thousand persons and resulted in bitter recriminations against the policy of the Party by veteran "home"

Communists, who felt that they had been shunted to the side-lines. It also witnessed a dramatic appearance by Mrs. Julia Rajk, who demanded full vindication for her husband and the punishment of those who were responsible for his execution.

The final meeting of the spring was held on June 27. It was the celebrated journalists' debate over which Marton Horvath, Geza Losonczy, and Gyorgy Mate presided. It had an overflow audience of several thousands and lasted from 7 P.M. to 3 A.M., at which time seventy would-be speakers still waited for their turn to address the crowd. In the supercharged atmosphere of the meeting, writers, journalists, and other intellectuals openly demanded the resignation of Rakosi and bade the government to end police interference with the freedom of the press. The character of the meeting was truly insurrectionary. Defenders of the regime were hooted down, and the secret police personnel scattered through the crowd were afraid to intervene.

The Party retaliated with a stern Central Committee resolution, and the Petofi Circle "drew in its horns." Its public activities ceased. The leaders fully expected that they and their sympathizers would be caught in a police dragnet and jailed.

In the brief span of its public existence, the Petofi Circle accomplished a great deal. Its magnetic attraction was best demonstrated by the rapidly growing numbers who attended its meetings. Considering that it received no written publicity and that it had no budget to publicize itself, its achievements were truly remarkable. The protocols of its meetings were not circulated in written form. They were passed on by word of mouth with incredible speed. The morning after a debate the capital buzzed with excitement over the latest exploit of the Circle. But the influence of the Circle did not reach beyond intellectuals, and its leaders had no ambitions to establish closer contacts with peasants and workers—at least not yet. They had no organizational network outside Budapest, and it was too much to expect of workers and peasants to take any interest in the type of intellectual debates it conducted.

The maneuvers of the Circle's leaders to circumvent the Party's restrictive regulations were devious and ingenious. The official executive board of the Circle was elected only at the end of May.[4] It was selected by the leaders in such a way as to thwart the Party's attempt to pack it. The slate was introduced at the public meeting on Marxist historiography and immediately voted on by acclamation so as to present the Party leadership with a *fait accompli*. Even so, the board had to include official representatives of the Party and its youth organization, and the task of the leadership was to work with and around these Stalinist stooges in a manner that would neither arouse their suspicion nor vitiate the purposes of the Circle.

The Party's efforts to control the Circle included the appointment of a committee to supervise its activities,[5] the infiltration of the Circle by secret police agents, the continuous shadowing of its leaders, and the threat of reprisals. The climate of opinion was not conducive to peremptory liquidation of the Circle and its active participants. The Party, despite its narrow, sectarian outlook, did not want to give the impression of being completely hidebound. But even the grudging permissiveness shown by Rakosi had an ulterior motive. Although he was now on the defensive, he schemed to entrap all the intellectuals opposed to him. He gave them a chance to reveal themselves and planned to arrest them at an opportune moment. That moment, he thought, had come after the June 27 debate of the Petofi Circle. But he was cashiered instead.

Aside from the Petofi Circle and the Writers' Association, other centers of opposition also sprang up. The country's intellectuals suddenly came alive, especially in the literary and journalistic fields. A number of publications staffed with opposition and even non-Communist personnel came into being and printed bold literary fare. Among such journals and periodicals were: *Beke es Szababsag*, where Meray and Aczel found employment; *Magyar Nemzet*, with Losonczy on its staff; *Uj Hang, Csillag, Muvelt Nep*, and, later *Hetfoi Hirlap*, an almost openly anti-regime paper with bourgeois journalists on its staff. Non-Communist writers also be-

---

4 The list of names is given in *La Vérité sur l'affaire Nagy*, pp. 64-65.

5 The members of the committee were Bela Szalai, Erzsebet Andics, Marton Horvath, Ervin Hollos, Sandor Nogradi, and Laszlo Orban.

gan to publish. Personal contacts between Communist and non-Communist writers were gradually developing.

Meanwhile, the morale of Party cadres steadily deteriorated. They were bewildered by indecisive and conflicting directives. Their job security was at its lowest ebb. Rakosi, who had the key to burning questions that were in everybody's mind, aggravated matters by his dilatory tactics. When he returned from Moscow, where he had attended the Party Congress, he acted as if nothing unusual had occurred or as if what had transpired there had no applicability to Hungary. He made a routine report to the Central Committee on March 12 in which he did not dwell on the evils of the cult of personality, although he extolled the virtues of "Leninist collective leadership." He affirmed the correctness of the policies that had been adopted a year before and went out of his way to attack "the irresponsible and demagogic [?] economic policy of right wing deviation pursued by the former Chairman of the Council of Ministers, Imre Nagy."[6] He made no mention of Rajk and ignored completely the whole question of victimized Communists.

He realized that for the time being he could not deal harshly with his opponents, and he took more abuse from them than he would have under normal circumstances. But he obviously hoped to be able to ride out the storm raised by Khrushchev's speech, underestimating both the fury to which it was yet to rise and Khrushchev's tenacity in the face of opposition from powerful members of the Soviet Presidium. He confidently looked forward to Khrushchev's fall, in which case all would be well. As long as he lived with such a hope, there was no point in admitting any past errors and there was certainly no sense in accepting any responsibility for his own complicity in the irregularities. Although his position grew more ludicrous every day, he held fast to it as long as he could.

At the end of March, he made the first grudging admission that there had been irregularities in the Rajk affair. He announced that the matter had been reviewed and that rehabilitations, in-

[6] For an English language text of Rakosi's speech, see *For a Lasting Peace, for a People's Democracy*, March 23, 1956.

cluding those of former Social Democrats, were making progress. Once again, he laid the blame on Peter and the secret police apparatus. Lame as his explanation was—indeed one wonders how it could have been believed by anyone—it was still not exposed as completely false. By this time, he alone among the East European Communists had failed to exonerate his victims of the trumped-up charges which alleged that they had conspired with Tito. Even the Czechs, who did not rehabilitate Rudolf Slansky and his major accomplices, had the good grace to retract that portion of the indictment.

Rakosi finally broke the pattern of his retreat on May 18. Addressing the Budapest activists once more, he acknowledged his complicity in the frame-up of Laszlo Rajk, but he coupled this admission with a counterattack in which he warned that the class struggle "continues in our country," thus necessitating the sort of vigilance he always had advocated.[7] Instead of resigning on the spot, he remained in office, and his authority was bolstered by M. A. Suslov, who was present at the meeting. Hungary had the distinction of being the only country in Eastern Europe with a self-confessed murderer of Communists at the head of the ruling Party.

It is difficult to determine precisely what the Russians had in mind by making Rakosi confess his guilt and by keeping him in office at the same time. Perhaps they thought that by putting the blame where it belonged, they would clear the air. Tensions would be dissipated and Rakosi would be saved. Clearly, they did not yet want to sacrifice him. If this was their reasoning, they miscalculated the mood of the people and of the Party function-aries. Now even the most obtuse among them had their eyes opened, and they were infuriated.

Many of them were ready to jettison Rakosi. But they acted like the timid lot they were and cowered before him. They had no leadership of their own, and they still would not entrust their fate to Imre Nagy and his coterie of radical intellectuals. They groped for a solution that would meet their requirements: a strongly centralized Communist Party with little inclination to en-

[7] *Szabad Nep*, May 19, 1956.

gage in reforms, under a native leadership that would minimize the alien character of the regime and reduce the degree of mutual estrangement between the functionaries and the population.

Another two months passed before Rakosi was removed. Even then, the Russians had to do it.

THE DISMISSAL OF MATYAS RAKOSI

The dismissal of Matyas Rakosi on July 18, 1956, surprised no one more thoroughly than Rakosi himself. The Central Committee meeting which accepted his resignation "at his own request" had been called for an entirely different purpose. Rakosi hoped to tighten his grip on the Party and to obtain an endorsement for a ruthless campaign against his opponents. Earlier in the month, he had forced through the Central Committee a resolution condemning the Petofi Circle. Now, he wanted more. His obduracy was fantastic. Prior to the meeting, Budapest was rife with the rumor that he had drawn up a list of four or five hundred persons whom he planned to have arrested, including most of the capital's leading intellectuals.

The story of Rakosi's resignation is well known; Mikoyan arrived unexpectedly and informed him that he was no longer first secretary of the Party. Rakosi protested and demanded to telephone Khrushchev, who confirmed what the unbelieving Rakosi could hardly comprehend. His services were no longer required by the Party to which he had given close to forty years of his life. He was permitted to withdraw gracefully, pleading ill health as the major cause of his retirement. But in a formal statement addressed to the Central Committee he accepted "responsibility . . . for mistakes that caused serious harm to our socialist development as a whole . . . made our Party's work more difficult, diminished its attractiveness, [and] hindered the development of Leninist norms of Party life."[8] Similarly, he acknowledged that it was his fault that "rehabilitation proceeded at times sluggishly and with intermittent breaks and that [there was] a certain relapse in the liquidation of the cult of personality [in 1955], and that sectarian and dogmatic views were not combatted resolutely."

8 P. Zinner, ed., *National Communism*, pp. 341-42.

While the actual circumstances of Rakosi's resignation are no secret, its antecedents are less clear. In the light of the events of the preceding two months, he had every reason to be astonished at the fickleness of the Russians. In May, they had given him strong encouragement, and, if Marshal Tito can be believed, in June, the Soviet leaders still held out for him as the most qualified person to head the Hungarian Communist Party.[9] What caused them to change their mind? Possibly they responded to urgent pleas from several members of the Hungarian Politbureau to avert an imminent collapse of the entire central leadership of the Party.

Gero, on being appointed first secretary in place of Rakosi, revealed that "for various reasons the Politbureau did not feel that it could rely on the unanimous support of the Central Committee. ... There was no full agreement among its members as regards the policy of the Party ... and ... relations to the Politbureau or to its individual members."[10] Gero's candid revelation does not say nearly enough. There must have been a deep cleavage in the central leadership and not merely a lack of unanimity among its members before a step so drastic as the removal of Rakosi was contemplated. Nor does Gero provide a clue as to whether Rakosi had a small majority in favor of his plan or whether there was a small majority against him. Finally, Gero sheds no light on the relation between developments in Hungary and in the Soviet Union, where a crisis over the anti-Stalin campaign had come to a head two or three days before the Hungarian Central Committee gathered. A decision may have been reached in Moscow to remove Rakosi quite independently from the initiative of the Hungarian Politbureau, and the two moves may have simply coincided.

From the beginning of 1956, the entire Communist world was in flux. The Congress of the CPSU was followed by the dissolution of the Cominform in April and by Tito's much-publicized

9 *Ibid.*, pp. 516-41. Tito in a speech at Pula on November 11, 1956, noted that as late as June, 1956, when he visited Moscow, Soviet leaders praised Rakosi as "an old revolutionary, honest . . . prudent," and said that "they knew of no one else on whom they could rely in Hungary." This was an extraordinary tribute to Rakosi and explains much about the course of events in Hungary between 1953 and 1956.

10 *Ibid.*, p. 345.

visit to the Soviet Union, from which Khrushchev apparently expected the cementing of ideological ties between the Yugoslav leader and himself and possibly even the announcement of Tito's return to the fold. This did not materialize, but Khrushchev continued to woo Tito conspicuously through the summer and early fall, as if he needed the Yugoslav leader's support for his internal struggles with the Stalinist opposition. It will be remembered that Molotov resigned from his post as Minister of Foreign Affairs just in time to clear the decks for Tito's arrival. During the month of June, Molotov was in eclipse.

Simultaneously, the disorganization of the various Communist parties reached dangerous proportions, and the Soviet leadership found it necessary to issue, on June 30, a declaration on the cult of personality in order to end the dangerous ideological drift among them. It gave an authoritative interpretation of the significance of the Khrushchev speech (without referring to or quoting from it), placed the problem of the cult of personality in proper perspective, and reaffirmed Leninist principles of organization and discipline.[11]

The intensity and the nature of the reaction to the anti-Stalin campaign must have rallied Khrushchev's opponents in the Kremlin. They counterattacked in the July plenary session of the Soviet Central Committee. Unconfirmed journalistic dispatches reported the circulation of a memorandum throughout Eastern Europe (presumably drafted by the anti-Khrushchev Molotov wing of the CPSU) that urged a return to more centralized policies, condemned Tito and other revisionists, and at least indirectly attacked Khrushchev.

If the struggle in the Soviet Central Committee was as bitter as alleged and if the threat to Khrushchev's leadership was serious, he had good reason to act without delay against the last remaining Stalinist stronghold in the Soviet bloc. He might have intervened in Budapest without any request from the local leadership, and, for all we know, he did. It has never been authenticated that the Hungarian leadership asked for help against Rakosi.

[11] See *The Anti-Stalin Campaign*, pp. 275-306.

There may be no truth in the foregoing assumptions; yet it is not far-fetched to posit the hypothesis that contending factions in Moscow were bidding for support in Eastern Europe. Mikoyan, who often served as Khrushchev's favorite trouble shooter, was sent on an urgent mission to several East European countries.[12] He stopped in Hungary to oversee Rakosi's dismissal and journeyed to Yugoslavia, Rumania, and Bulgaria as well.

The suggestion that Rakosi's removal was a necessary price Khrushchev had to pay for Tito's support does not ring true. The nature of the discussions between Khrushchev and Tito in June do not indicate a deal of this sort. Rakosi's replacement by Gero also tends to refute this line of reasoning. As far as Tito was concerned, Gero was Rakosi's twin, and much persuasion from Khrushchev was required to make Gero acceptable to the Yugoslav leader.

The selection of Gero raises several questions. It was an unfortunate choice that substantially offset the salutary effect of Rakosi's long-overdue departure. To the public, Gero was Rakosi's *alter ego,* and a popular saying in Budapest at this time was that "in place of a bald Rakosi, we got a thin one." The break in the continuity of leadership was more apparent than real. The Hungarian Central Committee accepted Gero and was buoyed by his appointment. This supine body had bestirred itself entirely out of an irrepressible feeling of hatred and revulsion against Rakosi personally. The spirit of reform did not permeate them either then or at any time before the outbreak of revolution.

The Russians, in their haste, may have settled for Gero as a stopgap until they could reassess the situation, or they may have thought that a mere change of persons would calm the troubled Hungarian scene. Their subsequent efforts to bolster his prestige would seem to indicate a desire to maintain him in a central position of leadership. Actually, the number of Communists in whom the Russians had any confidence was limited to one—Gero. No other "Muscovite" was suitable for the job, certainly not Nagy. None of the "home"

12 Nor was he the only member of the Soviet Presidium to be sent abroad at this time; Bulganin and Zhukov went to Poland, while Suslov attended the Congress of the French Communist Party on July 20.

Communists, the most prominent of whom had been jailed, was quite trusted by the Russians.

If Gero's selection was a mistake dictated by necessity, the reconstitution of the Party leadership was a neat effort at patching up a crumbling structure. The Politbureau was rounded out by the election of four new members—Janos Kadar, Karoly Kiss, Gyorgy Marosan, and Jozsef Revai. At the same time, Kadar was elected secretary of the Party. At one stroke he was elevated to the second highest position in the Communist hierarchy. Another rehabilitated Communist functionary, Gyula Kallai, was elected to the Central Committee and appointed chief of the cultural section of the Party Secretariat.

The restoration of Kadar to high office was obviously designed to reassure vacillating functionaries and to provide them with a much needed leader. Probably, it also was meant to isolate the right wing under Imre Nagy and to forestall the remote possibility of a coalition between it and the functionaries, which would have been hghly undersirable from the Soviet point of view. In Kadar, the Russians found a housebroken species of national Communist who suited their purpose ideally.

Meanwhile, as a sop to Nagy, Mikoyan assured him of the good will of the Soviet leadership and disassociated the Russians from the harsh measures Rakosi had taken against him. Transparent as Mikoyan's explanation was, Nagy, according to those who saw him immediately after his interview with Mikoyan, was completely taken in by it.

It is not known if any inducements were offered Kadar to join forces with Gero. Rakosi's removal gave Kadar great personal satisfaction, for he had been grossly abused by the deposed first secretary.[13] At the same time, Kadar had no sympathy for Nagy. It is said that Kadar took a more adamant stand than did Gero against Nagy's reinstatement in the Party.

All told, Mikoyan's purpose seems to have been to lay the founda-

[13] Even in the spring of 1956, Rakosi attempted to block Kadar's return to an important Party post for fear that he would ally himself with Gero. He played before the entire Central Committee the recorded conversation between Kadar and Rajk in which Kadar pleads with his friend, who was then in prison, to confess his guilt. Rakosi had the first sentence of the conversation erased from the recording. In it, Kadar says, "I have come at the request of Comrade Rakosi."

tions for some sort of unity in the Party—always a prime concern of the Russians. In this, he succeeded. The dangerous drift of Party functionaries was temporarily halted. More important, the opposition movement, which had been gaining ground, now faltered. Nagy was disarmed. His supporters were at a loss for further initiative. The prime objective on which they had concentrated was accomplished; Rakosi was out of the way. But reforms still needed to be implemented, and the opposition still lacked a suitable base of power. The question was what to do next?

Establishing closer rapport with the masses and returning Imre Nagy to the government seemed to be indispensable preconditions of further progress. The Petofi Circle set out on a new venture to organize branch offices in provincial towns so as to influence public opinion close to the grass roots. It also made contact with workers in a number of large industrial units. Having learned about the Circle from the June resolution of the Central Committee, the workers grew interested in its activities and asked for speakers from the Circle to address factory rallies. The return of Imre Nagy to the government, however, was complicated by obstruction at both ends—Nagy and the Party.

Nagy's prestige had risen throughout 1956. Although he was still under police surveillance, he moved about freely. His trips to the city from his suburban home and his walks in the main streets of the capital never failed to elicit the interest of fellow passengers and passers-by and usually led to expressions of good wishes and confidence in him.[14] The number of his visitors increased. A few came to see him because it was fashionable to do so. Others were impelled by serious motives. His home became the scene of frequent and regular gatherings attended by old and new friends— writers, journalists, artists, university teachers, and students.

He was without doubt the leader of the opposition. But it was a role he accepted reluctantly, and he did not exercise his prerogatives in the accustomed Leninist sense.

His concepts were not the most advanced, and he did not force-

[14] His birthday on June 19 served as an occasion for a political demonstration of sorts: a stream of well-wishers came to his door, defying the Party's ban on observing his anniversary.

fully impose his views on others. His idleness had been a period
of growth for him; he had had valuable time to mull over problems which otherwise would have gone unattended. His ideas had
become crystallized, and, in some respects, they could no longer be
reconciled with Marxist-Leninist dogma, in the correctness of which
he professed to believe. He argued vehemently with those who
pointed this out to him, and he engaged in spirited debates with
others who had developed much bolder, democratic ideas than his
own, explaining their revisionist errors to them.

Nagy was not a political leader concerned with strategy and
tactics. He could not avoid being consulted for his opinions, and
he knew about a great many of the plans that various groups and
organizations were making. But he did not direct them, and he
resented the attention that was paid him in the plans of these
groups. He did not want to be the focal point of all their hopes.
By no stretch of the imagination was he the mastermind of a conspiratorial ring. His stubbornness, his naïveté, and his occasional
fits of temper exasperated some of his close friends, but their
liking for him as a person did not diminish, and they usually
deferred to him.

He had an abiding faith in the Soviet Union · (and explained
Stalinist terror as an aberration), and, while he felt great animosity
toward the leaders of the Hungarian Communist Party who had
humiliated him, he also had a deep devotion to the Party and
great solicitude for it. His main concern was to be readmitted to
the Party, on his terms if possible, but not so as to embarrass it
and help to tear it asunder. The Party itself had no intention of
making concessions to him. For the moment, Imre Nagy stood at
dead center.

The nation, however, did not stand still. Public opinion now
exerted pressure on the Party as well as on the Communist opposition to move at a more rapid pace. While the people still had
no institutional outlets to assert themselves, they communicated
their attitudes and moods to the authorities in unmistakable terms.
Both the Party and the Communist opposition realized that popular demands must somehow be accommodated, and each proceeded

in its own way to do what it felt was necessary. The Party gave ground as slowly as possible; the opposition pressed new attacks that centered on the reinstatement of Imre Nagy.

In the summer of 1956, former democratic politicians once again became active participants in Hungarian politics in a consultative capacity. The Party leadership as well as the Communist opposition sounded them out for possible collaboration in order to benefit from the prestige they were still thought to have. Most of them, after long years of imprisonment, were too unsure of themselves to plunge into the thick of politics, especially on the terms offered by the Communists. The total contribution of these political leaders to the thaw that was all around them was negligible. They were at a handicap vis-à-vis the rest of the population. They first had to become adjusted to their environment, from which they had been separated for years and which had undergone tremendous changes. Only later could they hope to enter politics again, if they still had any ambition or courage left.

THE STRUGGLE FOR DEMOCRATIZATION CONTINUES: AUGUST-OCTOBER, 1956

As a concession to the public mood, the Communist Central Committee, before it adjourned from its July meeting, acted to expel General Mihaly Farkas from the Party and to strip him of military rank. He was accused of gross violations of socialist legality.

On July 30, the government was reshuffled. Hegedus retained the premiership. Gero resigned his post as first deputy premier and was replaced by Istvan Hidas. Gyorgy Marosan added the post of deputy premier to his newly gained seat in the Politbureau. The Minister of Education, Tibor Erdei-Gruz, was replaced by Albert Konya.

In August, the Party turned to the problem of intellectuals in a more sober manner than before. A Central Committee resolution printed in *Tarsadalmi Szemle*—the Communist theoretical journal—"concerning certain problems of Party policy toward the intelligentsia," summed up a variety of existing prejudices against "the old intelligentsia" and condemned them as harmful to the Party in that they deprived the people's order of much-needed expert talent.[15]

The resolution also noted the alarmingly low proportion of Party functionaries with a higher education (4.3 percent in the Secretariat of the Party and only 1.7 percent among the first secretaries of urban Party committees). It acknowledged that "excessive teaching of Party history" and not enough of philosophy and political economy had an adverse effect on the attitude of intellectuals. Yet at the same time, few people had had an opportunity to study at first hand the example set by the Soviet Union. "Of several hundred students at the Technical University at Budapest, there are only twenty who have been to the Soviet Union."

The situation with respect to the new generation of intellectuals was found to be somewhat more encouraging, but their inadequate educational background, their "political apathy and cynicism, caused partly by the shortcomings of political education at the Universities and partly by the obstacles they encountered in earning a proper livelihood after they graduated," also gave cause for concern, as did the excessive class consciousness of some members of the new intelligentsia.

On the basis of the foregoing analysis, the Central Committee listed some measures designed to improve the situation: increasing the attractiveness of the Party for intellectuals, dispelling some of the fears and misgivings of the old intelligentsia, and overcoming the split between the old and new generations of intellectuals; better utilization of the talents of technical experts with opportunities for their advancement; improved cultural exchanges with the Soviet Union and also with the West; increasing the availability of foreign scientific journals and information; substantial improvement in the material conditions of many intellectuals; and, finally, "discontinuing the compilation of confidential cadre material on people working in the intellectual professions."

The resolution failed to mollify the intellectuals. In the middle of September, they resumed their activities where they had left off in June.

[15] *Tarsadalmi Szemle*, No. 8, August, 1956, pp. 29-41.

In the meantime, Erno Gero departed for his annual holiday in the Soviet Union. He left the country on September 8 and returned on October 7. While in Russia, he joined in talks with Khrushchev and Tito in the Crimea, on September 30, and consulted with Mikoyan and Suslov on October 6.

On September 9, a delegation led by Janos Kadar and including Istvan Hidas, Zoltan Szanto, and Agoston Szkladan departed for China to participate in the Eighth Congress of the Chinese Communist Party. On their way home from Peking, they joined Gero in consultations with Mikoyan and Suslov and returned with him on October 7.

Gero, Kadar, Apro, Hegedus, and Kovacs then proceeded to Yugoslavia to cement relations with Tito, leaving on October 14 and returning only on the day the revolution broke out.

For five out of the six weeks preceding the revolution, several key members, including the two top men of the Politbureau, were absent from Budapest. Their absence might have been dictated by a number of very good reasons of Party and national interest. For Gero, it certainly was important to gain Tito's endorsement and to put Hungary's relations with Yugoslavia on a better footing. For Kadar, it probably was important to meet the leaders of the Communist world then gathered in Peking and to introduce himself to them as a newcomer in their midst. With hindsight, however, their decision to leave Hungary as this particular time under the direction of the "second team" seems irresponsible at best and foolish at worst.

Surely, conditions in the country were not so stable as to invite complacency. The unity of the Party was precarious. Without reliable central direction, in the face of mounting pressures from all sides, the Party apparatus showed further signs of disorganization and vacillation. The events that unfolded before the eyes of Communist functionaries—the solemn reinterment of Rajk on October 6, the arrest of Mihaly Farkas and his son on October 12, the readmission of Imre Nagy to the Party on October 14, and a wave of public manifestations of discontent—filled them with anxiety. They saw the writing on the wall and did not know how to react. An acute erosion of will set in; Party functionaries in all 'organizations including the police, wavered in their fidelity, not to the Party, which they wanted to preserve at all cost, but to the leadership of the Party as constituted. Many, overcoming their reluctance, at last gravitated toward Imre Nagy's reform program and toward Nagy as the person most likely to be able to save both them and the Party. But they did not go so far as to install Nagy in office by a palace coup.

Neither did the opposition take advantage of the absence of the chief Communist leaders from Budapest to bring about a radical overturn in the Party. It persevered in agitating for reforms from the outside and urged ever more forcefully the recall of Stalinist officials from the Party apparatus. A running debate about the necessity of a change of guard developed in the press between Geza Losonczy and Istvan Friss. Others joined the chorus.

The fall session of the Writers' Association on September 17 turned into a festival of freedom and truth, the writers vowing never again to stray from the truth and demanding complete artistic freedom. The session brought about the formal, national unity of the writers by the election to the Association's governing body of a number of non-Communists who for many years had been outside the community of writers, though among them were included some of Hungary's outstanding literati.[16] To be sure, not all shades of opinion among Hungarian writers were as yet represented. Conservatives were left out; those who were elected stood for populist, socialist, and democratic-liberal persuasions. Of equal interest was the exclusion from the new governing board of a number of Communists such as the "Muscovites" Illes and Gergely and the former Minister of People's Culture Darvas.[17]

Despite these limitations, the governing board of the Writers' Association gained a much broader base than it ever had before. The ratio of Communists to non-Communists (17–8) had never

[16] Elected were Lajos Kassak, Aron Tamasi, Laszlo Nemeth, Pal Ignotus (released from jail in March, 1956), Lorincz Szabo, Ferenc Jankovich, Jozsef Fodor, and Emil Kolozsvari-Grandpierre.

[17] Among the others thus excluded were Tibor Meray, Tamas Aczel, Sandor Nagy, Erno Urban, Tibor Barabas, Tibor Cseres, Gyorgy Boloni, Janos Foldeak, Sarolta Lanyi, and Istvan Kiraly. Some of these—e.g., Aczel and Meray—had been wild Stalinists but had joined in the writers' protest movement after 1954.

been as equitable as now, nor the Communists elected to the board as moderate in orientation. A significant step was thus made toward changing the Writers' Association from a typical Communist social organization to a genuine interest group with a measure of internal autonomy.

Meanwhile, the Petofi Circle acquired a number of provincial outlets that began organizing lectures and evening debates on the model of those conducted in Budapest earlier in the year. Thus, in Debrecen, a Kossuth Circle (identical in purpose with the Petofi Circle), formed in June, 1956, held its first public debate on October 14.

The topics selected for discussion now centered on Hungary's economic plight. The conclusions reached were neither startling nor necessarily novel. A great many people probably arrived at them individually at one time or another. But the function of these discussions was, once again, to articulate and generalize individually held views and to endow them with added prestige which they derived from corroborating testimony given by leading technical experts, scientists, and professors. In this manner, a feeling of economic nationalism was promoted ("Hungary the country of uranium") which in turn fed a desire for emancipation from economic dependence on Russia. A significant portion of popular demands during the revolution indeed concentrated on economic objectives.

Although the Circle performed splendid services in molding public opinion, it continued to display a caution that was characteristic of the Hungarian political scene. A case in point was the decision, at a meeting on October 17, to invite Zoltan Tildy, the former chairman of the Smallholder Party, to participate in a discussion of Hungary's agricultural problems. The possibility of asking Bela Kovacs, the former secretary general of the Smallholders, who had been imprisoned for eight years in Russia and Hungary, was considered and rejected in favor of the much "safer" Tildy, who was reputed to have collaborated with the Communists prior to 1948, when he was placed under house arrest. By passing over Kovacs, an opportunity for a telling political demonstration had been missed.

University students now also developed independent organizational activity. Until the fall of 1956, they had participated in the protest movement individually, as affiliates of other groups, but with the opening of the academic year they joined forces and, using their universities and student organizations as bases of operation, began to agitate as a distinct pressure group for educational reforms.

An analysis of their behavior reveals a mixture of political acumen and youthful irresponsibility. Some of them were wise beyond their age. They fully understood the broader context of the struggle that was being conducted in the country and acted accordingly. Others were interested largely in obtaining various student privileges that would enable them to lead more stylish lives. Nevertheless, they also challenged the authority of the Party in regard to educational matters and organizational controls over student life. They contributed a loud and important voice to the rising cry for reforms. Their numbers, their exuberance, their privileged status in society made them a factor to be reckoned with both by the Party (which just before the revolution made farther-reaching concessions to them than to any other group) and by the established centers of opposition. In the final days before the revolution, the university students seemed to be setting the tone and pace of opposition.

Beginning on September 23 (exactly a month before the outbreak of revolution), there was a speedup in the general tempo of developments. A definite sense of maturing crisis settled over the country, although no one dreamed of revolution either as a desirable or as a possible means of resolving problems.

On September 23, Gyorgy Marosan put out the first official feeler for the readmission of Imre Nagy to the Party. He broached the subject in an address delivered before a committee of the Patriotic People's Front. Alluding to the "unsettled" case of Imre Nagy, he said that, in the view of the Party leaders, Nagy's readmission could be secured on certain conditions.

On September 30, the press printed an announcement of the Presidential Council of the People's Republic, convoking the National Assembly for October 22, 1956. On October 3, the Central Committee of the Party announced that it had reached a decision to pay "last respects worthy of militants and revolutionaries ... to comrades who, as a result of political trials in past years, have been innocently condemned and executed, and who have already been rehabilitated earlier by the Party's Central Committee and reinstated in their Party membership."

On October 6, 1956—a symbolic date in Hungary's history[18]— there took place the ceremonial reinterment of Laszlo Rajk, Lieutenant General Gyorgy Palffy, Tibor Szonyi, and Andras Szalai, the chief victims of the purge trials of 1949. The deeper meaning of this macabre ritual was conveyed by an editorial in *Szabad Nep:*

> The silent demonstration began.... People were numbed not only by was a pledge not only that we shall preserve the pure memories [of the four dead leaders] but also that we shall remember the dark practices of tyranny, lawlessness, slander, and deception of the people....
>
> The silent demonstration began.... People were numbed not only by a deep sense of grief ... but also by burning hatred, by the memory that these comrades, these men were executed as enemies of the fatherland, of the people! We were led to believe—and we were willing to believe— the slanders about you! Forgive us for this, comrades!

Among the thousands who marched in the procession, Mrs. Rajk, of course, occupied a prominent place, as did Imre Nagy, who was at this time still in disgrace. The reinterment of Rajk turned into a silent national demonstration against the regime. It showed for the first time in many years that masses could flow through the streets unmolested by the police. The rediscovery of the collective experience of mass solidarity had an exhilarating impact on the people, imbuing them with new strength and confidence. The impassioned speeches of the day were avenging oaths against the crimes perpetrated on these innocent Communist victims (and, by implication, also on the non-Communist victims of the regime). They unmistakably branded Rakosi and his colleagues as murderers, thus precluding their return to power. Few people realized how desperately necessary it was to foil Rakosi's recall to leadership by his close associates, who still manned posts of influence within the Party. The homage paid to Rajk was a triumphant vindication

[18] It is the anniversary of the execution of heroes of the Hungarian struggle for independence of 1848-49.

for his widow, who had fought tooth and nail for almost a year to win this privilege. The Party leaders who finally acquiesced in her demands expected little or no public response to Rajk's re-burial. Instead, it became a dress rehearsal for the revolution.

On October 12, the arrest of Mihaly Farkas and his son Vladimir, a high-ranking secret police officer, was announced.

On October 14, coincidentally with the departure of the Hun-garian delegation to Belgrade, the reinstatement of Imre Nagy as a member of the Communist Party was made public. But the resolu-tion adopted by the Politbureau on October 13, which restored "Party member rights to Comrade Imre Nagy," intimated that all questions concerning "the mistakes actually committed by Comrade Nagy" as well as the exaggerated and erroneous findings of previous Party resolutions [condemning Nagy]" were not yet settled. The resolution recommended that these "open problems of the affair" should be taken up by the Central Committee so as to "clear up and conclusively close the matter in a principled manner." [19]

In other words, Nagy's reinstatement was still conditional. The road was not yet clear to his assuming high office. The Party seemed to have acted to immobilize Nagy in this crucial period, while deriving benefits from the gesture it made toward him. The Party's calculations were not entirely incorrect. Nagy was reluctant to press his advantage and counseled patience to his supporters.

Nagy's readmission to the ranks of the Party elicited favorable comment in the country's press. It was followed by the restoration of other posts and honors that had been withdrawn from him. On October 18, the Minister of Education informed Nagy of his reinstatement as professor of agricultural economy at the Karl Marx University of Economic Sciences in Budapest. On October 20, Nagy's regular membership in the Hungarian Academy of Sciences was also restored. Thereupon, he left for the country.

Excitement was now close to fever pitch. On October 17, uni-versity students formulated a series of specific demands with respect to their own affairs. These included a reduction of the number of mandatory courses on Marxism-Leninism, abolition of required study of foreign languages, replacement of a system of paramilitary

19 P. Zinner, *National Communism*, p. 389.

activities required of students in behalf of national defense, by wider opportunities for athletic activities, and, finally, improvements in board and lodging at university hostels or dormitories.

On October 19, the government met some of these demands and promised to consider others. At an extraordinary meeting of university rectors, the Minister of Education, Albert Konya, announced the discontinuation of compulsory Russian language study, proposed to expand the university curriculum from four to five years (except in the faculties of law and economics) in order to relieve some of the pressure from the students, promised a re-examination of national defense activities at the universities in conjunction with the Ministry of National Defense, and projected the formation of a "council on higher education" to consider university problems in general.

On October 20, the executive committee of the Party organization in the Writers' Association issued a resolution calling for a new Party Congress.

The resolution had been adopted at a meeting on October 17 and was printed in *Irodalmi Ujsag* on October 20. It was an unprecedented initiative on the part of a subordinate Party organization. In the resolution, the writers captured the essence of the Hungarian political situation and pointed to what seemed the only possible remedy:

Following the Twentieth Congress [of the CPSU] and the July resolutions, a nearly unanimous attitude developed among the people with regard to the crimes and mistakes of the past. But this attitude does not transcend the limits of condemning past negative phenomena. We deem it necessary that after the past has been completely and sincerely cleared up and the inevitable consequences from it have been drawn, a new, positive, forward-looking unity for action should be forged, whose initiator and standard-bearer can be none other than our cleansed Party.

Only a new, democratically elected Party leadership is capable of performing this task. For this reason we ask the Central Committee to schedule the next Party Congress in any event no later than three or four months prior to the general elections which are due to be held next year.

Also on October 20, the university students at Szeged broke their ties with the Communist Youth Association (DISZ) and founded their own organization, suited to "the needs of university students," under the initials MEFESZ (Hungarian University and Academic Students Association).

By this time, news of the Polish October had reached Hungary. It had an intoxicating effect on the entire population, especially the youth. In a burst of enthusiasm they wanted to show their solidarity with the Poles and to emulate the Polish example. On October 22, university students, writers, and members of the Petofi Circle met separately in their several organizations. (They did, however, consult one another and kept informed about their respective plans.) Out of these deliberations, which lasted into the early hours of the following day, came lists of demands to be presented to the government and the decision by the students to hold a public demonstration on the twenty-third to reaffirm the historic friendship between Poland and Hungary and to give evidence of the Hungarian people's unity with the Poles in their hour of trial and triumph.

The resolutions differed from each other textually and in the number of "points" into which they were divided. They were, however, identical in substance. The resolution reproduced here is that of the Petofi Circle. It is chosen, not because it was neces- sarily the most radical or most representative of the mood of the people or even of the students, but because it reflected the opinion of a cross section of the most persistent and sober elements in the Communist and left-oriented opposition to the Rakosi-Gero type of rule.[20]

"1. In view of the present situation in Hungary, the leadership of the Petofi Circle suggests that a session of the Central Committee of the Hungarian Workers' Party should be convened in the nearest possible future. (Comrade Imre Nagy should take part in the preparatory work of this session.)

"2. We consider it necessary that the Party and the Govern- ment disclose in all sincerity the economic situation of the country, revise the directives of the Second Five-Year Plan, and work out a

[20] The resolution cited here is based on a radio report of the Hungarian Telegraph Agency (MTI) as checked against the text of the resolution printed in *Szabad Nep* (October 23, 1956). The portions of the quotation in parentheses represent text which, though transmitted by MTI, was omitted from the *Szabad Nep* version.

concrete, constructive program in accordance with the special conditions existing in Hungary.

"3. The Central Committee and the Government should adopt every possible means to insure the development of socialist democracy in Hungary by developing the real function of the People's Front, by fulfilling the legitimate political aspirations of the working class, by introducing self-management in factories and a workers' democracy.

"4. To assure the prestige of the Party and State direction, we propose that Comrade Imre Nagy and other comrades who fought for socialist democracy and for Leninist principles should occupy a worthy place in the direction of the Party and Government.

"5. We propose Matyas Rakosi's expulsion from the Party Central Committee and his recall from other functions. (It is necessary that the Central Committee, anxious to establish tranquillity in the country, should bring to a halt present attempts at Stalinist and Rakosist restoration.)

"6. We propose that Mihaly Farkas's case be tried in public in accordance with socialist legality.

"7. We propose that the Central Committee revise certain sectarian resolutions—in the first place those of March, 1955, those of December, 1955, and those of June 30, 1956, concerning the Petofi Circle. (We propose that the Central Committee annul these resolutions and draw the necessary conclusions as regards the persons concerned.)

"8. Let even the most delicate questions be made public: the balance sheets of our foreign trade agreement (and the plans concerning the utilization of Hungarian uranium).

"9. (With a view to consolidating Hungarian-Soviet friendship, let us establish even closer relations with the Party, State, and people of the Soviet Union on the basis of the Leninist principles of complete equality.)

"10. We demand that the Central Committee of DISZ take a stand, at their meeting on October 23, on the points of this resolution and adopt a decision on the democratization of the Hungarian youth movement."

Under the title "New Spring Parade," the morning issue of

Szabad Nep (on October 23) commented editorially on the events of the preceding day. The unusually perceptive editorial merits quotation in full.

"Meeting follows upon meeting in our universities and our institutions of higher learning. Students of engineering, philosophy, law, and the creative arts are meeting at the universities of Budapest, Pecs, Szeged. These meetings of the youth are taking place in a passionate and stormy atmosphere, resembling a rampaging river overflowing its banks rather than an artificially channeled stream. Is this flood good? Is this fiery enthusiasm good? Let us admit that the past few years have made us forget about this sort of mass expression of opinion. Sectarianism and the Stalinist mistakes have dulled our sensitivity to mass opinion and mass movements which manifest themselves with elementary force, and even today there are those who cannot rid themselves of the old ingrained habits and regard these meetings of the youth with misgivings and distrust. Our Party and its press organ, *Szabad Nep,* align themselves with the youth, approve of these meetings, and wish these well-considered, creative discussions the best of success.

"We know very well that youth, and more particularly the university youth, was for years prevented from making its voice heard in national as well as in their own affairs. We know well that DISZ suffered organic shortcomings and, aside from slogans, was incapable of providing the youth with true, socialist substance. During these years much bitterness, many suppressed desires and wants were dammed up in our youth. Much justified dissatisfaction lay buried in the youth, and who can be surprised if this feeling, suppressed for more than half a decade, now bursts forth with elementary force. Those who would want our youth now to express its opinions cautiously and with calm restraint disregard the concrete historical antecedents and the given circumstances as well as the spirit of the Hungarian youth.

"The present meetings in many respects resemble the struggles of the Hungarian university and college students right after the liberation. The atmosphere of these gatherings reminds all of us of the university meetings and college discussions of the years after 1945, and today it is clear to everyone that those years bore healthy, good fruit. There are, however, also differences between the current meetings and those held after liberation. One such difference must be emphatically stressed. In the discussion after liberation only a *small portion* of the participating students believed in socialism and possessed a Marxist world view. Immediately after liberation bourgeois reaction still had considerable representation in the universities, and the children of peasants and workers constituted only a small percentage. The picture is today fundamentally different. At the current meetings, the *vast majority of the participants take part as firm believers in socialism.* At these meetings not 5 or 10 percent but a much larger percentage of worker-peasant students are represented, who take their place in the building of a socialist Hungary as proud bearers of the heritage of their fathers.

"There is still another circumstance to which we must pay attention. In the years after 1949 the country's political mistakes unwittingly led to an aggravation of the contradictions [differences] between students of working-class or peasant origin and students of intellectual or petty bourgeois family background. The present meetings are characterized by the fact that students of divergent social origin march forward hand in hand, demanding in unison the reform of university life and the consolidation of socialist democratism. The consolidation of the unity of the youth is among the results of these meetings, and it is for this reason too that we greet with pleasure the movement of university and college students.

"But there are other reasons as well why we warmly greet these meetings. The spokesmen of sectarian politics paid only lip service to the fact that active participation in politics on the part of the youth is in the vital interest of socialism. In practice they did everything to assure that our university and college youth should not think independently, should not use their heads, that there should be no possibility for the expression of independent opinion. We, having turned on the mistakes and crimes of the recent past, do not want to pay lip service alone to the stirring of our university youth, but want to align ourselves with them in deeds, by giving them all possible moral and material aid. We can do so all the better since these rallies have condemned in a most decisive way that sort of dabbling in politics which turns against learning, and since they have rejected that sort of public activity which would prejudice the students' studies.

"One of the characteristics of the present youth movement is that it combines a struggle for socialist democratism with a fight for better conditions of learning and for broader and more scientific information.

"The university youth has expressed its political attitude before the broad public. We welcome the position adopted by the university youth. We agree that those who have defiled socialist humanitarianism should be judged publicly. We agree that veteran fighters of the workers' movement should find a place in the leadership of the Party and the country. We agree that there is no room in the leadership for those who do not want or cannot consistently proceed along the road fixed by the Twentieth Congress of the CPSU and the July resolution of the Party.

"It would be easier for us to make promises and thus to quiet rising passions for a while. We will not do this. We do not want to mislead the youth. We must speak the truth even if it is, for the time being, unfavorable. At the same time we ask the youth to have confidence in the Party, because we want to satisfy every one of its justified demands.

"At the student rallies our youth has given proof of serious political maturity. This maturity is demonstrated not only by the fact that they are discussing matters of national policy, mostly confidently and in a healthy spirit, but also by the fact that they are searching for the road leading forward, and for the possibilities of a solution to problems.

"Their proposals bear testimony to the deep responsibility which permeates our youth as regards our People's Democracy. The majority of the students stand on the foundations of socialism. Students of law, philosophy, and engineering have often expressed their determination not to allow a wedge to be driven between university students and young factory workers. On the contrary, only yesterday the students of the Academy of Arts held a common meeting with the young workers of Csepel. It has happened, nevertheless, that on a few occasions at these university meetings a few dim-witted young men have tried to poison the atmosphere by chauvinistic counterrevolutionary slogans. We are proud of the masses of university and college youth for having isolated these troublemakers in a most determined manner and for taking a stand against troublemaking of that kind.

"There are people who seem to see a danger of bourgeois restoration in the heated debates of these meetings. These worries we feel have no serious foundation. Those who have attended these meetings have been able to hear and see that our university students have gone into battle not against but for the people's democratic system and for a purified socialism. In order to increase the effectiveness of this struggle and to further the realization of their aims, let us warn our young people to continue to be on their guard, as they have been up to now, lest counterrevolutionary manifestations be made at their meetings. Let them stand up, as they have stood up, against every kind of attempt at restoration.

"Let them be on guard under all circumstances lest their democratic and socialist unity be disrupted by some sort of provocation. They must not forget even for a moment that their struggle is being waged to advance the cause of socialist democratism. In the present circumstances every counterrevolutionary utterance left unanswered and every bourgeois provocation becomes grist for the mill of sectarianism.

"They must be aware of their great responsibility: if they fight consistently against sectarianism, they also fight against the danger of bourgeois restoration. By standing up against bourgeois endeavors, they also pull the ground from under the feet of the sectarians.

"We welcome the correct aspirations of our university and college students. We welcome this tremendous and democratic parade of our youth of which we can say, quoting the ever beautiful lines of [the poet Endre] Ady:

> " 'Fire, blood, fever, news, happy transformation,
>   Only creative effort burns in your eyes
>   Eternal spring, eternal revolution
>   Oh, be resplendent ever more resplendent.' "

Hungary was on the verge of momentous events.

PART THREE

The Revolution

10. The First Phase, October 23

THE beginning of every revolution is traceable to a physical act of violence that has both actual significance as a test of strength between the forces opposing each other and symbolic meaning as a point of no return in resolving the differences between them. This act of physical violence is comparable to the behavior of a critical mass at the instant when previously inert energy is released. The transformation, though quantitative in form, is qualitative in content. The mechanism involved in triggering a revolutionary outburst is less perfectly understood than the process that leads to a nuclear explosion.

THE OUTBREAK OF VIOLENCE

In Hungary, the point at which mass demonstration turned into armed rebellion was reached on October 23, between 8 and 9 in the evening, in front of the central headquarters of the national broadcasting corporation. Mob action was not limited to this spot. The Stalin statue—a passionately despised symbol of national humilitation—was by this time in the process of being toppled by frantic groups of youths, laboring under the lackadaisical gaze of a secret police detachment.

But it was in front of the broadcasting headquarters that tension between opposing forces snapped. It was here that combat broke out first. It was here that the first bricks were thrown from the street, shattering window panes, that the first tear gas bombs were hurled into the crowd and back into the headquarters building again, that the first shots were fired and the first casualties sustained by both sides. It was from here, perhaps even before blood was actually shed, that the anguished cry, "They are massacring the

Hungarians," spread like fire through the superheated atmosphere of the city.

The first groups of demonstrators gathered before the broadcasting headquarters at about 6 P.M. They were part of the great crowd that had already made history by marching through the streets of the city in response to the students' and writers' appeal for a mass demonstration, ostensibly intended to show solidarity with the Poles but actually meant to induce a political overturn in Hungary such as had just taken place in Poland. In the course of the afternoon, the crowds that assembled in the streets were harangued by inflammatory speeches.

The demonstration began at the statue of Sandor Petofi, the famed revolutionary poet of 1848. Here the actor Imre Sinkovits recited Petofi's poem exhorting Hungarians to "rise . . . for the motherland . . . now or never" and vowing that Hungarians "will no longer be slaves." The recitation of the poem must have had an electrifying effect on those who heard it. It is true that, without a loudspeaker only part of the crowd actually heard Sinkovits; but the place where he spoke exuded historic symbolism, and it was scarcely necessary to hear the recital to experience the effect of the inflaming words.

From the Petofi statue, the demonstrators crossed the bridge to Buda, to the statue of Joseph Bem, a Polish general, also of revolutionary fame, who assisted the Hungarians in 1848. Here Peter Veres, the president of the Writers' Association, read out a sixteen-point program of demands against the authorities. It amalgamated the grievances of the population as expressed in various programs formulated in the past two days.

The gist of the demands was the restoration of Imre Nagy to high position in the government; internal reforms consonant with the policies of the "new course" initiated by Nagy in 1953; and a readjustment of political and economic relations with Russia that would respect Hungary's national sovereignty. The overthrow of the "people's democratic" system was in no sense implied, although the authorities, by their actions, clearly showed that, in their view, to meet the demands of the people would amount to abdicating their power.

From the Bem statue, the crowd once more crossed the Danube to the heart of Pest. The streets were now filled with an ocean of humanity, more and more people having stopped work to join the demonstrators. Some were obviously apprehensive and soon returned to the safety of their homes. Others were driven more by curiosity than by any well-defined political motives: even if nothing were to come of the demonstration, to let off steam felt good.

By the time the demonstrators had completed their march from Pest to Buda and back again, darkness had fallen; they stopped before the House of Parliament, entirely filling the huge Kossuth Square. By this time, a heady spirit prevailed. National slogans passed from mouth to mouth. The Hungarian tricolor, without the hated Soviet emblem, had appeared out of nowhere very early in the afternoon.

Awareness of Hungary's national traditions was not erased from consciousness during the years of Communist rule. If anything, the survival of the memory of these traditions was assured by the exaggerated efforts of the Communists to identify themselves with the revolutionary glory and myth surrounding 1848. But in the day-to-day struggle for existence, few people derived strength from a conscious identification with past national glory, and even fewer acted as the direct descendants of national heroes like Petofi or Kossuth. This sort of identification took place, on various levels of consciousness, only in the heat of an acute national crisis such as erupted on October 23, 1956, and it then quite properly turned against the Communists as usurpers of the libertarian legacy of 1848.

The great majority of the crowd remained before the House of Parliament, demanding that Nagy be brought out to address them and awaiting the government's reaction to the day's happenings, which was to be forthcoming in a speech by Erno Gero scheduled for eight o'clock. Smaller groups detached themselves from the main body of demonstrators and went their own way to various centers of "attraction," such as the Stalin statue, the broadcasting headquarters, and the Party's press building.

The groups that went to the broadcasting headquarters were

not bent on violence. They had no thought of storming the building and of seizing its technical plant. They wished only to broadcast the sixteen-point program to the country. They also sought to place microphones in the street for the purpose of sampling the crowd's opinion. The authorities denied both requests.

The crowd, instead of dispersing, grew thicker and more menacing. Rumor spread that members of a delegation sent into the building to present the claims of the demonstrators had been detained and even shot. No one could verify the rumor. Tempers grew shorter. Shouted exchanges between the milling mass—confined as it was in a narrow street—and various officials who ventured out on a second-floor balcony in an effort to appease it further aggravated matters. The chanted slogans grew more radical, the language and catcalls grew fouler. Individual persons, protected by darkness and by the anonymity of the mob, also grew bolder. The lighted red star atop the building made a particularly tantalizing target of abuse. A young man shinnied up the façade of the building to the second floor to plant a Hungarian flag on the balcony's parapet. Very likely he acted as much from exhibitionism as from patriotic fervor, but it did not matter. At such a time purity of motive is neither required nor indeed is it ascertainable. Except in cases where crowd violence is consciously incited and manipulated by trained agitators dispatched to the scene of action by a conspiratorial group or political party—and history abounds in examples of this sort of maneuver—the acts in which a mob engages must be considered at face value, as spontaneous deeds, whatever unexpected turns they may take.

The behavior of an aroused mass is generally characterized by its unpredictability. But it is reasonable to expect that its mood is more susceptible to the influence of the loudest and most raucous participants, not the meekest and most sober. Whatever the personal motives and political convictions of these self-styled ringleaders might be, and whatever impact they might have on the crowd, they can hardly be assumed to be acting as conscious agents of history in behalf of rationally conceived political ends.

The confluence or interrelationship between consciousness and spontaneity in highly volatile revolutionary situations is still little understood, yet it is of supreme importance.

There is no point in pretending to know more than is knowable about the problem of spontaneity and consciousness in the Hungarian situation. A great deal of evidence is still missing. But the available information (including divergent Communist interpretations that make a crude attempt to impute conscious direction by reactionary forces from the very outset) strongly suggests that the crowd in front of the broadcasting headquarters acted spontaneously. Its composition was about the same as that of the afternoon demonstration—a rough cross section of the population of Budapest. It had no clear ideas of the consequences of its actions. It had no notion of bringing down the government. Its anger was vented on the hated symbols of the regime that were within reach of retaliation. But for all its lack of directed political goals, it was no less effective as the catalyst of revolution.

Curiously, the defenders of the broadcasting headquarters (who included secret police and army detachments) also acted spontaneously, at least to some extent. They responded to an acute situation of anxiety in a confused manner. There is no telling precisely what orders the secret policemen had about dispersing the crowd, or whether anyone authorized them to fix bayonets and fire into the throng with live ammunition. In any event, as the pressure of the crowd mounted (some say that the heavy wooden gates were being forced with an old sedan belonging to the broadcasting corporation), the secret police fixed bayonets, moved out of the gate in traditional wedge formation to clear the street, roughed up the mob, and fired, causing casualties. The time was about 8:45.

This act of violence by the secret police, coming as it did on top of Gero's short, strident, and disappointing speech (broadcast between 8 and 8:12 P.M.), ignited a general conflagration. There was now no holding back the capital's enraged population.

As the search for firearms and ammunition grew hotter, many spontaneous clashes occurred between the insurgents and the reinforcements called out by the government. Decisions had to be made on the spot. Skirmishes or truces ensued, depending on the moment and the place. Guns changed hands and persons switched sides from the government to the insurgents. Before dawn, Soviet motorized units entered the city. Their interference, though not decisive in the outcome of the struggle at this time, further aggravated the situation. A revolution was now in full progress, with the insurgents on the attack, laying siege to the broadcasting headquarters (which they conquered by morning), ransacking the central publishing house of the Party (both its editorial offices and the printing presses of its daily organ, *Szabad Nep*), and surrounding numerous other public buildings.

HOW THE LEADERS REACTED

The dangers of a spontaneous outburst did not escape either of the two major contending factions of Communists; but the university students who gave impetus to the demonstration were less worried about uncontrolled mass action than about the possibility of secret police provocation.

The supreme irony, not to say the tragedy, of the outcome of the day's events lay precisely in the interest shared by the major antagonists in keeping things under control and in their inability—for different reasons—to do so. In this sense, both sides lost the battle as soon as it was joined. Each fell victim to the forces in whose release they had collaborated, if at cross purposes.

On the morning of October 23, Budapest had been full of excitement and anticipation as a result of the rising vehemence of attacks on the government. The top leaders of the Communist Party, including Erno Gero, Antal Apro, Andras Hegedus, Janos Kadar, and Istvan Kovacs, were on their way back from Belgrade, reportedly a day ahead of schedule because of the heated political atmosphere at home. They arrived at 9 A.M. and, after brief, inconsequential ceremonies at the station, retired to Party headquarters.

At about the same time representatives of the Writers' Association, the Petofi Circle, and the university students met at the headquarters of DISZ to coordinate plans for the projected demonstration. In the course of their discussions, they checked several times with Geza Losonczy, an influential member of Imre Nagy's inner circle of friends. Nagy himself was out of town at a vacation resort on Lake Balaton. He had left Budapest on October 20. What had prompted his departure at so critical a time remains a mystery, unless he was totally disinterested in the events—which is unlikely. Perhaps he wanted to avoid all suspicion of plotting against the Party leadership while its chief representatives were out of the country. Whatever his motives might have been for absenting himself, he began his journey back into town in the morning of the 23rd, arriving at his suburban home about noon.

By this time, the Party leaders were apprised of the situation. Emissaries from the editorial staff of *Szabad Nep* went to Party headquarters before noon, independently of the groups planning the demonstration, in order to ascertain the mood of the leadership and to plead with it to be conciliatory. They found Gero and Kadar in the company of Marosan and Revai, an unpromising combination.

Marosan and Revai were talking like diehards, opposed to any concession or alteration in the Party's leadership and basic policies. Revai is reported to have been particularly vitriolic in his denunciation of the would-be demonstrators, threatening them with armed reprisal. In the heated exchange, Kadar, whose position will have to be evaluated at greater length later, once more appeared as a reluctant supporter of a policy tougher than the kind he would have been inclined to devise, explaining—as he had done in the past— that the situation was very complicated and not entirely what it seemed to be. Shortly thereafter, the official position of the Party leadership was broadcast; the demonstration was prohibited. The time was 12:53. The prohibition was repeated over the air at 1:15.

The Party's negative attitude spread consternation among the planners of the demonstration. A delegation led by Gabor Tanczos, the secretary of the Petofi Circle, hurriedly departed for Party headquarters to obtain a reversal of the decision. According to an eyewitness, the scene at headquarters was one of confusion and calamity. The atmosphere was not at all that of a command post confident of its strength and deliberate in its moves. Hysteria and near panic prevailed.

Ultimately, the Party leadership reversed its stand and rescinded the ban on the demonstration. The bulletin announcing the reversal was broadcast at 2:23, only thirty-seven minutes before the demonstration was scheduled to get under way. Despite the ban, groups of people were already gathering, and there was nothing to indicate that the Party leadership would not have been defied in any event. It is open to question whether the Party's cause would have been damaged more by steadfastly clinging to a ban that was defied than it was by public vacillation. The Party's irresolution infused the insurgents with an additional sense of excitement and derring-do.

The pressures under which the Party leadership reversed itself cannot be fully assessed. It may well be that the scales were tipped less by the arguments of the demonstrators than by the inability of Laszlo Piros, the Minister of the Interior, to guarantee that he could in fact successfully enforce the ban. Indeed the Ministry of the Interior itself was divided. Perhaps, even the loyalty of the secret police was in doubt at this juncture. Certainly, the population was no longer in awe of the Party's terrorism.

After reaching their decision, the various members of the Party hierarchy dispersed. While nothing like a detailed account of their movements exists, Gero is known to have closeted himself in his private office to prepare his address for that evening; Kadar appeared briefly at broadcasting headquarters in the early afternoon; Revai, allegedly on Gero's request, went to the editorial offices of *Szabad Nep,* which by this time were staffed almost exclusively with Imre Nagy's supporters. Betlen had cleared out the day before. His deputy, Marton Horvath, was less than staunch.

As the delegation led by Tanczos took their leave from Party headquarters, Antal Apro, one of the moderate members of the Communist high command, implored them to keep their demonstration under control. Apro's plea for self-policing, although it may seem ludicrous, was seriously meant and just as seriously considered. It was perhaps the most telling sign of the Party's impotence and of the difficulties the demonstrators were about to incur. Even before the genie was out of the bottle, it was clear that it was nearly impossible to contain him. There is good reason to believe that at this moment, just before the demonstration actually began, some of its instigators were already backtracking, or at least dissociating themselves from the events in progress. It was partly with an eye to controlling the demonstration that the Central Committee of DISZ, which met at 2 o'clock in the afternoon, adjourned in order to join the marchers in the streets.

Meanwhile, the scene of confusion and vacillation that characterized Party headquarters was almost duplicated at the quarters of Imre Nagy. While Gero and his aides were deliberating over their moves, Nagy and his intimate entourage, including Losonczy, Vasarhelyi, Gimes, and Janosi, were also meeting. Nagy was briefed as Gero had been about the events of the past few days. Similarly, Nagy, even as Gero, was subjected to great pressure to take a "proper" stance that did not accord with his own preferences.

Among other things, Gomulka's example was held up to him as a model to follow. Precisely what this implied, we do not know. The situation in the two countries differed as sharply as did the two men in question, and an overturn in the Party of the sort Gomulka accomplished was clearly impossible.

Perhaps Nagy was urged to place himself at the head of the demonstration. Perhaps he was asked to do no more than declare in favor of the demonstration and send an inspirational message to it. Perhaps he was counseled to take the initiative vis-à-vis the Party leadership in bringing about a change of command that would satisfy the demonstrators. Nagy declined whatever proposals were made to him by his advisors. His fear, actual or conveniently feigned, of being trapped in a "provocation" carefully baited by Gero is reported to have been his main argument for perfect passivity. (Word of a possible provocation had reached Nagy some time earlier through Imre Mezo, one of his supporters in the Party apparatus.) In any event, his reasoning and his behavior could hardly have been faultier. If the chief danger was that of a provocation by Hungary's Stalinists, the fact that a street demonstration was about to take place and that Imre Nagy's name was on everybody's lips as a symbol of the desired change would surely be sufficient cause for the Party leadership to arraign Nagy as the ring leader, regardless of his actual attitude toward the demonstrators.

Nagy's recalcitrance deeply disappointed his close friends. Except for his son-in-law, Ferenc Janosi, they left his home disgruntled and scattered through town. Gimes turned up at *Szabad Nep* and stayed there throughout the afternoon and night. Losonczy and Vasarhelyi roamed around town and ended up at broadcasting headquarters at about 7 P.M.

The manner in which Nagy's adherents moved in and out of public buildings, consulting with and being consulted by the officials in charge, was further evidence of the fluidity of the situation. Although none of them was a member of the Party leadership, they enjoyed *quasi* official status and wielded a measure of authority. At *Szabad Nep*, Gimes was certainly more influential than was Revai, who kept him company throughout the better part of the night. In turn, the role in which Losonczy was cast at broadcasting headquarters underlined the anomaly of the position of the "right opposition." At the very least, Losonczy tried to mediate between the self-proclaimed spokesmen of the crowd and the officials of the broadcasting corporation. He wished to mitigate tension, not increase it. In vain, he tried—at about 7:30—to enlist Nagy's prestige to the same end, urging him by telephone to come to broadcasting headquarters and address the crowd. Shortly thereafter, he left the building. Had he been impelled by motives of seizing the center of mass communications on behalf of Imre Nagy, or, still worse, had he acted on a carefully conceived plan to wrest power from the Gero leadership, he would have certainly behaved differently. As it was, he departed a dejected and forlorn figure, bemoaning the turn events had taken and the stubbornness of his senior colleague.

In these circumstances, it is absurd to speak of the cohesiveness of the "camp" of Imre Nagy or of its guiding authority in the events of October 23. Nagy and his immediate entourage were anything but a purposeful group acting in unison. They were physically dispersed and, though within easy reach of one another by telephone, they did not reconvene to assess the situation and devise a common plan of action. They were not of one mind as to the proper steps to take and were condemned to paralysis so long as Nagy himself, whom they treated with touching and gentle deference (Losonczy addressed him as Uncle Imre over the phone), refused to move.

When Nagy finally committed himself, in response to repeated urging that he address the throng before the House of Parliament, he did so half-heartedly, still not knowing what attitude to take. That the House of Parliament was essentially a hostile citadel in which he was surrounded by Party stalwarts such as Hidas, Mekis, and Erdei; that the technical facilities for his addressing the crowd were abominable—there was no loudspeaker system at his disposal, and few heard what he said—perhaps mattered less than the fact that he had nothing of any consequence to say either to the crowd or to the people who surrounded him. At nine in the evening, he was as unprepared to cope with the situation as he had been earlier in the day.

Following his stint before the House of Parliament, he met informally with a group of students and then departed for Party headquarters. The circumstances of his departure are obscure. It has been suggested that he went under duress, but no corroborating evidence has come to us.

Nagy's retiring to Party headquarters was the last of a long series of political blunders. At Party headquarters, he was effectively isolated and at the mercy of his opponents. Still worse—regardless of the actual conditions that governed his appointment as premier the following morning—he appeared to be doing the Party's bidding and thus confused rather than clarified the issues at stake. He alienated even some of his staunchest supporters, who forthwith disclaimed the limitations of *partiinost* (fealty to the Party), which still shackled Nagy. It is said that from October 23 to October 26 Nagy was a "prisoner." His freedom of movement might well have been controlled; but it is certain that he was at least as much a prisoner of his own attitudes as of the hostile forces surrounding him. It was not until October 26 that he extricated himself from the Party and transferred the seat of his activities to the House of Parliament, and even then he was able to do so only by virtue of decisive Soviet intervention in the internal affairs of the Party.

Imre Nagy's fate influenced and was largely shared by the organized groups that supported him. The Writers' Association, the Petofi Circle, and the university students' clubs were in fact organized groups, while Nagy and his close associates were not. But none of these groups was prepared for political action, only for the tasks of publicists. Nor were their leaders suited to operate outside the publicistic realm.

Overtaken by the events, they reacted in a variety of uncoordinated ways. Most of the intellectuals in question participated in the demonstrations as ordinary members of the crowds. As the situation crystallized and shooting began, they dispersed to the Writers' Association and to familiar coffee houses, where they engaged each other in heated and largely futile debate and tried to get their own bearings. Through numerous acquaintances in the Party, they tried to find out the Party's disposition and, if possible, to influence it. The writers—Zoltan Zelk, Laszlo Benjamin, Sandor Erdei, Lajos Konya, and Lajos Tamasi—on their own initiative visited Party headquarters four times during the night, supplicants armed with memoranda imporing the Communist high command to pursue a course of reason. Their efforts were of no avail. Another group, also acting on its own initiative, was more successful in persuading Sandor Kopacsi, the chief of the regular police in Budapest, to join the revolution on October 24. For the rest, the intellectuals scattered without a clear notion of what to do or how to do it.

Thus, during the early hours of the revolution, Imre Nagy and his close associates were at the lowest ebb of their effectiveness. Never long on political sagacity, lacking any organizational base whatever, they temporarily disappeared from the scene as active agents. The "man of the hour" cut a pathetic figure against the heroism of his people.

The spectacle of Imre Nagy and his supporters was matched by the equally dismal performance of the Communist Party, which to all intents and purposes disintegrated overnight. It was able neither to issue coherent orders from the center nor to preserve the integrity of its organizational and power structure at the edges.

The astonishing rapidity of the collapse of the Party machinery and of affiliated organizations is the most remarkable aspect of the first phase of the revolution. Faced with a popular riot of unforeseen proportions, the talents of the Communist leaders appeared to desert them. Far from anticipating contingencies, they failed even to keep pace with developments as they occurred. The external evidence of their actions betrayed irresolution and bewilderment.

The maladroit backtracking in the Party's pronouncement on the demonstration in the morning and noon hours was followed by other political and psychological blunders. One was the revelation that the security organs were quite unprepared to deal with the mass demonstration. Another was the substance and delivery of Gero's nationwide broadcast address. The gravest of them all was the hasty summoning of Russian troops to join in the fracas.

As far as it has been possible to determine, commanders of Hungarian military units outside Budapest were put on the alert in the early afternoon, but no specific orders were issued with regard to the disposition of troops. The military in Budapest received similar instructions. The disposition of security forces had the look of a halfway measure: additional guards were assigned to a number of public buildings, but neither their number nor their preparedness was sufficient to cope with a mass rising of the people. They had but a limited supply of ammunition. They lacked detailed instructions on how and when to intervene against the population. Before the sortie made by security troops from the broadcasting headquarters, these units kept well out of sight of the demonstrators. Given the unpredictable nature of the situation, it would have been difficult, of course, to devise a suitable strategic plan to meet all contingencies. But a greater degree of coordination would have been possible and only reasonable, had the authorities been less disoriented.

Gero's radio address to the nation has been almost unanimously proclaimed as a turning point in the revolution. It came at the close of a day of unprecedented riot and release. The demonstration had run its course. The atmosphere was charged, but no explosion had as yet taken place. Imre Nagy had failed to take the initiative in pressing a tactical advantage to force a showdown in the Party. The Party was not firmly in command, but all eyes were riveted on it and all expectations hinged on the cue Gero would give. By what he said, he could still powerfully influence the course of events if not fully determine it.

He himself must have been conscious, however incompletely, of his opportunities. The situation he found at Budapest on returning from Belgrade was vastly different from that which he had left behind a week earlier. The immediate political questions that required his urgent attention overshadowed memories of his foreign venture. Gero could, in fact, justifiably feel angry and confused. The Belgrade trip had been the high point of nearly two months of intricate maneuvering that took him out of the country for the better part of that period and as far as Yalta in the Crimea. Judging by external evidence, he had the support of Khrushchev, who in turn succeeded in enlisting Tito's aid to bolster Gero's leadership in Hungary. Kadar and a few other leading Hungarian Communists were apprised of this decision while in Moscow on their return journey from Peking. It contributed to Kadar's submissiveness at a time that was ripe had he been ready to make a bid for power in the Party. Of the means devised to strengthen Gero, his trip to Belgrade was the most ostentatious. It meant the formal healing of a breach that had existed between the two countries since 1948. It implied Tito's approval of Gero, and it thus cut—or was intended to cut—an important avenue of moral support from any incipient Hungarian "national Communist" movement. If Tito approved of Gero, he could not at the same time encourage the overthrow of his regime.

The rapid shift of events in Budapest marred these elaborately laid plans. Hungarians could hardly have been less concerned about the negotiations with Yugoslavia or their implications.

Gero's confusion, apparent in the manner in which he handled the police ban on the demonstration, became even more apparent in the way he handled his scheduled address to the nation. If reports about the actual staging of the broadcast can be believed, the address was to be pre-recorded on tape at Party headquarters and broadcast from the central studio at 8 P.M. As the afternoon wore on, Gero repeatedly postponed the recording. Finally, he delivered the speech in person, by remote transmission from Party headquarters.

A text of the speech he was to deliver is said to have existed before his return from Belgrade. Obviously, that one was unsuitable after the unforeseen change in the internal political situation. A new text had to be prepared. What would Gero say and how would he say it?

The brevity of the speech attests to the haste with which it was readied. Considering that it was replete with clichés and contained no programmatic announcement of the kind that would have required careful thought prior to being committed to paper, one concludes that it was not the mechanical aspects of preparing the speech that were responsible for the delay. In the end, deliberate choice could not have made the message less apt to the occasion. From its opening utterance to the closing harangue, it could only harden the hostility of his audience:

"Dear Comrades, dear friends, working people of Hungary. The Central Committee of the Hungarian Workers' Party adopted important resolutions in July of this year. The membership of our Party, our working class, our working peasantry and intellectuals, our entire people, received these resolutions with approval and satisfaction." This was the opening paragraph of Gero's speech. What could have taunted the population more than to be reminded at the start that the Party still clung to the July resolutions as its policy program and to be told the patent lie that this program had won the approval of the nation? Yet Gero, by way of reinforcing his statement, ended on the very same note on which he had begun, exhorting the population to implement the resolution "With Party Unity for a Socialist Democracy."

In the body of his speech, Gero condemned "those who strive to spread the poison of chauvinism among the youth and who, having abused the democratic freedom assured by the state . . . have carried out a demonstration of nationalistic character." The sole intimation he gave of the Party's concern over the situation was in a passage in which he heralded the convocation "in the next few days of a plenary session of the Central Committee." "Until such time," he bade the Party and nation to maintain "utmost vigilance . . . lest hostile elements disrupt the efforts of the Party and impede the clarification of the situation."

Although only a small portion of Gero's speech dealt with the

demonstration, it was this brief passage that attracted greatest attention and caused most profound indignation. In fairness to Gero
one must record that the words he used were not quite as harsh as
they were reported to be by those who actually heard the speech
and passed on its contents to thousands throughout Budapest. But
aside from this passage, the general effect of the speech was to complete a long-standing alienation between the people and the government.

In fact, so maladroit was Gero's address that it has prompted
speculation whether it could have been meant as deliberate provocation. The theme of provocation has recurred frequently enough in
the testimony of refugees to warrant consideration, if only conjec-
turally. The theme feeds on three sources: Gero's known past as a
master of utterly ruthless intrigue; a confidential message passed
on to Imre Nagy early in October, 1956, purporting to warn him
against an attempt by Gero to provoke him; and the reportedly
haughty demeanor of several Stalinists (including Gero's lieutenant,
Prime Minister Andras Hegedus) on the night of the demonstration, which led one observer to believe that the intervention of
Soviet troops was prearranged.[1]

The possibility of provocation by Gero cannot be ruled out, although cool logic would dictate against it. If Gero wanted to trap
Nagy, the demonstration as it unfolded was certainly more than
he needed to frame the former prime minister. If Gero wanted to
assure himself of Soviet backing as the indispensable man in the
face of unrest, he could have accomplished more by handling the
situation judiciously than by precipitating armed struggle. With
the Polish situation still very touchy, the Russians, far from welcoming an aggravation in the internal situation in Hungary, would
have favored an attenuation of conflicts there.

Of course, Gero was not necessarily operating according to cool
logic. It is possible that out of sheer desperation over the rapidly
deteriorating domestic crisis he conceived schemes to turn apparent

[1] As far as we can tell, reports of Hegedus's demeanor on the night of the
demonstration can be traced to a single individual, a writer sympathetic to
Nagy who was at Party headquarters and informed his friends of happenings
there by telephone.

defeat into victory. Perhaps he went so far as to imagine himself in the role of kingmaker in Russia, toppling Khrushchev as the person responsible for the troubles of the socialist camp and enthroning Molotov as the ruler of the Communist world. Whatever his motives were, it is clear that he acted hastily in conditions not of his own making.

He was probably willing to gamble heavily in order to preserve his status in the Party, but it is unlikely that he foresaw the later consequences of his actions and yet deliberately plunged the country into general chaos, damaging the cause of Communism not only in Hungary but throughout the world. To be sure, he fought tenaciously to retain the leadership of the Party, even after the outbreak of the revolution. He was ultimately removed by A. I. Mikoyan, who acted as the executor of the Soviet government's will for the second time in less than four months. It was Gero's personal misfortune to have erroneously assessed the forces at work in Hungary and to have misjudged the intentions of the Soviet leadership. The crowning act of a series of blunders was his rash decision to appeal for Soviet military assistance.

The exact time and the circumstances under which the appeal was made remain unknown. In the evening hours, as the gravity of the situation was borne in on the Communist leaders, their panic mounted. Graphic evidence of their state of mind is once again provided by the sequence of broadcast announcements concerning the convocation of a meeting of the Central Committee of the Hungarian Workers' Party to discuss pressing matters. In the course of a regular news broadcast at 7:30 P.M., it was reported that the Central Committee would be convened on October 31. The announcement was repeated immediately after the conclusion of Gero's address. A few minutes later, at 8:23 P.M., a bulletin was broadcast, interrupting the regular program of music then being transmitted, to correct earlier statements; the Central Committee, it was announced, would be called "in the next few days." The bulletin was repeated at 10:03. Nineteen minutes later another bulletin was flashed over the airwaves, announcing a decision of the Politbureau of the Hungarian Workers' Party to call an immediate session of the Central Committee "to assess the situation and to discuss measures required by it." The bulletin was repeated at ten-minute intervals.

THE FIRST SOVIET INTERVENTION

It is likely that Soviet troops were called no sooner than 10:30; it may have been somewhat later. Whether Moscow was consulted (and, if so, in what manner) or whether the local Soviet commander had discretionary powers to commit his troops up to a point, are questions that have yet to be answered. In any event, some time between 1 and 2 A.M., Soviet motorized units that were normally stationed thirty-five to forty miles from the city appeared in the streets of Budapest and joined the struggle. Their intervention at this time was not decisive. Neither their number nor their actions suggested any massive assault upon the insurgents.

The indecision of the Soviet military during the first night of fighting is understandable. There was inadequate intelligence as to the scope and type of the street fighting. Fighting in narrow city streets in the dark against unknown numbers of opponents required caution. How to act with firmness when the political stance of the Soviet government was not yet clarified? But a clarification would not be forthcoming until after Soviet emissaries had a chance to evaluate the situation on the spot. Messrs. Mikoyan and Suslov—representing perhaps opposing viewpoints in the Soviet Communist Presidium—arrived in Budapest only on October 24.

The Soviet military, however, continued to play an ambiguous part in the events of the next few days. While it engaged the insurgents and sustained (as it also inflicted) some casualties, it refrained from launching real assaults against the insurgents. Its primary assignment seemed to be to safeguard Soviet diplomatic and military installations—notably airports—and to protect selected Hungarian Party and government strongholds.

On October 25, a column of Soviet tanks inadvertently became involved in the bloodiest single encounter of the revolution. It took place in Kossuth Square in front of the House of Parliament. A group of demonstrators, in defiance of the government's martial law, had gathered at the head of one of the bridges at Buda and proposed to march to the House of Parliament. The Soviet tanks, heading in the same direction, interposed no obstacle in the demonstrators' way; indeed, they arrived at the square at the head of the multitude in what seemed to be manifest fraternization. At any rate, the tank crews made no effort at dispersing the crowd or firing at it. They were stationed at the center of the square when fire was opened on the milling crowd from the neighboring rooftops. In what has been described as a scene of tragic confusion, some members of the Soviet crews were wounded or killed; the rest returned the fire, sweeping over the heads of the crowd and possibly— by accident or by design—into the crowd. No one knew who was firing at whom or for what reason.

The rooftops were manned by secret police detachments. The order to fire may have been given by jittery officials from nearby Party headquarters who were apprehensive lest the mob lay siege to the isolated inner sanctum and threaten the lives of its occupants. The unarmed crowd in the square sustained heavy casualties. Estimates of the number of dead and wounded range from several score to several hundred. Whichever figure is nearer the truth, the massacre was a turning point in the revolution. It inflamed the spirit of resistance and put an end to any temporizing about the actual leadership of the Party. Until then, Gero retained the reins of power at Party headquarters. A scant half hour after the massacre, his replacement by Janos Kadar was announced.

The reasons for the behavior of the Soviet military at this stage have never been satisfactorily explained. Perhaps the number of troops stationed in Hungary was insufficient to put down the uprising. Perhaps the troops were unreliable: rumors of defections among the Soviet military personnel were rife, and there may have been a number of actual instances.[2] But in the last analysis, the reason for the behavior of Soviet troops must be sought in the political stance of the Soviet government. As far as it is possible to deduce the attitude of the Soviet authorities from circumstantial evidence—bolstered by such tantalizing tidbits as Khrushchev's allusion to the Presidium's divided mind about the second, massive interven-

---

[2] No respondent interviewed in connection with our project was able to provide authenticated evidence of defection.

tion—their disposition was to avoid the commitment of military forces and to minimize disturbances in Hungary rather than aggravate them.

Mikoyan is said to have severely reprimanded Gero for prematurely and irresponsibly involving Soviet troops in the fracas. The Soviet emissary clearly perceived that the participation of Soviet troops was an unnecessary irritant that further inflamed an already aroused public and transformed civil strife that was controllable without danger to the minimum security requirements of the Soviet Union into international strife of much more menacing implications. The very type of intervention that had taken place created the worst possible situation for the Soviet Union.

For so long as the Soviet government was divided as to the proper course of action, it was well advised to steer clear of any direct interference. If massive Soviet military intervention were called for, the issue would have been much less muddled had Soviet forces not been involved in any manner prior to the final, decisive action. If matters could be settled without Soviet military "assistance," the half-hearted commitment of Soviet troops could at best prove embarrassing. The withdrawal of the troops while the insurrection was still in progress would be tantamount to a serious if not intolerable loss of face.

Although the Soviet military was not unequivocally withdrawn from battle, the indecisive role it played had precisely the effect of creating a myth among the insurgents that they had actually defeated the troops of the occupying power. In a sense this was true, for what is the use of troops if they cannot—for whatever reason or consideration—fulfill the function assigned to them? In a military sense, it was not true that the Soviet forces were defeated. They suffered but minor casualties; their fighting capacity was unimpaired; they had complete freedom of movement throughout the country and controlled the major rail and air transportation centers. Yet the cocky mood engendered by the illusion of having defeated the Soviet military grew as the revolution wore on.

11. Victory in the Balance, October 24-30

THE people's exhilaration reached a peak for the first time late at night on October 23. Toward dawn on the 24th excitement abated and fatigue set in. The break of day also brought sobering thoughts as to the consequences of the night's revels. Most people could not believe that they had actually engaged the regime in armed battle and had done so well against it. Partly because of their lack of organization and partly because of the very rapid but natural attrition of their fighting spirit, the insurgents did not consolidate the next day their hold on the public buildings which they had seized in their first assault during the night. At no time after the night of October 23 did the insurrection regain the character of a massed, armed rising. Its military action was reduced to sporadic small-scale encounters fought by isolated groups that formed on the spur of the moment and frequently disbanded as rapidly as they were formed. Their spheres of operation were usually limited to a particular city block or a major intersection. Only the so-called Dudas group, of which more later, possessed sizeable quantities of arms. Moreover, none of the fighting units was headed by a professional soldier. Those soldiers who participated in the fighting did so on their own initiative. The several fighting units were at no time coordinated in a national militia under unified command. Formal control of the armed forces remained in the hands of officers loyal to the Gero regime. It was only on October 30 that the first steps were taken toward the creation of a high command composed of representatives from various walks of life, including those army officers who sided with the revolution. The new high command did not succeed in developing either a citizen's army or a professional army before the revolution was smashed.

The military weakness of the revolution did not cripple it. It did not require military power to topple the government. In the end, when the Soviet Union decided to intervene resolutely, better military preparedness on the part of the insurgents would only have increased the toll of casualties without changing the outcome.

In the morning of October 24, the revolution entered its second phase. The wave of excitement that had gripped the capital during the night gave way to apprehensive disbelief in the reality of what had happened. Only sporadic rifle fire broke the calm of the capital. There suddenly was an eerie emptiness in the streets, imposed by martial law, which the government had decreed at 8:45 A.M. (The first announcement prohibiting demonstrations and public gatherings had come four hours earlier, at 4:30 A.M.)

What sustained the revolution during the three days from the 24th to the morning of the 27th was the grit of a few isolated fighting units in the capital that maintained a semblance of continuing resistance; the spread of the revolution into the countryside; and, most important, the impotence of the Communist Party leadership to make any effective decisions, let alone to enforce them. This impotence reflected a profound inner conflict leading to psychic paralysis.

THE COUNTRYSIDE JOINS THE REVOLUTION

The spread of the revolution into the countryside signaled both the collapse of central authority and the spontaneous nature of the rising. Revolution did not envelop the entire country at once. Unrest did not break out universally and uniformly as if according to plan. There was no organizational link between the progenitors of the revolution in the capital and those in the countryside. The followers of Imre Nagy were almost wholly concentrated in Budapest. Whatever influence they had outside the city was due to instinctive affinity felt for the ideas they propagated. Nor did the revolution in the countryside begin with mass demonstrations of peaceful intent organized and initially led by Communists.

In the countryside, the revolution had a distinct anti-Communist flavor from the outset. For a combination of reasons, it was at once more radical and less violent than in the capital. Physical violence was limited to a handful of localities where the military commander or the secret police official in charge chose to resist the demand of the population that he surrender. Resistance of this sort led to bloodshed (notably at Mosonmagyarovar, where some eighty persons are said to have been mowed down by machine gun fire directed at a crowd by the secret police) and to occasional instances of popular vengeance on the perpetrators of such atrocities (as in Miskolc). On the whole, however, the local Communist authorities yielded their offices and their arms to the people in what was a peaceful transfer of power. Soviet military units stationed in the countryside also behaved passively, having made *ad hoc* arrangements with the local population concerning mutual respect for each other's safety. Only one or two cases of Soviet military moves against Hungarian army units are on record.

The spineless behavior of the Communists in the countryside seems to have had several causes. With the collapse of central authority, their positions became untenable. The local Communist authorities were never sufficient to safeguard Communist power against massive popular unrest. No government can possibly staff a police force large enough to check an actively restless population in every inhabited locality.

In the capital, the impersonality of social contacts had provided a measure of immunity from public wrath for the Communists, as did the fortified character of a few key buildings that served as headquarters of the movement. In the countryside, the Communists were far more exposed to public opprobrium. Their faith in the Party had been shaken by a long period of declining public esteem. Now left to their own devices, they had to act as they saw fit. Some of them might have been sufficiently disillusioned with the Party to throw in their lot with the revolution. Others, the great majority of them, acted in the interest of self-preservation. Only a few chose to serve as the praetorian guard of the Party. Some attempted to flee. The Communist Party in the countryside simply melted away. Membership in the Party had long since lost whatever meaning it had had. The corps of functionaries was swiftly swallowed

up by the multitude. (To be sure, the situation was only slightly
more propitious in the capital; but a concentration of functionaries
at any one place was more conducive to Party fidelity.)

The initiative in the countryside was in the hands of students
wherever there happened to be a college; of workers; of almost
anyone who had either organizing ability or prestige among the
local population. The pattern of revolutionary committees throughout the country was not uniform. In general, revolutionary committees adopted the name of "national council" (*nemzeti bizott-
many*), although in some cases (e.g., Debrecen) they went under
the name of "socialist revolutionary council." They were generally
composed of workers, peasants, and intellectuals. As a rule, representatives of the various subcouncils were delegated to the revolutionary council by the respective revolutionary committees of workers, peasants, etc. The northern and western parts of the country
led the rest as to the speed with which revolutionary councils were
formed and the radicalism and articulateness of their demands.
The industrial towns of Miskolc and Gyor made real strides toward
the amalgamation of local revolutionary councils from the districts
which they dominated as well as from more distant areas.

Gyor, the home of Attila Szigeti, the most imposing political
figure of the revolution outside the capital, became the center of
gravity of revolutionary agitation.[1] Although it did not threaten
to rival Budapest or to free itself of the authority of the central
government, it set the tone of a great many political demands and
put the central government on notice that the support of the "parliament of revolutionary councils" at Gyor would be contingent on
these demands being met. Both at Miskolc and at Gyor the insurgents seized the radio station and turned it into their own instru-

[1] Szigeti was a self-styled politician. Of gentry origin, he joined the populist
movement as a "non-writing" member in the 1930s. He served as a parliamentary deputy of the National Peasant Party after 1945 and was a member
of its governing presidium. He became a fellow traveler and was allowed
by the Communists to retain his parliamentary seat for a time following the
seizure of power in 1948. But he was later "exiled" to Gyor and finally demoted to the directorship of a state farm. He reemerged during the revolution
and asserted vigorous and constructive leadership in Gyor, helping to disarm
the AVH and to squelch an attempt at a rightist putsch. Kadar sought to
enlist his services after the revolution was crushed, but Szigeti demurred. He
was imprisoned, where he eventually committed suicide.

ment before October 26. The Budapest radio station was then still held by the government. Finally, it was a delegation from Miskolc—led by the former Communist regional secretary, Rudolf Foldvari, an early supporter of Imre Nagy—which, on October 26, first placed before the prime minister a specific proposal for the withdrawal of Soviet troops by January 1, 1957.

As the revolution continued to spread, gaining in intensity and momentum, the focus of attention in Budapest shifted from the streets to the headquarters of the Communist Party. It was here that the final scenes of the drama were enacted. Outside Party headquarters the situation was fluid but not quite desperate. Except for the Party's printing plant,[2] no public building of importance had as yet fallen to the revolutionists. None of the ministries was occupied by the insurgents. The technical facilities of the main studios of the broadcasting corporation in downtown Budapest were out of commission, but emergency studios, connected with the central transmitter at Buda, were able to carry a full uninterrupted normal load. In this manner, the government retained control of the dominant airwave of the country. The transmissions of the first few days failed to intimate the scope of the political upheaval. They were reserved for government and government-approved denunciations of the insurrection and for exhortations recommending peace, calm, and forbearance.

No public utility was impaired. With motor transportation curtailed and the freedom of movement of the people hampered, if not entirely stifled, by stringent curfew regulations, the telephone became the principal medium of communication. Never before in the history of the capital were the capacities of the telephone exchange so heavily taxed. Restricted to their homes and emboldened by the belief that under the circumstances the secret police were too busy to spend much time monitoring telephone conversations, the population of Budapest reveled in private exchanges of opinion and information. Some refugees claim to have made several hundred telephone calls during the thirteen-day period of the revolution.

---

[2] *Szabad Nep,* the daily organ of the Party, was not published for two days. When publication was resumed, the paper was edited by insurgents.

THE PARTY IN TRAVAIL

In the meantime, Party headquarters was seized with feverish activity. The session of the Communist Central Committee, begun sometime after 10 P.M. on October 23, broke up in the early morning hours of the 24th. It resulted in the reshuffling of the Central Committee and of the Politbureau, the issuing of proclamations that confirmed the call for assistance of the Soviet military, and the declaration of martial law. It also took a decision to appoint Nagy Premier of the government.

The actions taken during the first night failed in their intended effect. Concessions in the form of personnel changes came too late to placate the population. The retention of Gero as first secretary alone was insulting to the people. Soviet intervention poured oil on the fire, and martial law did not cow the insurgents.

The rush of activity at Party headquarters did not abate during the ensuing three days. The labors of the mountain, however, brought forth the proverbial mouse. The details of what must have been stormy interchanges among the Communist leaders have not come to light, but the public record, although skimpy, provides eloquent testimony to the progressive paralysis of the Party's nerve center.

The presence of two high-ranking Soviet emissaries, Mikoyan and Suslov, from the morning hours of the 24th until some time in the afternoon of the 26th did not help the situation. The gap between Party headquarters and the world outside grew ever wider. Those on the inside finally lost all sense of the reality of the world about them. The ranking members of the Communist hierarchy remained sealed off at headquarters day and night. Others, including representatives of the Writers' Association, drifted in and out of the building, serving as a channel of communications between the two worlds; but they had no noticeable impact on the deliberations conducted by the powers inside.

Imre Nagy's supporters barely had a chance to apprise him of the temper of the nation. They saw him only briefly under unfavorable circumstances. They found him brusque to the point of rudeness and unreceptive to their ideas.[3] The premier's isolation from his supporters was in part a function of the physical conditions prevailing at Party headquarters, but, in part, this temporary but significant alienation was due to his own self-imposed attitude. At a time of crisis, he—like all the other old warhorses of the movement, especially those who had gone through the tough Moscow school—reverted to a platform of orthodoxy that was as disappointing to his more impetuous younger comrades as it was comforting to the Soviet leaders. Whether or not they had full confidence in Nagy or his ability to rescue the situation is a moot question.

Nagy may not have been the ideal premier from the Soviet point of view (just as Gomulka was not in Poland). His tenure of office may have been regarded by the Soviet leaders as a temporary expedient forced upon them by circumstances. Still, at that time, the Soviet Union had not given up hope of saving the situation without military intervention. Problematic as it was how Nagy would handle matters, he was left in charge in good faith as the last best hope of the Communist cause, and not as a person who would predictably side with the revolution and lead the insurgents to the destruction of the entire Communist-built edifice.

Not that Nagy was merely passive in doing the Soviet's bidding. Wrangles between him and the "Soviet comrades" have been reliably reported. These disagreements touched on matters of principle on which Nagy could not compromise. For example, he steadfastly refused to assume public responsibility for issuing the call for Soviet military assistance. He was less reluctant to accept responsibility for declaring martial law, although on October 30 he disclaimed any complicity in this matter as well.

But in general, Nagy's disposition during the first three days of the revolution was not that of an official testing the limits of tolerance of the Soviet Union. There was no sense of incipient betrayal of the Communist cause about him. Neither he nor

[3] For example, a suggestion advanced by Miklos Gimes advocating the acceptance of the principle of multi-party political system as part of a Communist reform platform was vehemently rejected by Nagy.

his eventual detractors foresaw the enormous transformation he was to undergo during the days that followed.

In reality, Nagy's position in the Party, and even in the government, was anything but powerful. Hegedus remained as deputy premier until his flight to the Soviet Union on October 26. In the Party, Nagy was carefully hemmed in by Communists who stood somewhere between the contending sectarian and reformist factions. Their chief exponent was Janos Kadar, who became first secretary of the Party on October 25. Only two of Nagy's followers, Ferenc Donath and Geza Losonczy, received high Party posts. Both were made members of the Central Committee. Losonczy became an alternate member of the Politbureau. Donath became one of three new secretaries of the Party.

The composition of the Politbureau as announced on the morning of the 24th reflected the temporizing character of the changes within the Party. It had eleven full members (Antal Apro, Sandor Gaspar, Erno Gero, Andras Hegedus, Janos Kadar, Gyula Kallai, Karoly Kiss, Jozsef Kobol, Gyorgy Marosan, Imre Nagy, Zoltan Szanto) and two alternates (Geza Losonczy and Sandor Ronai). The Muscovite-Stalinist contingent was reduced to a single representative, Gero, who retained his post as first secretary and by all accounts continued to wield overriding influence at Party headquarters. The most prominent victims of the reapportionment of representations in the Politbureau were Istvan Kovacs, and Jozsef Revai. Hegedus was Gero's faithful retainer. Szanto was an old "Muscovite" who represented a moderate position. Seven members of the new Politbureau were functionaries. Some had been in prison (Kallai, Kadar, Marosan). Others had served the Rakosi regime well even if they lacked enthusiasm for Rakosi personally. It is interesting to note that all seven betrayed the revolution and six of them still constitute the core of the Hungarian Communist leadership as members of the Politbureau elected at the Party Congress on December 5, 1959. Only one (Kobol) was eliminated from the Politbureau and the Central Committee because of his sympathies for Nagy. Another (Gaspar) was demoted to alternate member of the Politbureau. Of the two alternates, Losonczy was an outright supporter of Nagy. He in fact was the most vocal of the reformists and associated himself with the demands of the revolution at an earlier time and more fully than did his mentor. The other alternate, Sandor Ronai, was an ex-Social Democrat turned rabid Communist. He has been elevated to full membership in the Politbureau.

At first, neither Losonczy nor Donath accepted the office to which they were "elected" *in absentia* and without their knowledge. After a day's delay, however, they assumed their duties at Party headquarters.

On October 25 at 12:32 P.M., the second change in the Party hierarchy was announced by the government-controlled radio. Gero's dismissal broke the stranglehold he had on the Communist leadership. From then on, Kadar and Nagy were the only public spokesmen of the Party. Kadar's address to the nation as chief secretary of the Party, at 3:12 P.M. on October 25, did not mention Gero's dismissal. It contained no recrimination against Rakosi. His analysis of the events admitted an intermingling of honest elements driven by honorable if misguided motives and of counterrevolutionary forces. He asserted that the Party leadership was unanimous in its determination to beat back the attack of the counterrevolution and promised the examination of the most inflammatory issues after the restoration of law and order. Nagy in his speeches on October 24 and 25 took a similar line, although he was somewhat more explicit in identifying the type of reforms the Party would consider.

Essentially, the public position of the Party leadership was unyielding. It made reforms contingent on restoring order. But its appeals sounded ineffectual and even pathetic. The bulletins it issued about the imminent liquidation of counterrevolutionary forces were optimistic. The repeated extension of the deadline on an amnesty to those insurgents who laid down their arms betrayed, however, the inability of the Party to regain the initiative and vitiated the intended effect of martial law.

On October 26, at last, the Communist Party abandoned the pretense of being in control of the situation. A proclamation issued in behalf of the Central Committee for the first time offered concrete concessions without extracting a price for them. The an-

nouncement of an important proclamation was first made by
radio at 10:05 A.M. The text was not read until 4:13 P.M. The
delay is reported to have been caused by Nagy's objection to the
wording of several passages, notably to a reference linking him with
the calling of Soviet troops. The final text contained no mention
of the events surrounding the outbreak of the revolution.

In the proclamation, the Central Committee, "led by Imre
Nagy," proposed to the Presidium of the National Council of the
Patriotic People's Front to recommend to the Presidential Council
of the People's Republic the election of a new government that
would be based on the "broadest national foundations." The new
government was "to open negotiations with the Soviet Government in order to settle relations between the . . . countries on the
basis of independence, complete equality, and noninterference in
each other's internal affairs." As a first step toward this end,
"Soviet troops will, after the restoration of order, immediately return to their bases."

So far, there was no hint of any acquiescence in a multi-party
system, but the Patriotic People's Front—essentially a Communist-
manipulated mass organization—was endowed with more meaningful political functions than in the past. Similarly, there was
no hint of a withdrawal of Soviet troops from Hungary, let alone
of Hungary's withdrawal from the Warsaw Pact. Only the return
of Soviet troops to their bases in Hungary was promised, and that
after the restoration of calm. Still, the tone of the proclamation
was conciliatory. It continued in that vein by condoning the formation of workers' councils "through the intermediary of the trade
union organs." The sphere of jurisdiction of the workers' councils, however, was not defined.

Further, the proclamation granted "amnesty to all those who
had taken part in the armed struggle," provided they laid down
their arms by 10 P.M. on the same day. At the same time the Central Committee professed its "adherence to the principles of socialist
democracy" and vowed to "annihilate without mercy those who
fail to lay down their arms within the set time limit." Finally, the
elaboration of changes "in the economic and political sphere will
begin immediately after order has been restored."

Even as the proclamation was broadcast, Mikoyan and Suslov departed from Budapest, as did Gero, Hegedus, and a few other high-ranking Communists. The Hungarian Communists disappeared from Party headquarters stealthily, unknown to Nagy, who is said to have discovered their absence toward the evening hours. Thereupon he transferred his seat to the House of Parliament.

At 8:45 P.M. on October 26, the Budapest city committee of the Communist Party broadcast an appeal to its members to stop the bloodshed and restore order. The new leadership of the Party was offered as the best guarantee that the just demands of the population would be met. The first phase of the collapse of the central organs of the Communist Party was complete.

Swift as the Party's transformation was, it was not fast enough to keep pace with the events. It took three days to effect a few relatively simple personnel changes that were clearly unavoidable. Had they been executed instantaneously, they might have saved the Party from total collapse. The explanation for the delay once again rests on circumstantial evidence: Gero's stubborn clinging to his office; bickering between opposing factions; disorientation occasioned by inadequate news of developments throughout the country; and, ultimately, a helpless waiting for clarification of Moscow's position.

On October 27, a member of a workers' delegation from Dunapentele (a vast industrial complex of foundries and steel mills) joyfully and somewhat hyperbolically reported the "flight of the last representative of Stalinism" from Hungary. A reorganization of the government was announced at 11:18 on the morning of the same day.

THE CABINET: CHANGING COMPOSITION AND METHODS OF OPERATION

The new cabinet of October 27 still contained an elaborate roster of familiar Communist names, along with a sprinkling of new names—Communists and non-Communists alike—that gave it a refurbished appearance. The portfolio of Foreign Affairs was held by Imre Horvath, a Communist. The Ministry of the Interior was in the charge of Ferenc Munnich, a veteran Communist with experience gained in the Spanish civil war. Karoly Janza, the Minister of National Defense, had served as Deputy Minister in the same department since 1950. Antal Apro, a Deputy Prime Minister, needs no further description. Istvan Kossa, the Minister of Finance, and Lajos Bebrits, the Minister of Transportation and Communication, were also Communists with an unsavory record of service. Antal Gyenes, the new Minister of Crop Collections, however, was a thoroughly reputable Communist who had worked as an unskilled laborer at the height of the Rakosi terror. Gyorgy Lukacs, as Minister of Culture, and Antal Babits (a professor of great prestige) as Minister of Health, lent a measure of respectability to the cabinet. They mitigated the unfavorable impression created by the presence of so many Communists in it. But the most eye-catching innovation was the presence in the cabinet of two former Smallholder leaders—Zoltan Tildy was made Minister of State, and Bela Kovacs, the former secretary general of the Smallholder Party, became Minister of Agriculture. Of somewhat less importance, but not without interest, was the presence of the controversial Ferenc Erdei, former crypto-Communist National Peasant leader, in still another Deputy Premiership.

The size of the cabinet seemed preposterous in the circumstances. What the government needed was a compact directing body. Moreover, the presence of certain luminaries was obviously more ornamental than functional, intended only to gain the confidence of the population.[4]

In deference to public pressure, several members of the government were dismissed during the following two days, among them Lajos Bebrits, to whom the revolutionary councils of the active and alert northwestern counties took strong exception.

THE THIRD PHASE: OCTOBER 26-30

While the Communist Party and the government were in deep travail, the revolution gathered momentum and refined the content of its fundamental aims. Tabulations of publicly aired demands—in terms of the frequency with which they were reiterated

4 Bela Kovacs, for instance, who was at Pecs when requested to join the government, arrived in Budapest only on November 1 and never had a chance to take part in the government's deliberations.

and of the specificity of their content—show that between October 26 and 28 the revolutionists concentrated on obtaining a cease-fire and on inducing the government to accept in principle the major points of the programs set forth on October 23. As soon as these were met by Imre Nagy in a cease-fire proclamation at 1:20 P.M. (on October 28) and in a public address at 3:25 the same afternoon, the focus of attention shifted to the attainment of internal political reforms: a multi-party system, free elections—in sum, the whole range of democratic freedoms. When these were fully met on October 30 in still another government proclamation which signaled the total internal victory of the revolution, interest shifted to the speedy settlement of Hungary's relations with the USSR.

THE SHIFTING PATTERN OF REVOLUTIONARY ACTIVITY

By October 26, the number and type of revolutionary organizations had greatly increased. Notable among them were the workers' councils that were springing up in factories throughout the country more or less simultaneously. The impetus for the creation of these councils cannot be traced to a single source. Intellectuals and workers alike, quite independently from one another, seem to have conceived of the idea at about the same time. They were familiar to a degree with the Yugoslav system of workers' councils, but it is not clear how closely they wished to copy the Yugoslav model. The councils had no precisely defined responsibilities. In practice, they exceeded by far the sphere of jurisdiction of the Yugoslav councils.

The councils replaced the bankrupt trade-union hierarchy in the factories [5] and also assumed managerial responsibilities that extended over the whole range of economic and social welfare problems pertaining to their respective plants or shops. While the councils were initially not charged with explicit political functions, some of their activities—such as the disposition they made of managerial personnel appointed by the Communists and

[5] This was, of course, only a temporary expedient, pending the establishment of a free trade-union organization. As far as we know, no one seriously thought of permanently replacing the trade unions as proper instruments representing the workers' interests by a pyramidal system of workers' councils.

the part they played in organizing the defense of factories—clearly had political connotations. After November 4, the councils were to gain additional political significance.

Coincidentally with the rise of the workers' councils, but not in causal relation to their development, revolutionary organizations of students and intellectuals also came into being: but they lacked resolution, and their influence was declining. They acted more as individuals or members of informal circles of friends than as affiliates of a particular interest group or professional association. This was especially true of the university students, who were the first to abandon fighting and as a result lost contact with one another on a university-to-university basis. They did not represent a coherent force, capable of formulating an over-all view or of mobilizing for any sort of concerted action.

The withdrawal of students from the street fighting altered the composition of the groups that persisted in armed resistence against the Soviet military. These groups were now, for the most part, made up of young workers (generally apprentices), and of teen-age high school students. They also included *Lumpenproletariat* elements. The typical freedom fighter with gun in hand did not cut a particularly appealing figure. His motivation for fighting did not always rest on noble patriotic sentiments. Many of the teenagers considered it great fun to blow up Soviet tanks with home made "Molotov cocktails." Many of the *Lumpenproletariat* elements were working off their resentments against society in general.

Official Communist propaganda has sought to discredit the entire revolution by emphasizing the presence of criminals and hoodlums among the freedom fighters and by exaggerating the part they played in the revolutionary events. It is well to remember in this connection that active street fighting was by no means a decisive or even an important aspect of the revolution after the first night. It is equally important to note that individual acts of bravery lost none of their value for lack of proper motivation on the part of the people that performed them.

As for revolutionary initiative, it rested with the countryside rather than with Budapest, which was still in a state of siege.

Movement was difficult and dangerous, especially at the principal points controlled by Soviet motorized units and in areas where sporadic fighting continued. The secret police, although shorn of authority and operating more or less on its own, displayed both tenacity and cleverness in infiltrating insurgent fighting units and haphazardly formed revolutionary groups. It was not until late evening on October 28, or possibly early morning the following day, that a joint order of the Ministers of National Defense and of the Interior ordered the army and the police to "obey the government and . . . show respect for the people." It is still not clear if the order applied to the secret police and was honored by it. The suspicion is that it did not, and that the secret police remained a law unto itself.

It was only on October 31 that coordinated activity by the secret police ceased in the capital and that secret policemen began to surrender at points designated by revolutionary committees. Evidence of isolated acts of secret police infiltration, however, were reported till the very end of the revolution. For example, police spies were said to have wormed their way into the newly established headquarters of the Smallholder Party. Although the administrative nerve center of the secret police, housed in the building of the Ministry of the Interior, fell to the insurgents, it is still unclear whether the operational center of the AVH was ever conquered. The chances are that it continued to operate, albeit with much diminished efficiency.

The countryside, on the other hand, was almost wholly free of Communist and Soviet military interference. Miskolc and Gyor were in strategic positions to formulate and dictate revolutionary demands and did so. While it is impossible to know what signal Nagy responded to, his proclamation of a cease-fire in the early afternoon of October 28 followed by only one hour and five minutes a broadcast ultimatum by the Gyor radio demanding a cease-fire by 8 P.M. The boldness and recalcitrance of the two provincial centers of the uprising, manifest in the claims they put forth and in the defiant tone with which they greeted Nagy's "capitulation," sharply contrasted with the note struck by the Revolutionary Council of Intellectuals—comprising the revolutionary councils of university students, writers, journalists, the Petofi Circle, the NEKOSZ, and MEFESZ—which still was the loudest voice of the insurrection in Budapest.

THE CEASE-FIRE AND THE GOVERNMENT PROCLAMATION OF OCTOBER 28

The cease-fire order of the government commanded Hungarian military forces and security troops to stop shooting at the insurgents. This brought fighting formally to a halt and quickened the pulse of daily life in Budapest.[6] In five days of skirmishing, 3,500 casualties were sustained by both sides. Of these—according to official estimates made on the spot—250 were dead. The cease-fire, may well have been ordered in direct response to urging from the provinces. In the circumstances, it was the only thing possible for the government. To prolong armed conflict would have served no good purpose. The restoration of peace was indeed a precondition for the resumption of normal life.

The manner in which peace was restored did not quite correspond to the earlier expectations of the Communists, including Imre Nagy. It was obvious that the isolated pockets of freedom fighters would not give up in response to repeated offers of an amnesty. It was equally obvious that the Hungarian army and police could not be effectively engaged in battle against the insurgents and that the Russians would not even if they could. With the passage of time, the morale of the Soviet troops declined sharply as they began to adjust themselves to the situation in which they were caught. With the Hungarian Communist leadership gone and the Russian political emissaries apparently agreed to weather the storm without Soviet military involvement, fighting had to be stopped. The terms on which this was done—no re-prisals whatever against the insurgents—represented a capitulation by the government.

The government proclamation, read over the radio by Imre Nagy at 3:25 P.M., was the final submission to the insurgents' will. The terminology and content of the proclamation differentiated it

---

[6] The cease-fire was meant to apply to Soviet troops, but they and groups of insurgents continued to act as they saw fit.

sharply from preceding announcements. Missing were the Communist jargon and the specious explanation of revolutionary events. Prominently featured in the speech, and first in order of precedence among the concessions promised by the government, were the material grievances of the urban and rural working people. Wages, work norms, minimum pay, family allowances, and pensions were all due for revision. A solution of the "grave housing crisis" was promised, as was the "extension of democracy" to enterprises through workers' councils.

In the countryside, Nagy offered to aid in revitalizing production in cooperative and individual farms and to rectify "serious illegalities" in the organization of collective farms and the commassation of land. The principle of cooperative farming, however, was not clearly disavowed.

In the political sphere Nagy was still less explicit. He gave assurance of "government support" for the "new organs of democratic self government that have sprung up at the people's initiative." But he did not go beyond saying that an attempt would be made to "find a place for them in the administration." He also touched on the delicate question of the organs of security. The creation of a new army "without delay" was one of his stated aims. As to the secret police, its dissolution would be decreed "after the reestablishment of order" and the organization of a new unified state police force.

Nagy also offered to restore the Kossuth emblem and the observance of March 15 as a national holiday.

On the burning issue of Soviet troops and of relations with the USSR, Nagy asserted that "the Hungarian government has come to an agreement with the Soviet government that Soviet forces shall withdraw from Budapest and that simultaneously with the formation of our new army they shall evacuate the city." He also said that the government would "initiate negotiations in order to settle relations with the Soviet Union . . . among other things with regard to the withdrawal of Soviet forces stationed in Hungary."

The vagueness of Nagy's political program was immediately noticed, and it was perhaps for this reason that during the next two days demands centered upon the closer definition of the content of domestic political reforms. Why Nagy chose to be vague on these issues can only be guessed at. Perhaps he wanted to hold the line until the revolution subsided and relations with the Soviet Union were normal again. He may have feared that to admit the collapse of all political control would invite Soviet intervention. It is inconceivable that at this time he would have been personally unsympathetic to granting the full range of democratic freedoms or that he could have hoped to avoid granting them.

Nagy's differentiation—accidental or deliberate—between the immediate evacuation of Budapest by Soviet troops and their withdrawal from the country after negotiations of unspecified duration also aroused adverse comment and fed suspicions. Here again it seems improbable that Nagy's intent was to deceive. He probably used an ambiguous formula in the hope that it would clear the atmosphere without blatantly insulting the Russians.

THE ROLE OF IMRE NAGY

With every passing day, the dissolution of the Communist Party grew more evident. On October 28, as a sequel to Nagy's first series of concessions, the direction of the Party was entrusted to a six-member caretaker presidium consisting of Kadar (chairman), Apro, Kiss, Munnich, Szanto, and Nagy.

The disintegration of any semblance of centrally directed formal Communist Party control, however, did not necessarily mean the cessation of all Communist influence on Imre Nagy and his government. When Nagy abandoned Party headquarters, its other occupants also scattered. Some, like Jozsef Darvas, went home into hiding; others, like Andor Berei and his wife Erzsebet Andics, departed for the Soviet Union. Still others accompanied Nagy to his new command post at the House of Parliament and remained in his immediate vicinity. The actual power they wielded and the precise roles they played cannot be determined. In the circumstances, they cannot have been very great. But they were privy to the negotiations that were going on in the House of Parliament day and night. They were closer to the center of things than were most others. Men like Apro, Kiss, Munnich, and, of course, Kadar, conferred with Nagy on a more or less continuing basis. Their advice was sought, and they were often consulted on matters that were, strictly speaking, well outside their spheres of competence.[7] By contrast, many a former supporter of Nagy had difficulty in gaining admission to the House of Parliament, which was guarded by Communist motorized detachments.

The prime minister was besieged by an unending stream of delegations from diverse revolutionary councils. He personally received as many as he could. It was through them that he learned of the mood of the country and the demands of the people and it was under the unceasing pressure of their demands that he yielded point by point in domestic matters and eventually in foreign affairs as well.

Prudence demands that the details of Nagy's personal trans- formation during these few days go unrecorded for lack of evidence. While it is possible to state confidently that in the end he caught something of the fire of the revolutionary excitement surrounding him, and that he was the leader of the revolution in fact as well as in name, it would be presumptuous to give an account of the motives that impelled his actions.

Nagy's immediate circle included Geza Losonczy, considered by many the real moving spirit of the government, and Zoltan Tildy, the former Smallholder President who acted virtually as the premier's alter ego and displayed unusual energy and sagacity. For practical work, Nagy relied on a six-man secretariat composed of Communists who had gone a long way toward abandoning the Party and its ideology. Some were victims of the Rakosi terror. Jozsef Szilagyi, whom Nagy met and befriended as a junior col- league during his stint as a university professor, acted as the premier's personal secretary. Ferenc Donath was in charge of radio and information matters. Gyorgy Heltai, a neighbor and social acquaintance of the premier's, was in charge of foreign affairs with the title of deputy minister. Ferenc Janosi, Nagy's son-in-law, was responsible for military matters. Gyorgy Surecz, a young man of working-class background who befriended some of Nagy's close

7 For example, Kiss and Apro took part in the crucial discussions on No- vember 1 concerning the declaration of Hungary's neutrality. Not a single non-Communist was present.

associates and became a follower of his, handled Party affairs. Finally, the writer, Gyorgy Fazekas, brother-in-law of Sandor Kopacsi, the chief of the Budapest police, had less explicitly defined duties.

Rounding out the official family were Istvan Dobi and Istvan Kristof, the Chairman and Secretary respectively of the Presidential Council of the Republic. They were in constant attendance in the House of Parliament, and although their functions were ceremonial, they provided a formal, legal sanction for the government as the highest functionaries of the legislature. They did not belong to Imre Nagy's "circle": their allegiance to the revolution itself was questionable. Both made the transition to the counterrevolutionary government, installed by the Russians, without a break in stride. They continue to hold their posts to this date.

Nagy also resuscitated Zoltan Vas as commissioner of supplies with the special task of provisioning the city of Budapest. Vas's reappearance recalled the heroic days of 1945, when he had won glory for mastering the disastrous supply situation of the capital. But, as a Communist of checkered career and reputation, he aroused a considerable amount of displeasure among the revolutionaries. He subsequently disappeared without any formal notice being given of his dismissal and at an unspecified time.

Nagy's secretariat acted as liaison between the premier and the outside world. But it could not relieve him of enough responsibilities, even for trivial matters, to allow him time for quiet contemplation. The cadence of his actions, as already stated, was largely determined by the flow of revolutionary delegations to the House of Parliament. Two distinct phases in his activities are nevertheless discernible. Until November 1, his attention was caught and held by the flow of visiting delegations. After November 1, his energies were concentrated almost entirely on deliberations with his associates and with diplomatic representatives—especially the Russian Ambassador—involving a single issue, the settlement of Hungary's relations with the Soviet Union.

On the whole, Nagy did not impose his own views on his callers. Nor did his views prevail. Rather, it was he who acceded to the demands placed before him. Still, he grew in stature as the revolution unfolded, and his position grew more secure. The net effect of the visits of revolutionary delegations was to reaffirm popular confidence in him as a worthy representative of national interests.

Thus, at the nominal seat of power, a confused situation prevailed. With the Communist Party out of power, Communists of varying hues occupied most of the pivotal governmental positions, although their own personal fates in the event of a permanent victory for the revolution would have been anyone's guess.

Outside the government, Communists—even those who abandoned the Party and wholeheartedly joined the revolution in deed and in spirit—rapidly lost all influence. They yielded before the onrush of popular forces expressed through a multitude of other revolutionary organizations. Some of these were new creations. Others were reincarnations of former democratic associations, parties, interest groups, or professional societies. The apparent dichotomy between the government and the country at large merely underlined the fundamental unity of purpose that had been born in the heat of revolution. The surprising thing was not that there was such a startling difference between the political composition of the central authorities and that of all other organizations and institutions, but that so broad a harmony prevailed between them.

In the circumstances, it could hardly have been otherwise. All but a few Communist diehards were caught up in the fever of the revolution, and the spontaneous nature of the uprising precluded precisely the seizure of power at the very apex of the institutional pyramid of the country. The dearth of democratic politicians of national stature was as much responsible for this as was the timidity and irresolution of those who happened to be available. The wisdom and resoluteness of the participants in the revolution varied, generally speaking, in inverse ratio to their distance from the center of power. Men of stature were for the most part made timid by the recollection of their unhappy political careers, which included incarceration in many instances. Their attitude was a mixture of wonderment and disbelief. Having once been pushed to the periphery of public life, not to say of human existence, they reacted to subsequent events too slowly to be effective in the runaway pace of the revolution. Understandably, they also hedged against the future. They never quite believed that the Russians would acquiesce in the victory of the revolution. Naturally, they accepted public responsibility only reluctantly.[8]

Time was too short to bring forth new national leaders. Again, the astonishing thing was not that so few men of prominence appeared on the scene, but that so many capable persons were raised to leadership so quickly on intermediate regional and institutional levels. The speed with which things seemed to order themselves held out excellent promise for recovery after the victory of the revolution. The government too, confused and ineffectual as it was, operated more smoothly than might have been expected. Toward the end of the second week of the revolution, it showed definite signs of mastering the situation, and, by joining with the strivings of revolutionary organizations from below, it gave encouraging assurance of an early return to ordered national existence.

THE ROLE OF INTELLECTUALS RECONSIDERED

The pace of revolutionary developments bewildered the intellectuals and left them simultaneously exhilarated and apprehensive. The mood of the intellectual community in Budapest was reflected in a manifesto drawn up on October 28, *after* they heard the government declaration that accepted the demands of the revolutionaries in principle.[9] Hailing the "final victory" of the Hungarian people in its "heroic struggle for freedom," it set down a nine-point program of reforms. Point 1 specified the "ordering of Hungary's relations with the USSR" and the withdrawal of

[8] A case in point was Jozsef Kovago, a Smallholder leader and former mayor of Budapest, who had been imprisoned by the Rakosi regime. The revolutionary City Council of Budapest restored him to the position he once held, but he flatly refused to take office and left one of his deputies in charge. See his account in *You are All Alone* (New York, Praeger, 1959), pp. 228-29.

[9] It was made public the following day in the form of an open letter signed by Istvan Pozsar, Jozsef Molnar and Janos Varga in behalf of the Revolutionary Council of Students; Sandor Erdei, Gyula Sipos, Tibor Meray, and Sandor Haraszti in behalf of the writers; Miklos Vasarhelyi and Ivan Boldizsar, for the newspapermen; Tamas Nagy, Mate Major, Ivan Kadar, and Gyorgy Markos for the university instructors; Laszlo Kardos, Antal Gyenes, and Otto Tokes as spokesmen of the NEKOSZ; Gabor Tanczos and Balazs Nagy for the Petofi Circle; Gyorgy Judics for the MEFESZ; Laszlo Bencze and Jozsef Somogyi for the artists; and Pal Jardanyi and Endre Szervanszky for the composers.

Soviet forces from the entire territory of the country. It made
no reference to the Warsaw treaty and obligations stemming there-
from. Point 2 reiterated the oft-heard demand that "all unfavorable foreign trade treaties be abrogated." Point 3 called for general, secret, and free elections; it was bolstered by point 9, which
called for "full freedom of press, speech, and assembly." Although
no specific reference was made to the restitution of a multi-party
system, the advocacy of free elections and freedom of assembly
could hardly be construed as anything but implicit recognition
of the inevitability of such a development. Point 4 concerned
itself with securing the usufruct of industrial production for the
workers. It specifically warned against returning "factory and
land . . . to capitalist and landowner." Points 5-8 also dealt with
economic and social problems, seeking to satisfy the material
wants of workers and peasants, to safeguard the legitimate interests
of artisans and shopkeepers, and to prevent the revival of large-
scale free enterprise. The question of cooperative farming was
passed over in silence.

There was nothing retrograde about the manifesto. It was a
great advance over the stance taken by intellectuals during the
first two or three days of the revolution, when they in fact pleaded
the government's cause by asking for the restoration of law and
order as a precondition for the meeting of revolutionary goals.

At the same time, the manifesto was not as militant as were
the demands of the insurgents from the countryside. It seemed to
assume that now that the government had aligned itself with the
revolution, all would be well in due course. It did not convey a
need for additional vigilance and pressure on the government to
see that these demands were met. Its spirit, not its formal content,
was at variance with the proclamations then being issued outside
the capital. The impression it gave—incorrectly—was that its sign-
ers were satisfied, that they wished to stem the tide of revolution,
not augment it. In this respect the temper of the intellectual
community in Budapest differed from that of the aggregate of
revolutionary councils throughout the country. The significance
of this discrepancy should not be exaggerated, for, in the end, all

such differences in temper were obliterated by the defeat of the revolution.

The stance of the Budapest intellectuals is nevertheless worth considering, for they represented the cream of the country's elite. Caution must be exercised when attributing collective attitudes to them. They engaged in all manner of activities—mostly liaison, publicity, and pamphleteering—but some simply went home to contemplate the future and to look after their families. Others immersed themselves in literary creation.[10]

Consider Tibor Dery, who stirred up much of the intellectual ferment preceding the revolution and was generally respected as a man of backbone and convictions; he was completely passive during the revolution. There is no record of his having taken any initiative in the revolutionary council of intellectuals. He missed their meetings and contributed nothing to their programmatic pronouncements. Tamas Aczel, the vocal and agile Stalin Prize winner, also appears to have withdrawn from overt participation in the revolutionary events. By contrast, Sandor Erdei and Zoltan Molnar, whose names figured less spectacularly in the prerevolutionary events, were the true moving spirits of the Writers' Association during the revolution proper. They in fact held the Association together at a time when many of its members lost the splendid sense of institutional solidarity they had felt for it in the period preceding the revolution. The diminution in institutional identification with the Association, of course, was due to the substitution for it of a higher sense of solidarity—with the whole nation. But this was a shapeless sort of identification, lacking any well-defined institutional form. It left plenty of leeway for individual responses to the given situation and encouraged especially the creative artist to give vent to his long-suppressed desire for individual expression.

Despite the break-up of any formal unity of the intellectual community of Budapest, intellectuals generally shared a formal

10 Despite its short duration, the revolution was immortalized in quite an extraordinary volume of hortatory literature composed on the spot. Witness, for example, the issue of *Irodalmi Ujsag* published on November 2 at the height of the victory of the revolution. It contains a representative sample of the product of writers of diverse political affiliations and of very different literary styles. The editing of this issue of *Irodalmi Ujsag* was the high point of the revolutionary activity of several writers.

reserve.[11] They did not lack enthusiasm for the revolution, but few if any of them were able to shake off nagging apprehensions about the dangers of a resurgence of internal strife should the revolution veer too far to the right—a possibility they thought unlikely, although they did not rule it out completely—and about the possibility of Soviet retaliation, which would be inevitable if the revolution were carried too far. It was largely for these reasons that they tried to moderate radical trends.

The realization that pleas for moderation were probably useless only enhanced a sense of weakness already felt; for the revolution painfully exposed the sterility of their ideas.

Neither the Communists, who had an opportunity to express their views prior to the revolution, nor the non-Communists, who had had to keep silent, had anything original or even viable to offer. The quality of their diagnosis was not matched by prescription of cure. In part, of course, this was due to the fact that they had concentrated almost single-mindedly on the removal of existing evils. In part, they were paralyzed by their circumspection, which made them pit the stark realities that impeded the fulfillment of Hungarian national aspirations against the ideal aims of the people —complete freedom. They saw, or perhaps only sensed, that the ideals striven for by the people could be realized only in a world differently ordered from the one in which they were living and over which they had no control. In this regard, they reflected a superior realism bordering on cynicism which they acquired as a result of disillusioning experiences during the preceding decade and a half. This does not mean that they did not fervently wish for the realization of these ideals or that they were wholly without illusions concerning the nature of the enemy. They, too, managed to

[11] Least affected by the dispersal of the intellectual community was the Petofi Circle. Not that it retained great institutional significance. By November 3, when it elected its new presidium composed largely of non-Communists, it too had lost much of its attractiveness and retained an influence that was largely symbolic. Yet, of all organizations that antedated the revolution, it came closest to supplying the revolution and more importantly the incipient postrevolutionary administration with a general staff. Slowly (by the standards of the revolution) and almost by a process of automatic sifting, persons formally and informally affiliated with the Petofi Circle emerged in a variety of capacities in government offices, revolutionary councils, and public institutions.

convince themselves—at least superficially—that in the end all would
be well and that by some miracle dreams would come true. They
were, in short, hedging. On the one hand, they were carried by the
momentum of the revolution and by their sense of duty to society;
on the other hand, their fears of the repercussions of victory
mounted as evidence of Soviet intentions accumulated.

The role of the intellectual in Hungary has been traditionally
framed in terms of duty to society. The precise nature of the relations between the intellectuals and the nation was—it will be remembered—a central point of the deliberations at Szarszo. The very
same issue was now enacted. The betrayal of this trust by a large
segment of the intellectuals weighed heavily on their consciences.
As we have seen, the opposition they manifested toward the Communist regime in the period 1953–56 was strongly motivated by a
desire to atone for their past sins. The revolution provided them
with a further opportunity to redeem themselves. To this end they
sought to suppress doubts that would have brought them into
opposition to the popular will once more. (This applied to Communists rather than to non-Communists, many of whom had a clean
slate as far as their personal behavior was concerned.)

Some of the non-Communists, men like Laszlo Nemeth, had acquired an almost saintly reputation as a result of their ascetic withdrawal from public life and their steadfast refusal to succumb to
the Communist regime's pressure and enticement. The simple spiritual message of Nemeth—Hungary for the Hungarians—so hotly
debated at Szarszo, now commanded awe; not because of its intrinsic
brilliance but because of the contrast in which it stood to other,
often well-reasoned and well-intentioned viewpoints that were
proven by practical experience to be defective.

The differences that once separated Communist and non-Communist intellectuals lost much of their immediate significance. Many
Communists, chastised by the fiasco of their involvement, abandoned all dogmatic affiliation with the Party and espoused instead
a sort of shapeless liberalism that exalted the freedom of man.
Many non-Communists in turn acknowledged that the Communist
era, despite its sorry record of terror and depredation, brought
many lasting positive achievements: the thorough eradication of

the undesirable traces of an old society to which the Hungarian intellectuals stood unalterably opposed, definite social and economic welfare gains, and, last but not least, the emancipation of popular consciousness.[12]

There is no doubt that Communist oppression created its own antidote by rapidly sensitizing the nation to social, economic, and political values. At bottom, then, Communist and non-Communist intellectuals were in substantial agreement on the contours of the good society. The composing of differences in viewpoint among them, however, only exaggerated their frustration, for they lacked the means to implement their ideas, and they found that under the circumstances they wanted both too much and too little, depending on the vantage point from which they were judged.

[12] Striking confirmation of the consensus among intellectuals on social, political and economic issues may be found in an article by Laszlo Nemeth on "Parties and Unity" (Partok es Egyseg), which appeared in the November 2 issue of *New Hungary* (Uj Magyarorszag). According to Nemeth, Hungary "has in the past decade progressed quite far along the path of socialism; it has in fact become a socialist state. Not to take this into account . . . would be a tremendous failing."

12. The Revolution Victorious, October 30-November 3

On the whole, Nagy's speech of October 28 was well received. It was interpreted as signalizing the victory of the revolution. People rightly felt that the road was clear to the just reordering of their lives. Less than forty-eight hours later, at 2:28 P.M. on October 30, Nagy announced that, "in the interest of further democratization . . . the cabinet abolishes the one-party system and places the country's government on the basis of democratic cooperation between the coalition parties reborn in 1945." At the same time, he clarified the role of "democratic organs of local autonomy" by announcing that the government "recognizes them . . . relies on them, and asks for their support." Dangerous gaps in the political program of the government were now filled in.

Nagy also clarified the government's intention "to begin negotiations immediately with the Government of the USSR about the withdrawal of Soviet troops from Hungary." At the same time, he "appealed to the headquarters of the Soviet forces immediately to begin the withdrawal of Soviet troops from the territory of Budapest."

Tildy, Erdei, and Kadar followed Nagy to the microphone to announce the final victory of the revolution and to call on the members of their parties to begin organizing anew. Of the four addresses —including Nagy's—Tildy's was the most moving, the most humane, and the most informative. Greeting his listeners as "Hungarian brethren," he opened his statement saying that "the nation's will, the national revolution has won." He compared the heroic struggle and its results favorably with the fight for freedom in 1848. He then spelled out some of the measures the government had already ap-

pròved and others it contemplated. He announced the recall of
the Hungarian delegate to the United Nations, Peter Kos, and the
dispatch of another delegation that would "represent the government in office." He proclaimed the abolition of compulsory deliveries of agricultural goods (a decree to that effect was issued by
Antal Gyenes, Minister of Crop Collections, later in the day) and
expressed the conviction that in this manner the countryside would
supply the cities with food more amply than ever before. Finally,
he made it clear that by abolishing the one-party system the government "implied that the people must freely, without outside
interference, decide the country's future. That is, free elections
have to be prepared."

It seemed that the victory of the revolution was indeed total.

METAMORPHOSIS OF THE GOVERNMENT

One evidence of its triumph was the creation of an inner cabinet
of Ministers of State which included Nagy, Tildy, Kovacs, Erdei,
Kadar, and Losonczy. It was to be enlarged by one Social Democrat, designated by his party. This inner cabinet also proved of
transitional character. But it is worth noting that its active non-
Communist members—Tildy and Erdei—were politicians of strong
leftist orientation who had incurred the displeasure of their respective parties.

Further changes at the top of the government hierarchy comprised the dismissal of the Prosecutor General, Gyorgy Non, the
recall of the Hungarian delegates to the United Nations—Foreign
Minister Imre Horvath and special representative Endre Sik—and
the assumption of the portfolio of Foreign Affairs by Nagy himself
on November 1.

The final and most drastic reorganization reflecting a reborn
four-party coalition took place on November 3. Nagy, Tildy,
Kovacs, Losonczy, and Kadar (!) were joined as Ministers of State by
Anna Kethly, Gyula Kelemen, and Jozsef Fischer for the Social
Democratic Party, B. Istvan Szabo, as the third Smallholder, and
Istvan Bibo and Ferenc Farkas for the National Peasant (renamed
Petofi) Party. Colonel Pal Maleter was advanced to the portfolio
of Defense. The only casualty in the inner cabinet formed on

October 30 was Erdei, whom his party disowned. He and the rest of the previous cabinet who had held specific departmental posts were said to have been dismissed at their own request.

The government in its reconstituted form came into being just in time to preside over the final act of the revolution. It was in office less than twenty-four hours before it was ousted by the Soviet military. During that time, it held no plenary session and arrived at no collective decision on any issue of national importance.

CLEAN SWEEP OF THE REVOLUTION

Together with swift changes in the composition of the government, the remaining obstacles to freedom fell rapidly and a mood of exhilaration seized the population. In quick succession, the gates of the most heavily guarded prisons (*Kobanya, Marianosztra, Szolnok*), holding political prisoners and common criminals, were flung open and their inmates released. On October 30, the central broadcasting station was placed under the direction of writers who were in the service of the revolution. Revolutionary councils began to form in central government offices in Budapest, including the Ministry of National Defense and the headquarters of the regular police. Until then, the nerve centers of these organizations had been left intact by the revolution.[1] The revolutionary council of the armed forces instituted the first formal purge of Communist officers (many among those most compromised had, of course, already lost all power, and some had even left the country), including the Minister of National Defense, Karoly Janza, the First Deputy Minister, Lajos Toth, Generals Jeno Hazai, Ferenc Hidvegi, Istvan Szabo, and others. Revolutionary councils sprang to life in the

[1] Also, on October 30, a group of freedom fighters laid siege to the building that housed the headquarters of the Budapest City Organization of the Communist Party. The defenders capitulated after several hours of skirmishing during which they tried vainly to obtain reinforcements. Upon emerging from the building, several of the defenders were brutally murdered by the insurgents. Among those killed was Imre Mezo, a Party secretary, one of only two fairly high functionaries who consistently and sincerely supported Imre Nagy and sided with the revolution. The death of Imre Mezo embittered many Communists, who were at this time unusually impressionable. In the circumstances, it was impossible for them not to exaggerate the implications of the deplorable massacre that had claimed the life of one of their friends, although it was atypical of the general conduct of the revolution.

Academy of Sciences (with Zoltan Kodaly, the famed composer, at its head) and at various university faculties, lawyer's guilds, and other professional associations. Last but certainly not least, at 10:05 P.M. on October 30, the Prince Primate of Hungary, Jozsef Cardinal Mindszenty, was liberated from the house arrest under which he had been held since his formal release from prison in July, 1955. On the following day, the government officially rescinded the legal validity of the proceedings against him and voided all restrictions on the Cardinal's exercise of his "civil and ecclesiastic rights."

Initiative now began to shift from the countryside to the capital and from revolutionary bodies to the political parties that were being revived.

In Budapest, the adult middle-class population ventured forth in large numbers for the first time since the outbreak of revolution, although curfew regulations were officially lifted only on the following day, October 31. The reluctance of the middle class in Budapest to brave the hazards of rifle and machine gun fire and the stringent restrictions imposed by martial law did not necessarily betoken either cowardice or lack of sympathy with the revolution. The persecutions and privations they had suffered in the past counseled prudence as long as the victory of the revolution hung in the balance. Moreover, they were conscious of the fact that their active participation would give the uprising a counterrevolutionary character which the Communists would exploit against it. With the exception of a few heedless individuals, the middle class stayed on the sidelines. Its identification with the revolution, however, was complete. People who had never felt any particular kinship with the masses now were seized with indescribable excitement. Without any question, the middle class, long alienated or antagonistic to the peasant and laboring classes, now contributed its share to the forging of national unity. The revolution left an indelible mark on the memory of middle-class people and transformed them into radical patriots. It also showed that they had ceased to count as a political factor in Hungary.

In practical terms, the release of restraints meant a manifold increase in the general confusion. Budapest was full of newspapers expressing a variety of viewpoints. There were political mass rallies and public meetings of revolutionary councils to attend. That order was maintained in such circumstances, that looting was held to a minimum, that injury to persons and to personal property was registered in isolated instances only, bespeaks the purity of the revolution and the fundamental self-discipline of the population in the absence of any effective police patrol.

No mass movement is pristine, and the purity of the revolution ought not to be microscopically examined for individual blemishes. Certainly there were transgressions and embarrassing incidents, sometimes of anti-Semitic character. But they were so infrequent and aroused such revulsion on the part of those who happened to witness them as not to besmirch the extraordinary self-conscious record of the revolution.

Naturally, it is impossible—and, for the goals set within this study, unnecessary—to trace in detail the happenings in Budapest and elsewhere during the few days of freedom won by the Hungarian nation. To illustrate the prevailing atmosphere, brief accounts of a few characteristic episodes will suffice. They may also serve as guidelines for the evaluation of some of the weightier long-range issues that faced the country in the event that the victory of the revolution should be permanently secured.

THE DUDAS INCIDENT

A showdown between Jozsef Dudas and Imre Nagy in the evening of October 30, resulting in Dudas's chastisement, underscored both the scope and the limits of the influence attained by the most illustrious of the self-appointed leaders of the revolution in Budapest.

Aside from Colonel Pal Maleter, who achieved fame overnight as a military hero of the revolution, there were only three leaders of fighting groups whose names were known outside their immediate surroundings—Janos Szabo, the kindly, elderly, unpretentious "commander" of a motley group of youngsters operating in and out of Haymarket Square in Buda; Kalman Pongracz, a rough, tough *Lumpenproletariat* type who led a determined band of rowdies at Corvinus Place in an industrial section of Pest; and Dudas. Of the three, Dudas alone had political ambitions. He made the most spectacular conquests, having occupied the central printing press of the Communist Party on October 29 and set up headquarters there. He also laid siege to the Budapest Party headquarters on October 30 and stormed the Ministry of Foreign Affairs, which was undefended at the time and nominally already in the hands of Imre Nagy, who had reserved that portfolio for himself.

Dudas was not entirely an upstart. He had a long and checkered past in the Communist and Smallholder parties (he himself claimed in an interview granted during the revolution to have belonged to the Social Democratic Party before the war), and his political activities had earned him confinement in prison and later in the labor camp at Recsk. There he reportedly underwent a religious conversion. Following his release in 1954, he returned to a working-class environment as a laborer. But he was a natural leader, combining personal magnetism, visionary characteristics, and a penchant for demagoguery. As a result, he acquired a following among the workers with whom he was in touch. The role he played in arousing the workers before the revolution has never been determined. During the revolution, he emerged "out of nowhere" with a sizable contingent of armed men. He is said to have had as many as 3,000 fighters under his command, and he succeeded in capturing several Hungarian army tanks with which he besieged the Budapest Party headquarters. His exploits quickly earned him almost legendary stature. Rumors identified him as a fascist and attributed extraordinary ruthlessness to his men: they massacred their victims; had looted the National Bank and carried away fabulous sums of money and gold. The substance of these reports could never be verified, and they probably had no basis in fact.

What is true is that he had political aspirations and that he founded what he called a "countrywide national council" which posed as a roof organization of all national councils throughout the country. In point of fact, his council represented no one but

himself and his immediate entourage. He did edit, publish, contribute to, and distribute a newspaper, *Fuggetlenseg* (Independence), that was well edited with the fortuitous assistance of some
university students who had but the most tenuous connections
with his movement. He also controlled one of the internal telephone tie lines which linked Party and government institutions
throughout the country independently of the regular network. This
lent him a certain prestige. He was able to ring various places in the
country and to address whomever happened to pick up the phone
with a voice of authority, whose sole credentials rested on control of
a line of communications that was known to be privileged. In this
manner, he might have managed to influence some of his listeners
without their being aware of who he was or what he stood for.
Impressive as were his resources, they afforded him no overriding
political influence.

On October 30, after Nagy's capitulation to the demands of
the revolutionists, Dudas betook himself to the House of Parliament to claim representation in the national government as Minister of Foreign Affairs or of National Defense. His meeting with
Nagy was stormy and protracted, not only because of Dudas's fiery
temperament but also because of frequent interruptions. In the
end, Dudas was put in his place. His demand for representation
was denied, and, on November 2, he himself was taken into protective custody for a few hours to cool off. Thereafter, his star
waned as rapidly as it seemed to have risen. The rebirth of political parties undermined his competitive position for political
influence.

The Dudas incident is illustrative of the impersonality of the
revolution. His program essentially expressed the demands of the
people. But as an individual seeking a voice in the affairs of the
state on the basis of an incipient, new institutional frame (his
national council), he failed, whereas anonymous spokesmen of
revolutionary organizations representing the people's will in its
rawest form succeeded in imposing their views on the government.
In fact, then, the voice of the people was heeded. The road to
personal success, however, had to follow the old, familiar institutional channels.

THE MEETING OF WORKERS' DELEGATIONS
FROM UJPEST AND CSEPEL

From about the third or fourth day of the revolution, a general strike had engulfed the country. It was a formidable weapon in the hands of the workers. The workers were fully aware of its destructive economic consequences, the brunt of which would be borne by them, but they were also conscious of its political potentialities, and they were searching their consciences as to which factor they should assign greater weight.

Seventy workers from Ujpest called on their comrades at Csepel to thrash out this issue, which was of national importance—whether to continue using the strike weapon as a means of pressure on the government or whether to go back to work and thereby indicate to the nation that in the eyes of the working class the legitimate ends of the revolution had been met. These two groups represented the hub of industrial Hungary. Their meeting took place in the evening of November 1, after a hectic day of conferences among delegates representing a profusion of organizations. It lasted for six hours and had all the earmarks of a democratic Donnybrook. It was unruly and disoriented. A great many of the comments made were petty and not to the point. Yet the participants were imbued with a deep sense of responsibility, and they were tortuously working their way to a solution of an immensely important problem.

The significance of the meeting derived from the fact that here for the first time freely elected workers' delegates met in congress to discuss issues that transcended by far even the vital problems of self-management in factories by means of workers' councils.

The meeting, which did not arrive at a decision, was symptomatic of the workers' independent participation in politics. It also pointed to the next developmental phase of the revolution—the restoration of order and the creation of conditions conducive to the resumption of normal national life. By the same token, the revolutionary council of the Ministry of Education on November 2 issued regulations withdrawing history textbooks from circulation, ordering the teaching of Soviet geography in a manner comparable to that of other countries, suspending compulsory Russian language studies, restoring unfettered religious instruction, and discontinuing the special Russian secondary school in Budapest bearing the name of Maxim Gorky. Other institutions and organizations confidently scheduled meetings for days in advance to consider problems of organization and policy. Meanwhile, a back-to-work movement in factories and offices was gaining momentum.

Amid the tumult of revolution, positive constructive trends thus quickly began.

EXPLORING THE MINISTRY OF THE INTERIOR AND SECRET POLICE HEADQUARTERS

A strongly contrasting picture is offered by the story of the fall of the Ministry of the Interior, which also housed the administrative offices of the secret police, and by the disposition—or rather the lack of disposition—that was made of this complex of buildings during the revolution.

Far from invalidating each other, these contrasting pictures reinforce the general image of the revolution as an undirected mass upheaval that harbored and reconciled within itself sharp divergences and contradictions.

This institution was the dread administrative center of the terror apparatus of the regime that had inflicted so many wounds on the population and elicited such unmitigated hatred in return. Housed in a complex of massive buildings in downtown Budapest near other Party and government offices, it fell to the revolutionists without the firing of a single volley, with only two janitors left behind to defend it.

A group of revolutionaries—no one knows precisely who, but there were contingents of the regular police and a number of students among them—first entered the building on October 29. The physical appearance of the offices held plentiful evidence of strenuous preparation by the secret police for fierce armed struggle: ammunition and weapons were strewn about, with machine guns mounted on desk tops. Also, there was evidence of preparations to keep up with the rapidly changing revolutionary developments by mingling with the people and infiltrating revolutionary groups:

forged papers and various types of uniforms and civilian clothes were found in abundance. At the same time, there were unmistakable signs of hasty evacuation in advance of the arrival of the first contingent of revolutionaries. The accounts of the janitors corroborated what could be surmised from examining the contents of wastebaskets; these were full of shredded but not destroyed documentary material, as were the bins in the basement. The buildings had been abandoned between October 26 and 27. In all probability, they stood empty on the 28th.

Abandoned though the buildings were, a massive array of electrical machinery on the top floors, described as mysterious but almost certainly consisting chiefly of automatic telephone monitoring devices, remained connected and emitted a disquieting humming noise interrupted by occasional clatters.

Following the arrival of the insurgents, no attempt was made either to seal the buildings or to take systematic inventory. No officer was appointed to see that the documentary material was catalogued or merely preserved. The perfunctory guard of policemen vanished on about October 31. It was replaced by an erratic guard of armed students.

The "exploitation" of the buildings was also left to teams of students, who divided up tasks among themselves. Nominally, they were selected for the task by revolutionary committees. Actually, they were dispatched much as an army detail would be by a noncommissioned officer from among recruits who happened to be loitering around the orderly room at the time they were needed. Anyone could at his own initiative attach himself to the detail.

This did not mean that a mob of curious scavengers swarmed over the buildings. On the contrary, the groups were quite small. Nor were the students irresponsible. They tried, as best they could, to assay the material they found. But it took a while to orient themselves, and they had to make decisions without reference to higher authority. They hardly knew where to begin and how to dispose of the things they found. Lists of informers were reportedly sent to the government. Otherwise, they barely sampled the contents of the secret police files, possibly because they did not know the filing system. More important, the bulk of the most interesting items existed only in recorded form on tape. In order to make use of them, transcription was necessary. This, of course, they were not equipped to do.

There seemed to be no urgency about the taking of a systematic inventory: the victory of the revolution guaranteed that, as things settled down, duly authorized personnel would take possession of the buildings and explore their contents. On the other hand, those who returned repeatedly to the Ministry of the Interior could not help having a spooky feeling about the place—the very site of the secret police, the very emptiness of the premises, the mysteriously humming machinery, remembered wartime stories of mined buildings (especially at Stalingrad) that blew up at the touch of a telephone, a recording machine, or a light switch; they experienced a growing uneasiness, as the days went by, sensing that all was not well, that the Russians would return, and that it would be unwise to be caught redhanded, of all places, in the headquarters of the secret police. These feelings were enhanced on November 3 by imagined or actually heard footsteps in the basement that could not be traced to any identifiable source and by the presence in the doorway of two or three civilians, not observed before and obviously not belonging to the student groups. By this time, no one was in a mood to inquire from the strangers who they were, let alone to challenge their right to be there. The student teams, considering discretion the better part of valor, cleared out of the buildings almost furtively. Twice during the revolution this most valuable piece of real estate changed hands without armed struggle, without a face-to-face encounter between the opposing forces, and without any substantial damage to its precious content.

THE LIBERATION OF CARDINAL MINDSZENTY

The liberation of Cardinal Mindszenty from house arrest at Felsopeteny, a small village in northwestern Hungary, was unquestionably an important event. The Cardinal's arrest in 1948, his sensational trial early in 1949, and his subsequent incarceration stirred the imagination of the whole world. The crude, contemptuous treatment accorded an ecclesiastic figure of such rank aroused popular indignation in Hungary and abroad. That the Cardinal, with his extraordinarily strong, forthright, and unyielding personality, was chosen as its chief non-Communist victim, to be broken in public, only broadcast the infamy of the Rakosi regime.

The martyrdom of the Cardinal remained a much talked-about issue abroad. Presumably, in the eyes of Hungary's Catholic believers, if not of the entire population, it symbolized their grievances. Yet the liberation of the Cardinal was not among the most vociferous demands of the revolutionists. That it did not appear in the programs drawn up at the outset of the revolution is understandable enough. These programs were drafted by Communists. No matter how tenuous their connection with the Party or how genuine their patriotism, their religious feelings were not profound. They were anticlerical in disposition, and the Cardinal was not a favorite character of theirs, even if they acknowledged and deplored the legal injustice of his detention. The most charitable view they took of him was that of an anachronism.

That the Cardinal's release and restoration to office did not become one of the focal points of the public's demands after the outbreak of revolution was somewhat more surprising. This does not necessarily mean that the Cardinal's fate was of no concern to large numbers of people. Perhaps those most acutely concerned— the older generations of rural folk—belonged to a segment of the population that was least able to make itself heard. Perhaps it was feared that the Cardinal's premature return to his see would endanger both his person and the whole revolutionary movement. In any event, there is no readily discernible evidence of widespread worry over his whereabouts and his welfare during the first week of revolution. Political, economic, and social issues clearly took precedence —to such an extent that on October 29 Attila Szigeti, in response to a question by foreign newspapermen about the Cardinal's status, registered sincere surprise and innocently expressed the opinion that he was at liberty.

The impetus for the Cardinal's release came from Zoltan Tildy, a former Protestant minister, in a conversation with a delegation of workers in the afternoon of October 30. In a matter of hours, the Cardinal was free. The following morning, shortly after 8 A.M., he was back at his palace at Buda. By all accounts, his return to Buda was triumphant. Believers accorded him an enthusiastic, almost jubilant welcome. Yet, his reappearance in the public forum elicited misgivings as well, not only among anticlerical elements but also among younger, emancipated Catholic laymen and clerics.

This was to be expected. The Cardinal had always been a controversial figure. Almost eight years of isolation from the outside world were bound to increase the distance between him and the very institution he headed. The local Church had undergone changes in time. Viewpoints had evolved that did not necessarily accord with the Cardinal's own. Reunion after long separation and resumption of old familiar duties after many years of absence are invariably bitter-sweet occasions. Eager anticipation is mixed with trepidation even under the most benign conditions. The Cardinal's return did not take place in the most propitious circumstances.

His presence complicated an already highly complicated situation. How would he act? What would he do? Would he espouse the revolution or disavow it? Would he be ruled by rancor and bitterness toward his enemies and even others who forsook him? Or would he act in a spirit of magnanimous forgiveness? What niche would he wish to carve out for himself in the nation's life? Did he have political ambitions? What were his political views? Many felt they knew and were not hopeful.

No one could or did treat the Cardinal with less than deference. But anything and anyone that threatened to sow discord in a magnificently united nation was suspect. The Cardinal might do precisely that. A stiff, unbending man, he would not adjust easily to the fluidity of the situation. His pride would forbid him to embrace the government wholeheartedly. His lack of political sagacity would cause him to make tactical errors detrimental to himself and perhaps to the national welfare.

The worst fears concerning the effect of the Cardinal's return to public life proved groundless. He did not strike the discordant tone that some were afraid of. Neither did he unequivocally align himself with the government. He kept aloof, putting dignified distance between himself and those whom he described as "the legatees" of the old system. The instructions he gave to his followers in private, the plans he made for the future are unknown to us.

Nor did they much matter. None of the projects he might have been preparing had a chance to materialize.

The Cardinal's views are known from two public addresses, a brief one in the evening of November 1 and a longer, admittedly political statement which was broadcast in the evening of November 3, a scant eight hours before the Soviet assault on the capital. In his first statement, he disavowed hatred for anyone. He made it clear that he was willing to forgive if not to forget. He referred to his "miraculous freedom" and extolled the "people's struggle for freedom" for which he saw no "parallel in history."

The Cardinal's address on November 3 was clearly in response to mounting pressures on him to declare himself on important issues. He did so following a lengthy sitting of the bench of bishops in the afternoon.[2] In his address, he covered a wide range of subjects, from international relations to national politics and the status of the Church. He correctly estimated that the crux of the matter in the Hungarian situation was what the Russians decided to do. He emphasized Hungarian suffering in the past and reaffirmed the time-honored theme of Hungary's special position in that part of the world as a bastion of the West. At the same time, he denied national enmity toward anyone and professed a desire to live in honorable peace with all.

He specifically disclaimed that Hungary was experiencing a "revolution" and called it a "national struggle for freedom"; he did not say what the difference was. Possibly he wished to accentuate the international rather than the domestic aspects of the revolution. But he did not ignore domestic matters. The position he took on them can best be described as stern. His main concern seemed to be to define the consistent righteousness of his stance and to delineate his relation to the "people's struggle for freedom" (which he embraced totally) and the actions of individuals (from whom he carefully differentiated himself). In contrast to others who now made a vogue of reevaluating their positions and views, he had nothing to revise.

2 On November 1, Zoltan Tildy and Pal Maleter paid their respects to him on behalf of the government. It was, as far as is known, the only personal contact he had with representatives of the government.

"Today it is customary to break with the past and speak truthfully. I cannot quite put it that way. By the grace of God, I have ...retained the convictions I held prior to my imprisonment. I cannot even admit that I will now at last speak truthfully, for I always spoke the truth." Disclaiming any desire to sit in judgment of others, he nevertheless warned the participants in and the legatees of the Communist political system, who now heaped scorn on that system and strove to exonerate themselves and make amends for past errors, that he reserved the right to call them to account should they break their promises.

He set himself "apart from, and by virtue of [his] ecclesiastic position, above" party and partisanship. He called for free elections under international supervision, open to any party that wished to participate. In the same breath, he implored the nation to preserve its unity and in fact to reject the political parties. "This country needs a great many things, but least of all political parties and party chieftains." His use of the word *partvezer*, denoting chieftain, instead of the more familiar *vezeto* (meaning simply leader), may have been accidental. It could also have been a deliberate attempt to show his contempt for the species of political leader with whom he never had good relations.

On vital questions of social and political progress, he expressed himself in familiar terms. Referring to a pastoral letter of the bench of bishops of 1945, he asserted that the Catholic Church "does not set itself in opposition to the justified direction of historic progress, on the contrary, it facilitates healthy evolution in every respect." He did not spell out what he meant by "healthy evolution," although he stated that the Church helped to develop "democratic achievements, and stood on the ground of private property, appropriately and justly limited by social interests."

As for the status of the Church itself, he simply declared, brooking no contradiction or argument, that "along religious lines" all such terrorism and repression as were characteristic of the late system would be eradicated. "We rightfully expect the immediate ordering of free Christian religious instruction, and the return to the Catholic Church of its institutions and associations, including its press."

Of the entire speech, the sentence last cited, which came almost at the end of the Cardinal's address, elicited the most widespread critical comment. It gave rise to speculation whether the Cardinal implied the restitution of the landed property of the Church or not. His detractors all too willingly assumed that he would demand exactly that and saw in it confirmation of their suspicions of the Cardinal's fundamentally reactionary disposition. Actually the text itself and the manner of the Cardinal's delivery did not permit any such imputation. It is possible that he wished to keep the door open on the question of Church property at least for bargaining purposes; but to conclude that he would take an inflexible stand on so delicate and far-reaching an issue was to deny the Cardinal any benefit of doubt.

Whatever his motives, he might have been better advised to leave no doubt in his listeners' minds. On the whole, his address was moderate and correct, but no more than that. A dispassionate, neutral observer could hardly find serious fault with it. In the given atmosphere, it did not quite measure up to expectations. Proper as it was for the Cardinal to be less than wildly enthusiastic about the government and the political leaders who were once again assuming national office, he might have gone just a little further in expressing his solidarity with them. Harking back to 1945 pastoral letters, no matter how impeccable their content, was under the circumstances not very helpful. It could easily be mistaken for an attempt to turn the clock back to 1945, and this no one really wanted.

He need not have gone as far as Cardinal Wyszinski had gone in Poland. The backgrounds against which the two men acted were as different as were their temperaments. But Mindszenty could have, without demeaning his own status, bestowed a measure of moral prestige on Nagy and his entourage instead of putting them on probation. As it was, his speech left a great many people dissatisfied. His critics saw no reason to change their opinions about him, and even his supporters expressed regret that he did not come out more resolutely in favor of the revolution and the purification of the human spirit that accompanied it. Many of his supporters, of course, refrained from voicing their criticism out of respect for and loyalty to the Cardinal. The major defect of the speech, then, was its equivocal character. It meant all things to all people. The Cardinal would have been well advised to make a simpler, less haughty statement, but, to do so, he would have had to step out of character. This was asking too much of a man as set in his ways as the Cardinal was.

The timing of the speech minimized what effects it might have had. It came too late to serve as a pretext for the Soviet decision to intervene (less than an hour after the Cardinal spoke, the ring of steel closed around Budapest) and to arouse passions for or against the Cardinal among factions of the Hungarian people. It showed quite clearly that the Cardinal would be a potent and contentious figure. As the only surviving great man of the past, with his personal prestige enhanced by the certain emergence of a strong Christian Social political party for the first time in the history of Hungary, he would have left his mark on the country. More likely than not he would have posed problems at once delicate and formidable of resolution. As things developed, he had no visible influence on events.

On November 4, five days after he was set free, the Cardinal was forced to flee for his safety. He sought and found asylum at the United States legation in what turned out to be for him another indefinite—perhaps lifelong—confinement. For, despite the best will of his hosts, he is as effectively imprisoned there as if he were in a Communist jail. Effectively separated from his flock and at no cost to the Hungarian authorities, he is likely in the course of time to lose stature in the eyes of the people. The psychological advantage this time is with the Hungarian regime, which seems to be fully aware of it and is content to let matters rest as they are.

THE REBIRTH OF THE PARTY SYSTEM

The rebirth of the Party system, substantially what it had been in 1945, represented the high-water mark of the revolution's political success. It also introduced a new dimension into its political complexity.

On October 30, in conjunction with the announcement of the reintroduction of a multi-party system, Kadar in substance acknowledged the total disintegration of the Communist Party and the necessity for rebuilding it on new foundations. On November 1, the formation of a new Communist Party was announced "in accordance with the wishes of many true patriots and socialists who fought against the despotism of Rakosi." Kadar, who proclaimed the formation of the new Party, also pledged that "it would cleanse itself of the crimes of the past once and for all." He acknowledged the vastly diminished drawing power of the Party, but consoled its would-be followers by stressing the importance of quality over quantity, while disabusing them of any notion they may have entertained of special privileges deriving from Party membership.

The temporary leadership of the Party, charged with preparatory work for its organization, consisted of Ferenc Donath, Janos Kadar, Sandor Kopacsi, Geza Losonczy, Gyorgy Lukacs, Imre Nagy, and Zoltan Szanto. This group was very different from the composition even of the caretaker presidium of only four days ago. Of those designated on November 1, Kadar alone continues to hold office. Donath, Kopacsi, Losonczy, and Nagy were apprehended and tried; Lukacs and Szanto live in obscurity. The editor of the Party's new daily, *Nepszabadsag,* was Sandor Haraszti. He too was imprisoned once more.

Surprisingly, Lukacs and Szanto were said to have objected to the formation of a new Communist Party that both interrupted the formal continuity of the Party's history and flouted its fundamental organizational and ideological tenets. At all events, the new Party in its intended composition never came to life. It was snuffed out by the crushing of the revolution and gave way to still another Party, constructed along more acceptable "Leninist" lines, although it kept the name "Hungarian Socialist Workers' Party" (Magyar Szocialista Munkaspart [MSZMP]), selected for the still-born party.

That the Party disappeared as a social and political mass organization is a recognized fact. That many of its top leaders scattered and that its central apparatus ceased to function in any meaningful way is also an acknowledged fact. But Party headquarters was not abandoned to the insurgents until the very last day or two of the revolution, when—preparatory to the slashing riposte by the Russians—leading Communist functionaries were quietly removed from the capital. Until then, Kadar and the men closest to him, rather than Nagy, were in charge of the headquarters, with secret police doing what was required to insure its physical security. Given the hectic nature of the events of these days, physical possession of this invaluable piece of real estate, with its records and files and its closed communications system that connected it with various institutions throughout the country and abroad, was of immense importance to the Communists as privileged sanctuary. Although the actual happenings inside the building in the course of the revolution are still shrouded in mystery, it is known that Mikoyan and Suslov held important conferences there, well protected against intrusion by undesirable listeners. Kadar's defection on November 1 must also have been easier because of the existence of an operational base, where plans could be made surreptitiously, without danger of detection.

Even as the Communist Party was seeking to lay the foundations for its existence under new and different circumstances, its erstwhile coalition partners, the Smallholder, National Peasant, and Social Democratic parties in quick succession reconstituted themselves, as did a number of splinter groups with an explicitly Catholic orientation. The astonishing speed with which long-defunct political organisms came to life confirmed the enormous value of precedent, the magnetic attractiveness of the familiar and the remembered as against the new and the unknown. Old party leaders emerged from obscurity to resume their labors almost as if these had never been interrupted, like the fairy tale princess who awakens from a hundred years sleep. Party members, in turn, eagerly responded to the call to old flags. Heartening as this demonstration of political acuity may have been, it was not entirely edifying. It raised many problems that cut to the core of the political structure of the state, including the type of representation the people were to have and the social bases of power distribution.

The revival of the 1945 coalition threatened to reintroduce partisanship and bickering among contending political rivals. This would offend the magnificent harmony born in the heat of revolution and would not serve the nation's best interest. Seen from the distance of some years, the flaws of the coalition period, quite apart from the perfidious maneuvers of the Communists, are more readily apparent. All parties, in fact, bore the stigma of complicity for the destruction of what might have been, and probably was, a rare opportunity for a democratic political system in Hungary. No party was exempt from charges ranging from chicanery to ineptitude.

The public, instead of evincing sympathy for the political parties that had been victimized by the Communist regime, tended to take a harsh view of their imperfections and reacted instinctively against the resumption of "politics as usual." Party leaders themselves were well aware of their sins of omission and commission. They hastened to assure the nation that coalition politics would be resumed in a new spirit. Still, what guarantee was there? The aptitude of the leaders had not improved appreciably if at all, since 1948. Temporary restraints on partisanship, during the revolution, were likely to wear off quickly once normal conditions were restored. Even during the revolution, to divert the energies of the population into four or more channels was obviously not the same as to concentrate these energies into unified revolutionary councils.

Political parties are to a large extent self-seeking agencies whose function it is to define issues of contention, not to blur them. While this is necessary and constructive within a smoothly operating parliamentary system in which the terms of competition are tame and scrupulously adhered to, it is not an unmitigated good in all situations. In Hungary a great many people regarded the parties as ideal vehicles for the redressing of past wrongs. This was understandable. An individual claim made before a revolutionary council, which for the moment was the direct, living embodiment of the social conscience and of the raw political power of the polity of which the claimant was a member, stood less chance of being acted on favorably than did a demand supported by the impersonal machine of a political party.

Try as they would, the parties could not avoid becoming repositories of grievances. Party headquarters witnessed unsavory incidents not duplicated elsewhere. The activities of the parties themselves of necessity also concentrated on staking out claims—requisitioning of buildings and cars, repossessing the party press, and hiring staffs—not on the pursuit of revolution. To be sure, there was not much to pursue during these days. Major objectives had been won. The remaining crucial decisions could not be handled by mass action.

Party activity nevertheless was not promising. Unhappiness with the party system was registered from opposite poles of the political spectrum (and for different reasons) by Cardinal Mindszenty and by Jozsef Dudas, by students as well as by some local revolutionary councils.

The attitude of the students deserves further comment. They saw the party system encroaching on their self-attributed prerogatives. Being for the most part too young to have had any prior affiliation with political parties—except the Communist—the students were excluded from exercising any influence in them. The rise of the party system automatically relegated the students to an inferior political place. They naturally resisted such a development out of self-interest. But the party system also had broader social and ideo-logical connotations.

By virtue of the composition of their leadership and of the clien-tele to which they appealed, the political parties as they were then being re-formed (and there was no assurance that they would be substantially modified) gave weight to those elements in society—older, conservative generations, mostly of middle-class origin—that were least intimately involved in the preparation and execution of the revolution. Young revolutionists and workers were underrepre-sented in the political parties, although the Smallholder Party included among its second- and third-echelon officials a number of people in their thirties.

The unbalanced social, ideological, and age representation achieved by the parties promised conflict that might have come to pass—but, like so much else, did not.

Despite misgivings in various quarters, the revitalization of political parties proceeded apace. Proof of the infectiousness of party-organizing activity was supplied by the founding on Novem-ber 1 of a Revolutionary Party of the Youth. It gave the students a party of their own and reflected their decision to join a trend that they might have deplored but could not avert.

Reports from the provinces indicated that the parties were in no imminent danger of developing oversized heads in the capital without bodies to support them throughout the country. In a matter of two or three days a network of local cells began to take shape. But differences between the capital and the countryside persisted. While the formal roster of the government already conformed to the four-party coalition, seats in local revolutionary councils were as a rule not apportioned accordingly. The coalition itself varied. Whereas in the capital it included the Smallholder, National Peasant (Petofi), Social Democratic, and Communist parties, in some places in the countryside a Christian Social Party replaced the Communist as one of the charter members. Finally, some localities, Sopron for instance, showed eminent good sense in reporting the formation of parties and at the same time announcing that in order to avoid the frittering away of energy, the parties would refrain from any organizing activity for the time being.

The rate of development of the parties varied, of course. Each had internal difficulties to cope with. Of them all, the Smallholder Party appeared to be the most robust. The National Peasant Party dropped its name, which had become a liability, and adopted that of the revolutionary poet Petofi as its own. It had the most illustrious leadership, composed exclusively of outstanding literary figures, but its mass appeal was questionable. The Social Democrats, true to form, showed the greatest irresolution. They also had the most formidable obstacles to overcome.

The Smallholders had to cope with the simultaneous presences (one felt and one actual) of Ferenc Nagy and Bela Kovacs. The former personified the problem of relations with the emigration, a touchy subject. The latter epitomized the problem of conscience for the party.

Embarrassingly, Ferenc Nagy—in a display of poor political judgment—appeared in Vienna and initiated negotiations about his return to Budapest, using emissaries who entered the country from exile. His overtures were peremptorily turned down, and the Hungarian government, to avoid uncalled-for repercussions, requested the Austrian authorities to cooperate in removing Nagy from the vicinity of the Hungarian frontier. This was done and for the moment a crisis over the intrusion of émigré politicians on the national scene was averted.

The problem of Bela Kovacs did not arise as acutely nor was it resolved as neatly. Leaders of the Smallholders who gathered at Budapest elected him chairman of the Party. They owed him as much for his long years of imprisonment. Besides, he was presumed to be the most popular Smallholder leader in the country. Kovacs did not reach Budapest until November 1. A statement he made the day before at a Smallholder rally at Pecs—his home town —could hardly inspire confidence in his would-be colleagues concerning his attitude toward them and his disposition toward the Party itself.

Acclaimed by the assembled crowd, he reminded them that he did not "come among them as a Smallholder . . . for he had been expelled from the Party." He also disabused them of any notion of turning the clock back "to 1939 or 1945." In his opinion, the world of "counts, bankers, and capitalists" was finished, and those who wished for its restoration could not call themselves Smallholders. "The past ten years were difficult, but they held useful lessons for the Smallholders."

Those who talked with Kovacs were impressed by the changes he had undergone. Once a fiery and volatile man, he was now sober and deliberate. His intentions could only be surmised. Aside from a deep-seated loyalty to the exiled Ferenc Nagy, which apparently had weathered the political vicissitudes and personal disappointments suffered by Kovacs, he did not harbor the kindest feelings toward a number of Smallholder leaders. Their reunion was bound to reopen wounds and perhaps even lead to recrimination. One of Kovacs's pet schemes before his arrest in 1947 was the Peasant Alliance that straddled parties. Possibly he might wish to concentrate his efforts on reviving the Alliance as a substitute for peasant parties. Alternatively, some claimed, he was entertaining the idea of creating a new party, distinct from either the Smallholders or the National Peasant Party.

Aside from the issues personified by Nagy and Kovacs, the Smallholder Party faced other unresolved problems of personal and programmatic nature. Like all other parties, the Smallholders harbored among them a number of formerly prominent leaders who had betrayed the party or come close to it. The question was, what to do about them? Should they be expelled or should mitigating circumstances be taken into account? Outright traitors like Ortutay and Dinnyes presented no real problem. It was different with men like Istvan Dobi (although his sins were considerable) and Zoltan Tildy. Strictly speaking, both had collaborated with the Communists, Dobi more openly and with greater success, for he was the beneficiary of high public office as Chairman of the Presidential Council of the Republic. Tildy had collaborated less conspicuously and suffered privation. Despite their records, both could be useful to the Smallholder Party. For example, it was Dobi who made contact with Kovacs in regard to joining the cabinet, and Tildy particularly distinguished himself by his behavior during the revolution.

The National Peasant Party also had painful personal difficulties to contend with. One of its better known and more talented leaders, Ferenc Erdei, had made himself odious by his brazen cooperation with the Communists, aggravated by the suspicion that he had been a crypto-Communist all the time (i.e., from 1943 or 1944 on). Yet it was Erdei who issued the call for the re-formation of the party in the course of a series of broadcasts by government leaders on October 30. Whether or not Erdei aspired to lead the party is a moot point. In his right mind he could not hope to do so. His act, therefore, may have been devoid of personal ambition and may have reflected a desire to render a service to the party in partial atonement for his sins toward it. In any event, protests against Erdei's participation in the party in any capacity were so numerous that he felt called on to apologize for having taken it on himself to initiate the party's restitution. He explained that it had seemed the most natural thing to do since no other Peasant Party leader was on the spot.

Needless to say, neither Erdei nor Peter Veres, the former president of the party, was reelected to office. But Veres, whose offenses were less—he served the Communist regime as a perennial, docile, accommodating chairman of the Writers' Association—was picked for membership of an over-all steering body superimposed on the political executive of the party. Erdei's exclusion from his party did not immediately terminate his usefulness to Imre Nagy. He re-

mained a Minister of State until November 3 and was designated as
one of the members of the Hungarian negotiating team that was to
discuss the terms of Soviet withdrawal from the country.

At an organizing session on November 1, the National Peasant
Party selected both its steering committee and its temporary politi-
cal executive. The roster of the former body read like a Who's Who
in Hungarian populist literature. It included the writers Geza Feja,
Gyula Illyes, Dezso Kereszturi, Janos Kodolanyi, Laszlo Nemeth,
Zsigmond Remenyi, Istvan Sinka, Lorincz Szabo, Pal Szabo, Aron
Tamasi, and Peter Veres. A politician, Ferenc Farkas, was chosen
secretary general. On November 3, Ferenc S. Szabo and Gyula
Zsigmond became deputy secretaries general. The political executive committee included Istvan Bibo and Attila Szigeti among
others.

The impressive list of names in the steering body assured neither
overwhelming popularity for a party that had a dismal if not wholly
deserved reputation to live down, nor, unfortunately, superior political wisdom. A statement released in the evening of November 1
proposed harebrained schemes, such as a plebiscite within three
days—to be conducted by territorial revolutionary councils—in order
to determine the nation's will in the matter of foreign relations,
and the establishment of a supreme national council, headed by the
composer Kodaly, to replace both parliament and government. Both
schemes fell through.

The problems of the Social Democratic Party were different from
those of other parties. The question of the disposition of renegade
leaders—Szakasits, Marosan, Ronai—never came up. Whether these
ultimately went to prison or not, they had moved beyond the pale
when they became active Communists, as they did in 1948. They
could not retrace their steps and return to the fold of Social Democracy. For once, too, the opportunity to make mistakes occurred not
in accepting a Communist bid to join hands in a common effort,
but in not rising to the occasion rapidly and resolutely enough.

The Social Democratic leaders, in a simultaneous display of deference and misplaced stubbornness, got off to a bad start. At midnight on October 30, when other parties were well on their way to
organizing, the Social Democrats were "petitioning the premier to

take possession once more of [their] headquarters and [their] newspaper." At the same time they announced that "as to the Premier's
desire for the Social Democrats to join the government, they will
give [their] answer after the formation of [their] party." Thereupon, Miss Anna Kethly, the Social Democratic chairman-designate
and a veteran of many inconclusive skirmishes, immediately departed for Vienna, where an international Socialist gathering was
in progress. She returned on November 2. Her party then graciously
consented to join the government. Apart from these personal va-
garies—and no one could really blame the much maligned Social
Democrats for wanting to renew international friendships before
buckling down to the work that awaited them at home—the party
faced crises over ideology and membership. As on other occasions
in the recent past, its chief problem was to differentiate itself from
the Communists, who in their new incarnation once more threatened to preempt the appealing tenets of social democracy without
succumbing to the organizational flabbiness and programmatic ter-
giversation associated with it.

Disillusioned Communists were not a likely reservoir of Social
Democratic support. A surprisingly large number of them expressed
contempt for the Social Democrats as a superannuated political
group that had nothing to offer to anyone. Whether they spoke
from conviction or simply mouthed Communist propaganda, their
verdict was devastating. The Social Democrats had a steep uphill
battle to wage in such a political sweepstakes. Their short-term
prospects seemed decidedly weak. Some observers claimed that their
long-run chances looked more promising.

The significance of the growth of other parties in addition to
the aforementioned "traditional ones" cannot be evaluated with any
degree of accuracy. We have virtually no information to go on in
estimating their attractiveness and staying power. The fact that
many of these parties were of a Catholic orientation was rather
gleefully noted by the adherents of the major parties who, for the
most part, belonged to other denominations or professed no strong
religious attachments. The implication was that, politically at least,
the Catholics did not present a united front and thus showed their
immaturity. In part, this attitude stemmed from a need for self-

assurance that Catholic opinion would not crystallize around a single party. Indeed, many of the refugees whose opinion was sampled for the purposes of this study, when pressed to speculate on what would have been the probable outcome if a free election had been held, said that by virtue of an "automatic swing of the political pendulum" some sort of Christian Social grouping stood the best chance of amassing a plurality of the votes. In a sense, this would have amounted to a repudiation of the old party system while confirming the validity of a multi-party system in principle.

The resumption of political party activity thus introduced into the revolutionary scene a variety of controversial questions. It undoubtedly marred some of the surpassing unity achieved by the revolution. The contribution made by the parties to the revolution was nil. Programmatically they had nothing new or constructive to offer. They were the beneficiaries rather than the benefactors of the revolution. They seemed ready to partake in a division of the spoils without commensurate contribution to the struggle that preceded their attainment. They represented a spurious sort of legitimacy based on questionable rights deriving from institutional precedent.

Yet the reemergence of the party system was as inevitable as it was unwelcome to some. There is no telling what form the system would have taken ultimately. In addition to the likelihood of the coalescence of various Catholic groups in a Christian Social party, there was talk of the merger of the two peasant parties or of their being supplanted by the Peasant Alliance. In the end, inertia bolstered by personal incompatibilities might have caused things to settle in the old grooves. But these were questions for the future to decide, as was the question whether the country's political structure should be based on a council or a party system.

The interrelationship between the political parties and the revolutionary councils as two possibly conflicting forms of political democracy has attracted attention as one of the distinctive features of the revolution. From the brief glimpses gained of actual trends in Hungary, it seemed certain that the parties would win hands down over the revolutionary councils once normal conditions were restored.

The council system in the abstract conforms to the ideal of total democracy better than does any other institutional frame as yet devised by man. It operated with remarkable success in Hungary, bringing to the fore unknown heroes of the population, possessing unsuspected talents. The ease with which it developed and the smoothness with which it functioned bespoke a new-found maturity of the people. It was a lesson not easily to be forgotten by the totalitarian and not lightly to be dismissed by the student of politics.

The vitality of the council system, however, is predicated on the maintenance of an elemental, direct relationship between rulers and ruled. It demands a continuous flow of the kind of political commitment which in practice can be achieved only in short bursts of intense enthusiasm. The ebbing of political interest is sure to induce a decay in the council system. The preservation of revolutionary purity is only a noble dream.

A further and perhaps fatal drawback of the council system is its intrinsic unsuitability for the building of an elastic and responsive pyramidal nationwide power structure. It tends to break down with the transfer of authority from one level to another and higher level of jurisdiction and with the selection of representatives to these higher bodies. The necessity of indirect selection—or delegation, if you wish—of representatives to the higher echelons of government obviates the very purpose of the council system. The functional efficacy of a council decreases in inverse proportion to the distance between it and the objects it administers.

The individual representative who stands in undifferentiated relation to his immediate environment and makes its problems his own does not necessarily stand in the same relation to the nation. While on a level of considerable intimacy, the individual representative is likely to identify his interests with that of the community; on the more impersonal, national level it is more frequent for the representative or leader to identify national interest with his own. To equate the nation with the sum total of its territorial units is sheer phantasy. There is a quantum jump in nearly every respect between the problems and patterns of association of a community and those of a nation. A simple arithmetic summation of the parts is likely to yield a total that is smaller than the sum total of these parts.

Great as the virtues of the council system are, it is limited in efficacy to brief periods of time and to small units of territorial or functional self-government. Its success depends on conditions of perfection, including high morality and nearly unanimous consensus, that no large-scale polity can sustain over time. As an operational embodiment of Rousseau's general will, which predominates when a high degree of concord exists in assemblies and near unanimity of opinion prevails, the council system fails when these prerequisites do not obtain, for it creates more problems than it can solve.

By contrast, the party system thrives in the normal range of imperfections of any given society. It fills the gaps left by the council system. For all its faults, it is the most serviceable instrument of national politics. The party system can minimize or maximize the imperfections of a given society. But, contrary to the belief of some, it is not the source of these imperfections. It is eminently suited to the making of political consensus. It also provides a line of vertical communications outside the channels of governmental and administrative organs proper for which the council system makes no provisions whatever. The party system alone is capable of sustaining a continuous national process of political competition which, when all is said and done, is the lowest common denominator of freedom.

The alternative to the party system is neither the council system nor indeed a hybrid system combining the two. Not that there is theoretical incompatibility between them, but their practical mating is difficult. The alternative is the one-party totalitarian dictatorship or a less structured authoritarian dictatorship based on personal rule with a minimum of institutional underpinning.

Important as it is to explore the conflict or interrelation between councils and parties as fundamental historic forms of political democracy, to see the principal significance of the Hungarian revolution in the clash between these two forms is a fallacy of misplaced abstractness. Notwithstanding the desirability of analytical generalization, the meaning of the revolution cannot be reduced to sociological and political abstractions. The reading into the Hungarian situation of general principles on an exaggerated scale reduces the flesh and blood aspects of the revolution to schematic interpretations that bear little useful relation to reality.

As matters turned out in Hungary, the party system collapsed under outside pressure before it had a chance to fortify itself. The councils had the last word. After November 4, in a brief and heroic gesture of defiance against superior physical power, councils—based on, but substantially different from, those in existence prior to the second Soviet intervention—emerged as the sole source of political authority in the country. The "victory" of the councils over political parties confirms rather than refutes the validity of the observations made in the preceding pages. They operated under unusual conditions, during a brief span of time characterized by an unusual moral unanimity.

13. The Revolution in Danger, October 30-November 3

THE triumph of the revolution had been achieved in the presence but without the defeat of the forces of a foreign great power. Neither the disposition of these forces nor the posture of the government that controlled them had as yet been satisfactorily clarified. As the revolution was sweeping ahead unchecked by any internal resistance, and as it was preparing to consolidate its gains and to given them an institutional frame, its most pressing problem remained to be solved.

Emboldened by their achievements, the revolutionaries now formulated harsh terms for the settlement of their relations with the Soviet Union: Hungary's unilateral denial of obligations stemming from the Warsaw treaty, and strict time limits—ranging from sixty to ninety days—for the withdrawal of all Soviet troops from Hungarian soil.

Between October 30 and November 3, the attention of Imre Nagy and his close advisers was engaged almost exclusively by problems attendant upon the ordering of Hungary's relations with the Soviet Union.

Nagy's appeal to the Soviet command to begin the withdrawal of troops from Budapest was the only anxious note in his otherwise joyful message of October 30, confirming the political victory of the revolution. The appeal intimated that the evacuation of troops from Budapest, announced as a fact two days earlier, was encountering inexplicable delay. Actually, tank units did not abandon their stations in front of major public buildings, e.g., the Ministry of National Defense, until the noon hours of October 31. Then their withdrawal might already have been a part of strategic redeployment rather than genuine abandonment of the capital.

Together with confusing and disquieting news from the country-side of Soviet troop movements in and out of Hungary at various frontier points, the general disposition of Soviet troops and their intentions marred the enjoyment of domestic freedoms just won.

Still, the momentum of the revolution was so great that even the most sober-minded persons suppressed nagging apprehensions, the grounds for which had been learned over a decade. In the face of clear evidence to the contrary they believed that they could flout their giant neighbor with impunity, insulting and humiliating him to boot. What was worse, they once again were gullible in assessing Soviet statements, promises, and proffers of peace, amity, and negotiation—as they had been a decade before. Even elementary precautions were put aside, as in the Hungarian military delegation's ready agreement to meet with the Russians at their headquarters late in the evening of November 3 to discuss terms of Soviet withdrawal. It will be remembered that the Hungarian delegates did not return from this meeting. They were summarily arrested in the middle of the night, even while their captors were poised for a massive attack on their country. Not that Soviet military intervention could have been avoided or resisted by a change in the locale of the meeting, but surely Ivan Serov, the Soviet security chief, could not have raided the meeting secretly and by surprise had it been held in the House of Parliament, as was an earlier meeting that morning; moreover, precious hours might have been gained in learning about the imminence of Soviet attack.

Worst of all, however, the behavior of the Hungarian delegation was symptomatic of a turn of mind that permits itself to be trapped over and over again by the same trick of the opponent. How many times will the Russians have to arrest visiting delegations before their opponents—or friends, as the case may be—will take proper precautions? Irony of ironies, news about the beginning of negotiations, which spread in Budapest on the afternoon of November 3, raised hope to an unprecedented pitch. The fact that negotiations had been joined was interpreted as evidence of "good faith" on the part of the Russians. That evening a great many people went home for the first time in ten days to settle down to what they termed "a good night's rest at last."

DEMANDS FOR NEUTRALITY AND WITHDRAWAL FROM
THE WARSAW PACT

No sooner had Nagy finished his radio address of October 30 than he was confronted with demands to declare Hungary's neutrality (to which Nagy agreed in principle) and to denounce the Warsaw treaty (Nagy said that this was impossible without parliamentary approval). Neither of these demands was new. They had been discussed as possibilities by circles of friends (including Losonczy) as far back as the winter of 1955 and spring of 1956. Nagy, in the writings he submitted to the Communist Central Committee, had broadly hinted at neutrality.

During the revolution it took only a few days for the slogan *Ruszkik haza* ("Russians go home") to be refined to specific proposals of a juridical nature, designed to accomplish and safeguard by international convention the fundamental aim of national sovereignty. It was to be expected that as the last barrier to complete internal freedom fell, the breaking of Hungary's bondage to the Soviets would be the next order of business. The "logic" of revolution demanded no less. Calls for neutrality and the abrogation of the Warsaw treaty rose to a mighty crescendo on October 30, with an increasing number of revolutionary councils, including that of the Ministry of Foreign Affairs, joining the chorus. The lead, if any primacy could be established, probably belonged to Gyor.

The scene in the Premier's office was tumultuous. A number of delegations were present and engaged in heated debate. Nagy himself was understandably edgy. He was proud of the announcement he had just made and wished to be praised for it. Instead, additional demands were heaped on him, which he must have recognized as likely to strain the patience of the Russians. The victory of the revolution, now within reach, was about to be forfeited by unreasonable extremism. Despite Nagy's annoyance, his responses were genuine enough. He did not seek refuge in legalism. He was sincerely at a loss as to how to go about declaring neutrality, and his addiction to legal proprieties made him loath to condone a revolutionary step that was morally justified but could not be defended on legal grounds. It could conceivably jeopardize the very legitimacy of the government.

Nagy's attitude clearly aligned him with other tragic figures in history, caught in the swirl of revolution and horribly mistreated by it. Nagy was further handicapped by not knowing the provisions of the Warsaw treaty. It was not clear to him what rights he had as Premier of Hungary and what privileges had been granted the Russians. Challenged by hecklers to explain why he needed parliamentary approval for the abrogation of the pact, he momentarily lost his temper, denounced anarchy, and threatened to resign. An unkind soul in the assemblage wisecracked that that would be just fine; he was hustled from the room. The meeting broke up on this note. But, as if to impress the Premier with the urgency of the demands, a five-man delegation from Gyor, led by Attila Szigeti, warned him that if he demurred, a parliament of revolutionary councils, representing substantially all of Western Hungary, which was meeting in a two-day session at Gyor, might revise its stand toward the government and break with it.

The die was now cast. The Premier stood in the middle between irreconcilable forces rapidly converging on one another and on him. It was his unhappy duty to avert a clash, to seek a solution for an insolvable conflict. Torn between what his heart urged him to do and what his reason dictated, he struggled but briefly. In the early afternoon of October 31 he spoke extemporaneously to a crowd before the House of Parliament and announced that "today we opened negotiations for the withdrawal of Soviet troops from the country and for the renunciation of our obligations stemming from the Warsaw Pact." He reiterated as much to foreign newspapermen who interviewed him shortly thereafter. His statement, however, was not broadcast to the nation until 6 o'clock in the evening. Some time during the day Nagy informed Mikoyan and Suslov, who had returned to Budapest in the evening of October 30, of his decision. Nagy's references to the "opening of negotiations" imply that he had alerted the Soviet emissaries already in the morning. The question was taken up again in the afternoon.

Unfortunately it has been impossible to reconstruct a detailed time table for October 31, a crucial day in precipitating the final crisis between the Soviet Union and Hungary. The sequence of developments was obviously very rapid and requires close analysis. Nagy's relatively quick turnabout from the position he held in the afternoon of October 30 must be explained. Did he act in response to domestic pressures or did he decide to move decisively because he finally became convinced of the insincerity of the Soviet Union in dealing with him? It would appear that he had no more reason to distrust the Russians on the 31st than he had had on the 30th. Contradictory moves on their part merely muddled the picture.

That troops were pouring into the country and that the evacuation of Budapest was at least temporarily halted were clear facts. But the deployment of troops may not have had the ominous implication they acquired two or three days later. At least Nagy need not have interpreted them that way. More important, the Soviet high command need not have intended them that way at that particular moment.

THE SOVIET POSITION RECONSIDERED: CONCILIATION AND THE MENACE OF INTERVENTION

The precise instant at which the Soviet Union decided to intervene in Hungary has not yet been fixed with satisfactory accuracy. Khrushchev has since then indicated on a number of occasions that the Soviet Presidium had been of a divided mind on the wisdom of intervention.[1] What he did not clarify was how long the division persisted and when the binding decision to strike hard was reached. The dispatch of troops could have been, and in all likelihood was, ordered in advance of such a final decision, either in anticipation of the decision or as a measure "just in case."

Simultaneously with the troop movements into Hungary, the Soviet government took steps of a conciliatory nature. An editorial in *Pravda* of October 28, though ostensibly rebuking the "counterrevolution" in Hungary, struck an optimistic note. It spoke of the "collapse" of the counterrevolution and referred approvingly to the activities of "Comrades" Janos Kadar and Imre Nagy. The editorial clearly reflected the assessment arrived at by Mikoyan

[1] *Nepszabadsag*, December 3, 1959.

during the preceding days. It contained a projection of the situation desired by the Soviet Union, a device the Communists often resort to. Although it does not correspond to reality, it gives valuable clues as to the likely moves the Soviet government will take. Indeed, a declaration of the Soviet government of October 30 (published in *Pravda* the following morning), on the "Principles of Development and Further Strengthening of Friendship and Cooperation between the Soviet Union and Other Socialist States," conveyed a spirit of accommodation and concession.[2] It included specific references to the question of troop withdrawal from Hungary:

"Having in mind that the further presence of Soviet military units in Hungary could serve as an excuse for the aggravation of the situation, the Soviet government has given its military command instructions to withdraw Soviet military units from the city of Budapest as soon as this is considered necessary by the Hungarian government.

"At the same time, the Soviet government is prepared to enter into appropriate negotiations with the government of the Hungarian People's Republic and other members of the Warsaw Treaty on the question of the presence of Soviet troops on the territory of Hungary."

The declaration, of course, did not touch on the question of Hungary's neutrality or its withdrawal from the Warsaw Pact. It is doubtful if the Soviet leadership could have even discussed matters in that framework. Nor was the declaration free of ambiguities hedging against possible developments that were not in accord with its spirit. Thus, Soviet troop withdrawal from Budapest was still projected in the future, though perhaps the immediate future, whereas the Hungarian government had insistently demanded it for some days and even reported that it had effectively begun. The change in status of the troops stationed in Hungary on the basis of the Warsaw treaty, in turn, was to be considered in multilateral conference of all the interested parties and, presumably, in a calmer atmosphere. The presence of a sizable

2 P. Zinner, ed., *National Communism*, pp. 485-89.

number of Soviet troops in Hungary would certainly strengthen the bargaining position of the Russians and would leave something for them to "reduce" without withdrawing completely.

It is possible, though highly unlikely, that the entire document was a sham designed to placate potentially restive East European peoples with the promise of substantial improvement in their relations with the Soviet Union and to assuage the temper of the Hungarian people while preparations for the crushing of the revolution were rushed to completion. A more plausible explanation is that the document was intended to calm the Hungarian people, but with a view to inducing it to accept a basis for a negotiated settlement rather than to set it up for the kill.

The specific terms of the document lent themselves to various interpretations. The concessions offered and the adjustments spoken of were indefinite. The chances were that once the Russians restored normal relations, they would slowly regain the upper hand, and the wishes of the Hungarian people would receive partial satisfaction at best. But the basic intent of the declaration of October 30 must be seen in the light of the Soviet Union's continuing desire to save the situation short of total engagement. The document does not reflect the substantial deterioration in the situation that took place in Hungary during the very period when its contents were being discussed in the Kremlin.

The declaration of October 30 came too late to stem the flow of revolution in Hungary. It was a scrap of paper by the time it was issued. The pace of the revolution made it so. The Soviet leadership misjudged and underestimated the mood of the Hungarian people. For once, the well-oiled machine of a totalitarian state could not keep up with the rapidly changing events. The deliberations of the Soviet Presidium, which had to take into account the broader international implications of the situation, were too ponderous to cope with the problems on the spot. By October 30 and 31, the choice open to the Soviet Union had in fact narrowed to the making of far-reaching and humiliating concessions that were clearly unpalatable to it or to the ruthless crushing of the revolution. The Hungarian insurgents held the initiative. They were also more intransigent at this time than their Soviet opponents.

The foregoing is not meant to imply that the Soviet Union acted in good faith toward Hungary or that it showed reluctance out of humanitarian considerations to strike down the insurgents. It had to make the best of things. Its reluctance was based on self-interest and on a large measure of doubt, greater than we would have assumed and greater than was warranted by the possible counter moves the West might make in response to military intervention in Hungary. The Anglo-French-Israeli military action against Egypt on October 30 in this sense considerably eased the anxiety of the Soviet leadership. But this is not to put the burden of Soviet intervention in Hungary on the unfortunate Suez Canal venture. By this time only force could have prevented Hungary's defection from the socialist camp. Without Suez the Soviets simply would have had to use force at greater risk to themselves.

In the context of the situation it is not surprising that what the Soviets unquestionably meant as a major diplomatic statement went virtually unnoticed in Hungary. It was not given priority over the airwaves and, what is more arresting, it was not once referred to publicly by Imre Nagy. Once would think that if the Premier had thought the declaration useful in taming the force of the revolution, he would have given it widespread publicity, if only to test its impact on the population. There is no evidence that he considered giving it a try. Instead he transmitted the people's ultimatum to the visiting Soviet dignitaries.

The information that we have from second-hand sources about the conduct of the Soviet-Hungarian talks on October 31 is as unsatisfactory as it is disturbing in its implications. The gist of it is that "Mikoyan agreed to everything." The one piece of solid evidence available, a report by a university student turned journalist during the revolution, who happened to be at Party headquarters just as Mikoyan and Suslov were leaving, corroborates the general impression that all went well and amicably. The student describes the Soviet leaders as emerging from Kadar's office at Party headquarters, relaxed with looks of satisfaction on their faces, shaking hands all around (including the reporter's) and entering Soviet armored cars for their journey home.

Now, it seems incredible that Mikoyan and Suslov could have

taken thus calmly the news of Hungary's intention to pull out of the Warsaw treaty. Yet there is no intimation of their having lost their temper or of their having given the Hungarian Communists a dressing down. There is no intimation that they were horrified at Nagy's (and Kadar's) inability to hold the line and at the general worsening of the situation. Their calm and ready agreement to anything and everything would make perfect sense only if they had come with the foreknowledge of a decision to smash the insurrection—in fact, bearing instructions for the Soviet military and the Hungarian Communists to that effect. To assume this, of course, would invalidate the thesis advanced in the preceding pages. Barring such foreknowledge, Mikoyan and Suslov must be adjudged superb tacticians and masters at concealing their sentiments. One would expect no less of two seasoned Communists who had survived for decades in the jungle world of the Soviet hierarchy. Still unanswered are the questions when and how the Soviet decision was made and what role in it was played by Mikoyan and Suslov.

There are rumors of telephone conversations between Mikoyan (from Party headquarters at Budapest) and Khrushchev. In view of the ease with which telephone conversations are monitored, it would seem unlikely that anything of substance passed between the two men even if they did talk. There were other opportunities for an exchange of views by teletyped code from the Soviet Embassy. Unfortunately, we do not know whether Mikoyan and Suslov stopped at the Embassy, and, if they did, when and for how long. Given the delicateness of the question involved, it is doubtful if Khrushchev could have passed on to them a snap decision ordering a military assault on Hungary. So we are left to wonder, with an added complication arising from the attitude displayed on the afternoon of November 1 by Communists like Kadar, Munnich, Apro, and Kiss, all of whom turned coat and became leaders in the countergovernment established on November 4, and from the sudden and unexplained disappearance of Kadar and Munnich on the evening of November 1.

Is it conceivable that on the afternoon of November 1 all four of the abovementioned Communists should readily endorse the

Premier's suggestion to abrogate the Warsaw treaty and declare Hungary's neutrality, that Kadar should go so far as to remonstrate provocatively with the Soviet Ambassador, threatening to fight "with gun in hand," in the streets if necessary, unless the Soviet military withdrew, and that a few hours later they should steal away from the House of Parliament to join the Soviet forces, unless they acted on prearranged plan? Would Kadar take instructions from the Soviet Ambassador, contrary to his understanding of Mikoyan's and Suslov's commitments, made the day before? Why the uncalled-for display of verbal bravery by Kadar if not to dissimulate? Kadar was not a man known for such outbursts.

The conclusion suggests itself that all this was play acting on the basis of instructions left by Mikoyan and Suslov on October 31, before their departure from Budapest. From then on, one may surmise, the Soviet representatives with whom Nagy maintained contact, notably the Soviet Ambassador in Budapest, Y. V. Andropov, and the Communists who had been chosen to do the Russian's bidding merely played for time. They awaited the deployment of the troops needed to crush the revolution at one blow. This contention is corroborated by the fact that at 10 o'clock in the evening of October 31, armored vehicles surrounded and sealed off the municipal airfield of Budapest (Ferihegy). At daybreak the following morning, Soviet foot soldiers occupied the buildings and offices, cutting off all air traffic in and out of the capital.

On the other hand, it could be argued that in so fluid a situation the Russians could hardly have trusted Kadar and others sufficiently to inform them of their future role more than twenty-four hours in advance of their actual departure from the scene. If that be so, one must assume that Kadar was after a fashion "kidnaped"—with Munnich acting as the Russians' chosen instrument to bring about the defection—not really knowing where he was being taken and for what purpose. If the timing and the manner of Kadar's defection are subject to speculation, the reasons underlying his selection for the task of forming a Communist countergovernment are clear beyond doubt. His past performance had shown him to be a suggestible and manipulable person. He had the added attractiveness of being, despite everything, the least odious and best known Communist leader among those not hopelessly lost to the revolution. It would not take much to break down his resistance, if indeed he had any, to betray the revolution. Convincing explanations of the danger of a counterrevolutionary victory would assuredly induce him to support the Communist cause.

The others—Munnich, Apro, and Kossa—also belonged to the group of Communist functionaries who were caught in a crossfire by the revolution, neither loyal to it nor committed to the perpetuation of the Rakosi regime. It is possible that in order to win them over, the Russians threatened to bring back a part of the old Stalinist guard. Actually this alternative would not have served the Russians well, and it may not have been necessary to invoke it as a threat; as events were unfolding, the Communist functionaries must have seen for themselves what was ahead. There was no future for them in a reborn Hungary. At best they could hope to avoid imprisonment and to return to the menial jobs for which their working-class background qualified them.

Further conjecture at this point would seem to serve no useful purpose. The facts as they are known, though they are spotty and fail to illumine motives and to dispell discrepancies, give a reasonably coherent account of the frantic negotiations between the Hungarian government and the Soviet Ambassador throughout November 1 and 2, and of the opening of talks of a mixed Soviet-Hungarian military commission on November 3. These talks were the last point of contact before the Soviet attack.

HUNGARY ABROGATES THE WARSAW PACT

On November 1 Imre Nagy saw the Soviet Ambassador five times and talked with him once by telephone. In a move without precedent the Hungarian Premier asked the Soviet Ambassador to call on him in the House of Parliament at 9 o'clock in the morning. Normally, the Premier would have paid his respects at the Soviet Embassy or the ambassador would have informed him. In this encounter, Nagy remonstrated with the ambassador over continuing Soviet troop movements into Hungary. He offered proof of these movements in the form of intelligence reports. The ambassador professed ignorance and offered to consult with his government. He returned to the Premier at 11 A.M.—a scant two hours later—with the explanation that the moves were not of a military nature; they involved police units of the MVD, and their sole purpose was to insure discipline among the Soviet troops stationed in Hungary and scheduled for withdrawal. The morale of these troops had deteriorated considerably since the outbreak of revolution, and it was advisable to guard against untoward incidents during their withdrawal.

Nagy, dissatisfied with the answer, as he well might be—a more specious explanation could hardly have been offered—pressed for the absolute cessation of troops movements across the frontier. He asked if the Soviet government still stood by its declaration of October 30 and cited provisions of the Warsaw treaty, with which he had at last familiarized himself, placing Soviet troops under the jurisdiction of the military commander of the host country. Andropov suggested that he inquire further from his government about the troop movements. He called the Premier forty minutes later to tell him that the Soviet government still stood by its declaration of October 30 and that it requested the Hungarians to designate two commissions—one political, to discuss questions relating to the abrogation of the Warsaw treaty, the other military, to discuss technical and military questions pertaining to the troop withdrawal. Nagy again inquired about the troop movements. Andropov gave no answer.

The tone of the exchanges marked a sudden chilling of the allegedly amicable atmosphere that had surrounded discussions with Mikoyan and Suslov the night before. What had caused Nagy to become apprehensive overnight? Why should he suddenly be seized by doubts if the night before Mikoyan had "agreed to everything"? Either Nagy had nothing to worry about, or else he should have sought direct contact with Moscow to clarify an evident misunderstanding of the terms of Mikoyan's agreement. Dealing through an intermediary seemed incongruous, yet there is no evidence of further direct contact between Nagy and Moscow.

The situation was very bad indeed. The Soviet Ambassador acted with transparent disingenuousness. Nagy was obviously profoundly disturbed. He resorted to the only diplomatic weapons at his disposal. He abrogated the Warsaw treaty and declared Hungary's neutrality.

Shortly after his telephone conversation with the Soviet Ambassador, Nagy called a meeting of leading members of the Communist Party. Antal Apro, Ferenc Donath, Sandor Haraszti, Janos Kadar, Karoly Kiss, Geza Losonczy, Gyorgy Lukacs, Ferenc Munnich, and Zoltan Szanto attended. The Premier informed them of the state of affairs. The Party leaders noted that the Soviet Union had already violated the Warsaw Pact by sending in additional troops. They expressed concern lest the troops provoke new and disastrous bloodshed. They decided that the only solution for Hungary was to abrogate the Warsaw treaty and declare neutrality. Lukacs and Szanto alone demurred. Their reasons can only be guessed at. As old Moscow hands they probably felt that the proposed measures would irritate the Russians and invite fierce retaliation without offering the slightest protection of Hungary's interests. What the others thought—since they agreed to the measures—is even more problematic. Nagy seemed to be carried away with the righteousness of the decision and extolled the benefits the Soviet Union would derive from a neutral but genuinely friendly Hungary. It seems incredible that he should have actually convinced himself that the Russians would find a "free but friendly" country on their borders palatable; but, by all accounts, he did so convince himself.

In any event, the measures were approved and the Deputy Minister of Foreign Affairs (our source of information on the events of these hours) was ordered to draft the necessary diplomatic documents.[3] Meanwhile, to observe absolute propriety, Nagy convened the cabinet, including the chairman of the Presidential Council of the Republic, and informed it of the proposals made by the Communist Party leadership. These were accepted and legitimized by the titular head of state, Istvan Dobi.

[3] Gy. Heltai, "Nagy Imre es a Varsoi Szerzodes" (Imre Nagy and the Warsaw Treaty), *Irodalmi Ujsag*, London, June 15, 1959.

Hungary was about to act in ways for which history holds few parallels. Small states rarely abrogate treaties with big ones unilaterally. Although such a move was of questionable wisdom, since it was not suited to accomplish the ends it sought, the Hungarian government did not have a better alternative open to it. A general mobilization would have been unthinkable and futile. The Premier might have considered making a strongly worded speech alerting the nation to the imminent danger facing it. In fact, special bulletins of the news were broadcast later in the day in which the Premier did announce his declaration of neutrality. The public was not kept entirely in the dark, but neither was it fully informed of the thinking of the government. In refraining from mobilizing public opinion, Nagy was probably motivated by a desire to avoid incidents that could lead to the slaughter of an unarmed population. At the same time, Nagy hoped against hope that he might be successful; the Russians, if ever so slightly, were encouraging him in this belief.

In the afternoon the Soviet Ambassador again requested to see the Premier. He was told, in the presence of the cabinet, about further Soviet troop movements and about the decisions reached by the Hungarian government. It was on this occasion that Kadar vowed to fight with gun in hand in the streets against the Russians. After the meeting, a telegram was dispatched to the Secretary General of the United Nations apprising him that "the President of the Council of Ministers [of Hungary] . . . informed the Soviet Ambassador that the Hungarian Government immediately repudiates the Warsaw treaty and at the same time declares Hungary's neutrality, turns to the United Nations, and requests the help of the four great powers in defending its neutrality." The telegram also requested that "the question of Hungary's neutrality and the defense of this neutrality by the four great powers" be placed on the agenda of the forthcoming session of the United Nations General Assembly. The foreign missions were informed verbally of the actions of the Hungarian government. (But Nagy had not consulted them in advance about the diplomatic moves he contemplated. The revolutionary atmosphere and his own wrought-up frame of mind at this juncture precluded such sober, deliberate canvassing of opinion. In any event, the Western legations in Budapest hardly would have been able to give him a constructive or an encouraging reply.)

This was the first appeal for such assistance that had issued from any quarter in Hungary since the outbreak of the revolution. It asked for no more than diplomatic protection. Until that moment, in the heat of revolution, carried away by visions of victory, no one had given the question of outside assistance any serious consideration. It simply had not occurred to the people; none seemed required.

It was not until after the Soviet assault on November 4 that cries for armed assistance went out. For until the very last minute, the people, though apprehensive about Soviet motives, believed with Nagy that matters could be handled by negotiation, that the Soviet military would withdraw, and that some form of diplomatic move by the United Nations, such as the arrival of the Secretary General or of a fact-finding commission at Budapest, would suffice to induce the Russians to respect Hungary. (Some Hungarians persisted in this belief long after the revolution.)[4] It was a belief partly supported by Communist propaganda, which depicted the West, especially the Federal Republic of Germany, as an armed camp ready to move at a moment's notice.

"Knowledge" of the armed might of the West gave the Hungarians a comforting background against which their cockiness could find full expression. In an ironic aftermath to the revolution, escapees who found their way to Germany expressed acute disappointment at the absence of any signs of armed preparedness and any spirit of belligerence. They felt, retrospectively, let down

---

[4] A large number of Hungarian political refugees who fled in 1956 maintain to this day that the presence of a United Nations delegation in Budapest would have stayed Soviet military intervention. In this connection it is worth noting that at one point—reportedly on Friday, November 2—a rumor spread through Budapest to the effect that the arrival of a United Nations delegation was imminent. A group of newspapermen drove out to the airport to greet it. While they found the airport occupied by Russians, they managed to "ascertain" from the Hungarian personnel that a flight bearing the United Nations representatives had been given clearance to land, but that inclement weather had forced the craft to land at Bratislava (Slovakia); the Czechoslovak authorities had refused permission for the craft to take off for Budapest. It is inconceivable how such information could be believed even by a single individual. Yet it was currently reported by newspapermen.

and a little cheated, although they admitted having been the victims of Communist propaganda.

The population learned of the day's diplomatic exchanges, including the abrogation of the Warsaw treaty and the appeal addressed to the United Nations, through a special bulletin broadcast at 6:12 P.M. At 7:50 in the evening, Nagy made a brief radio address in which he told the nation that the government, "imbued with profound responsibility toward the Hungarian nation and history, and giving expression to the undivided will of the . . . millions, declares the neutrality of the Hungarian People's Republic." He made no direct mention of the Warsaw Pact, although neutrality was automatically incompatible with membership in it. He merely added that the "people desires the consolidation of the achievements of its national revolution without joining any power blocs. The century-old dream of the Hungarian people is thus fulfilled."

It is interesting to note that Nagy cast the declaration of neutrality in the light of a positive, crowning achievement of the revolution and not as a measure of desperation to fend off impending disaster.

Momentous as these developments were, more were to follow in the remaining evening hours of November 1. Late at night, Andropov called on Imre Nagy again, to sound out the Premier if he were willing to accede to a Soviet suggestion that he withdraw his message to the United Nations if the Russian government agreed to withdraw its troops. Nagy readily concurred in what seemed to be a somewhat innocent and more than equitable *quid pro quo.* Concomitantly, the Soviet Embassy announced that Russian mechanized units had surrounded all airfields in Hungary to insure the orderly withdrawal of troops. Hungarian air units declared themselves ready to resist superior Soviet force, but desisted at the order of the government, which "in full knowledge of its responsibility forbade them to open fire."

KADAR DISAPPEARS

At about the same time, a still-mysterious chapter in the life of Janos Kadar was unfolding. Some time during the crowded day a decision was arrived at to begin with the reorganization of the

Hungarian Workers' Party on new foundations. Among the members of the provisional directing body, Kadar provided the only link with the former leadership. The announcement of the reorganization and of the problems attendant upon it was read over the radio at 10 o'clock in the evening by Kadar. He was reliably reported to have been driven away in an unidentified car toward the Soviet Embassy and then to have dropped from sight about an hour or so before the broadcast was made. This in itself is not necessarily contradictory. The time of his disappearance could have been toward 11 rather than 9, or else his speech could have been prerecorded and broadcast from tape at a convenient hour.

The content of his address, however, deserves close scrutiny for the apparent incongruities in it. Although he glorified the uprising for having "shaken off the Rakosi regime [and] . . . achieved freedom for the people and independence for the country, without which there can be no socialism," he made no reference whatever either to the repudiation of the Warsaw Pact or to the declaration of neutrality.

He also introduced, for the first time in several days, the notion of counterrevolution. In his view, "the uprising of the people [had] come to a crossroad. The Hungarian democratic parties will either have enough strength to stabilize [their] achievements or [they] must face an open counterrevolution. The blood of Hungarian youth, soldiers, workers, and peasants was not shed in order that Rakosiite despotism might be replaced by the reign of the counterrevolution." He then sounded the alarm of "the grave . . . danger . . . that foreign armed intervention may allot [Hungary] the tragic fate of Korea." But instead of decrying the source from which the danger of intervention stemmed, he counseled that to avert it "we must eliminate the nests of counterrevolution and reaction. We must finally consolidate our democratic order." To this end, he turned to "the newly formed democratic parties, and first of all the other workers' party, the Social Democratic Party, with the request to overcome the danger of a menacing counterrevolution and intervention from abroad, by consolidating the government."

In his final summation, Kadar struck a patriotic tone. He referred to the fact that the "people have proved with their blood their intention to support unflinchingly the government's efforts for the complete withdrawal of Soviet forces. We do not want to be dependent any longer. We do not want our country to become a battlefield." (Note the curious inversion of priority between people and government in demanding the withdrawal of Soviet troops.)

In the light of what happened subsequently, one is strongly tempted to read into Kadar's speech an ominous meaning which it may not have intended. Nevertheless, some of his terminology and some of his interpretations rang decidedly untrue in the prevailing climate of opinion. With only slight modification, his interpretation of the danger of counterrevolution could have served to justify Soviet intervention. The official Communist line adopted after the defeat of the revolution conformed precisely to this reasoning. Was Kadar, if ever so cautiously, laying the groundwork for it? More important, was he consciously indulging in the subtle art of "esoteric communication," trying to pass on information to Communists whose cooperation he wished to enlist, to be on the alert for the turn of events that was about to take place? Is it not straining credulity to find altogether accidental Kadar's dwelling on two themes not publicly emphasized by anyone else—counterrevolution and Soviet intervention?

The answers to these questions may never be known. Kadar's movements during the days he was missing and the repercussions of his disappearance remain obscure. Some say that he went to Uzhorod in the Carpatho-Ukraine,[5] others that he went to Szolnok (a short distance from Budapest in East-Central Hungary). There are those who believe that he returned to the House of Parliament a number of times. Inexplicably, he was included on the roster of the Cabinet Council announced on November 3.

Contradictory views also persist about the reaction of the officials in the House of Parliament to Kadar's disappearance. Some

---

[5] It has since become clear that Kadar and other Communists who joined him found asylum for a short while at least in the capital of the Carpatho-Ukraine, near the Hungarian border but in Soviet territory.

claim that Nagy expressed surprise on November 4, when he was apprised of Kadar's defection. It hardly seems possible that the absence of such a key figure over two days should go unnoticed. But it is puzzling that the fact was not registered in some more public manner. We have found no intimations in what way, if any, Kadar's disappearance affected the thoughts and actions of Imre Nagy and his entourage.

HUNGARIAN-SOVIET NEGOTIATIONS ARE JOINED

On November 2, Andropov and Nagy had further exchanges, though less feverish than on the preceding day. The ambassador, on seeing the Premier in the morning, told him that the Soviet government took note of Hungary's announcement of the abrogation of the Warsaw treaty. He asked that the Hungarian government designate its negotiators for the political and military talks. He also suggested that the Hungarians pick the site for the political talks, whereas Budapest would be suitable for the military negotiations. The Hungarian government responded in three *notes verbales.*

The first reviewed the general situation and recalled the Hungarian government's effort to induce the Soviet Union to open negotiations for the withdrawal of troops from Hungary. It spelled out the principles of future cooperation between the two states on the basis of complete equality, sovereignty, and noninterference in each other's affairs. It also designated a five-member delegation of political negotiators headed by Geza Losonczy and including Ferenc Farkas, Jozsef Kovago, Andras Marton, and Vilmos Zentai.

The second *note verbale* designated a four-man military delegation composed of Ferenc Erdei, Pal Maleter, Istvan Kovacs, and Miklos Szucs. (The last three were military men; Istvan Kovacs ought not to be confused with the first secretary of the Budapest organization of the Communist Party.) It suggested that discussions be opened immediately in the House of Parliament in Budapest.

The third note registered further protests against continuing Soviet troop movements. It specified that these moves were taking place in an East-West direction, and that Soviet troops were occupying railway lines and stations on their way. As a consequence, the Hungarian government felt obligated to inform the foreign missions of the nature of these moves once more and to call them to the attention of the United Nations.

A telegram from Imre Nagy to the United Nations Secretary General, dated November 2, 1956, again complained against Soviet military moves. It asked the Secretary to urge the great powers to recognize Hungarian neutrality and to place the problem on the agenda of the Security Council.

The actions of the Hungarian government now betrayed a sense of greater urgency but not of panic. There was no evidence of any preparation whatever for meeting an emergency. Outside the walls of the House of Parliament the revolution was running out its course, moving toward the restoration of order and the resumption of work, heedless of and undisturbed by the diplomatic maneuvers attendant upon the Soviet military menace. Isolated voices, that all was not yet won, were drowned out in the general din of the victorious revolution. November 5, a Monday, was the logical date set for the beginning of normal life under freedom and national sovereignty.

At noon on November 3, a mixed Hungarian-Soviet committee began discussing technical questions pertaining to the withdrawal of Soviet troops. The meeting adjourned early in the afternoon. An interim report, broadcast at 3:20 P.M., recorded satisfactory progress and noted a Soviet promise that no new troop trains would cross the border into Hungary. The commission was to reconvene at 10 P.M. What the broadcast did not say was that at the request of the Russians the locale for that meeting was moved to the headquarters of the Soviet military command at Tokol, on an island in the Danube. The request, in the form of a polite invitation stressing reciprocity, seemed too harmless to turn down.

14. The Crushing of the Revolution

FROM 10 P.M. on November 3, the Hungarian negotiators had no contact with their government. They were never to be heard from again. Toward dawn, on November 4, members of the government who spent the night in the House of Parliament were tipped off by telephone from the Yugoslav Embassy about the impending attack. By that time, they could hear the rumble of heavy mechanized equipment and occasional gunfire from the distance. A round of frantic telephoning ensued, alerting other members of the government for their safety and calling them for a last emergency session of the government. Few of them made their way there. A select number of other dignitaries, including Cardinal Mindszenty, were also warned by telephone so that they might save themselves as best they could. The scene at the House of Parliament was an utter bedlam. At 5:20 A.M. Nagy announced to the nation that "in the early morning hours, Soviet troops launched an attack against the capital with the obvious intention of overthrowing the lawful, democratic Hungarian government. Our troops are fighting. The government is doing its duty."

Actually, Budapest had no organized defense. General Bela Kiraly, the titular commander of the city, had no troops to speak of under his command. He never received a clear-cut order to resist. Nor did the government remain at its post for long. At 5:56 A.M., Nagy issued an appeal to the Hungarian military delegation, "who went to the Soviet Army Headquarters at 10 P.M. last night and have not yet returned, to return immediately and to take charge of their posts." At 7:12, the government appealed to the Russians not to shoot, to avoid bloodshed. "The Russians are our friends and will remain so." At 7:57, the Hungarian

Writers' Association broadcast its now famous appeal to the world for help. At 8:07, the Budapest radio fell silent.

Shortly thereafter Soviet troops seized the House of Parliament. Its occupants had for the most part fled. What they did, where they went, was strictly a matter of individual choice. Some, including the Premier, availed themselves of an offer of asylum extended by the Yugoslav Embassy. Others, sensing that the embassy might turn out to be a trap, chose the possibly more hazardous alternative of remaining at large. They melted away in the crowd, taking advantage of the general confusion until they could get their bearings. By the early morning hours, the government of Imre Nagy had ceased to exist.

In the meantime, from "somewhere" in Eastern Hungary came word of the formation of a "revolutionary worker-peasant government" headed by Janos Kadar. In the dawn hours, Ferenc Munnich broadcast an "open letter" to the "Hungarian working people." Speaking in his own behalf and in behalf of others, he said:

"We the undersigned Antal Apro, Janos Kadar, Istvan Kossa, and Ferenc Munnich, Ministers, former members of the Imre Nagy government, proclaim that on November 1, 1956, we severed all our relations with that government, resigned from our positions, and initiated the formation of the Hungarian revolutionary worker-peasant government.

"This grave step was prompted by our realization that the government of Imre Nagy had come under the sway of the reaction and become impotent. Within the frame of that government we had no further opportunity for action in the face of the ever-growing strength of the counterrevolutionary threat that menaced with extinction our People's Republic, our worker-peasant power, and our socialist achievements."

Then Kadar announced the formation of the new government.[1] Its members included the abovementioned four Communists and Imre Dogei, Gyorgy Marosan, and Sandor Ronai. Other port-

[1] The time and point of origin of these broadcasts are still in doubt. Earliest monitoring reports place Munnich's speech at 5:05 A.M. and Kadar's at about 6 A.M. Because of the wavelength on which they were originally transmitted, these announcements were probably not heard by the nation until later in the day when they were rebroadcast at thirty-minute intervals.

folios remained open "for the time being." Kadar did not disavow
the revolution. He took pains to dissociate his government from
the discredited Rakosi-Gero clique. The program he set forth, in
an obvious effort to allay the fears of the people, embodied many
features of the original demands of the revolution. It catered to
hurt national pride, promised "the securing of national independence and . . . sovereignty," and outlined a series of administrative,
economic, and social reforms. It also gave specific assurance of no
reprisals and no "persecution of workers under any pretext for having taken part in the most recent events." While Kadar did not go
so far as to endorse a multi-party system, he asserted that "representatives of other parties and non-Party persons loyal to the
People's Democratic system who are ready to defend the achievements of socialism" would be asked to fill government posts "after
the restoration of legal order."

Much of this was stock phraseology designed to bemuse the gullible. Kadar's formulations were strikingly reminiscent of the
terms set by the Communists for coalition cooperation in the initial
stages of power seizure immediately after the war. The promise of
moderation was there, dependent on Communist good will, as was
the premise of multilateral accommodation based on prior acceptance of the defense of socialist achievements such as the Communists
defined them. It was on these terms that Stalin deferred to Western
insistence in 1945 and agreed to the coopting of democratic representatives to the Rumanian and Bulgarian governments. The terms
of the concession robbed it of any meaning whatever. Kadar now
ostensibly embarked on a similar venture, for indeed he found
himself in a situation in which he must reconquer power before he
could hope to proceed with the further construction of socialism.
Although the specific circumstances markedly differed from 1945,
the task was in essence the same.

The proclamations of the Kadar government did not mean that
it was capable of taking action to keep its promises. The government existed in name only. It did not control the executive machinery of the state, nor did it have the personnel to staff that
machinery. Some time was to elapse before the government became
operational. The members of the government took their oaths of

office on November 7 and then moved as rapidly as possible to gather a staff and to repair their organizational machine.

In the meantime, the Soviet military was in actual control of the country. Its battle plan called for a simultaneous attack on all urban centers to stamp out any territorial base of the revolution. The plan was successfully carried out against an unarmed nation. The Soviet juggernaut met only improvised resistance on the part of mixed groups of students, workers, and some military personnel. These pockets of resistance were quickly reduced to isolated industrial strongholds which stood their ground in some places for a week or more. Considering the disproportionate superiority of Soviet power, the grit, determination, and effectiveness of the defenders were heroic.

AFTERMATH

The Soviet assault on Hungary did not snuff out the revolution at once. Although organized military resistance collapsed before it was even begun, the great convulsions of the body politic that characterized the revolution did not subside at one stroke, nor did the spirit of the revolution, combining both defiance and naïve, baseless hope, die without a struggle. For a period of several weeks, Hungary lived under a veritable *interregnum*, with the Soviet military wielding effective power, the Hungarian government in the throes of painful reconstruction, the object of derision and ridicule, and the workers' councils, spontaneous bodies of the people's will, exercising *de facto* political power to the point of being consulted by the Soviet military as well as Hungarian government organs.

It was a period not unlike the climactic days of the revolution itself. It was at once frightening, fantastic, and chaotic. In the interstices between anarchy and renascent power, individual chances could be taken that normally would not be attempted in a totalitarian state. Accidental recognition in the street by a Soviet or Hungarian policemen led to many an arrest;[2] at the same time, conspiratorial circles of friends met frequently, albeit in a haphazard way and in an atmosphere of increasing unreality.

2 Among those thus arrested was Sandor Kopacsi, the chief of the Budapest police, who had sided with the revolution.

It was only after the middle of November that a systematic smoking out of revolutionary intellectuals began and that the exodus of intellectuals from Hungary took major proportions. But the trancelike state of mind which possessed them was to linger both with those who left and with those who stayed behind. Some who refused to flee did so in the belief that their services would be needed to preserve the achievements of the revolution.

It was difficult to come to terms with reality, to reconcile oneself to the fact that the revolution was extinguished and would leave but few traces behind it. The dictate of right reason demanded that the largest concessions won by the revolution should be honored by the Russians as well as by the parasitic Kadar regime. Somehow Nagy had to be taken back into the government, his friends and colleagues given posts commensurate with their status. It was in the manifest interest of the Russians themselves, let alone the Hungarian authorities, to foster reforms. For a brief time, counting on the sensibility of the Russians and the incapacity of the Kadar regime, the revolutionary intellectuals nurtured the hopé that a Hungary freer even than Gomulka's Poland could be salvaged from the situation. This was also the burden of the proposal advanced by Istvan Bibo, the last Minister of State to remain at his post in the House of Parliament. In a memorandum drafted on November 4, he set forth a slightly refurbished version of the third road formula for Hungary. This memorandum has since become a sort of bible for those refugees of the revolution who advocate a realistic solution of the Hungarian problem. Perhaps they needed it to sustain hope in their own tattered souls. (In any event, a few also continued clandestinely to publish a newspaper, "October 23," which embodied Nagy's ideals; only five issues appeared, all before December.) Others, notably the writers, clung to other hopes.

The writers once more girded to defend a lost cause. They alone of all revolutionary groups retained an organizational base in the Writers' Association. All other institutions affiliated with the revolution, and especially those created by it, collapsed virtually overnight. The revolutionary council of students went out of existence on November 4. The Petofi Circle, as might be expected, forfeited all claim to existence, although its members maintained some sort of informal and personal contact. The Free Trade Union Association could not organize itself before it was recaptured by the Communists. Territorial revolutionary councils fell prey to the Russians and to the returning Communist functionaries without any possibility of resistance. The Writers' Association and the workers' councils, for different reasons, became the sole institutional legatees of the revolution.

The Writers' Association was a source of inspiration and wisdom. Its advice was actively solicited, and it was looked to by the people for some sign indicating the proper attitude to adopt. Lacking any power whatever, the Association was limited to the issuing of appeals and manifestoes, to making informal suggestions and to negotiations with the authorities.

On November 2—two days before the revolution was crushed—the Association had enlarged its presidium by the inclusion of six new members, bringing the total to thirty-one;[3] the entire presidium had then been declared to constitute the Revolutionary Council of the Association. Thus the writers had been among the last to create a revolutionary body in their midst, but they could point with pride at the continuity in the roster of their representatives—elected in September, 1956—whose composition had required no alteration whatever. No other organization could boast of similar fidelity.

It is true that on November 2 the Writers' Association had been at the nadir of its influence, content to stand on the sidelines and to encourage the youth of the country as the personification of the revolution.[4] The writers had outlived their usefulness, retaining only their remarkable unity, and even that was in danger as Communist writers began to feel left out. Their thoughts turned inward, to the appraisal of their own personal fortunes. They realized now for the first time that their voluntary espousal of the revolution

---

[3] They were Geza Feja, Dezso Keresztury, Janos Kodolanyi, Istvan Lakatos, Gyorgy Ronay, and Istvan Sinka.

[4] The front page of the November 2 issue of *Irodalmi Ujsag* is a case in point: here Laszlo Nemeth and Tibor Dery—the deans of non-Communist and of Communist writers respectively—sang the praises of the country's youth in two lead articles.

would not protect their rights for future recognition. Some of them arrived at the inescapable conclusion that they would suffer the consequences of their involvement with Communism. Shorn of all privilege, they would have to prove themselves by the quality of their literary products. For some, this would present no problem; for others, it would.

The crushing of the revolution erased these divisions and falterings. The issue once again was how to oppose tyrannical power. This imbued the writers with a sense of responsibility for the welfare of the nation. Their memorable meeting on November 12 reflected this sense of importance. But, once again, the intellectuals had little of practical relevance to offer. The writers extolled the purity of the revolution, deplored the political party system, approved of the social progress registered in the past ten years, and decided that Kadar was a scoundrel with whom one either had to break relations or compromise. On the crucial question—that of offering armed resistance and encouraging the continuation of a general strike—the writers, after some deliberation, mercifully offered no recommendation. It was not theirs to commit the lives of others. The decision of striking and fighting properly belonged to those directly involved, the workers. Although these had sought out the Writers' Association for advice, in the end they made their own decisions and acted on their own premises.

A continuation of the armed struggle on a nation-wide scale was, of course, out of the question. Nor did the workers' councils seriously consider it as a means by which to force concessions on the authorities. The question of strikes was another matter. The impulsive preference of the workers was to keep on striking and so to press the government for political and economic concessions.

The workers' councils thus became the last institutional citadel of the insurgent nation. For this reason far greater responsibility and authority devolved upon them than they had ever contemplated. That they were able to maintain themselves where other organizations failed was due to the solidarity and cohesiveness of the working class itself, especially around industrial centers and in large factories.

It was one thing for the Soviet forces summarily to reoccupy a town hall and to sweep away the local revolutionary council; it was quite another thing for them to dislodge by force a workers' council whose base of operation was in the middle of an industrial complex employing thousands of workers. To dislodge the workers' councils individually would have entailed the mobilization of military force in excess of what the Russians had and the recruitment of much larger numbers of scabs willing to do the Russians' bidding than could be rounded up from among the working class. The oft-heralded but seldom demonstrated power of the working class that stems from its concentration, cohesiveness, and superior self-consciousness was apparent beyond the shadow of a doubt in the Hungarian situation of November, 1956.

To increase the effectiveness of the workers' councils, those within the general area of greater Budapest agreed to place themselves under the guidance of a higher, elected representative body that spoke for all of them. In this manner the Workers' Council of Greater Budapest was formed on November 14. The idea of a "National Workers' Council" was still-born because of the difficulties of communication and liaison with industrial centers outside the capital—Gyor, Miskolc, Debrecen, and others. An effort was made to maintain contact clandestinely, but it did not work out satisfactorily. Differences in approach between the Greater Budapest Workers' Council and other workers' councils developed. For example, the Budapest council decided to resume working on November 19 as a sign of good will, on condition that the government for its part would begin negotiations for the withdrawal of Soviet troops and readmit Nagy to the cabinet. Workers' councils elsewhere did not go along.

The workers' councils operated under grievous difficulties. They were harrassed in the most brutal fashion by the Soviet military and by the Hungarian authorities, who resorted to police and military interference, to infiltration agents, to deliberate misinformation, and to directives issued by the Trade Union Center (which had in the meantime been reestablished under Communist control) and who further wore down the councils' resistance by means of meetings, procrastination, and false promises.

But quite aside from these extraneous obstacles, the workers'
councils—including that of greater Budapest, which had begun to
develop an administrative apparatus with its own offices—also
labored under self-imposed difficulties. Though they lacked a
precise political program, they were not fully reconciled to the
political role in which they were cast. In any event, they regarded
their political functions as temporary and sought to free themselves
of them by securing the return of Imre Nagy to the government:
he would take care of things. The threat of a counterrevolution
was not out of the question, and it caused them anxiety; in other
words, some of the arguments advanced by the authorities were persuasive. Still worse, as the strike wore on, an increasing number
of workers and leaders alike saw it as a double-edged weapon. It
paralyzed the country's economy, but it also threatened to starve
the workers themselves into submission. With winter approaching,
food, shelter, and clothing were political arguments. A compromise
with the government was inevitable.

At the beginning of its existence, in the early part of November,
the Kadar government was utterly powerless. It was caught between
the Soviet high command, which insisted on the rapid and ruthless
restoration of controls, and the population, which in no way hid
its contempt for the new regime and simply refused to acknowledge
its existence, let alone its legitimacy. Kadar was known to have
quarreled with and to have been threatened by the Soviet military;
at the same time he was unable to induce the Hungarian people
to comply with any of his wishes.

The abduction of Imre Nagy and his colleagues on November 22
upon their leaving the asylum of the Yugoslav Embassy, on what
was presumed to be a safe-conduct, represented a turning point in
the Kadar government's efforts at mastering the situation. To be
sure, Nagy was abducted by Soviet constabularies. His "mysterious
disappearance," for which the government had only lame explanations, caused further indignation—but it did not lead to a sudden
groundswell of active opposition. With Nagy effectively isolated
from his followers, a dangerous center of infection was eliminated.
As if emboldened by this step, the government moved more resolutely to crush the remnants of the revolution.

The government continued to intimate that it desired the co-operation of other political parties and leading personalities, but the conditions attendant upon cooperation were such as to make them unacceptable to any self-respecting non-Communist. As in his statement of November 4, Kadar made cooperation contingent on acceptance in advance and without reservation of the Communist interpretation of socialist reconstruction. To be sure, Kadar would not have rejected the association of leading non-Communists with his regime, since it would have imparted a measure of prestige to it, but he showed no inclination to make any genuine concessions. He acted as though his real intention was to dissipate the energies of the opposition elements and to forestall their unification: indeed, an offer of accommodation, no matter how spurious, always disrupts the will and resolution of those to whom it is made. In any event, nothing came of the repeated offers of cooperation either at this time or later.

Instead, the Communist Party proceeded to reaffirm the principle of one-party rule and to revalidate the 1948 merger of Communists and Social Democrats. On December 6, the Party was able to hold a Central Committee meeting at which a theoretical apologia for the October catastrophe was elaborated (in essence it has remained the Communist line on the revolution and its antecedents with only occasional, minor shifts in emphasis) and a program was laid down.

Simultaneously, the government moved with force against the workers' councils, beginning with the arrest of leaders in the provinces. It was this move which precipitated the last showdown between the councils and the government. In response to the arrests, the Council of Greater Budapest called a clandestine meeting to which representatives of the provincial councils were also invited. At the meeting it was decided to proceed with a general protest strike of forty-eight hours duration on December 11 and 12. The government, tipped off by informers, struck rapidly by apprehending the leaders of the Workers' Council of Greater Budapest in the morning of December 9—a Sunday. In the evening of the same day the government ordered the dissolution of the Budapest council and of all workers' councils above the factory level. The order was consistent with a decree-law issued the day before which outlawed all territorial and functional revolutionary committees and councils.

The strike began on schedule despite the disruption of the work of the Greater Budapest Council. But it was the last major manifestation of concerted opposition by the workers. The leaders of the Greater Budapest Council—Sandor Racz and Sandor Bali, who had been released shortly after their detention on Sunday, December 9—were again apprehended on December 11 as they presented themselves in the House of Parliament for negotiations with Kadar, at his invitation and with the guarantee of safe-conduct. Thereupon the Central Workers' Council of Greater Budapest collapsed. After the forty-eight-hour work stoppage the back of the strike movement was also broken. The resumption of economic production was a giant step toward "normalcy."

From then on the flame of revolution flared only briefly and in isolated instances, as at Csepel in January, 1957, when the workers protested against the appointment of a number of managers selected by the government. With the resignation of the workers' council of Csepel at the end of January, on the ground that it was unable to fulfill its task because of continuous harrassment by the authorities, the active phase of resistance came to an end there as well.

A similar fate overtook the Writers' Association, which attempted a heroic rearguard action. Late in November it revived the Revolutionary Council of Intellectuals, in whose name it issued appeals to the government. On January 17, 1957, the Writers' Association was temporarily suspended. On April 21, 1957, it was permanently disbanded by the government. In the meantime, the incarceration of the spiritual progenitors of the revolution went on apace. The revolution now survived only as it was locked in human hearts.

Epilogue

Epilogue

THE crushing of the Hungarian revolution introduced a new era in the relations among Communist parties. Drift and deterioration were halted. There followed a steady if unspectacular restoration and even an extension of Communist control well beyond anything experienced before.

The Soviet intervention in Hungary was as effective as it was brutal. Communists throughout Eastern Europe, including Tito, condoned it. The victory of the revolution would have threatened them all. More important, the successful Soviet intervention (and the corollary inactivity of the West) caused a definite reorientation in the thinking of the people. The Hungarian effort showed them the national and international limits of disruption of Communist control. Instead of nurturing further hopes of liberation against the wishes of Moscow, they came to recognize that any amelioration in their condition must be achieved through and with the consent of Moscow. Eastern Europe became pacified.

In the absence of expectations of cataclysmic changes, tensions between governments and their peoples abated to the benefit of both. Relations between individual East European states and the Soviet Union were also adjusted on a basis of greater reciprocity.

The need for immediate and far-reaching concessions that was implied by the Soviet Government Declaration of October 30, 1956, passed rapidly as Hungary was subdued. But the Soviet government did not go back entirely on the promises the declaration had made. The terms of economic cooperation in the Soviet bloc were revised. The worst exploitative features of Soviet policy were removed in favor of a more equitable commodity and price structure of foreign trade. Grants in aid, loans, and other assistance were forthcoming to shore up sagging economies, especially in Poland and Hungary.

The intent of these changes was to give the East European states a sense of participation in the building of a new type of international community within which they would retain their individuality while they cooperated in ventures that were designed to benefit them all.

To be sure, the limits of individuality were carefully circumscribed. A declaration issued by twelve Communist and Workers' parties in Moscow in November, 1957, confirmed the validity of "basic laws applicable to all countries embarking on a socialist path" and listed these as "leadership of the masses of the working people by the working class, the core of which is the Marxist-Leninist party, in bringing about a proletarian revolution in one form or another and in establishing one form or another of the dictatorship of the proletariat; alliance of the working class with the bulk of the peasantry and with other strata of the working people; the abolition of capitalist ownership and the establishment of public ownership of the basic means of production; gradual socialist reorganization of agriculture; planned development of the national economy with the aim of building socialism and communism; raising the working people's standard of living; the accomplishment of a socialist revolution in the sphere of ideology and culture; and the creation of a numerous intelligentsia devoted to the working class, the working people, and the cause of socialism; the elimination of national oppression and the establishment of equality and fraternal friendship among peoples; defense of the achievements of socialism against encroachments by external and internal enemies; solidarity of the working class of a given country with the working class of other countries—proletarian internationalism." [1]

The program of the Communist Party of the Soviet Union adopted by its Twenty-second Congress in October, 1961, reasserted that "the socialist revolution and the strengthening of the unity of the world socialist system on the basis of proletarian internationalism is an imperative condition for the further progress of all its member countries." It went on to say that the relations among the countries of the socialist commonwealth were characterized by "full

1 *Pravda*, November 22, 1957.

equality, mutual respect for independence and sovereignty, fraternal mutual assistance and cooperation." [2]

The practical side of cooperation through the Warsaw Pact and the Council of Mutual Economic Aid, as well as through less permanent bilateral and multilateral schemes, places definite restrictions on the national sovereignty and individuality of the East European states. It would be surprising if an alliance between one "super power" and a number of second-rate powers would allow the full equality of its members, regardless of the ideological considerations that might be involved.

The overwhelming economic and military superiority of the Soviet Union compels a hierarchic relationship.[3] But the crushing weight of Russia is no longer felt as acutely anywhere in Eastern Europe as it had been felt in the not too distant past, when it ruffled local tempers and impeded the development of friendly relations. The socialist bloc is far from achieving real cohesiveness, let alone monolithic unity. Differences persist among the East European countries as well as between them and the Soviet Union. But under the façade of differences, forces are at work to achieve greater unification. It remains to be seen how far this process will go, how long it will last, and what its ultimate results will be.

For the moment, one can only record that in the five years following the upheavals in Poland and Hungary, the Communist systems demonstrated a capacity for making adjustments—a sort of totalitarian variant of peaceful change on the international and national plane. It differs from the peaceful change germane to free societies chiefly by its manipulative rather than self-regulatory character. But it serves the same purpose, to make minor modifications consistent with recognized necessity (or felt need) in order to preclude catastrophic changes that would threaten the very survival of the existing order.

2 *Ibid.*, November 2, 1961.

3 This superiority is bolstered by the enforced presence of Soviet troops in Poland and Hungary, and at least nominally in Rumania (despite the official announcement of the withdrawal of Soviet garrisons from that country in 1958). The mere presence of troops, of course, proved once in the past to be insufficient to repulse massive opposition.

One of the main beneficiaries of these new trends in the Soviet bloc was Janos Kadar, who, with Soviet assistance, was able to strengthen his tenuous hold on the country. Soviet military forces aided him in the establishment of domestic tranquillity, at a time when he had not a shadow of power at his disposal to deal with the revolutionists at large throughout the country. Soviet economic assistance helped him to stave off imminent collapse of the Hungarian economy and to repair quickly the damage caused by revolutionists so as to erase visible signs in the capital and elsewhere that were reminiscent of the glorious days of the revolution. Effusive endorsements by Khrushchev bolstered Kadar's status and made it possible to rebuild the Communist Party from the shambles into which the revolution had turned it.

The revolutionists were dispersed and brutally broken. Those who did not flee to the West in time (during the first thirty to sixty days after the revolution, when it was still possible to escape to Austria and Yugoslavia) were either deported to the Soviet Union or tried by summary courts in Hungary. Some were executed; others were given harsh prison sentences.[4] Writers, journalists, and members of the Petofi Circle—the entire intellectual leadership of the opposition—were subjected to police harassment, and many of them were jailed, including Tibor Dery, Gyula Hay, and Zoltan Zelk. Only an insignificant number of those who had played an active part in the developments preceding the revolution fled to the West.

Reprisals against the revolutionists came to a horrifying climax in June, 1958, when Imre Nagy and eight of his close associates were tried secretly on a number of charges including high treason. Nagy and three others (Jozsef Szilagyi, Miklos Gimes, and Pal Maleter) were executed. Sandor Kopacsi was sentenced to life imprisonment, and four others (Ferenc Donath, Miklos Vasarhelyi, Ferenc Janosi, and Zoltan Tildy) were sentenced to prison terms ranging from twelve to fifteen years. One of the main defendants, Geza Losonczy, did not survive a second incarceration. The trial and execution of Imre Nagy completed his martyrdom. He became a genuine national hero in the eyes of Hungarians at home and abroad. No Communist before him had achieved such distinction.

4 For example, Jozsef Dudas was executed in January, 1957.

Together with the heroes of the revolution, its villains also disappeared from the scene. Rakosi and Gero have not been heard of since. Presumably they live in the Soviet Union. Revai, who found asylum in Russia, returned to Hungary in 1957 and died in 1959. Some of the lesser "Muscovites" were retained in important administrative posts, but Kadar rebuilt the Party from the large corps of functionaries who had never sided with Nagy and who had been less than enthusiastic about Rakosi.

A year after the Nagy trial, Kadar felt that his administration had been sufficiently fortified to permit the release of some political prisoners. An amnesty was decreed in 1959 and another in 1960; as a result, Dery, Hay, and four of Nagy's co-defendants (Donath, Vasarhelyi, Janosi, and Tildy [5]) were set free together with hundreds of other persons.[6] Additional thousands, however, remained incarcerated, and the government continued to round up intellectuals and to throw them into jail as if it were still fearful of having too many of them at liberty at one time.

Despite the obvious repressive character of the regime, it was, neither in its policies nor in its personnel, a simple extension of the hated Rakosi regime. Although it is hardly possible to speak of freedom in a society devoid of political and legal rights, the conditions of day-to-day existence in Hungary were less restrictive for the average citizen than in any other East European country except Poland. The attitude of the people was one of resignation and apathy such as usually follows an unsuccessful revolutionary outburst. The memory of the revolution had no discernible effect on their will to resist. But it must be assumed that the moral legacy of the revolution survives among them and that it may yet serve the Hungarian nation well in a renewed bid for freedom.

Seen from a distant perspective, the 1956 revolution appears as one in a series of revolutions and near revolutions that have punctuated Hungary's history over the past century. There is a direct link between the revolutionary surge of 1848–49 and that of 1956. It is not maudlin romanticism to compare these two events—and

[5] Tildy died in August, 1961.

[6] Within the terms of these amnesties, former Stalinists were also released— Gabor Peter in 1959 and the two Farkas's in 1960.

not only because the gallant efforts of Hungarians in both cases succumbed to the intervention of Russian arms.

More than a hundred years after the 1848 insurrection, the Hungarian people are found once again striving for identical aims— national independence, social emancipation, and political democracy. It has been their abiding misfortune never to have had a successful revolution and never to have found fulfillment through gradual evolution. Their existence in a hostile or at least alien national environment is an important cause of this misfortune, although it is not the only reason why Hungarians have been unable to attain national sovereignty and to institute democratic humanitarian reforms at the same time.

These two sets of problems, the attainment of sovereignty and the establishment of democratic humanitarian reforms, have been inextricably interwoven at each of four critical junctions in Hungary's recent history—1848, 1918, 1945, and 1956. Every time Hungary failed miserably to cope with them, and the result was either suppression of national aspirations, or retrogression and retardation of social and political processes, or both.

The partial fulfillment of Hungary's aspirations to national sovereignty in 1867 had a disastrous effect on democratic reforms. It brought about a resurgent feudalism in a period when the trend of progress in Europe was toward industrial democracy and social equality.

Hungary was not only falling behind; it was moving in a direction opposite to that of the civilized world. There followed the revolutions of 1918. (They really were two revolutions that merged into one—a socialist democratic and a communist.) Their failure engendered new repression and stagnation. The collapse of the old order in 1945 raised high hopes that Hungary would at long last break out of the vise in which historic circumstances had held it; but these hopes too were frustrated by a new tyrannical system that shocked the people, since it denied them both national sovereignty and democratic reforms, although it did promote a sense of social emancipation.

It is safe to say that if the Communists had fulfilled either aspiration, even in part, the intensity of feeling against the regime would not have run so high as to bring about an explosion.

Examined at closer range, the 1956 revolution loses some of its transcendent qualities, but none of its importance. It was a moment in the history of Hungary and, perhaps, a moment in the history of all mankind. It teaches a number of lessons germane to an understanding of the politics of our time.

The part played by the Communist Party in the incubation period of the revolution deserves particularly close scrutiny. Its monopolistic position and the power it exercised over its members profoundly affected the content of the dialogue that developed in Hungary, the manner in which it was carried out, the degree of participation in it of various groups, and the response it evoked among the population.

The Party was cast in a dual capacity, agent and object of reform. It was clearly divided into opposing factions, but it retained organizational unity and thereby created a series of problems. For one thing, the sincerity and the intent of statements that appeared under the Party's sponsorship were instinctively suspected by the public. People surmised that the Party might feign moderation to strengthen its hold on the country. If this were true, genuine and bogus demands for reform would be indistinguishable. For another thing, the Party—i.e., its controlling sectarian faction—had at its disposal procedural means in the form of "democratic centralism" [7] and discipline that effectively influenced the substance of debate, limited its range, compartmentalized and confined it to Party councils, and, most important, confronted would-be oppositionists with serious political and moral dilemmas.

The practical value of "democratic centralism" proved itself

[7] Democratic centralism is a term that literally embodies a contradiction, the thesis and antithesis of a dialectic formula. The practical synthesis which has emerged from this meaningless verbal formulation clearly nullifies the democratic element (the principle of elective officers from the lowest to the highest levels of Party organizations) in favor of centralism, which demands unquestioning and universal acceptance of the decisions of the majority of the highest governing organ of the Party. Factional struggles—i.e., real competition for power by legitimate means—on the part of a minority to become a majority and thus to impose its will are ruled out of bounds. Once a majority is achieved —by force or otherwise—it is unassailable—except by superior force if such can be mustered, since it tends to perpetuate itself by coopting new members when necessary. In other words, democratic centralism safeguards the prerogatives of a self-appointed and self-perpetuating leadership against all legitimate challenges to its authority. The principle is defined with unmistakable clarity in *Kommunist*, No. 18, 1957.

beyond doubt. Reform-minded Communists were in a small minority among Party officials. They had no way of asserting themselves.
In order to be heard, they had to be in power. To come to power,
they had to oust the incumbent leadership. This could not be
accomplished in any legitimate way except through the change of
heart or defection of a controlling majority of the leadership. Barring that, the opposition had to have recourse to assistance from
the Russians (which it could not secure) or to the use of force
(which it could not muster and which in any event was a breach
of discipline).

It seemed that as long as the Party leadership adamantly opposed
innovation, did not yield to reason and open its ranks to members
of the opposition, the reform wing of the Party was condemned
to futility. Its last resort was to go outside the realm of the Party,
appeal to the public directly, and make common cause with it—
a heretical deed, a moral betrayal of the Party which few Communists could bring themselves to commit.

The moral and political issues involved in going outside the
Party to enlist public support in behalf of the Communist reform
program were gravely debated by the most serious and most aggressive members of the opposition as late as the spring of 1956. As
Communists, even if not of the most militant type, they appreciated
the value of an illegal organizational network to bring about a
change of command in the Party. They considered the creation of
one, but rejected it on the grounds that it would limit the scope
of their struggle to an intraparty affair without any reference whatever to the population and would of course run the gravest of risks
of detection and summary liquidation.[8] They thus decided to form
a link with the public in an effort to bring pressure to bear on the
Communist leadership, not to overthrow the people's democratic

8 It was a mistake to neglect the creation of an illegal organizational network
in *addition* to the open public activity of the opposition. For had such an
illegal network existed, and had it gone undetected until the fall of 1956, it
might have been able to engineer a transfer of power in the Party similar to
that which took place in Poland and in this manner avert popular uprising.
Whether or not an illegal network would have been of much use once revolution
broke out is highly problematical. In any event, oppositionist Communists have
lived to regret their failure to pay more attention to organizational questions.

system or to undermine the status of the Communist Party, but merely to reform it. They did not make this choice easily. It was a tactical decision dictated by exasperation.

In this belated effort, the opposition failed. The absorbing tragedy of reform-minded Communists was precisely that they could neither arrange for a transfer of power in the Party nor harness popular indignation to their own ends in time to avert national catastrophe.

Those who fail are always judged harshly, and not only by their detractors. The right-wing opposition did not give a good account of itself. Among its members, there were few strategists and tacticians. They were intellectuals who imperfectly understood the game of politics. Their leader, a Communist of life-long standing, had never been of militant temperament, and he neither understood nor cared for the rough and tumble of close-quarter political struggle.

Lest they be judged too harshly, it is necessary to state that the job of intellectuals is not to lead political movements but to fan the breeze for political fires. The successful transfer of power in Poland was not accomplished by intellectuals but by Party cadres, including persons who had been in disgrace and others who had stayed out of trouble. In Hungary the cadres did not prove tractable. For this the intellectuals hardly can be held responsible. The result might have turned out differently had Rajk been alive or had Kadar and Kallai shown more fortitude.

The gulf between Communist intellectuals and Communist cadres is large everywhere and is probably kept that way on purpose by a sagacious leadership. The Party recruits its cadres among the lower classes and trains them in accordance with the requirements of the positions of power they are to hold in the command structure. They acquire much practical experience and receive an education in service institutions as their careers warrant.[9] Their preparation and their general orientation are vastly different from those of

[9] With due allowance for an almost antithetical ethos of success in America and in the Soviet Union, the Communist cadre, as a prototype, is the opposite number of the self-made man.

intellectuals, even of intellectuals raised entirely under a Communist system.[10] In Hungary, neither the intellectuals nor the cadres had been raised entirely under the Communist system. Awareness of their social origins heightened the distrust between them.[11]

The intellectual distance between writers and working-class cadres was particularly great. The problem was less acute in the case of former populists who clustered around the Petofi Circle: they had much in common with the administrative-technical cadres of the Party, but had no affinity for the political cadres, such as Party secretaries and secret police officers. Rakosi's ruthless cadre policy paid unexpected dividends. It helped to split the Party into two hostile camps. The antagonism between these camps prevented them from coalescing against him and also barred them from achieving mutual accommodation that would have saved the Party from disaster.

The indecisiveness of the right opposition cannot obscure Rakosi's preeminent responsibility for the turn of events. He refused to accede to gradual modifications that would have helped to release pressure. An orderly transfer of power in the Party required a minimum cooperation from him, which was not forthcoming. His truculence in large part accounted for the extraordinary isolation of the ruling elite from the people, including the mass of Party members, and for its inability to find acceptable accommodation with any segment of the population except Party functionaries. His obduracy persisted until the end of his active career. It contributed to the universal hatred felt toward him. Few Communist leaders anywhere have been as thoroughly despised as he was. Gero continued in the same vein.

The Soviet Union acted at cross purposes in Hungary. The record of its actions reveals both disingenuousness and an astonishing degree of misjudgment or ignorance of the local situation. The

10 So far only the Soviet Union has produced a generation of intellectuals raised entirely under a Communist system.

11 In this context, it is worth noting that while social distance between groups diminished considerably in Hungary in the period of Communist rule, intellectual distance between them decreased much less rapidly. Even in the heat of revolution when many barriers between different groups were temporarily obliterated, insurgent workers did not fully trust insurgent students, and the latter did not always consider the workers to be fully their equals.

support the Soviet Union lent Rakosi was inconsistent with its universal goals. These were better represented by Nagy and by the opposition, whom the Soviet Union overtly helped to suppress but to whom in fact it gave covert (though incidental rather than deliberate) support. The net effect of Soviet policies was to abet the efforts of the opposition by projecting a general framework of practical adjustments and saving the day for it just when Rakosi was about to destroy it. In this manner the Soviet Union helped to envenom relations in the Party, eroded the confidence of functionaries, and postponed decisive solutions of urgent social, political, and economic problems. The Party lost its capacity for resolute action. This incapacity to function was an absolute prerequisite for the outbreak of revolution.

According to Lenin, revolutions will occur when the rulers cannot and the people will not continue in the old way.[12] In Hungary, both conditions were met.

The unwillingness of the population to be governed in the old way reflected years of accumulated grievances. These were aggravated in a number of different ways, particularly by recurring cycles of exaggerated hopes and miserable frustrations. Marxist ideology and Communist propaganda contributed to the spread of discontent by the rosy promises which they held out prior to the seizure of power and by their continued lip service to idealized social goals in the face of a reality which was palpably at odds with these goals. Exposure to Communist indoctrination raised people's expectations and supplied them with tools and theoretical standards for condemning the regime's performance.

An exact scale of individual deprivation cannot be easily determined. But grievances caused by great and prolonged personal

[12] V. I. Lenin, *Left-Wing Communism, An Infantile Disorder* (International Publishers, New York, 1940), p. 66. Lenin's simple working definition appears adequate, although it does not identify the terms of incapacity and unwillingness and does not provide a clue as to how these conditions are achieved.

Because the Communist system is distinguished by an unprecedented monopoly of control over all media of social action and integration, an internal breakdown of its authority is an even more important requisite for the proliferation of unrest that might lead to revolution than is the erosion of the will and ability to rule of any other type of tyrannical government.

insecurity, affronts to individual dignity and self-respect, and humiliation of the national ego seemed to have a consistent priority over dissatisfaction with material conditions of life. People felt a revulsion against the lies which saturated their existence, and they despised the atmosphere of moral depravity which surrounded them.

Among economic grievances, the exploitation of Hungary as a country by the Soviet Union, symbolizing the subjugation of the people, sometimes was paramount to any feeling of personal hardship. Frequently, when respondents pleaded economic hardship as a prime reason for discontent, they tended to exaggerate the degree of deprivation they suffered and drew invidious comparisons with an imagined state of well-being at other times within their memory. Thus economic discontent seemed to be strongly colored by politically and psychologically motivated hostility toward the rulers. In estimating political allegiance, no correlation between material privation and disloyalty can be established. High income and comfort, as in the case of artists, writers, and professional people, especially physicians, did not preclude the persistence of intensely hostile anti-Communist attitudes. Similarly, a modest improvement in the material well-being of workers and peasants failed to mollify their opposition.

Even so there is no certainty that revolution would have occurred without the "Polish October," which fired the people's imagination, or that insurrection could not have been averted at the last minute by a well-considered gesture on Gero's part. The evidence of historic events is always overwhelmingly in favor of that which happened as against that which failed to materialize. This must in no sense be understood to imply historic inevitability. The prerequisites must be met before certain events can occur. The fulfillment of prerequisites, however, does not guarantee that events will culminate as preordained.

The structure of popular grievances gave the revolution the predominant character of a national and democratic uprising rather than of a social revolution in the traditional sense of classes contesting for supremacy.

Although the Communists have denounced it as a counterrevolution, it was anything but that.[13] The revolution provided unexcelled evidence of the dimensions of change in social structure and attitudes that had taken place in a little over ten years. Chief among these was the growth of the workers' political consciousness, which clearly belied the Leninist thesis that the working class cannot rise above economic consciousness without the guidance of its vanguard, the Communist Party. Many revolutionaries harbored deep hatred for Hungary's former ruling classes. Others, including intellectuals and students, regardless of Party affiliation, had a sincere devotion to a humane type of socialism. They had no use for bourgeois institutions as they had known them in their country or as they had understood them to be in the West. Their Western orientation consisted of a desire to have cultural and intellectual intercourse with the West on their terms, but not to imitate Western political, social, and economic institutions.

Among the participants in the revolution there was no evidence of nostalgia for the Horthyite regime or for its values. On the contrary, those who had a chance to express themselves condemned the old order and asserted with satisfaction that its undesirable remnants had been wiped out expeditiously. They wanted to substitute acceptable new values and patterns of human existence for the old ones, which the totalitarian Communist system had promised but failed to do.

The revolution had no opportunity to embody the ideas of its participants in a comprehensive and detailed program. The precise form and the specific content of a suitable political and social order would have had to be worked out as time went on. Un-

---

13 The label of counterrevolution by the Communists is not surprising. Within their frame of reference it could not be otherwise. They do not recognize the possibility of a step forward from socialism, by which they mean the social and political organization of society under their rule. To admit the possibility of a higher synthesis from a resolution of conflicts under socialism would wreak havoc with the entire dialectic concept of history as a progression of class struggles. To admit the possibility of an improvement on socialism under auspices other than their own would deprive them of exclusive custodianship of the historic destiny of mankind and totally undermine their claims of legitimacy. Any change, therefore, from socialism signifies retrogression and is by definition counterrevolutionary.

doubtedly, their formulation would have created difficulties. The unity and harmony of social classes in the revolution very likely would have been dissipated rapidly as soon as normal conditions set in. Under Communism, Hungarian society was said to have lost its stratified character. It was reduced to two hostile groups, a small number of usurpers of power and a large exploited mass of people. This observation was correct in that intergroup conflicts were dwarfed by the common negative factor of antagonism toward the regime. But group contradictions had not been obliterated, and there was no discernible consensus on a large number of positive issues, such as the preferred type of agricultural ownership, the scope of private enterprise in industry and commerce, the methods and modes of its control, and the limitations on social differentiation based on entrepreneurial initiative. Neither the resolution of economic and social issues nor the implementation of procedural safeguards for the preservation of freedom would have gone smoothly. Although the need for such safeguards was now more thoroughly appreciated than at any previous time, the country was no better prepared to govern itself responsibly in freedom than it had been in 1945. But it is the right (and the price) of freedom to live dangerously, and the Hungarians earned this right splendidly by their revolution.

The question whether the victory of the revolution could have been preserved gives rise to conjecture. One cannot say what action on the part of the West might have saved the revolution, just as one cannot determine whether the United States would have been able to rise to the occasion even under a different administration and in less awkward circumstances.

Since the outbreak of violence was not related to any specific impulse from the outside, it caught the Western governments by surprise. The confused and rapidly changing situation could not be evaluated reliably and with sufficient dispatch to cause a responsible government to remonstrate with the Soviet Union. For several days there was nothing about which to remonstrate.

By the time the need for rescue became desperately urgent, it was too late, not because the Anglo-French-Israeli adventure in

Egypt had given the Soviets a free hand,[14] but because the Soviet Union had built up a military force in Hungary far superior to anything the West could marshal. This deployment, which began before the Suez adventure was precipitated, gave Russia an advantage that could not be challenged without the risk of general war.

The psychologically optimum moment for the West to intervene with any hope of effectiveness would have been before October 30, when the revolution was still an internal Hungarian affair and when the Soviet Union was hesitating as to the proper course of action. The purposes would have been to warn the Russians against invading Hungary, thereby transforming the internal conflict into an international war, and to reassure them that the West would not exploit events in Hungary for any further inroads against Soviet security interests.

This type of intervention by the United States was clearly unthinkable, irrespective of the approach of presidential elections. Neither the administration nor the public were psychologically or otherwise prepared for it. One may even question the desirability of their developing a combat frame of reference that would allow them to act in a fluid situation without adequate knowledge of the facts.

The inability of the West to rescue the revolution was thus caused not by its lack of moral fibre but by a combination of circumstances in which time and distance played a crucial part.

The United States can be faulted for its enunciated policy of liberation. For whatever was meant by those who propounded it (and precisely what they did mean has never been satisfactorily determined), it could be understood only in one sense by those to whom it was addressed. They had to assume a stance on the part of the United States that did not and properly should not exist.

This is not to imply that the Hungarian people rose against their tormentors on the premise of United States policy. There

---

[14] It may or may not be true that in the final analysis Hungary was the victim of the Anglo-French-Israeli venture in Egypt. If the international situation were viewed from a very broad perspective, one might be entitled to say that the Hungarian revolution saved the world from general conflagration. Had the Soviet Union not been preoccupied with its troubles in Eastern Europe, it might have intervened more forcefully in the Middle East.

is nothing in the labored genesis of the revolution to indicate that this was so. But a nation with responsibilities such as the United States cannot afford to have its stated aims grossly misunderstood, or easily subjected to willful misinterpretation.

The experience of the Hungarian revolution underscores the inseparable nature of national and international politics in our time, a condition that has been aptly labeled international civil war. Unless this is recognized by the makers of United States policy and some means are found to cope with the complex problems that derive from a blurring of these traditional distinctions, other revolutions may also end in defeat.

Although the revolution of 1956 was a unique historic event, there is no reason to believe that it could not be repeated. Its uniqueness lay not in a function of peculiarities organically rooted in Hungary's distinct past but in a combination of particular and universal influences, among which national and personal peculiarities also played a part. Both the revolution and its antecedents bear close resemblance to large-scale political upheavals at other times and in different historic settings. Moreover, signs of conflict similar to those which preceded the explosion in Hungary were discernible elsewhere in Eastern Europe in a more subdued form.

The exact circumstances in which the Hungarian revolution occurred are not likely to be recreated either there or in any other country. But the Communist system of government causes tensions despite the propensity for adjustment and accommodation it has recently demonstrated. The dialogue in the Party continues. Revisionism is as old as the Communist movement. Finally, by virtue of its absolutist character, Communist totalitarianism is subject to periodic crises of succession. All these factors may combine again to promote the likelihood of revolution. Study of the Hungarian precedent might help us to recognize the danger signals far enough in advance to create an international environment hospitable to the assertion of aspirations toward freedom.

Bibliographical Note

THE LITERATURE about the Hungarian revolution and related developments is large and still growing. It is not my purpose to provide a comprehensive bibliography of all the known titles. Nor is it my desire to enumerate all the works I consulted, since many of the publications were of marginal relevance only in the preparation of this study. I wish merely to identify and to evalute briefly the major sources and to cite a few books and articles as a possible guide for further reading.

The transcribed interviews comprise ten-thousand pages of reading material. This was supplemented by ten reports of approximately twenty-five pages each, prepared by particularly knowledgeable respondents at the request and for the sole use of the Project, and three background papers prepared by participants and research assistants in a graduate seminar on the revolution and its antecedents.

In addition to these sources, I found most useful, for the period of the revolution, the monitored broadcasts of Hungarian radio stations at Budapest and at such provincial towns as Miskolc, Gyor, Szombathely, and Debrecen. The transmissions of these stations comprise the only comprehensive and authentic record of the development of the revolution in the capital and in the countryside. Newspaper reporting was of necessity intermittent and incomplete, and due to the pressure of time and the chaotic conditions that prevailed, even important speeches by political leaders and government proclamations were often not preserved in writing. Thus the usual archival material is missing and were it not for the monitored transcripts, documentary references to the revolution would be spotty indeed. The broadcasts include all the statements made by government figures, all official proclamations, revolutionary demands, announcements, reports of the formation of revolutionary councils and the composition of their membership, exchanges of messages among them, interviews, appeals, and even poetry. The complete unedited file of broadcasts from 10 A.M. on October 23 to midnight on November 5, 1956, covering 1,125 pages, was placed at my disposal shortly after the crushing of the revolution. I used them extensively for the selection of documents in the volume, *National Communism and Popular Revolt in Eastern Europe* (New York, 1956), which I edited, and I studied them carefully in the preparation of this essay.

The quotations in Part Three are drawn either from the corresponding section of my documentary publication (pp. 398-481) or from the original documents which I did not include in that volume.

The Revolt in Hungary, A Documentary Chronology of Events, October 23—November 4, 1956 (New York, 1957) is an English translation of excerpts from broadcasts. *The Hungarian Revolution and Struggle for Freedom in the Mirror of Domestic Broadcasts, October 23 to November 9, 1956* (A Magyar Forradalom es Szabadsagharc a Hazai Radioadasok Tukreben, 1956 Oktober 23—November 9, New York, 1957) is a compilation made by Mr. Laszlo Varga of the full record of broadcasts during the revolution. I have not made a verbatim comparison between the text of this volume and the transcripts in my possession.

The *Report of the Special Committee on the Problem of Hungary,* issued by the General Assembly of the United Nations (New York, 1957)· and based on depositions by refugees, is also a very valuable source on the revolution.

A four-volume paperback publication, *The Counterrevolutionary Forces in the Hungarian Events of October* (Ellenforradalmi Erok a Magyar Oktoberi Esemenyekben, Budapest, 1957–58) presents the Hungarian government's version of revolutionary events. A fifth volume, *The Counterrevolutionary Conspiracy of Imre Nagy and His Accomplices* (Nagy Imre es Buntarsai Ellenforradalmi Osszeekuvese, Budapest, 1958) deals with the trial of Imre Nagy and his co-defendants and includes the indictment against them.

An interesting series of six articles in *Nepszabadsag,* January 22–27, 1957 (the official daily of the Hungarian Communist Party since the revolution), "The Siege of the Radio" (A Radio Ostroma), describes the outbreak of violence in front of broadcasting headquarters on the night the uprising began.

The Soviet interpretation of revolutionary events is given in V. Zakarchenko, *Budapest, October–November, 1956* (Budapesht, Oktiabr–Noyabr, 1956, Moscow, 1956), S. K. Krushinskii, *What Happened in Hungary* (Chto Proizoshlo v Vengrii, Moscow, 1956), Mazov *et al., About the Events in Hungary, Facts and Documents* (O Sobitiakh v Vengrii, Fakti i Dokumenti, Moscow, 1957), A. Belokon, *The Truth About Hungary* (Moscow, 1956), and V. Leonov, *The Events in Hungary* (Moscow, 1957).

Individual commentaries on the revolution include Mr. Tibor Meray's *Thirteen Days that Shook the Kremlin* (New York, 1959), which surprisingly relies on information gathered outside Hungary after the revolution rather than on Mr. Meray's own observations and thoughts on the spot in the heat of the revolution. Mr. George Urban's *The Nineteen Days*

(London, 1957) is a close account of the unfolding of the revolution, based on broadcasts and on human interest material collected by the British Broadcasting Corporation, Mr. Urban's employer. Mr. Peter Fryer's *Hungarian Tragedy* (London, 1956) contains many sharp observations by the correspondent of the London *Daily Worker* who broke with Communism as a result of the Hungarian experience.

For developments prior to the revolution, including the years 1945–56, I had recourse selectively to the official publications of the Hungarian Communist Party, particularly its newspaper, *Szabad Nep*, and its theoretical journal *Tarsadalmi Szemle*. I also used the files of *Irodalmi Ujsag* as these appeared pertinent.

The standard sources on the Communist seizure of power by Hungarian democratic politicians who either fled their country or defected from its service in the late 1940s include François Honti's *Le Drame Hongrois* (Paris, 1949), Stephen Kertesz's *Diplomacy in a Whirlpool* (Notre Dame, 1953), Imre Kovacs's *Im Schatten der Soviets* (Zurich, 1948), Ferenc Nagy's, *The Struggle Behind the Iron Curtain* (New York, 1948), and Dezso Sulyok's *Zwei Nachte ohne Tag* (Zurich, 1948). In addition to these I found interesting the account of an ex-Communist journalist Bela Petrovics, *J'ai Echappé aux Rouges* (Paris, 1951).

The published minutes of the 1943 Szarszo conference, *Az 1943 Evi Balatonszarszoi Magyar Elet Tabor Eloadas es Megbeszeles Sorozata* (Budapest, 1943), which in the view of some of the participants with particularly good memories are an expurgated version of the proceedings, nevertheless constitute a remarkable historic document. Unfortunately it is difficult to obtain. To the best of my knowledge it is available only in a few private collections in the United States. Yet familiarity with its contents appears to me essential to an understanding of the main literary and political trends that underly Hungary's recent development.

A volume by Job Paal and Antal Rado, *Resurrection at Debrecen* (Debreceni Feltamadas, Budapest, 1947) gives an unexcelled description of the events surrounding the formation of the first post-war government of Hungary, and it conveys a vivid picture of the prevailing political climate, the personal behavior and the expectations of leading government figures.

Dezso Nemes's *The Liberation of Hungary* (Magyarorszag Felszabadulasa, Budapest, 1st edition, 1955, 2d revised edition, 1960) gives the authoritative Communist interpretation as of both dates of publication. It is an invaluable source especially on internal Party developments, including the part played by various leading individuals, factional strife and policy formation. It is not, as its title would indicate, limited to the liberation of Hungary, but begins its narrative earlier, during the war years, and the 2d edition brings the story up to date. Its value is enhanced by numerous divergences in fact and evaluation between the two editions, which place key personalities and developments in a previously unsuspected perspective and afford insights into Communist historiography. There is also a Russian edition of this work, *Osvobozhdenie Vengrii*, (Moscow, 1957) which anticipates many of the changes of the 2d revised Hungarian edition.

Specifically on Imre Nagy, his own "theses" published under the title *Imre Nagy on Communism: in Defense of the New Course* (New York, 1957) are indispensable, as is the semi-documentary volume, *La Vérité sur L'Affair Nagy* (Paris, 1958), prepared by some of his friends and associates abroad as a refutation of the charges raised against him and his co-defendants by the Hungarian authorities.

The volume by Miklos Molnar and Laszlo Nagy, *Imre Nagy Réformateur ou Révolutionnaire* (Geneva, 1959), attempts a more or less systematic assessment of the premier's personality and of his political career together with a partial evaluation of the group or groups who supported him. It is an interesting contribution, but is based on recollection rather than study of the documents and it leaves a great deal unsaid either because the authors' knowledge is incomplete or because their fear of incriminating friends still in Hungary is too great to permit them to write down all they know. This fear is a major factor affecting the publications of all responsible Hungarians who fled after the revolution. Their desire to protect and in no wise to contribute to any possible harm to their comrades in Hungary has understandably caused them to conceal much information about events throughout the entire period of Communist domination. The most serious political refugees and those with the most inside information so far have had the least to say.

A study of the revolt of the Hungarian intellectuals by Mr. Istvan Meszaros, *La Rivolta Degli Intelletuali in Ungheria* (Torino, 1958) is the best general treatise on the subject.

The volume by Tamas Aczel and Tibor Meray, *The Revolt of the Mind* (New York, 1959) offers illuminating glimpses of the travail of Communist writers, but it is by no means a systematic analysis of the career of any single person or of the development of the Writers' Association. It consists of a series of almost disconnected vignettes, and is distinguished more by what it omits than what it says. It is likely to mislead the reader who does not know the general setting in which the events described by the authors take place.

A little-known work by three Hungarian literati, Gyorgy Faludy, Maria Tatar, and Gyorgy Paloczi-Horvath, *Tragodie eines Volkes* (Vienna, 1957) contains useful insights and observations.

A great number of short studies and articles deal with the problem of Hungarian intellectuals. Even a selective listing of the more significant ones would be impossible here. *La Révolte de la Hongrie*, a special issue of the French review *Les Temps Modernes* (November-December, 1956,

and January, 1957) devoted entirely to Hungarian intellectual developments presents the best anthology of Hungary's pre-revolutionary and
revolutionary literary product and the most trenchant commentary on it.
Mr. Istvan Csicsery-Ronay's *The Revolution of the Poets* (Koltok Forra-
dalma, Vienna, 1957) contains a representative selection of poems in
Hungary from 1953 to 1956.

A composite picture of the part played by Hungarian youth in revolutionary developments is given in M. Nicolas Baudy's *Jeunesse D'Octobre*
(Paris, 1957). Twelve "temoignages" by young people are followed by
the author's psychological profile of Hungarian youth based on answers
by 347 respondents (including 83 girls) to 24 questions about their background, experiences, and social, political, and intellectual attitudes.

A constant flow of important reminiscences and re-evaluations may be
found in journals and periodicals published by persons who fled after the
revolution. *Irodalmi Ujsag* (London), which was suspended in Hungary
after the revolution, is the journal of the Hungarian Writers' Association
in exile. *Uj Latohatar* (Munich) is devoted to literary and political problems. *The Review* (Brussels) is a quarterly, edited by former Communists, friends of Imre Nagy. It devotes serious attention to social,
economic, and political analyses and to the publication of documents
about the workers' councils.

Among first hand accounts written by outsiders Mr. Alexander Bain's
reportorial work, *The Reluctant Satellites: An Eye Witness Report
on Eastern Europe and the Hungarian Revolution* (New York, 1960),
stands out, as does Dora Scarlett's *Window onto Hungary* (Bradford,
England, 1959). Miss Scarlett is a former British Communist who became
disillusioned after the Hungarian revolution. She worked in the English
language section of the Hungarian radio in Budapest from February,
1953, until the revolution and fled, with the assistance of British consular
authorities, on November 15, 1956. Her comments on the Hungarian
social scene are very apt.

Mr. Francois Fejto's *Behind the Rape of Hungary* (New York, 1957)
is a competent but superficial summary of events from 1945 to and including the revolution by an extremely well informed author. Mr. Fejto,
a former Communist, has resided in France for many years and writes
about Hungary from the outside with an insider's viewpoint. The French
and Italian editions of his book are richer in detail than the English
version. Mr. Paul Kecskemeti's *The Unexpected Revolution* (Stanford,
1961) and Mr. Ferenc A. Vali's *Rift and Revolution in Hungary* (Cam-
bridge, Mass., 1961) were published too late to be of help to me.

Among secondary sources of article length, the following merit special
consideration: ·

Hannah Arendt, "Totalitarian Imperialism: Reflections on the Hungarian Revolution," *Journal of Politics*, February, 1958.

Harris L. Coulter, "The Hungarian Peasantry: 1948–1956," *The American Slavic and East European Review*, December, 1959. An excellent survey of social, political, and attitudinal changes in the Hungarian country-side based primarily on the interview material.

George Ginsburgs, "Demise and Revival of a Communist Party: An Autopsy of the Hungarian Revolution," *The Western Political Quarterly*, September, 1960.

William E. Griffith, "The Revolt Reconsidered," *East Europe*, July, 1960. This review article raises some pertinent questions and provides many useful bibliographical references.

Paul Kecskemeti, "Limits and Problems of Decompression: The Case of Hungary," *The Annals of the American Academy of Political and Social Science*, May, 1958.

Janos Meszaros, "On the Eve of a Revolution," *Journal of Central European Affairs*, April, 1958.

Index